Mental Health and Social Work

CAREER DIRECTORY

Inside

Visible Ink Press proudly presents the first edition of the *Mental Health and Social Work Career Directory*. The hallmark of this volume, part of VIP's Career Advisor Series, is the essays by active professionals. Here, industry insiders describe opportunities and challenges in all segments of mental health and social work, including:

- Substance abuse counseling
- Music therapy
- Art therapy
- Counseling psychology
- Clinical psychology
- Developmental psychology
- Neuropsychology
- Family psychology
- Forensic psychology
- Psychiatry
- Infant mental health
- Child welfare work
- School social work
- Employee assistance
- Marriage and family therapy
- Medical social work
- Aging/gerontology
- Research
- Policy and planning
- Community organizing

In fully up-to-date articles, they describe:

- What to expect on the job
- Typical career paths
- What they look for in an applicant
- How their specialty is unique

Provides Job Hunting Resources

Once this "Advice from the Pro's" has given you a feel for mental health and social work careers, the *Directory* offers even more help with your job search strategy:

- **The Job Search Process** includes essays on determining career objectives, resume preparation, networking, writing effective cover letters, and interviewing. With worksheets and sample resumes and letters. **FEATURES:** Resumes are targeted to the realities of mental health and social work.

- **Job Opportunities Databank** provides details on hundreds of organizations that hire at entry-level. **FEATURES:** In addition to the entry-level information, entries also include information on all-important internship opportunities.

- **Career Resources** identifies sources of help wanted ads, professional associations, employment agencies and search firms, career guides, professional and trade periodicals, and basic reference guides and handbooks. **FEATURES:** Resource listings include detailed descriptions to help you select the publications and organizations that will best meet your needs.

Master Index Puts Information at Your Fingertips

This *Directory* is thoroughly indexed, with access to essays and directory sections both by subject and by organization name, publication title, or service name.

Mental Health and Social Work

CAREER DIRECTORY

A Practical, One-Stop Guide to Getting a Job in the Helping Professions

1ST EDITION

Bradley J. Morgan and Joseph M. Palmisano, Editors

Diane M. Sawinski, Associate Editor

DETROIT • WASHINGTON, D.C. • LONDON

CAREER ADVISOR SERIES

MENTAL HEALTH AND SOCIAL WORK
CAREER DIRECTORY

1st Edition

A Practical, One-Stop Guide to
Getting a Job in the Helping Professions

Published by **Visible Ink Press**™
a division of Gale Research Inc.
835 Penobscot Building
Detroit, MI 48226-4094

This publication is a creative work fully protected by all applicable copyright laws, as well as by misappropriation, trade secret, unfair competition, and other applicable laws. The authors and editors of this work have added value to the underlying factual material herein through one or more of the following: unique and original selection, coordination, expression, arrangement, and classification of the information.

Visible Ink Press™ will vigorously defend all of its rights in this publication.

Copyright © 1993 by **Visible Ink Press**™

Some data were included from *Ward's Business Directory*, copyrighted by Information Access Company.

No part of this book may be reproduced in any form without permission in writing from the publisher, except by a reviewer who wishes to quote brief passages in connection with a review written for inclusion in a magazine or newspaper.

ISBN 0-8103-9445-6

Art Director: Cynthia Baldwin
Cover and Design: Mary Krzewinski
Career Advisor Logo Designs: Kyle Raetz

Printed in the United States of America

All Rights Reserved

10 9 8 7 6 5 4 3 2 1

Contents

INSIDE *ii*   ACKNOWLEDGMENTS *xi*   INTRODUCTION *xiii*
HOW TO USE THE JOB OPPORTUNITIES DATABANK *xvii*   HOW TO LOCATE CAREER RESOURCES *xix*

PART ONE

Advice from the Pro's

1 The Counseling Psychologist
Donna L. McKinley, Ph.D., ABPP, Vice Chancellor for Student Affairs, University of Michigan—Dearborn
Describes the role of a counseling psychologist in a variety of different settings. **1**

2 Exploring a Career in Substance Abuse Counseling
Gregory A. Blevins, Ph.D., Professor of Alcohol and Drug Abuse Sciences, Governors State University
Explains how treatment of substance abuse is an area of increasing growth and development. **5**

3 Family Psychologists Look at the Larger Picture
Carol Philpot, Psy.D., Professor and Associate Director of Clinical Training, School of Psychology, Florida Institute of Technology
Provides insight into this relatively new specialty in clinical or counseling psychology. **11**

4 Preparing for a Career in Family Therapy
Robert F. Stahmann, Ph.D., Professor of Family Sciences, Brigham Young University
Explores career opportunities in the newest and most rapidly growing of the mental health professions. **15**

CONTENTS

5 Wanted: Psychology Professors—Women Should Apply!
Joan C. Chrisler, Ph.D., National Coordinator, Association for Women in Psychology

By starting now to gain the experience and credentials required, a woman can look forward to a career as a psychology professor. **21**

6 On Becoming a Psychologist: One Woman's Story on Surviving as an African-Cherokee American
Brenda Andrieu, Ph.D., ABPP

This personal account will inspire minority students seeking a career in psychology. **27**

7 Music Therapy: Paths for Growth and Change
Caryl Beth Thomas, M.A., ACMT, Vice President of Public Services, American Association for Music Therapy

Music therapy combines artistry and science to help individuals improve, maintain, or restore a state of well-being. **33**

8 Art Therapy: A Unique Career Opportunity for Native Americans
Kathleen D. Westcott-Emerson, Anishnabe-Ikwe, M.A., ATR, Native Art Therapist

This field presents a unique and valuable opportunity for Native Americans interested in social services who value traditional Native wisdom and creative processes. **39**

9 Developmental Psychologists: Studying and Promoting Development Across the Life-Span
Dolores T. Benn, M.A. and Celia B. Fisher, Ph.D., Graduate Program in Development Psychology, Fordham University

Provides first-hand knowledge of the branch of psychology that studies the process of human development. **47**

10 Career Opportunities as a Clinical Psychologist
John D. Robinson, Ed.D. MPH, ABPP(CL)

Whether treating schizophrenia or substance abuse, the importance of clinical psychologists in all areas of need will continue to increase. **53**

11 The Study and Measurement of Brain Functions
C. Munro Cullum, Ph.D., Clinical Neuropsychologist and Assistant Professor, University of Colorado Health Sciences Center

Learn about the exciting field of neuropsychology—the study of brain-behavior relationships. **57**

12 **Forensic Psychology: Psychology in the Courtroom**
Alan M. Goldstein, Ph.D., ABPP, Diplomate in Forensic Psychology
Forensic psychology involves the application of psychological research, theory, methodology, and knowledge to address legal issues. **61**

13 **Psychiatry: An Opportunity to Ease Human Suffering**
Theresa Anna Yuschok, M.D., Duke University Medical Center
Provides a concise overview of the various career paths that psychiatry offers. **67**

14 **Social Work: Carving Out My Own Special Piece**
Sonja R. Berry, CSW-ACP
An accomplished social worker offers advice on initiating your own private, independent practice. **71**

15 **Infant Mental Health: An Exciting, Emerging Field to Consider**
Marjorie Frank, LCSW, Virginia Frank Child Developmental Center
Consider a rewarding career that seeks to address the physical, social, emotional, and developmental needs of babies and their families. **77**

16 **So You Want to Be a State Child Welfare Worker?**
S. Donna Helm Murphy, Staff Development Supervisor, Missouri Division of Family Services
A public child welfare agency offers a variety of fulfilling employment opportunities. **81**

17 **Social Work in the Schools**
Steve Turner, MSW, School Social Worker, Gull Lake Public School System
Explains the many rewards and challenges associated with school social work. **87**

18 **Marriage and Family Therapists—Healing Wounded Families in a Changing World**
Henry C. Malone, ACSW, CSW, Licensed Marriage and Family Therapist
Offers expert advice on preparing for a satisfying career in marriage and family therapy. **93**

CONTENTS

**19 Diversity and Challenge:
Social Work Careers in Employee Assistance**

Bridget Arens-Jones, ACSW, Employee Assistance Program, Lutheran Hospital

Employee Assistance Programs (EAPs) provide assessment, counseling, and resource referral services for employees and their dependent family members. **99**

**20 Medical Social Work in a Physical Therapy Clinic:
A Unique Opportunity**

Jennie Petrovich, M.S.W., Greater Lansing Rehabilitation Agency

A medical social worker assists patients and physical therapists to make the rehabilitation process go smoothly and efficiently. **105**

21 Why Social Work Practice in Corrections?

Marjorie Hammock, Chief of Social Work Services, South Carolina Department of Corrections

This challenging career track offers employment in most courts, local jails, juvenile and adult probation centers, and juvenile and adult corrections facilities. **111**

**22 Career Opportunities in Aging/Gerontology:
Expanding Opportunities**

Wilma L. Greenfield-Moore, Ph.D., Chairperson, Department of Social Work, Florida Atlantic University

The projected boom in our aging population will spur rapid expansion of this social work specialty. **117**

23 Social Work Researchers: Studying Ways to Better Help People

Cynthia A. Loveland Cook, Ph.D., ACSW, Senior Research Health Scientist, Richard L. Roudebush Veterans Administration Medical Center

Research helps the social work profession develop a scientific basis for practice and provides information to better plan and implement treatment. **121**

24 Improving Our Society through Policy and Planning

Sunny Harris Rome, M.S.W., J.D., Lobbyist, National Association of Social Workers

Social work policy and planning offers the opportunity to affect the well-being of people through the political process. **127**

25 Community Organizers: For a Change

Terry Mizrahi, Ph.D., Hunter College School of Social Work

Describes a career path that focuses on working collectively with people to solve a host of social problems. **131**

PART TWO

The Job Search Process

26 **Getting Started: Self-Evaluation and Career Objectives**
Defines what a "job search process" is and explains how to evaluate your own strengths and weaknesses. **139**

27 **Targeting Prospective Employers and Networking for Success**
Covers how to begin your job search, how to identify companies you would like to work for, what networking is and how to do it, informational interviews, and six good reasons to network. **149**

28 **Preparing Your Resume**
Provides an overview of resume preparation, reviews the records you will need, explains how to create your first resume, and provides tips on what to avoid. Also includes resume worksheets and examples of the three primary resume types. **161**

29 **Writing Better Letters**
Explains the importance of a good cover letter and provides information on other letters you will need to successfully complete your job search. Includes examples of letters for every job search situation. **189**

30 **Questions for You, Questions for Them**
Reveals the intricacies of the interview process and explains how you should prepare for any job interview. Provides sample questions and answers, including information on illegal interview questions. **205**

PART THREE

Job Opportunities Databank

31 **Job Opportunities Databank**
Entry-Level Job and Internship Listings **221**
Additional Companies **289**

CONTENTS

PART FOUR

Career Resources

32 **Career Resources**

Sources of Help Wanted Ads **295**
Professional Associations **304**
Employment Agencies and Search Firms **318**
Career Guides **319**
Professional and Trade Periodicals **324**
Basic Reference Guides **326**

PART FIVE

Master Index

33 **Master Index** **343**

Acknowledgments

The editors would like to thank all the pro's who took the time out of their busy schedules to share their first-hand knowledge and enthusiasm with the next generation of job-seekers. A special thanks to Kathleen M. Daniels, Assistant Director of the Career Planning and Placement Office at the University of Detroit Mercy, who provided much needed help with the job search section.

Thanks are also owed to the human resources personnel at the companies listed in this volume and to the public relations staffs of the associations who provided excellent suggestions for new essays. Nicholas Palo of the American Board of Professional Psychology and Jan Peterson of the National Association of Social Workers deserve special mention.

Introduction

"Corporate America has developed a deep, and perhaps abiding, reluctance to hire."
—*Business Week*, February 22, 1993

As the above quote indicates, getting and keeping a job these days can be a demanding proposition. Despite an economy that is finally recovering from the latest recession, many firms are still downsizing and are reluctant to increase staff levels.

What this means is that the job search is an increasingly competitive process. To beat the competition, job seekers need information. By using the *Mental Health and Social Work Career Directory*, job seekers gain the information they need to make the best possible decisions during their job search. This *Directory* is a comprehensive, one-stop resource that includes:

- Essays by industry professionals that provide practical advice not found in any other career resource
- Job search guidance designed to help you get in the door in mental health and social work
- Job and internship listings from leading mental health and social work organizations in the United States
- Information on additional career resources to further the job hunt
- A Master Index to facilitate easy access to the *Directory*

The *Directory* is organized into four parts that correspond to the steps of a typical job search—identifying your area of interest, refining your presentation, targeting agencies, and researching your prospects.

Sidebars located throughout the *Directory* are intended to amplify the text or provide a counterpoint to information presented on the page. They'll help you build a context for your career and job-search efforts by bringing you discussions of trends in the book publishing industry and the business world, labor statistics, job-hunting techniques, and predictions about our future worklife. These and other tips and tidbits were gleaned from a wide range of sources—sources you can continue to draw upon for a broader understanding of your chosen field and of the job-search process.

INTRODUCTION

Advice from the Pro's: An Invaluable Tool

Instead of offering "one-size-fits-all" advice or government statistics on what the working world is like, the *Mental Health and Social Work Career Directory* goes into the field for first-hand reports from experienced professionals working in all segments of mental health and social work. This **Advice from the Pro's** is offered by people who know what it's like to land that first job and turn it into a rich and rewarding career. Learn about:

- how to become a substance abuse counselor from Gregory A. Blevins of Governors State University.
- opportunities available for women to become psychology professors from Joan C. Chrisler of the Association for Women in Psychology.
- establishing an independent private social work practice from Sonja R. Berry, CSW-ACP.
- and 19 other areas of specialization, including:

Music therapy	Child welfare work
Art therapy	School social work
Counseling psychology	Employee assistance
Clinical psychology	Marriage and family therapy
Developmental psychology	Medical social work
Neuropsychology	Aging/gerontology
Family psychology	Research
Forensic psychology	Policy and planning
Psychiatry	Community organizing
Infant mental health	

The essays cover the most important things a job applicant needs to know, including:

- Which college courses and other background offer the best preparation
- Specific skills that are needed
- What organizations look for in an applicant
- Typical career paths
- Salary information

The Job Search Process: Making Sense of It All

What is the first thing a new job-hunter should do?

What are three different types of resumes and what should they look like?

What questions are off-limits in an interview?

These important questions are among the dozens that go through every person's mind when he or she begins to look for a job. Part Two of the *Mental Health and Social Work Career Directory*, **The Job Search Process**, answers these questions and more. It is divided into five chapters that cover all the basics of how to aggressively pursue a job:

- **Getting Started: Self-Evaluation and Career Objectives.** How to evaluate personal strengths and weaknesses and set goals.
- **Targeting Companies and Networking for Success.** How to identify the organizations you would like to work for and how to build a network of contacts.

- **Preparing Your Resume.** What to include, what not to include, and what style to use. Presents samples of the three basic resume types and worksheets to help you organize your information.
- **Writing Better Letters.** What letters should be written throughout the search process and how to make them more effective. Includes samples.
- **Questions for You, Questions for Them.** How to handle an interview and get the job.

Job Opportunities Databank: Finding the Job You Want

Once you're ready to start sending out those first resumes, how do you know where to start? The **Job Opportunities Databank**, Part Three of the *Directory*, includes listings for more than 350 general and psychiatric hospitals, long-term care facilities, nursing homes, private counseling centers, and state human services agencies in the United States that offer entry-level jobs in mental health and social work. These listings provide detailed contact information and data on the organizations' business activities, hiring practices, benefits, and application procedures—everything you need to know to approach potential employers. And since internships play an increasingly important role in the career research and employment process, information on the internship opportunities offered by the organizations listed is also included.

For further information on the arrangement and content of the **Job Opportunities Databank**, consult "How to Use the Job Opportunities Databank" immediately following this introduction.

Career Resources: A Guide to Organizations and Publications in the Field

Need to do more research on the specialty you've chosen or the organizations you'll be interviewing with? Part Four of the *Directory*, **Career Resources**, includes information on the following:

- Sources of help wanted ads
- Professional associations
- Employment agencies and search firms
- Career guides
- Professional and trade periodicals
- Basic reference guides and handbooks

Listings now contain contact information and descriptions of each publication's content and each organization's membership, purposes, and activities, helping you to pinpoint the resources you need for your own specific job search.

For additional information on the arrangement and content of **Career Resources**, consult "How to Locate Career Resources" following this introduction.

Master Index Speeds Access to Resources

A **Master Index** leads you to the information contained in all four sections of the *Directory* by citing all subjects, organizations, publications, and services listed throughout in a single alphabetic sequence. The index also includes inversions on significant keywords appearing in cited organization, publication, and service names.

INTRODUCTION

For example, the "American Psychological Association" would also be listed in the index under "Psychological Association; American" Citations in the index refer to page numbers.

Information Keeps Pace with the Changing Job Market

This edition of the *Mental Health and Social Work Career Directory* contains essays in the **Advice from the Pro's** section that were contributed by leading professionals in the mental health and social work industry on subjects of particular interest to today's job seekers. All employers listed in the **Job Opportunities Databank** were contacted by telephone or facsimile to obtain current information, and **Career Resources** listings were obtained from selected material from other databases compiled by Gale Research Inc.

Comments and Suggestions Welcome

The staff of the *Mental Health and Social Work Career Directory* appreciates learning of any corrections or additions that will make this book as complete and useful as possible. Comments or suggestions for future essay topics or other improvements are also welcome, as are suggestions for careers that could be covered in new volumes of the Career Advisor Series. Please contact:

> Career Advisor Series
> Visible Ink Press
> 835 Penobscot Bldg.
> Detroit, MI 48226-4094
> Phone: 800-347-4253
> Fax: (313)961-6815

Bradley J. Morgan
Joseph M. Palmisano

How to Use the Job Opportunities Databank

The **Job Opportunities Databank** comprises two sections:
Entry-Level Job and Internship Listings
Additional Companies

Entry-Level Job and Internship Listings

Provides listings for more than 350 general and psychiatric specialty hospitals, long-term care facilities, nursing homes, private counseling centers, and state human services agencies in the United States. Entries in the **Job Opportunities Databank** are arranged alphabetically by organization name. When available, entries include:

- **Organization name.**
- **Address and telephone number.** A mailing address and telephone number are provided in every entry.
- **Fax and toll-free telephone number.** These are provided when known.
- **Business description.** Outlines the organization's business activities. The geographical scope of the company's operations may also be provided.
- **Corporate officers.** Lists the names of executive officers, with titles.
- **Number of employees.** Includes the most recently provided figure for total number of employees. Other employee-specific information may be provided as well.
- **Average entry-level hiring.** Includes the number of entry-level employees the organization typically hires in an average year. Many have listed "Unknown" or "0" for their average number of entry-level jobs. Because of current economic conditions, many firms could not estimate their projected entry-level hires for the coming years. However, because these organizations have offered entry-level positions in the past and because their needs may change, we have listed them in this *Directory*.
- **Opportunities.** Describes the entry-level positions that the organization typically offers, as well as the education and other requirements needed for those positions.

USING THE DATABANK

- **Benefits.** Lists the insurance, time off, retirement and financial plans, activities, and programs provided by the organization, if known.
- **Human resources contacts.** Lists the names of personnel-related staff, with titles.
- **Application procedure.** Describes specific application instructions, when provided by the organization.

Many entries also include information on available internship programs. Internship information provided includes:

- **Contact name.** Lists the names of officers or personnel-related contact who are responsible for the internship program.
- **Type.** Indicates the type of internship, including time period and whether it is paid, unpaid, or for college credit. Also indicates if an organization does not offer internships.
- **Number available.** Number of internships that the company typically offers.
- **Number of applications received.** Total number of applications received in a typical year.
- **Application procedures and deadline.** Describes specific application instructions and the deadline for submitting applications.
- **Decision date.** Final date when internship placement decisions are made.
- **Duties.** Lists the typical duties that an intern can expect to perform at the organization.
- **Qualifications.** Lists the criteria a prospective applicant must meet to be considered for an internship with the organization.

Additional Companies

Covers those organizations that elected to provide only their name, address, and telephone number for inclusion in the *Directory*. Entries are arranged alphabetically by organization name.

How to Locate Career Resources

The **Career Resources** chapter contains six categories of information sources, each of which is arranged alphabetically by resource or organization name. The categories include:

▼ Sources of Help Wanted Ads

- **Covers:** Professional journals, industry periodicals, association newsletters, placement bulletins, and online services that include employment ads or business opportunities. Includes sources that focus specifically on mental health and social work concerns, as well as general periodical sources such as the *National Business Employment Weekly*.
- **Entries include:** The resource's title; name, address, and telephone number of its publisher; frequency; subscription rate; description of contents; toll-free and additional telephone numbers; and facsimile numbers.
- **Sources:** *Job Hunter's Sourcebook* (published by Gale Research Inc.) and original research.

▼ Professional Associations

- **Covers:** Trade and professional associations that offer career-related information and services.
- **Entries include:** Association name, address, and telephone number; membership; purpose and objectives; publications; toll-free or additional telephone numbers; and facsimile numbers. In some cases, the publications mentioned in these entries are described in greater detail as separate entries cited in the Sources of Help Wanted Ads, Career Guides, Professional and Trade Periodicals, and Basic Reference Guides and Handbooks categories.
- **Sources:** *Encyclopedia of Associations* (published by Gale Research Inc.) and original research.

▼ Employment Agencies and Search Firms

- **Covers:** Firms used by companies to recruit candidates for positions and, at times, by individuals to pursue openings. Employment agencies are generally geared toward filling openings at entry- to mid-level in the local job market, while

executive search firms are paid by the hiring organization to recruit professional and managerial candidates, usually for higher-level openings. Also covers temporary employment agencies because they can be a method of identifying and obtaining regular employment. Includes firms that focus specifically on mental health and social work, as well as some larger general firms.
- **Entries include:** The firm's name, address, and telephone number; whether it's an employment agency, executive search firm, or temporary agency; descriptive information, as appropriate; toll-free and additional telephone numbers; and facsimile number.
- **Sources:** *Job Hunter's Sourcebook*.

▼ Career Guides

- **Covers:** Books, kits, pamphlets, brochures, videocassettes, films, online services, and other materials that describe the job-hunting process in general or that provide guidance and insight into the job-hunting process in mental health and social work careers.
- **Entries include:** The resource's title; name, address, and telephone number of its publisher or distributor; name of the editor or author; publication date or frequency; description of contents; arrangement; indexes; toll-free or additional telephone numbers; and facsimile numbers.
- **Sources:** *Professional Careers Sourcebook* and *Vocational Careers Sourcebook* (published by Gale Research Inc.) and original research.

▼ Professional and Trade Periodicals

- **Covers:** Newsletters, magazines, newspapers, trade journals, and other serials that offer information to professionals in mental health and social work.
- **Entries include:** The resource's title; the name, address, and telephone number of the publisher; the editor's name; frequency; description of contents; toll-free and additional telephone numbers; and facsimile numbers. Publication titles appear in italics.
- **Sources:** *Gale Directory of Publications* and *Broadcast Media* and *Newsletters in Print* (published by Gale Research Inc.) and original research.

▼ Basic Reference Guides and Handbooks

- **Covers:** Manuals, directories, dictionaries, encyclopedias, films and videocassettes, and other published reference material used by professionals working in mental health and social work careers.
- **Entries include:** The resource's title; name, address, and telephone number of the publisher or distributor; the editor's or author's name; publication date or frequency; description of contents; toll-free and additional telephone numbers; and facsimile numbers. Publication titles are rendered in italics.
- **Sources:** *Professional Careers Sourcebook, Vocational Careers Sourcebook,* and original research.

Advice from the Pro's

CHAPTER ONE

The Counseling Psychologist

Donna L. McKinley, Ph.D., ABPP,
Vice Chancellor for Student Affairs
University of Michigan—Dearborn

"I just don't know what I'm going to do with my life. My parents want me to be sure to get a college degree in something that will land me a job, and I've taken some business courses. But I hate them so much that I'm thinking of dropping out of school."

"We were so in love when we got married. When I look back on it, I guess we really did have very different interests, but each of us was willing to go along with the other. Now, we hardly have a kind word for each other. I put all my energy in my job and the kids, and he's just never home. Is this marriage salvageable?"

"This patient has very high blood pressure and is at great risk for life-threatening heart disease. I'd like you to work up a personal stress management program with her before I release her from the hospital. I think she may also need some personal counseling after she goes home."

"Two students from our residence hall were killed in an automobile accident last weekend. Three other students had planned to go on the trip with them and are feeling guilty because they weren't along to share the driving. Most of the students in the hall are affected in some way by this tragedy. Nobody's getting any school work done, and final exams are coming soon. Is there anything you can do to help?"

"Individuals in our work group are producing, but the team as a whole is getting nowhere. In fact, there hardly seems to be a team at all. One person talks to the team leader about a new idea, and someone else cuts it down and points out all the problems. I think we could do better for the company if we could figure out how to work together. It would also be a lot more fun to come to work."

This is just a sample of the kind of situations addressed by counseling psychologists. The role of a **counseling psychologist** is to help people learn about themselves, solve problems, make decisions, and live satisfying lives. Counseling psychologists work in a variety of different settings, but the goal is always to create the environment and circumstances that allow the individual to live to the fullest capacity.

Career Preparation

Entering the field of counseling psychology requires completion of a doctoral degree in counseling psychology. The degree may be a Ph.D., Ed.D., or Psy.D., depending on the location of the graduate program. Most, but not all, doctoral programs in counseling psychology are accredited by the American Psychological Association.

An undergraduate degree in psychology prepares one to apply for admission to a graduate program in counseling psychology, although some programs will accept other undergraduate majors. Good communication skills are essential. Involvement in a research project as an undergraduate is good preparation for the rigors of graduate school. Volunteer or work experience in a human services setting, such as a hospital, summer camp for troubled adolescents, or residence hall, and undergraduate research experience provide good opportunities to test out one's interest in this field and also are viewed positively in admissions decisions.

Graduate programs in counseling psychology include course work, research, and clinical training. Completion of the doctorate takes four to five years. Graduate education prepares a counseling psychologist to use tests, interviews, and other tools to assess an individual or group's functioning, provide counseling and psychotherapy to individuals and groups, conduct research to further understanding of psychological phenomena and the impact of the human environment on people, and develop educational and treatment programs to promote psychological health and development.

An internship is required for completion of the doctorate in counseling psychology. The typical internship is a full-time experience of one year in an organized training program that may also be accredited by the American Psychological Association. Internships exist in a variety of settings, including college and university counseling centers, psychiatric and medical clinics and hospitals, community mental health centers, and prisons.

An intern has direct responsibility for providing service to patients or clients. Typically, an intern will spend some part of each week conducting interviews with individuals who are requesting or being referred for the purpose of deciding what service is required. This process may include testing, observation, and interviews with other individuals as well as the client. The intern will also be assigned some clients as the service provider. For these clients, the intern must develop a plan, carry out a course of counseling, and evaluate the success of the counseling. In many settings, interns will have the opportunity to supervise less experienced counselors and to work with groups as well as individuals.

For most counseling psychologists, the internship is the end of formal training. Some pursue additional specialized training through a post-doctoral internship or fellowship. Such specialized training usually prepares the individual to work with a

---

Getting Your Feet Wet in Psychology

Volunteer or work experience in a human services setting, such as a hospital, summer camp for troubled adolescents, or residence hall, and undergraduate research experience provide good opportunities to test out one's interest in this field and also are viewed positively in admissions decisions.

specific population or use a particular method. Examples include forensic (legal) psychology, health psychology (using psychological interventions to assist individuals who have physical symptoms), neurological psychology (brain-behavior linkage), and family therapy. Many psychologists who pursue advanced training seek recognition as a Diplomate of the American Board of Professional Psychology through an application and examination process.

Working Conditions

The majority of counseling psychologists are employed in colleges or universities in counseling centers or as faculty members. An increasingly popular option is independent private practice, either in addition to university employment or as full-time work. Starting salaries in university settings are $28,000 to $30,000. The income potential in private practice is higher, but there is less security and often less variety in the work, and setting up a practice requires business and entrepreneurial skills, as well as the professional expertise in counseling psychology. Counseling psychologists may be employed in a number of other settings, such as Employee Assistance Programs in business and industry, medical clinics and hospitals, firms which provide organizational consultation, and police departments.

Working in a Counseling Center

For a counseling psychologist in a counseling center, a typical day includes a variety of activities. The psychologist will counsel some clients with concerns as varied as adjusting to being away from home to overcoming the effects of childhood sexual abuse. The counseling psychologist in this setting typically oversees the work of other individuals and will spend time observing, teaching, or problem-solving with them. These may be undergraduate paraprofessionals who are running a study skills clinic, graduate students in a counseling psychology program who are learning counseling skills, or a psychometrist who administers psychological tests to clients. On occasion, the psychologist may need to consult with a physician or psychiatrist about possible medication or hospitalization for an individual with a life-threatening problem, such as someone who has attempted suicide. Perhaps the day will end with the counseling psychologist conducting a workshop on some important skill, such as stress management or conflict resolution. On other days, there will be opportunities to conduct research and write, to consult with faculty and others on psychological issues, and to develop new educational approaches to promoting psychological health.

Working in Private Practice

Counseling psychologists in private practice spend most of their work time in direct counseling and psychotherapy with individuals, families, or groups. They may also conduct evaluations for use in legal proceedings. The psychologist charges a fee for service, which is paid by the client or by health insurance. Most psychologists in private practice do some work for free or at a greatly reduced rate as a contribution to society.

The Future in Counseling Psychology

Future career prospects for counseling psychologists are tied to changes in the healthcare industry. Extensive efforts are underway to make healthcare accessible and affordable for all Americans. While there is evidence that effective use of counseling and psychotherapy can reduce the need for or extent of medical care, it is not yet clear that this will be reflected in inclusion of counseling psychologists as recognized healthcare providers by all insurance companies.

What is certain, though, is that the focus of the practice of a counseling psychologist is on creating the conditions to support people to build on strengths and work toward positive outcomes. Whether it is overcoming health problems, resolving interpersonal conflicts, working to change policies that disadvantage certain groups, making changes in one's work or family situation, working through grief, or minimizing the effects of a disability, there are immense rewards from helping people to live their lives to the fullest.

▼

DONNA L. MCKINLEY completed her undergraduate work at Kansas Wesleyan University and her Ph.D. in counseling psychology at Ohio State University. She is a diplomate in counseling psychology from the American Board of Professional Psychology. Dr. McKinley has held professional positions at Capital University in Columbus, OH; University of Michigan-Ann Arbor; and Colorado State University. She is currently vice chancellor for student affairs at University of Michigan—Dearborn.

CHAPTER TWO

Exploring a Career in Substance Abuse Counseling

**Gregory A. Blevins, Ph.D.,
Professor of Alcohol and Drug Abuse Sciences
Governors State University**

Generally, when people think of careers in the substance abuse field, their thoughts tend to focus on counseling. While substance abuse counseling is an important aspect of the service continuum and is likely to be the most frequently available position in the field for the foreseeable future, there are also other types of positions available. For example, there is an increasing demand for prevention specialists. However, let us begin by exploring the career aspects of substance abuse counseling.

History of Substance Abuse Counseling

Over the last 25 years, substance abuse counseling has become increasingly refined and recognized as a distinct occupation. In part, this process can trace its roots to the manpower and training activities of the National Institute on Alcohol Abuse and Alcoholism (NIAAA) and the National Institute on Drug Abuse (NIDA). In addition, individuals working within the substance abuse field have formed organizations such as the National Association of Alcoholism and Drug Abuse Counselors (NAADAC), Alcohol and Drug Problems Association of North America (ADPA), and Employee Assistance Society of North America (EASNA). These organizations and others have been working toward defining the requisite skills and knowledge required of substance abuse professionals and developing standards for certifying individuals as meeting minimum competency levels. Overall, substance abuse counseling has and is evolving as a profession.

Functions of Substance Abuse Counselors

What do substance abuse counselors do? The National Certification Reciprocity Consortium (NCRC), which is a voluntary association of most of the certification boards in the individual states, defines substance abuse counseling as consisting of 12 core functions. These core functions are:

1. **Screening**—determining the appropriateness and eligibility of an individual for admission;
2. **Intake**—completing administrative and preliminary assessment procedures for admission;
3. **Orientation**—describing the program philosophy, goals, rules, services, costs, and client rights;
4. **Assessment**—identifying and evaluating a client's strengths, weaknesses, problems, and needs;
5. **Treatment Planning**—deciding with the clients which problems to focus on, what the goals will be, and how those goals are to be met;
6. **Counseling**—helping clients achieve their objectives by exploring problems and their implications, examining attitudes and feelings, considering alternatives, and decision-making;
7. **Case Management**—coordinating multiple services within and among agencies to achieve client goals;
8. **Crises Intervention**—responding to acute or short-term emotional or physical distress;
9. **Education**—providing information on alcohol and other drug abuse, related problems, and the services and resources available;
10. **Referral**—assisting clients to utilize support systems and community resources in meeting their goals;
11. **Report and Record Keeping**—maintaining and updating assessments, treatment plans, reports, progress notes, discharge summaries, and other client-related data; and
12. **Consultation**—working with substance abuse and other professionals to assure comprehensive, quality care for the client.

In fulfilling these core functions, the substance abuse counselor is expected to be familiar with federal and state regulations as well as the ethical standards of professional organizations. A key concern is maintaining confidentiality, since counselors often become aware of client information that could harm the client, including the fact that the client has sought help or is in treatment.

There is considerable variation among programs in how these counseling functions are fulfilled. Small programs may require the counselor to perform all 12 core functions (plus additional activities), while larger programs often permit specialization in one or a combination of the core functions (e.g., screening, intake, and assessment). Likewise, publicly funded agencies tend to have broader expectations for a counselor's performance (including some administrative responsibilities) than privately funded programs.

Clearly, substance abuse counselors are expected to possess a wide range of knowledge and skills, many of which are common to most health and human services professionals. What distinguishes the substance abuse counselor from other helping professionals is his/her understanding of the causes, correlates, and consequences of alcohol and other drug use. The overall goal of substance abuse counseling is to reduce or minimize the effects of alcohol or other drug use on the client's behaviors.

Working Conditions

Substance abuse counselors do much of their work in the afternoon, evenings, and on weekends. This is especially true of outpatient programs. In addition to the work hours, prospective entrants to this field should be aware that experienced professionals often complain about the record keeping and the seeming futility of working with some clients.

Manpower studies have suggested that about one-third of the counselors leave the field annually. Some of the problems encountered by substance abuse professionals include: becoming emotionally drained through their involvement with clients; fatigue in meeting the daily needs of clients; insufficient resources (personnel and funding) to provide appropriate, high quality services; ambiguity of tasks (what am I expected to *do* and what kind of *impact* am I having?); and inter-agency conflicts with other substance abuse agencies and with other health and human service providers.

> **ADVICE FROM THE PRO'S**
>
> **Average Work Week in Major Economic Countries**
>
> Ranked by: Average number of hours worked each week in 1991.
> 1. Japan, with 41.5 hours
> 2. Sweden, 40.0
> 2. United States, 40.0
> 2. Italy, 40.0
> 5. France, 39.0
> 6. Britain, 38.8
> 7. Germany, 37.6
>
> Source: *New York Times*

While these problems are not unique to the substance abuse profession, conflict between recovering (from alcohol or other drug abuse) and non-recovering staff has been a special issue. This conflict can appear in several ways, including differences in: perceived motivation for entering the field, perceived attitudes toward substance abusers, education and training accomplishments, and approaches to working with clients. The development of professional standards and certification is helping to *reduce* but not necessarily *eliminate* this conflict.

All in a Day's Work

A typical day for a substance abuse counselor consists of four to five hours of individual counseling sessions, one to two hours of group or family counseling, one hour of educational lectures, and two to three hours of record keeping. Weekend work is often part of the responsibility.

Salaries

Starting salaries, raises, and top salaries vary considerably across the states and with the characteristics of the agency (e.g., private versus public, hospital versus non-hospital, inpatient versus outpatient). Substance abuse services are part of the health and human service area and insurance industry practices and federal-state-local budgetary priorities greatly affect salary levels. Entry-level counselors with a bachelor's degree can expect to earn $15,000 to $20,000, while experienced counselors with master's degrees are at $45,000 to $50,000.

Career Paths

The typical career ladder in substance abuse counseling involves moving from a Counselor I to a Counselor II, clinical supervisor or senior counselor, program director, and agency administration. Such a progression assumes continuing education and training, along with experience. The actual rate of promotion is hard to predict: some professionals move into administration in as little as five years, while others never move beyond a Counselor I level.

Traditionally, substance abuse counselors have come from a variety of backgrounds and many have entered the field without a college education. However, this avenue is rapidly closing as the field becomes increasingly professionalized and those entering without specific educational credentials are likely to find their career paths severely limited. Nationally, associate, baccalaureate, and master's degree programs have been developed and potential employees are seeking their graduates. Typically, the college programs require a minimum of five to six courses in substance abuse, which may be cross-listed in psychology, counseling, social work, mental health, human services and related areas or, with increasing frequency, as chemical dependency, addiction studies, alcohol and drug abuse, or substance abuse courses.

Getting Started in Substance Abuse Counseling

The first step in considering substance abuse counseling as a career field is to engage in some self-exploration. Some of the people who have entered the field have done so without an awareness of *their own* motives, attitudes, values, and beliefs and, as a result, have found themselves (or have been discovered by supervisors, peers, and clients) to be working on personal issues through their clients. Thus, it is important to participate in some form of personal awareness or self-growth course or workshop before committing to the field.

The next step in preparing for a substance abuse counseling career is to acquire the specific knowledge and skills necessary to function effectively. Typically, this requires an understanding of: pharmacology of abused drugs; impact of chemical dependency on individuals, families, and social systems; the service delivery network including prevention, intervention, treatment, and aftercare; and the application of counseling techniques and theories to substance abusers, their families, and others who are interdependent with substance abusers.

Finally, with the foregoing in hand, one is ready to begin applying his or her knowledge and skills with actual clients. This should be done in a supervised setting with a skilled clinician. Obtaining a supervised internship in substance abuse agencies has been relatively easy, and part-time employment has been frequently used as a way of initiating a career. Substance abuse counselor certification requires a supervised work experience, and higher education programs require internships or practica for graduation. Most substance abuse agencies are willing to accept individuals for internships and part-time employment if they are prepared to provide appropriate supervision to the trainee. Interviewing with and participating in treatment agency is an excellent way to determine if this is the career area for you.

Career Options

What happens if I decide I do not want to stay in substance abuse counseling? There are at least two career options open to those who enter the substance abuse counseling profession but decide that they want to leave. The first is to move into another aspect of the health and human services area. Substance abuse counselors generally find that their knowledge and skills transfer well to other areas. However, the ability to move into another specialization will depend upon the particular criteria of that area. Just as substance abuse agencies have become increasingly reluctant to hire counselors and social workers who have little or no background in substance abuse, other counseling and social service agencies may require appropriate backgrounds beyond substance abuse education and experience.

The second career option for substance abuse counselors is to consider some other part of the substance abuse field. As mentioned at the outset, the substance abuse field encompasses more than counseling. In particular, there are opportunities for substance abuse specialists in school and community prevention programs, private and public employee assistance programs, criminal justice (parole, probation, correctional, and court services) programs, and new areas of application that are being developed constantly. For better (because there are career opportunities) or worse (because substance abuse continues to be a major national problem), the substance abuse field is an area of increasing growth and development.

▼

DR. GREGORY BLEVINS received a specialty certificate in alcoholism and drug abuse in 1975 and a doctorate in sociology in 1979 from Western Michigan University. Since 1982, he has been a professor of alcohol and drug abuse sciences at Governors State University, where both an undergraduate minor and a master's degree are offered. He has frequently been called upon as a trainer and consultant to local, state, regional, and national organizations on a variety of substance abuse related issues. He has co-authored two books, *Handbook for Volunteers in Substance Abuse Agencies*, published by Learning Publications, Inc. and *Substance Abuse Counseling—An Individualized Approach* with Brooks/Cole. Dr. Blevins is also a founding member of the International Consortium of Addiction Studies Educators (INCASE).

CHAPTER THREE

Family Psychologists Look at the Larger Picture

Carol Philpot, Psy.D.,
Professor and Associate Director of Clinical Training
Florida Institute of Technology, School of Psychology

While psychology is broadly defined as the study of human behavior, there are many subspecialties within the field, designated both by site of practice (clinical, counseling, school) and by focus (neuropsychology, child, family). Although family *therapy* as practiced by social workers, ministers, and a few maverick psychiatrists, has been around since the '50s, **family psychology** is relatively new as a *recognized* specialty in clinical or counseling psychology. Although the Division of Family Psychology of the American Psychological Association is only nine years old, the field now boasts a major APA journal, *The Journal of Family Psychology* and offers the ABPP status, the highest honor awarded to a clinician who has mastered an area of expertise.

What Does a Family Psychologist Do?

One of the exciting things about psychology is the range of activities in which one can engage while in the field. These include but are not limited to: professional practice, which includes assessment and treatment; consulting with organizations and businesses; teaching at all levels of education; writing (both for professional journals and academic books and for newspapers, popular magazines, or self-help books); research (in either an academic or clinical setting); serving as an expert witness in court; running a clinic or hospital; supervising the clinical work of others; designing and directing treatment programs; lobbying in Congress or serving as an advisor to governmental programs; and even appearing on television and radio talk shows as an expert. It is not possible to describe the typical day of a psychologist because s/he may choose to do any one of the above or a combination of several, either simultaneously or sequentially, during his/her career.

What makes the family psychologist different is his/her *systems* orientation to understanding human behavior. Family psychologists believe that psychological distress cannot be understood separate from the social context of which it is a part and that efforts to alleviate human distress must create change in transactions among the persons of subsystems currently involved in the maintenance of distress. That is, (to borrow a metaphor from Wegscheider-Cruse) families are like mobiles. If every piece is in perfect condition and balanced just right, the mobile functions well. Each piece hangs separately, yet connected; all parts are able to move and change in the breeze, but they do not function totally alone. If any one piece gets tangled or broken, the whole mobile goes askew and all parts are affected adversely. If these parts were human, they might well try all sorts of maneuvers to get the mobile rebalanced so that they could continue to dangle in their previously comfortable manner. However, there are many different ways in which to balance a mobile and a new arrangement might be more appropriate for the errant piece, one that would not put so much stress on any one part. Unfortunately, human mobiles are creatures of habit and tend not to think creatively; they struggle to recreate what they already know. Therefore, they get stuck, and it often takes a mechanic to untangle the mess and find a new balance which allows each part to grow and prosper.

This is an obviously simplistic explanation of a very complex process. So what does that mean in concrete, practical terms? An example may help.

A seven-year-old boy is brought to the therapist because he is exhibiting angry and defiant behavior both at home and at school. A child therapist who does not think systemically may well set up a behavior modification program which rewards incompatible good behavior and extinguishes the negative behavior. However, if Mom and Dad are in a power struggle and Dad is covertly supporting his son's rebellion against Mom because he resents her control but is afraid to confront it directly, the program will fail unless he also teaches Dad and Mom how to deal with each other openly and negotiate a satisfactory compromise. In fact, the situation may be further complicated by good older sister who wants her brother to stay in the role of bad boy because she is elevated to a superior position and can get away with murder. If he begins to make progress, you can be sure she will find a way to sabotage him unless she is provided some other means of being a special child which does not depend upon his dysfunction.

Thus, therapy which is done with the individual alone is less likely to be successful and enduring than that which changes the entire system. For this reason, family therapy has become the treatment of choice in a large variety of cases and is considered by many to be the *future* of psychology.

It is also true that family patterns are passed down from one generation to another; thus dysfunction which began with one's great grandmother can affect one's great granddaughter as well. For this reason, family psychologists study families to determine what factors seem to facilitate happy and healthy lives and which factors do not. They can then advise families, schools, and governmental programs on how best to devise prevention programs, rather than waiting for dysfunction to occur.

Innumerable Career Options Await You!

One of the exciting things about psychology is the range of activities in which one can engage while in the field. These include but are not limited to: professional practice, which includes assessment and treatment; consulting with organizations and businesses; teaching at all levels of education; writing (both for professional journals and academic books and for newspapers, popular magazines, or self-help books); research (in either an academic or clinical setting); serving as an expert witness in court; running a clinic or hospital; supervising the clinical work of others; designing and directing treatment programs; lobbying in Congress or serving as an advisor to governmental programs; and even appearing on television and radio talk shows as an expert.

What makes the family psychologist different from other psychologists is his/her focus on *relationships* and the impact of those relationships on mental health, both in the present and the future.

ADVICE FROM THE PRO'S

How Do I Become a Family Psychologist?

Specialization in psychology, as in medicine, takes place after one has received the basic training required of all psychologists. To become a psychologist, one must first obtain a bachelor's degree, preferably with a psychology major, and then attend graduate school for approximately three to five years, depending on the program, followed by internship, after which the doctoral degree (Ph.D., Ed.D., or Psy.D.) is awarded. This must be followed by one year of post-doctoral experience in most states before one is allowed to take the licensing exam. Once the exam is passed, the psychologist can practice independently, setting up his/her own practice much as a medical doctor does. Although students may receive course work in family theory, research, and practice during graduate school, intensive study in that area would probably take place at the internship and post-doctoral levels.

Entry-Level Jobs

Although the training period sounds like a very long one, individuals can actually work in the field as they learn, first as mental health technicians (at the A.A. and B.A. degree levels), and later as psychotherapists (at the master's degree level) in hospitals, schools, and clinics under the supervision of a licensed psychologist. Although several states provide licensing for practice at the master's degree level for mental health counselors or marriage and family therapists, *psychology* continues to require the doctoral degree to practice independently. The doctoral degree in psychology broadens the range of opportunities for practice and increases the earning potential.

Earning Potential

Since family psychologists perform such a wide variety of functions, income varies according to setting and geographical location. Those who choose to remain in academia to teach and do research may enter at the assistant professor level, earning somewhere between $33,000 and $35,000 for a nine-month contract. Hospital administrators and program directors might earn $40,000 to $50,000 a year or more. Those who begin work with an established practice may be guaranteed $50,000, with a potential to make much more.

Established private practitioners can make as much as $200,000 a year or more, charging between $90 and $150 an hour for their time, depending upon years of experience, reputation, and geographical location. Successful researchers bring in two- and three-million dollar grants from which they can pay themselves comfortable salaries. Top lecturers can command $2,500 a day for their services. In addition, many psychologists collect royalties from test-scoring systems, textbooks, self-help books, audio and video self-help tapes, or special programs they have developed and marketed. The potential in the field is great.

Personal Qualifications

In addition to the educational requirements which demand intelligence, perseverance, organization, good work habits, and a great deal of stamina, there are also other personality factors which are very important for this field. In the field of psychology, it is almost imperative that one be socially adept, very comfortable with all types of people, and be able to put them at ease very quickly. Psychology, perhaps more than any other field, requires an open-minded, non-judgmental, empathic, and caring personality, one who can accept differences in values, lifestyles, and goals as healthy variety, as long as individuals are not being harmed. Likewise, family psychologists need to be emotionally stable and well-grouped, having a good sense of their own boundaries, to protect themselves from burn-out and depression, while dealing daily with the pain of others. Psychologists are problem solvers who must have analytic minds and enjoy constant change and challenge. No two families are exactly alike. Days are never routine. One cannot predict what might be presented when the conference room door closes. Family psychology is not for the faint-hearted. It can be demanding and exhausting, but it can also be very rewarding.

▼

Dr. Carol Philpot is a professor of psychology and associate director of clinical training at the School of Psychology, Florida Institute of Technology. She designed and directs a three-course family psychology tract within the School of Psychology. She also maintains a part-time private practice specializing in marital and family therapy, divorce therapy and mediation, remarriage, and gender issues. She is past-president of the Division of Family Psychology of the American Psychological Association. She has presented widely and published in the area of gender sensitivity training, gender sensitive psychotherapy, divorce and remarriage, premarital counseling, and family systems theory. She is an American Association for Marriage and Family Therapy-approved supervisor and a consultant to *Bridal Guide* magazine.

CHAPTER FOUR

Preparing for a Career in Family Therapy

Robert F. Stahmann, Ph.D.,
Professor of Family Sciences, Brigham Young University

What is Marriage and Family Therapy?

Family therapy or marriage and family therapy (MFT) is the youngest and most rapidly growing of the mental health professions. MFT has grown from the status of an area of treatment practiced by a few pioneering individuals in traditional mental health professions, such as psychiatry, psychology, and social work, to a profession in its own right. Currently, 30 states license or certify marriage and family therapy as a mental health profession separate from other professions. A definition of marriage and family therapy is the process of providing professional psychotherapy to individuals, couples, and families, either singly or in groups. Marriage and family therapy includes individual, premarital, relationship, marital, divorce, and family therapy for the purpose of resolving emotional disorders, modifying interpersonal and intrapersonal dysfunction, and promoting mental health.

Marriage and family therapists are trained in the diagnosis and treatment of mental and nervous disorders, as are other mental health professionals, such as psychologists, psychiatrists, and social workers. However, marriage and family therapists have specialized training and knowledge in such areas as human growth and development, marital and family interaction, sexual dysfunction, parent-child relationships, and the dynamics of family systems. This training gives MFT's a particularly appropriate basis for helping people and dealing with normal developmental stages, such as pre-marriage, marital adjustment, children moving from childhood to adolescence, adults moving from productive employment into retirement, or aging. MFT's also work with problems and crises such as death in the family, unexpected illness, divorce, alcoholism and/or substance abuse, unemployment, and child and/or spouse abuse.

What Training is Required?

The master's degree is the minimal credential required to practice MFT. While it is possible to get a master's degree in a field related to MFT and then *add on* MFT course work in order to eventually meet MFT practice requirements, my discussion is focused on graduate study in MFT. What I present here also applies to getting into doctoral-level MFT graduate work.

The application process at different graduate schools will vary, and a prospective student should write to each school of interest in order to obtain specific information and application forms. I suggest doing this early enough in the undergraduate training in order to allow time to take any courses that may be required or suggested for admission.

In applying for graduate school, first be aware that the application deadline is usually during the winter before the academic year that the student will begin the program. Thus, it will likely be that all materials, such as application forms, transcripts, letters of reference, Graduate Record Exam (GRE) test scores, etc., will be due to the graduate school in January or February. Plan early!

As suggested previously, it is wise for a prospective student to correspond with MFT programs of interest during the junior year of undergraduate work. This gives time to meet specific course requirements, learn details of the graduate program, and meet the application deadline. Most MFT programs begin the academic program each fall and require full-time study. This is the case because the combination of didactic and clinical work in the MFT curriculum is very demanding of time and intellect.

Admission is usually competitive with often times more applicants than students admitted. While didactic courses in the MFT curriculum can serve 15 to 25 students, the practicum courses must be limited to no more than six students per faculty member, in order to provide adequate supervision of clinical work with clients. Thus, a prospective student is well advised to apply to more than a single graduate program. Specific areas that graduate admissions committees are likely to consider are:

1. Undergraduate major in a social science or at least a concentration of course work that includes the prerequisites for that particular graduate program.

2. Grade point average (GPA) of at least a 3.0 on a 4.0 scale. Often graduate schools look at GPA on the most recent 60 semester/quarter hours of course work as well as overall GPA.

3. Letters of reference are important because they can provide various views of past and potential performance. Obtain them from a variety of people who can give information about interpersonal qualities as well as academic performance and potential.

4. It is likely that an admissions exam such as the Graduate Record Exam (GRE) or Miller Analogies Test (MAT) will be required. Find this out in time to prepare for the test and take it so that the results will be available to the graduate admissions committee on time.

5. A letter of intent or interest is often required. Sometimes a biographical sketch is requested. Admissions committees find these useful in helping to determine whether the graduate program will likely meet the prospective student's goals and interests. Thus, these statements should be carefully and honestly written by the prospective student.

6. Some graduate schools require the prospective student to visit the campus for an interview. I believe, whether required or not, it is a good idea for the student to make such a visit to enable the student to get a feel for the faculty, physical facilities, and graduate program. It also obviously gives the faculty a chance to see the prospective graduate student as more than an application file. Students can prepare by thinking of questions about the school, curriculum professional activities of recent MFT graduates, etc. Be sure to schedule an appointment with the faculty, rather than just *drop in.*

7. While the application may not require a resume, I suggest that a student submit one as part of the application materials. Remember, the task of the admissions committee is to know the student through the application materials submitted. A resume, well thought out and written, is useful and impressive.

What Is the Graduate School Curriculum?

Of course, there are individual differences in the MFT graduate curriculum at different schools. Variations are based upon the specific goals of the school or state licensing requirements. Yet, the following curriculum, based upon standard accreditation guidelines, is typical of most offered in a two-year master's degree program.

1. **Marital and Family Studies** (three courses)—Family development and family interactional patterns across the life cycle of the individuals as well as the family. Courses may include the study of: family life cycle; theories of family development; marriage and/or the family; sociology of the family; families under stress; contemporary family; family in a social context; cross-cultural family; youth/adult/aging and the family; family subsystems; or individual, interpersonal relationships (marital, parental, sibling).

2. **Marital and Family Therapy** (three courses)—Family therapy methodology; family assessment; treatment and intervention methods; overview of major clinical theories of marital and family therapy such as: communications, contextual, experimental, object relations, strategic, structural, systemic, or transgenerational.

3. **Human Development** (three courses)—Human development; personality theory; human sexuality; psychopathology; or behavior-pathology.

4. **Professional Studies** (one course)—Professional socialization and the role of the professional organization; legal responsibilities and liabilities; independent practice and interprofessional cooperation; ethics; or family law.

5. **Research** (one course)—Research design; methods; statistics; or research in marital and family studies and therapy.

6. **Clinical Practicum** (one year minimum, 500 hours)—15 hours per week, approximately 8 to 10 hours in face-to-face contact with individuals, couples, and families for the purpose of assessment, diagnosis, and treatment.

A master's thesis and other courses are often required to complete the graduate degree. Thus, a master's degree in MFT will require 45 or more semester hours. Remember also, that prior to licensure or certification by a state, supervised post-degree clinical practice must be obtained. Generally, this is a two-year process involving at least 1,000 hours of face-to-face contact with couples and families, providing assessment and treatment.

What About Financial and Time Requirements for Marriage and Family Therapy Education?

It is important for potential students in marriage and family therapy (or any other professional program) to realize that graduate education is an expensive undertaking. The exact costs vary among different training programs, particularly in regard to tuition. The per semester or per credit hour tuition costs for graduate education are almost universally higher than the corresponding undergraduate tuition costs. MFT students receive a great deal of individual instruction and clinical supervision from professors. Use of this valuable commodity is one of the major reasons for the increased tuition costs. It is important to ask for specific tuition cost information when inquiring about a training program in which you are interested. Also, keep in mind that MFT education usually continues all year, so plan for the added tuition costs of school during the summer.

Graduate education is extremely time-consuming. The student has the usual demands of class attendance and preparation, research activities (thesis or dissertation), and often assistantship duties. While graduate students in almost any discipline have these same demands, MFT students have the additional requirement of client interaction. Requirements are that students at the master's level will complete 500 hours of face-to-face contact with clients. When the time necessary for the associated case planning, record keeping, and supervision is added to academic work, 10- to 14-hour work days are not uncommon for MFT students.

This level of involvement will cut significantly into the amount of time available for personal and family activities. The student will need the support and understanding of significant others, such as spouse or children, in order to be successful.

Many MFT programs, along with the universities with which they are affiliated, offer assistantships to their students. An assistantship most often consists of helping a professor with various aspects of a research project or teaching associated undergraduate classes. These assistantships offer the student an opportunity to earn money while gaining valuable experience that will help build a professional career. The graduate programs in which students are interested can provide information concerning the availability and amount of assistantships. Be aware that assistantships are usually not provided for every semester of the student's education.

Where Will I Work and How Much Will I Make?

ADVICE FROM THE PRO'S

Marriage and family therapists are finding employment in a world of ever-expanding opportunities. Many marriage and family therapists are self-employed, developing private practices that are both professionally and financially rewarding. There is a wide range of incomes for MFTs. Beginning salaries in agencies are similar to other mental health professionals, in general about $30,000 per year. Income later depends on the setting (agency or private practice) and professional reputation, with an annual income of $50,000 to $80,000 common. The public demand for the services provided by marriage and family therapists is continuing to grow at a rapid rate.

Other marriage and family therapists find employment opportunities in public and private hospitals where their services are in demand in adult, child, and adolescent treatment units, as well as traditional mental health settings such as community mental health clinics.

As alcohol and substance abuse have become to be seen as a *family problem*, marriage and family therapists have made a significant impact in the area of alcohol and substance abuse treatment. Breaking the cyclical and mutually reinforcing patterns of an alcoholic family is work well-suited to the trained and motivated marriage and family therapist.

More and more opportunities for employment are being found in the business sector. Family therapists are making significant inroads in staffing corporate Employee Assistance Programs (EAPs) that provide employees with counseling that helps them be productive on and off the job. Often, marriage and family therapists will act as independent consultants to businesses, providing them with the expert knowledge of how systems work and how they can be improved.

Of course, as the demand for marriage and family therapists grows, so does the demand for those with the skills to teach others to be therapists. Academic jobs (teaching, supervision, and research in the field) require a doctoral-level degree. For those with the appropriate training and skills, academic careers are currently available and are highly sought-after positions.

The Demands of Graduate School

Graduate education is extremely time-consuming. The student has the usual demands of class attendance and preparation, research activities (thesis or dissertation), and often assistantship duties. While graduate students in almost any discipline have these same demands, MFT students have the additional requirement of client interaction. Requirements are that students at the master's level will complete 500 hours of face-to-face contact with clients. When the time necessary for the associated case planning, record keeping, and supervision is added to academic work, 10- to 14-hour work days are not uncommon for MFT students.

DR. ROBERT F. STAHMANN received his B.A. from Macalester College in St. Paul, MN, and M.S. and Ph.D. degrees in counseling psychology from the University of Utah, Salt Lake City. He did a post-doctoral residency in marriage and family therapy at the Marriage and Family Counseling Service, Rock Island, IL, and post-doctoral training in sex therapy at the Sex and Marital Therapy Clinic, University of Utah College of Medicine.

He was a professor of counselor education and director of the University of Iowa Counseling Service from 1967-1975. Since 1975, he has been a professor of family sciences at Brigham Young University, Provo, UT, with primary teaching responsibilities in the graduate programs in marriage and family therapy. He has also served as director of the MFT program and chairman of the Department of Family Sciences at BYU.

Bob has authored or co-authored over 50 articles and book chapters in professional counseling literature and presented a similar number of papers and/or programs at national professional meetings. He is co-author of *Dynamic Assessment in Couples Therapy*, to be published this year, and of *Premarital Counseling*, published in 1980; co-editor and contributor to the book, *Counseling in Marital and Sexual Problems*, with editions published in 1977 and 1984; and co-editor of *Reading in Ethical and Professional Issues for Marital and Family Therapists*, published in 1980. He was also editor of the *AMCAP Journal* (1977-78) and an associate editor of the *Journal of College Student Personnel* (1970-77).

Bob is a licensed marriage and family therapist in Utah and maintains a limited private practice.

CHAPTER FIVE

Wanted: Psychology Professors—
Women Should Apply!

**Joan C. Chrisler, Ph.D.,
National Coordinator Association for Women in Psychology**

Psychology is probably one of the most interesting of the academic disciplines. After all, its subject matter is *us*! Psychologists study all aspects of human behavior—physiological, cognitive, behavioral, and social—both normal and abnormal. We can study behavior from a variety of perspectives, e.g., developmental (how behavior changes from infancy to old age) or comparative (how human behavior is the same or different from that of other species). Our work may be primarily experimental, as we strive to discover facts about people's behavior, or primarily applied, as we attempt to use our knowledge to help people change their behavior or feel better about themselves. The field is a broad one encompassing specialties such as education, health, consumer behavior, psychophysics, abnormal psychology, and the psychological study of women, children, the elderly, and ethnic minorities. The possibilities are endless...and endlessly fascinating.

Women in Psychology

There have been many successful women psychologists right from psychology's beginnings in America around 1890. Two of the early presidents of the American Psychological Association were women: Mary Whiton Calkins in 1902 and Margaret Floy Washburn in 1921. Today most undergraduate psychology majors are women, as are more than half of the graduate students. Will the increasing number of women change the field of psychology? No one knows. However, one thing is certain: young women will feel comfortable and welcome in their classrooms and later at their work sites.

The areas of psychology in which women have historically tended to specialize are developmental and child psychology, educational and school psychology, and clinical and counseling psychology. This is not surprising as these specialties are compatible with women's traditional roles as nurturers and childrearers. What *is* surprising is that these same specialties are still the ones that attract the most women today. The most popular career plan among undergraduate students is to become a clinical psychologist in private practice. As a result, clinical psychology has become the most difficult field of psychology to enter. Entrance requirements for clinical graduate programs have become very strict in recent years; many require Graduate Record Examination (GRE) scores in the 600s and grade point averages (GPA) of 3.5 or more (better than a B). These strict requirements have resulted in many excellent students becoming disappointed when they don't get into graduate school and leaving psychology to pursue another career.

Now, ask yourself some questions. If most psychology majors want to do applied work, who will do the research and make the new discoveries about human behavior? If most want to become psychotherapists and consultants, who will become professors and train the next generation of psychologists? Should I become a psychology professor? *Could* I?

Preparing to Become a Psychologist

No matter what area of psychology you want to enter, you'll have to plan on four years of college and four to seven years of graduate study. There are few career opportunities in psychology with a bachelor's or master's degree; you must have a doctorate to call yourself a psychologist. Doctoral work usually consists of three years of full-time course work, plus the completion of a research project that results in a written dissertation. Those studying clinical psychology must also count a year-long internship as part of their graduate work. Other applied specialties may also require internships. See the American Psychological Association's Guide to Graduate Study in Psychology and Related Fields for information on the entrance and program requirements of graduate schools in the United States and Canada.

As an undergraduate, you should major in psychology. Take as many core courses (e.g., abnormal, personality, social, physiological, cognitive, history and systems, developmental—these correspond roughly to the chapters in your general psychology textbook) as you can so that you gain a broad knowledge of the field. Don't take trendy courses (e.g., Death and Dying, Psychology of Advertising) unless they are directly related to what you plan to study in the future. For example, Death and Dying would be useful for developmental or health psychology. Take a statistics course regardless of how you feel about mathematics; this course is required by most graduate schools no matter what specialty you want to enter. You might want to minor in a field related to your special interest (e.g., sociology for social psychology, biology for physiological psychology, women's studies for psychology of women, education for educational or school psychology).

Graduate school entrance is very competitive, although it is easier to enter fields other than clinical because the numbers of applicants are fewer. In addition to good grades and good GRE scores (take a review course or buy a practice book and study it), you should try to get some experience that will make your application stand out. The best thing that you could do is get involved with research. Approach your professors to ask if they are working on any projects with which they need help. Ask if you could design and complete a project of your own as an independent study. It may be possible to find a summer research opportunity at your own or another college or university; ask the chairperson of the psychology department for information about summer research programs. Research experience is enormously beneficial, and graduate admissions committees are very impressed by it. If you are planning to enter an applied field, you might also want to do some volunteer work or find a summer job in a psychiatric hospital or other office or agency related to your interests. Join the American Psychological Association (APA), American Psychology Society (APS), or Association for Women in Psychology (AWP) as a student member. If your college has a Psi Chi chapter or psychology club, you should become an active member. This is a good way to learn about career opportunities and to show that you are already committed to the field. Prepare a resume with your experience and professional memberships on it and send it along with your graduate school applications.

A Professor's Life

Professors often describe their career with the phrase *the life of the mind* to emphasize our concentration on intellectual matters. Essentially, we get paid for reading, writing, thinking, and teaching. The challenge is lifelong learning; the pleasure is sharing what you've learned with your students. I think that teaching college and graduate students is much more rewarding than teaching children. The older students choose their courses so they are much more likely to be seriously interested in the subject matter. Anyway, psychology is such a fascinating discipline that it's easy for our students to share our enthusiasm!

Besides teaching two to four courses a semester, professors spend time advising students, working with student groups such as Psi Chi, working on college committees, conducting research, and writing articles or books. The varied activities keep the job interesting. A major benefit of the professorate is the flexibility of our schedules. It is possible to arrange to teach only early or late in the day or only on two or three days per week. This is especially helpful for women with young children, as is the benefit of the winter, spring, and summer breaks. In addition, every few years professors are entitled to a semester or a year-long sabbatical during which they are excused from teaching in order to spend more time on research or writing. If you are interested in an applied field (e.g., clinical, environmental, industrial/organizational, or school psychology), you may be able to arrange your schedule so as to have a day free for consulting or private practice.

Although you must count on about 10 years of higher education to become a professor, it is possible to start working in the field before you earn your Ph.D. Most professors get their start while in graduate school as teaching or research assistants, where they gain experience while working under the supervision of a senior faculty member. Such work usually earns a small salary plus tuition remission. After you have completed your course work and the required examinations and while you are working on your dissertation, you may be able to find your first faculty post as a part-time or full-time lecturer or instructor. When you earn your Ph.D., you will qualify for an assistant professor position, which is generally considered entry-level. Starting salaries range from $25,000 to $35,000, depending upon whether you are hired by a small or large, public or private institution and how much experience you have had. After approximately six years, you can apply for tenure and promotion to associate professor. The highest level is full professor, which is granted to those who have made major contributions to their discipline and/or the institution at which they teach. Many universities are slow to promote women to the full professor level; you should look into the track record of any institution at which you are thinking of taking an academic job.

You may have heard the phrase "publish or perish." This refers to the fact that professors are expected to produce knowledge themselves as well as to teach what others have produced. Producing knowledge means sharing it with the public (publication = public education) through articles, books, papers at conferences and other scientific meetings, and lectures to the general public. Publication is required to achieve tenure and promotion at most colleges and universities, but especially at research universities and elite liberal arts colleges. If you are primarily interested in teaching, you should look for a position at a community or liberal arts college. If you like both teaching and research, look for a position at an institution with a graduate program in psychology.

Another benefit of the *life of the mind* is the opportunity to travel. I have been all over the United States and Canada and visited a number of countries in Europe and Asia to attend conferences and scientific meetings or give guest lectures. I find it very exciting to belong to an international community of scholars, to exchange ideas and teaching strategies, and to share my research with colleagues at other institutions. I try to take some students with me to conferences whenever possible; ask your professors about conferences you might attend. It's never too early to meet other psychologists and learn about the latest research findings.

Best National Liberal Arts Colleges

Ranked by: Composite rating in five academic areas.
1. Williams College (MA), with a score of 100.0
2. Swarthmore College (PA), 99.9
3. Amherst College (MA), 99.7
4. Bowdoin College (ME), 98.5
5. Pomona College (CA), 98.3
6. Wellesley College (MA), 98.1
7. Wesleyan University (CT), 94.3
8. Haverford College (PA), 93.5
9. Middlebury College (VT), 92.2
10. Smith College (MA), 91.5

Source: *U.S. News & World Report*

The Future of Psychology

The future of psychology is bound to be a good one. A large percentage of the professorate will be retiring in the next 10 to 15 years, and many new professors will be needed. In addition, the field is expanding, and new areas of work and leisure are being studied from a psychological perspective. There may be consulting opportunities 10 years from now that we cannot even imagine. There will surely be room for you if you start now to gain the experience and credentials you will need to earn your doctorate in psychology. Good luck!

DR. JOAN C. CHRISLER received her B.S. in psychology from Fordham University, Bronx, NY. She received her M.A. and Ph.D. in experimental psychology from Yeshiva University, New York, NY. Dr. Chrisler is currently an associate professor of psychology at Connecticut College in New London. She specializes in health psychology and the psychology of women and collaborates with her undergraduate and graduate students on research on women's health. She has published numerous articles and book chapters and edited two books in her areas of interest, and is currently serving as the national coordinator of the Association for Women in Psychology. And yes, she loves her work!

CHAPTER SIX

On Becoming a Psychologist: One Woman's Story on Surviving as an African-Cherokee American

Brenda Andrieu, Ph.D., ABPP

Becoming a psychologist was not easy for me because no one in my family had ever gone to college. In high school, I was a very quiet, withdrawn student who made A's in subjects that I liked, such as math. But in the few subjects that did I not like or did not like the teacher, I did not do the work and received D's. Of course, I got some B's and C's, but I was never on the honor roll in high school.

I remember wanting to join the school club for future teachers, but being too embarrassed to apply for fear that my grades were not high enough. So, I never mentioned my interest to anyone and never joined. I remember walking home from school with a friend, mentioning to her that I might be interested in being a child psychologist (not really knowing what a child psychologist did). My friend said that I would never be able to be a child psychologist because I would need to have straight A's in all my subjects and take biology. Well, as I mentioned before, I did not have all A's and was terrified by the idea of cutting or touching dead animals in biology class, so I forgot about any notions of being a child psychologist.

Education and Early Training

Because most colleges offer courses in psychology, it is a relatively easy field to get started in. When I entered college, I took courses that interested me. I wanted to understand people and why they behaved in various ways. I also wanted to be able to help people who were having adjustment problems or were mentally ill. So I took enough psychology and sociology courses to complete degrees in both areas. I was still interested in teaching, but still lacked the courage to let anyone know or to apply for entrance into the teacher certification program. I was afraid that I would be rejected even though my grades were better than in high school (probably a B-average). Nevertheless, I graduated from college with *two* bachelor degrees, and

MENTAL HEALTH CAREER DIRECTORY

though *technically* it was a course requirement, I never did take biology (yes, there *are* exceptions to some rules).

While I was working on my bachelor's degrees, my father died and I was forced to take a full-time job as a caseworker with the Welfare Department's Aid to Dependent Children Division. I consider this my first professional job in the area of psychology. The requirements for this job in most areas of the country have increased since I entered the field, but when I began, I only needed two years of college and no work experience, and that's exactly what I had. There was also a written exam and an interview, and I passed those with flying colors! This first caseworker job developed my interviewing skills and gave me experience in identifying problems, assisting clients in working through difficult situations, and budgeting skills.

I know that many people think that most people of color are offered scholarships to go to college. This is not true. In reality, many people (myself included) cannot afford to go to college without working a full-time job while they are getting their education. Often Hispanic- and African-American and American Indian students have parents who are financially unable to contribute anything to their education or living expenses. There are obviously exceptions to this. Not all Hispanic- and African-Americans, or American Indians are poor, and not all come from families who are not college educated. Some students of color are very much supported by their families financially and emotionally in getting their education, but many are not.

If you are having financial trouble and wish to go to college, be sure to learn about the financial grants and loans that are available to minority students that are not dependent on grade point average. Apply for all of them—don't let money stop you from going to any college or university you want to in this country!

On to Grad School

After I received my bachelor degrees, I had a baby daughter. When my daughter was 12 months old, I entered a master's degree program which had just been created in Washington, D.C., by President John F. Kennedy. The program was conveniently located across the street from my welfare job, so I was able to work a full-time job during the day and take night courses for a master's degree in counseling and guidance. I was able to put my daughter into a day-care program and get a sitter for the evenings.

My personal experience in this area highlights the fact that many minority women have to go to school and bear the full responsibility for children—this makes going to college all the more difficult. After working, going to school, and taking care of their children, they still must study to keep up with the other students. It was my experience, however, that this burden gave me a maturity that made me rethink my priorities and become very serious about my responsibilities. I even became an A student!

When I finished my master's program, the faculty (who were predominantly African-American) supported me and helped me get into one of the best Ph.D. programs in the country. Entering that program was like learning a new language.

> **Investigate Your Financial Aid Options**
>
> If you are having financial trouble and wish to go to college, be sure to learn about the financial grants and loans that are available to minority students that are not dependent on grade point average. Apply for all of them—don't let money stop you from going to any college or university you want to in this country!

But, by then, I knew that I could do it! My confidence level was sky-high after all my successes, and I wasn't going to let anyone stand in my way.

Don't think it was easy to get into this program, however—it can be very hard to get into graduate programs. Letters of recommendation mean a lot. It can make all the difference in the world if the person who is recommending you knows someone in the department you are applying to and is well thought of by people in that department. Grades count too, but your admissions interview is even more important than grades. If you are granted an interview, the impression you make at that interview is crucial. If you are not able to interview, a strong portfolio that has samples of your work and discusses your ambitions and tells a little bit about who you are is vital.

While in my doctoral program, I worked 20 hours a week the first year as a research assistant and spent the next three years as a counselor in the Student Counseling Center. Through these jobs, I gained experience working with academic and psychological problems in both individual and group counseling sessions. I also administered psychological tests. My advisor referred me to these jobs which had been set aside for graduate students.

Eventually You'll Choose a Specialty

Within the field of psychology, there are many different specialties. People can be very different in their interests and abilities and still be very good psychologists doing very different things. As a graduate student in psychology, I chose the counseling major because it was an applied degree, and I felt that it would allow me to practice in a variety of areas. Applied meant that I would be able to see and treat people in therapy sessions, in addition to being able to teach or do research. My 20-hour job in the counseling center fulfilled my counseling internship requirement. Depending on what program you enter, you will have an internship requirement that is one to two years in length. In the counseling center, I functioned as a professional counselor, seeing students with personal and academic problems for individual and group sessions.

While working, my course load was also very heavy. I took courses in counseling and assessment and initially chose a supporting field of statistics before switching to social psychology. I had five major exams to test my knowledge of the areas that I was specializing in—history, motivation, social psychology, learning, and counseling. The last thing that I had to do was my dissertation, which involved conducting a research project, writing up the results, and having them printed in book form. I then had to defend this dissertation before a committee, after which I received my Ph.D.

The Importance of Mentors

It is still not unusual for people of color to go all through their college and graduate experiences without having others of color as instructors and without hearing of professional contributions by persons of color in their course work. During my undergraduate and Ph.D. courses, this was true for me, as all my instructors and all the administrators and support persons were white. In my master's program, however, I was fortunate because there were many instructors of African-American heritage. One of those instructors continues to be one of my best supporters today. I am no longer in contact with any of my white instructors—once I left their classrooms or their programs our relationships ceased. This is only one woman's opinion, but I feel this is definitely an argument for hiring people of color as role models for students of color.

My Career as a College Counselor—One Path You Could Choose

Currently, I am working in the counseling center at a small private New England college. I have been working here for five years. Each year is a little different. During the fall, winter, and spring, we have a young student population. Most of the students are between 18 and 22 years old, and they live on campus. For some of them, it is their first time away from home; others have been to boarding school and traveled throughout the world. Students come to my college from all over the world.

During the summer months, we have an older student population that also lives on campus and comes from all over the world. These older students come to our college because we have one of the world's best foreign language programs and an excellent English program. We offer B.A.'s, M.A.'s, and Ph.D.'s in Arabic, Spanish, French, German, Chinese, Russian, Japanese, Italian, and English.

In the counseling center, we see students who are having a hard time adjusting to being away from home or adjusting to new friendships, as well as more severe problems such as substance abuse, eating disorders, learning disabilities, identity issues, and other emotional issues. We see students individually in private offices and help them talk about issues and plan strategies for dealing effectively with difficult situations. We also plan group discussions and therapy sessions around issues that students are interested in working on, such as a survivors of incest support group.

I also provide psychological and educational testing for students. Tests are only conducted at the student's request. Sometimes students need special personality tests for entrance into graduate school or admittance into another kind of program. Other times students are having difficulty in their classroom with reading or writing assignments, and they wonder if they could have a learning disability. I give them tests to determine how much they know in certain areas, how they learn best, and whether they have a learning disability. After testing, I teach them about techniques that they and their professors can use to help them in completing and comprehending their assignments.

Counseling centers differ in the qualifications they are looking for when hiring a professional counselor. Some will hire students as peer counselors, and some will hire persons with a bachelor's degree, but most want at least a master's degree and some require the Ph.D.

Almost every school system and college/university employs counselors and school psychologists. Private schools hire psychologists through their own schools and departments. Public schools have additional qualifications which vary depending on the state and whether it is higher education or elementary/secondary school.

Public school systems often require school certification and experience as a classroom teacher, while most colleges, universities, and private schools do not.

Other Career Opportunities

Other areas where you can find work as a psychologist include industry, private practice, the military, and hospitals. A psychologist's income varies throughout the country and depends on the kind of work and the setting he or she is working is. Psychologists can be found working full time for less than $20,000 a year to more than $120,000 a year. The average is around $50,000 annually.

Psychologists are regulated by state licensure in all 50 states in America. All but two of those states—Vermont and West Virginia—require that you have a Ph.D. to practice unsupervised as a psychologist. Most states **do not** require that you have a Ph.D. to practice as a counselor.

The Future for Minorities in Psychology

People of color are greatly underrepresented in the field of psychology, whether it is as students, faculty, or staff. It is estimated that 25 percent of the population will be nonwhite by the year 2000, yet minorities make up only 20 percent of the undergraduate student population and nine percent of those graduating from graduate-level programs in psychology. The course work needs to become more multi-culturally oriented. The curriculum in psychology must relate to the people we are going to be working with. Minority faculty and staff comprise less than 5 percent of academic positions. There needs to be more American Indian, Asian-, Hispanic-, and African-American faculty and support staff so that students of color and Euroamerican students can learn to respect and value persons from different ethnic groups as role models.

I hope that I have encouraged you to learn more about the areas you are interested in and not be turned around because someone says you can't.

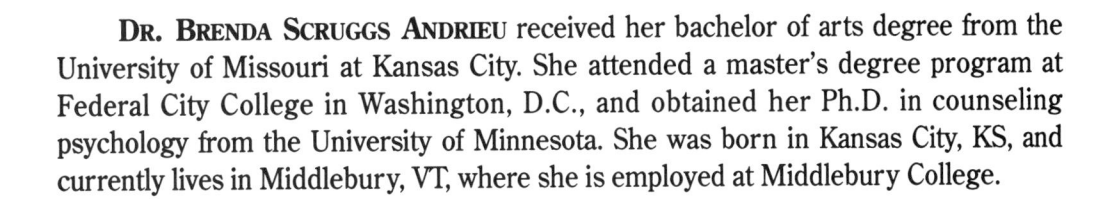

▼

Dr. Brenda Scruggs Andrieu received her bachelor of arts degree from the University of Missouri at Kansas City. She attended a master's degree program at Federal City College in Washington, D.C., and obtained her Ph.D. in counseling psychology from the University of Minnesota. She was born in Kansas City, KS, and currently lives in Middlebury, VT, where she is employed at Middlebury College.

CHAPTER SEVEN

Music Therapy: Paths for Growth and Change

**Caryl Beth Thomas, MA, ACMT,
Vice President of Public Services, American Association for Music Therapy**

"What is music therapy?" Every music therapist has been asked this question more than once. It is asked by all kinds of people: those with and without musical experience, the general public, and healthcare professionals as well. Music therapy is a relatively young and expanding field that does not enjoy the universal awareness of some other helping professions, such as nursing, social work, and physical therapy. Therefore, many people are not aware of this unique and exciting career.

Defining Music Therapy

Music therapy unites the fields of music and therapy to help individuals improve, maintain, or restore a state of well being. It is a goal-directed process that utilizes musical experiences and the relationships that develop through them as dynamic forces of change. A wide variety of mental, physical, emotional, and social needs or problems may be addressed in music therapy. In some instances, these problems or needs are approached directly through the music; in others, they are addressed through the therapeutic relationships that develop between the client, music therapist, and/or the group. Music therapists are often members of an interdisciplinary therapeutic team that analyzes specific problems and plans general treatment goals together. The music therapist then works with clients through assessment, treatment, and evaluation procedures.

Music therapy may involve the client and therapist in a wide range of musical experiences. The main activities utilized are improvising (spontaneously creating music), performing (singing and playing instruments), composing, notating (both lyrics and music), verbalizing, and listening to music. These methods may range from simple rhythmic instruments or songs that require no previous experience, to more complex work, based on the client's interests and level of comfort.

Education and Training in Music Therapy

The training received by music therapists is unique among college programs because of the dual requirements of a thorough knowledge and training in music, and an in-depth education of human development and approaches to treatment, such as behavioral, humanistic, psychodynamic, and biomedical. Therapists must understand basic biological sciences, sociology, anthropology, psychology, and be adept in oral and written communication. Music therapy programs are approved by one of two professional organizations: the American Association for Music Therapy (AAMT) or the National Association for Music Therapy (NAMT). There are approved bachelor's, master's, and doctoral-level programs, and curriculums vary depending on the particular college or university. NAMT schools have a curriculum based on 133 semester hours of study to earn a baccalaureate degree, whereas AAMT requires each institution to design its own curriculum based on essential competencies for the practice of music therapy. All training programs consist of a variety of course work, including musical foundations, music therapy foundations, behavioral/health/natural sciences, clinical foundations, general education, and general electives.

Music therapy foundations include courses in music therapy principles, the psychology of music, and practical clinical experiences (field work placements and at least one internship). Classes generally cover theories, observation and assessment techniques, treatment planning, therapy implementation, research literature, methods and materials interdisciplinary collaboration, and ethics. Students can expect to learn about the application of these topics to a variety of disability groups, through both observation and practical experience. The course work in music therapy is normally completed in four years if you are a full-time student and includes a six-month to one-year internship at a clinical facility. Graduate studies typically take two to three years and include a thesis or dissertation in addition to clinical internship.

Music courses include: theory, history, literature, ear-training, performance on primary and secondary instruments; required competency in piano, guitar, and voice; functional knowledge of orchestral and band instruments, music leadership skills; improvisation; and movement (such as in Dalcroze-Eurhythmics, Kodaly, or Orff-Schulwerk training).

Clinical foundations and behavioral/health/natural sciences include course work in psychology, sociology, human development, counseling, and research methods. It is recommended that studies in group dynamics, physiology, kinesiology, neurology, psychopathology, and biology be included.

General education consists of those courses required by the individual institution for baccalaureate degrees. A school's general curriculum often includes math, English, philosophy, physical education, and basic computer skills. Additional course work in the humanities, such as art, dance, theater, and movement are suggested.

A small portion of the curriculum may be devoted to general electives: studies chosen by the student. These courses may be in related areas of music, other creative arts therapies or modalities, psychology, health or natural sciences, or additional work in music therapy.

Depending on the school and its professional affiliation with AAMT or NAMT, students may have their internship placements during the senior year of undergraduate school or following completion of all course work. There is a wide variety of locations nationwide that represent a full spectrum of clientele. During the internship, the student refines his or her clinical skills under the supervision of a certified or registered music therapist. This experience simulates a full-time job in music therapy and provides the student with practical experience in most aspects of the music therapy practice.

Once all course work and practical experiences are completed, the student is eligible to apply to AAMT for certification (CMT) or to NAMT for registration (RMT). At this time, music therapists are also eligible to take the Certification Board exam, which is administered by the Certification Board for Music Therapists (CBMT), an independent accrediting organization. The test measures the candidate's knowledge about music therapy foundations and principles, clinical theories and techniques, general knowledge about music, and professional roles and responsibilities. Once the exam is passed, the candidate becomes board certified and is credentialed as either CMT-BC or RMT-BC.

Approximately 82 percent of practicing music therapists (from a 1989 investigation) hold bachelor's degrees. With an increasing number of graduate and postgraduate programs developing, some clinical settings have begun to require graduate degrees, but most entry-level positions continue to require undergraduate degrees.

For information regarding schools that offer music therapy programs, contact the American Association for Music Therapy (AAMT) or the National Association for Music Therapy (NAMT).

Career Opportunities

Music therapists work in a variety of healthcare and educational settings, including medical hospitals, clinics, group homes, centers for the developmentally disabled, early intervention programs, drug and alcohol treatment centers, physical rehabilitation, geriatric facilities, residential treatment centers for adults or children, prisons, schools, hospices, and mental health facilities. Some music therapists have private practices or serve as consultants. Others teach, supervise music therapy interns and other music therapy professionals, or become administrators. The majority of music therapists are employed in inpatient psychiatric facilities or in special education school programs, with a significant number working in nursing homes or other geriatric facilities, private practice, and universities (as teachers in a music therapy program).

Job opportunities vary depending on geographic location, with the highest concentration of jobs in metropolitan areas. Other factors in the number of job opportunities include availability of funding and regional and institutional practices. Employment opportunities appear to be most stable in public schools, state-supported institutions, nursing homes, and geriatric facilities. The highest concentration of music therapists is on the West Coast, in the Midwest, the

Top 10 Job Markets

Ranked by: Total new jobs by 1995.
1. Washington, DC, with 118,200 new jobs
2. Anaheim, CA, 108,800
3. Atlanta, GA, 104,600
4. Phoenix, AZ, 92,000
5. San Diego, CA, 77,100
6. Tampa-St. Petersburg, 76,300
7. Orlando, FL, 70,300
8. Dallas, TX, 69,300
9. Riverside, CA, 67,700
10. Minneapolis-St. Paul, 64,700

Source: *Money*

Southeast, and the Northeast. Employment opportunities can be expected to change with future developments in educational and healthcare trends.

Music therapists' salaries are comparable to those of other professionals in allied health professions, such as special education teachers and social workers, which again varies according to geographic location and its economy or the institution's practices.

Music therapists often work in a variety of job titles and departments, depending on the particular setting. Some institutions have a music therapy department and others may have a creative arts therapy department. Some positions come under the department of psychology, rehabilitation services, activity therapy, special resources, or other adjunctive services. Some job descriptions may include other therapeutic services than the primary music therapy work, such as social activities and programs, verbal groups, or other forms of creative expression such as art or movement.

A typical day for a music therapist in a hospital or clinical setting might include attending rounds in the morning with other members of the treatment team to discuss new admissions, treatment plans for the upcoming days or weeks, evaluations, and progress reports. There is generally some type of community meeting where all involved persons, staff and clients, meet to discuss the issues at hand and attempt to come up with plans for resolutions as a group. The rest of the day usually consists of ongoing group or individual sessions with clients, and ends with documentation for that days' activities and contacts with the clients.

An educational setting or long-term rehabilitation setting may have similar kinds of meetings for evaluations and treatment planning, but less frequently, since most individuals are involved in therapy over a longer period of time. For example, most school programs require Individualized Educational Programs (IEPs), which are usually updated two times after the initial plan during the school year. Long-term settings also tend to have more clients than others, where the turnover of clients may be much faster.

A music therapist may be responsible for as many as five one- hour or ten thirty-minute sessions during the course of a day. Groups vary in size, depending on the needs of the particular clients, but are ideally kept relatively small in order to meet as many individual needs as possible in a group setting. Individual sessions are recommended when an individual's needs cannot be best met in a group setting.

Looking Toward the Future

For more than 50 years, music therapy has been growing and changing, improving education and training standards, developing a body of research, and building a professional identity. There continues to be growing interest in music as a facilitator of change, both as an educational tool and as a means of self-discovery and self-expression. A recent bill was passed in Congress called the *Older Americans Act*, which provides federal funding for music therapy with the elderly.

The earliest references to music and medicine are found in preliterate cultures, and continue to be found in most societies up to the present day, so the use of music as a means of treatment or therapy is not new. The current renaissance of music and other art forms, in association with healing and wellness, supports the use of music therapy as an alternative to more traditional forms of therapy.

▼

CARYL BETH THOMAS M.A., ACMT received her bachelor of music education at the University of North Carolina at Greensboro, with a focus in special education. Ms. Thomas also received her master of arts degree in music therapy from New York University and completed the Advanced Clinical Training in Community Music Therapy at Creative Arts Rehabilitation Center of New York, NY. She has worked with adults, adolescents, and children in psychiatric facilities, residential treatment programs, and school settings in the greater New York City area. Currently she is working at McLean Hospital in Belmont, MA, a private psychiatric facility, the Community Music Center of Boston, supervising creative arts therapists and the student intern program, and private supervision of music therapists. She is vice president of public services for the American Association for Music Therapy and a member of the Massachusetts Music Therapy Alliance.

CHAPTER EIGHT

Art Therapy: A Unique Career Opportunity for Native Americans

**Kathleen D. Westcott-Emerson, Anishnabe-Ikwe, M.A., ATR,
Native Art Therapist**

There are two predominate disciplines in Western art therapy. While these two strands can be relevant to Native people, a third strand—**Native American art therapy**—is now emerging.

As you may know, traditional Native societies such as clan systems, naming, sub-societies, and kinship structures were all principally developed by Native people in their relationship with the natural and unseen spirit world. Today, while much of this has been lost in many tribes, the prospect of regaining societies that are based on these principles is proving to be vital to both Native and non-Native people.

Native American art therapy promises to play a critical role, not only in the processes of reclaiming primal knowledge, but also in healing the outcomes of having moved so far away from that knowledge. It will also be valuable to non-Native people because of the sacred ceremonial spiritual aspects of Native art therapy.

Three Distinct Forms of Art Therapy

At the present time, there are three distinct forms of art therapy: **Traditional** art therapy—a predominately Western European discipline influenced by the work of Sigmund Freud; **Archetypal** art therapy—based on post-Jungian archetypal psychology; and **Native American** art therapy—based on the structures and principles of Native ceremony and teachings.

The traditional art therapist makes a clinical inquiry. This art therapist may use the artwork as a departure point for verbal therapy or focus on a diagnosis through interpretation of the art work. The diagnosis is based on illness as defined by Western European psychological theories. A medical model of wellness and illness has evolved from these theories. American hospitals, alcohol and drug treatment centers, and counseling clinics are based on this medical model. Some of the tools of the traditional art therapist can include the House-Tree Person (HTP) and the Kinetic Family

Drawing. These are known as projective drawing tools, in which the client *projects* his psychological make-up into the drawn image. The elements of the drawing are then interpreted using a standardized key or manual.

The archetypal art therapist listens to the imagination as expressed in the art work. This listening takes place through exploration of the image as metaphor. Through interaction with the image, the client begins to hear what the art work has to say, offering new avenues for introspection via nonverbal communication. The archetypal art therapist stays with the image, personifying it through fantasy and metaphor, inviting the image into being. Mythology is an integral part of this program—traditional and contemporary myth are introduced in the course work as a means of giving depth and perspective to the creative process. The archetypal art therapist is also trained in the *traditional* theories and methodology mentioned above.

As an example, the traditional art therapist may look at a painting of a house without windows and interpret the image as suggesting hostility or withdrawal. The archetypal art therapist would consider what remains in darkness, what is not being seen through or into, what may be closed off from what is inside.

What Is Native American Art Therapy?

As a Native American art therapist, I have come to understand Native American art therapy in the following ways: *An art therapist practicing Native American art therapy understands the image as a bridge between the unseen world of our ancestors, our Holy People, and the spirit essence of all forms of life* (i.e., the plant world, animal world, the four sacred directions, the seasons, colors, and so on). Working with a client's images is done with the following understanding: Each person comes to this image-making process (art therapy session) with their entire community of relations that exist both in the seen and the unseen world. The image-making that takes place will provide a place and a time for these relations to have a voice, to share their point of view, to respond compassionately to that person's request and need, to describe without judgment or expectation the present circumstances, to assist in remembering the past, and to provide healing. The Native American art therapist facilitates the individual's opportunity to witness this gift of unconditional love and kinship. The result is a whole picture of the individual's essential self, the values and attributes that make up the individual's core being, and a description of the person's circumstances, seen as teachers giving insight into the distance traveled from the core self and the causes of that journey.

The very process of creating images is understood by the Native American art therapist as a process and a language that is sacred. It is through the creative process that we *inquire to the Great Mystery,* and it is through the creative process that we receive our answers, record what we receive, and then, in time, share our gift with others. Our image-making process includes the forms of our dance outfits, our songs and dances, our images (including weavings, pottery, baskets, paintings, and bead and quill work), our ceremonies, and our creation stories.

The Native American art therapist (depending on his/her tribe) may come to understand the house painted with no windows as an indication of the individual's need to look within, to turn to sage, the bear, the dream, the color black, to sunset or folding darkness, to fasting, and to the spirits of the Western direction for assistance in this looking. Depression and even thoughts of suicide often accompany this time and can be understood as indicators of such a need.

At all times, the art therapist holds, first and foremost, a respect for and an adherence to the art process and the art materials themselves. This respect is maintained with an understanding that the art process has integrity and is not separate from the client's capability to generate everything needed to bring about recovery and healing. The art process enables the client to generate information, insight, and understanding that would typically be blocked in verbal therapy, due to our well-practiced skills in defending and masking ourselves through words. As the therapy process takes place, the art therapist will rely on his/her extensive knowledge of various art media to determine which media is the most suitable for each stage of the process. The client will also make decisions about media based on what feels right.

While the Native American art therapist must have the skills and knowledge described above, s/he also works with the knowledge that each of these life experiences resides in a context of relatedness and that each of these image-making processes is a sacred act of communicating with some of the kinship ties formed around this particular client. In the course of moving through the issue presented, images and or dreams may appear in which one or more of the client's community of kinship ties will directly respond. This response will assist the client in receiving teachings about the principles held within his/her experience. For example, Cedar Woman may appear explaining directly to the client that what s/he is working on is intergenerational; that as the client resolves, heals, amends, this issue, Cedar Woman will take that resolution and send it through those generations yet unborn. The Native American art therapist and the client work with the knowledge that being taught in this way is inherent to the therapy/creative process and that the outcomes impact the lives of many.

Having What It Takes to be an Art Therapist

An ideal candidate for this profession is a person with life experience, community involvement, some experience and/or interest in working with people in the area of mental health, and one who is involved in and values creative processes.

The Role of the Client in a Native American Art Therapy Session

In the first session with the art therapist, the client briefly discusses the issue or situation that has brought him/her to therapy. The therapist then asks the client to express this issue or situation through art materials. The client and the therapist spend several moments quietly observing and listening to the image. The therapist then facilitates the description of the image-giving voice to the image without interpretation. A metaphor and/or a story emerge giving information about the situation or circumstances beyond the literal—usually a stuck place for the client—thus allowing for a deepening in understanding and a resolution.

For example, a woman who enters therapy because her adolescent son and herself repeatedly have the same fight begins with painting. Her painting is restricted to the page with a tiny painted area placed in the corner. It reveals something about her experience with her adolescent son that leaves her constricted and with much emptiness. She will be invited by the therapist to move her shoulders and arms, returning to the page and allowing the paint to lead her around the paper. The way in which she is moving may give insight into where the tightness and restriction is in her relationship with her adolescent son. The mother can relate what it feels like to move through places on the page that are restricted and tight, then leave the image and bridge this insight to her experience with her son. The issue that the mother brought to therapy has been moved out of the literal experience and into her body. This allows another perspective: a perspective that comes from the cellular level of her body, allowing what was unconscious to become conscious.

There are many differences and variables in an art therapy session. These differences are determined by the client. The client's culture, emotional flexibility, values, distinct personality traits, and thinking patterns will contribute to these differences.

Getting Trained as an Art Therapist

Bachelor's Programs

For Native American students that decide to enter the field of traditional art therapy, there are over 20 American Art Therapy Association-approved programs in the United States that provide excellent training. Names and addresses for these programs can be acquired by writing to the AATA. For those students seeking to enter the archetypal art therapy discipline, the University of New Mexico's Art Therapy Program is the only one in the country using the theories of archetypal psychology. This AATA-approved program deals with each applicant individually, and a non-traditional degree route would be honored. For information about this program, write to:

> Josie Abbenante, M.A., A.T.R.
> Director, Art Therapy Program
> Department of Art Education
> University of New Mexico, Albuquerque, New Mexico 87131
> 505-277-4112

Unfortunately, there are no Native American art therapy degree programs in the United States at this time. Currently, the University of New Mexico Art Therapy Program is the only program that offers course work in Native American art therapy. One course a year titled Cross Cultural Art Therapy (subtitled Native American Art Therapy) is available at the college. A three semester course is available through independent contract with the same instructor with credit available through the college. For more information contact:

> Kathleen D. Westcott-Emerson, M.A., A.T.R
> Ni Ha' Alchini Ba Educational Programs
> PO Box 3541
> Shiprock, NM 87420
> (505)368-5475

Master's Programs

After receiving a bachelor's degree in art therapy, a student must earn a master's degree leading to registration, in order to practice as an art therapist. Prerequisites for entering a master's degree program will vary with each university, however, you will generally be required to have a bachelor's degree in art education, art, psychology, or another field with prerequisites completed. Prerequisites include 15 credits in studio arts, with painting, drawing, ceramics, and art history required, and 12 credits in psychology, with abnormal and child psychology required. A master's program typically involves approximately 55 credits, including core courses, and 600 internship hours. Most programs require that each student be in therapy for at least one semester (16 session minimum) and for the duration of the internship. The internship is demanding: you will be working in the exact settings and populations that you will eventually be treating. Every aspect of your professional and personal self will be challenged.

Licensing Procedures

After graduating, you will be required to complete 1,900 hours (direct contact with clientele) of documented, supervised practice as an employed art therapist before qualifying for A.T.R. registration.

At the present time, art therapists do not have licensure in most states. For this reason, it is possible for an individual to call themselves an art therapist without training or a degree and without being registered if the organization they are working for is unaware of the national standards set by the AATA. Art therapists are working hard to attain licensure state by state. It is only a matter of time before the field will be regulated and it will no longer be possible to work as an art therapist without a master's degree and registration with the American Art Therapy Association. The state of New Mexico is the first state to legislate art therapy licensure throughout the state (effective 1993).

The training you receive as an art therapist qualifies you to be a competent counselor with a diversity of skills. You are prepared to move on to a Ph.D. in any area of human services. This particular training program increases your capacity to live as a compassionate, responsive human being.

Working in the Field

At an entry-level position (after interning), you can expect to be working in one of the following areas: an alcohol and drug treatment center for adults and/or adolescents; a residential home for handicapped people, such as head injury patients, or the severely retarded; a home for the elderly; a center for the homeless; a hospital administering to special populations, such as relationship and substance addiction, veterans, and adult and/or child victims of violence and ritualistic abuse. In these settings, you would be a member of a treatment team. In this capacity, you would be one of three to six specialists who meets with the clients in groups and in one-on-one sessions. You would provide the clients and the treatment team with individual assessments, input in planning a treatment program, and evaluation along the way. You would keep records in the client's chart or file. A typical day would include facilitating group art therapy sessions, individual art therapy sessions, a treatment team meeting, and charting client participation in treatment files.

An ideal candidate for this profession is a person with life experience, community involvement, some experience and/or interest in working with people in the area of mental health, and one who is involved in and values creative processes.

Difficulty or discomfort working as an art therapist can occur when working in an organization that is ignorant of the nature and effectiveness of this form of therapy. At times, art therapy is trivialized due to society's general devaluing and misunderstanding of the crucial role of creativity and imagination in our human life.

What You'll Earn

You can expect your beginning salary to be $24,000 to $28,900 a year, if you are working full time for an organization. After acquiring three to five years experience and determining what population you are best suited for, you may go into private practice or teach full- or part-time. In private practice, the hourly rate is between $25.00 to $75.00 an hour. If you specialize in an area that is in great demand with few active art therapists (Native American art therapy is one of these specializations), you can earn $250.00 to $800.00 a day, plus your traveling expenses working as a consultant.

Particular Concerns for Native Art Therapists

The field of art therapy is growing rapidly as knowledge of its effectiveness increases. John Perry, author of the book *The Far Side of Madness* states, "That is where the real work is being done" (i.e., in treatment recovery and healing). The medical model has not served the need for healing within the mainstream American population; this realization is expressed repeatedly by mental health and chemical dependency counselors, social workers, and art therapists in my own and my colleagues training throughout the United States and Canada. The reasons that are given include lack of cultural relevancy and lack of processes which acknowledge the spiritual, intuitive, and creative aspects of being fully human. Among Native people, the medical model is all but failing. Some of the reasons for this are the distinct cultural differences present between dominate society and Native populations.

Native communities that have made significant gains in addressing their problem have done so by claiming ownership of the problems and then setting out to alleviate them through intervention and prevention. Intervention and prevention have proven most successful when the strengths of both mental health professionals and the traditional healing practices which exist within tribal culture are combined. Working in coordination with one another, a more competent mental health system emerges, which facilitates access to both medical services and traditional healing approaches.

The discipline of art therapy has the opportunity to form itself around the structure, processes, and principles of Native ceremony. For the entire existence of human life, art has been a healing tradition. Native people have maintained this knowledge through continued practice in the form of ceremony, song, dance, prayer, and image-making.

It is important when working with Native individuals and communities that we provide our academically acquired skills and knowledge within the Native cultural knowledge, rather than imposing this Western model over the Native client's culture. We must know that to work out of whatever theoretical model we are employing causes further harm, unless the model is employed as an instrument of our client's cultural philosophy.

For these reasons, a Native American student looking for an art therapy program should look for a program that acknowledges and values these cultural differences. This would ensure that even if the program does not offer specific course work in Native art therapy, the program would support and encourage you to research your own tribe's knowledge and use of imagery, and would assist you in applying this knowledge to your degree requirements.

Summary

The training and profession of art therapy is one that allows you as a student and as a practicing art therapist to bring your own cultural philosophy and resources into your work. This is a unique and valuable opportunity for a Native person interested in a career in social or human services who values traditional Native wisdom and creative process. It is also an opportunity for us, as Native people, to do what we are being called upon to do: To heal ourselves and to apply the beauty, integrity, and the ancient wisdom of who we are to the needs of all people to heal and once again be whole.

▼

KATHLEEN WESTCOTT-EMERSON received her B.A. in elementary education and fine arts from Hamline University in St. Paul, MN and her M.A. in art therapy from the University of Wisconsin-Superior. For the past 13 years, Kathleen has worked as an art therapist in Native American alcohol and drug treatment centers for adults and teens in Minnesota and New Mexico. A key element of Kathleen's practice is the dream-vision and the creative process as understood by the Anishnabe people. In addition, Kathleen is a group facilitator for women in recovery for incest and sexual abuse and works as a consultant throughout the United States and Canada. She also has taught philosophy and social psychology from a Native perspective at the Institute of American Indian Arts in Santa Fe, NM, and continues to teach Native art therapy at the University of New Mexico, Albuquerque.

Ms. Wescott-Emerson would like to thank Josie Abbenante and Larry W. Emerson for their collaboration in writing this article.

CHAPTER NINE

Developmental Psychologists: Studying and Promoting Development Across the Life-Span

**Dolores T. Benn, M.A. and Celia B. Fisher, Ph.D.,
Graduate Program in Developmental Psychology,
Fordham University**

Development is described as the sequence of physical and psychological changes that we human beings experience as we grow older. Development starts with conception and continues throughout life, ending with death. **Developmental psychologists** are interested in understanding, predicting, and shaping the process of development. As such, developmental psychology is a significant and comprehensive field in the area of psychology.

Activities of Developmental Psychologists

Essentially, developmental psychologists are engaged in two distinct, yet overlapping, activities. First, developmental psychologists are active in the systematic study of human development. Through various research methods, these psychologists generate scientific knowledge about the behavior of individuals at all points across the life span. Second, developmental psychologists are interested in applying their knowledge to foster healthy development. Many developmental psychologists are active in both the generation of knowledge and its subsequent application in real world settings.

Developmental Psychology: Knowledge Generation

Developmental psychology is concerned with the scientific study of development. Psychologists in this field conduct basic research to understand the behavior of individuals throughout the life cycle. These psychologists strive to produce empirical information to describe and explain the developmental processes that are the foundation for age-related changes.

Developmental psychologists address three central issues in their research:

stability and change; biological and environmental influences; and individual differences. First, they are concerned with whether individual development is a gradual and continuous process or one characterized by discrete stage-like transformations. For example, they study how the child's moral decision making changes through adolescence and adulthood. Next, they are interested in the sources of development. That is, they investigate how nature (biological factors) and nurture (environmental factors) interact to produce change. For example, developmental psychologists examine both the characteristics of infants and the behaviors of their caretakers that promote emotional bonds. Lastly, developmental psychologists are concerned with intra- and inter-individual differences, the process by which one develops characteristics that make him or her a unique individual. In this regard, they may investigate individual differences in aggression and pro-social behavior.

Different assumptions regarding these issues have produced competing theories of development, each attempting to present a thorough interpretation of developmental processes. Through several research techniques and designs, developmental psychologists investigate a variety of psychological phenomena, such as perception, cognition, and language to test the validity of their theories. In this way, they attempt to describe and explain developmental processes across the life span.

Developmental Psychology: Knowledge Application

In recent years, applied developmental psychology (ADP) has emerged as a specialization within the field of developmental psychology, designed to train individuals who can offer practical approaches to optimize developmental outcomes in individuals and families.

Applied developmental psychologists attempt to understand the normative changes and challenges experienced by individuals and families as they develop along the life cycle. They seek to facilitate developmental processes and prevent the development of handicaps through: research in applied settings aimed at furthering our understanding of problems of societal import; the construction of developmental assessment instruments emphasizing normal rather than pathological development; and the design and evaluation of developmental intervention programs. In this way, developmental psychologists seek to promote the health and welfare of individuals and families.

With the emergence of ADP, developmental psychology has been directed at issues of immediate social relevance that concern a diverse range of populations. Some of these various populations include Black and Hispanic families, single and working mothers, developmentally delayed infants, sexually active adolescents, and the institutionalized elderly. Working with these populations, developmental psychologists have been able to address some of the many important developmental challenges facing individuals today, including: the developmental competence of pre-term infants; children's ability to provide eyewitness testimony; adolescent drinking behaviors; and the effect of chronic illness on the psychological adjustment of the elderly and their adult children. The field of developmental psychology is at an exciting and challenging point as the activities of developmental psychologists evolve into direct application.

Entering the Field of Developmental Psychology

Like other fields of psychology, developmental psychology requires a postgraduate degree (Ph.D.). Various developmental psychology programs have specific undergraduate entrance requirements for admission. In general, the requirements that must be met include: a bachelor's degree from a regionally accredited college or university; an undergraduate grade point average typically expected to be above 3.0; results of the Graduate Record Examination (GRE) consisting of the verbal, quantitative, and advanced psychology sections; and letters of reference. It may not be necessary to be a psychology major as an undergraduate to be admitted into a developmental psychology graduate program. However, an applicant may need to demonstrate some background in psychology by successfully completing selected courses, as well as meeting the above requirements. Such information can be obtained by directly contacting specific programs of interest. Furthermore, any work-related and/or research experience is certainly beneficial to one's application.

Most developmental psychology programs that offer a Ph.D. degree are full-time day programs. Because such programs require a great deal of one's time, outside employment must usually be limited to part-time. Students with either an interest or a financial need may apply for various merit-based departmental assistantships and/or fellowships that allow the student to do part-time work in exchange for tuition remission and/or a stipend. Again, such information can be obtained by directly contacting specific programs of interest.

Students are normally required to enroll in four courses per semester, and the course work is usually completed in three years. In addition to course work, students conduct research on a variety of topics under the direction of a professor(s). Those programs that place emphasis on the application of developmental psychology to real-world problems, or offer a subspecialty in ADP, provide students with an opportunity to gain experience through practica courses. The practica courses allow students to apply developmental knowledge and methodology in community-based settings.

Generally, to earn a Ph.D. in developmental psychology, students must meet certain requirements which include: completing a specified number of course credits; demonstrating satisfactory performance on qualifying examinations; maintaining a specified grade point average; completing a pre-doctoral research project; and completing a doctoral dissertation. In most cases, it takes a minimum of four years to complete a Ph.D. program in developmental psychology. As such, graduate school is a serious undertaking, as it is very time- and energy-consuming. Yet, at the same time, a graduate education in developmental psychology is satisfying and rewarding.

After earning a Ph.D., an individual may apply for a post-doctoral fellowship through a university or a research institute. The post-doctoral fellowship provides one with an opportunity to expand one's research or applied skills. Such positions may last from one to three years.

Academic Careers in Developmental Psychology

Psychologists interested in developmental psychology frequently hold academic positions in colleges or universities. In such positions, developmental psychologists not only teach, but also conduct research and seek to publish their findings and perform various services for the college or university. Most psychologists who have earned a Ph.D. begin as assistant professors. From this position, one may then be promoted to the position of associate professor, and then to that of full professor. After approximately six or seven years, most colleges or universities will review a professor's body of work so that a decision on tenure (a permanent position within the institution) may be made. Developmental psychologists also may find employment in research institutes, such as the National Institute of Child Health and Human Development (NICHD).

Careers in Applied Developmental Psychology

Psychologists interested in applied developmental psychology engage in activities that are best described on a continuum that spans from knowledge generation to knowledge application. At one end of the continuum, there are applied developmental psychologists engaged in knowledge generation. These individuals attempt to integrate developmental theory and real-world problems by testing the generalizability of these theories in natural settings. For example, research conducted across different cultures, settings, and economic conditions has begun to challenge the theoretical assumptions concerning the special significance of early and extended contact between mothers and infants to later growth and development.

Other applied developmental psychologists are engaged in a second set of activities, which includes exploring issues of developmental significance that may otherwise be neglected due to lack of research. These psychologists realize that the success of social policy and interventions depends upon a scientifically based understanding of constantly changing developmental processes. Accordingly, they engage in defining, describing, and explaining issues of relevance so as to best address developmental problems. For example, new research has indicated that there may be some relationship between common, mild, recurring middle ear infections and language development and behavior difficulties in late infancy and early childhood. Previously, the relationship between common, mild, recurring illnesses and development had been overlooked.

A third set of activities with which applied developmental psychologists are concerned includes the construction and use of developmental assessment instruments. In contemporary society, there is a rapidly growing cultural and generational diversity that calls for the development of sensitive assessment instruments to measure abilities and vulnerabilities in those from all walks and stages of life. Applied developmental psychologists use assessment instruments to identify developmental strengths and vulnerabilities, to measure progress, and to learn which interventions would be most suitable for an individual and his/her family. For example, observations of interactions between adolescents and their parents have been used to further our understanding of adaptive and maladaptive family communication.

Applied developmental psychologists are involved in a fourth set of activities that includes the design, implementation, and evaluation of developmental intervention programs. A developmental intervention is a planned attempt to change the developmental process with the goal of enhancing behavior. These interventions are rooted in developmental theory, knowledge, and methodology, and as such, they must be empirically based and evaluated. Examples of developmental interventions include infant stimulation and nutritional interventions, adolescent substance abuse programs, and cognitive skills training for institutionalized elderly.

A fifth set of activities that applied developmental psychologists are engaged in concerns the dissemination of knowledge to individuals and groups. In order to use empirical findings in applications, these psychologists explain and interpret such findings through scholarly publications, the mass media, consultations to professionals and organizations, a variety of educational workshops, and expert testimony provided to participants in the legal system.

> **ADVICE FROM THE PRO'S**
>
> **Top 10 Occupations**
>
> Ranked by: Greatest expected employment gains by 2005.
> 1. Computer systems analyst
> 2. Physical therapist
> 3. Operations analyst
> 4. Psychologist
> 5. Travel agent
> 6. Computer programmer
> 7. Occupational therapist
> 8. Management analyst
> 9. Respiratory therapist
> 10. Marketing, advertising or public relations manager
>
> Source: *Money*

Salaries

Starting salaries in the field of developmental psychology range from $28,000 to $35,000 per year. Experienced developmental psychologists may earn $70,000 to $90,000. These salaries may be enhanced by grants and consultations.

A Look into the Future

The scientific study of developmental processes provides psychologists with a powerful method to understand and improve the human circumstance at any point in the life span. Developmental psychology is a dynamic field that continues to progress so that the developmental needs of individuals and their families can be understood and met.

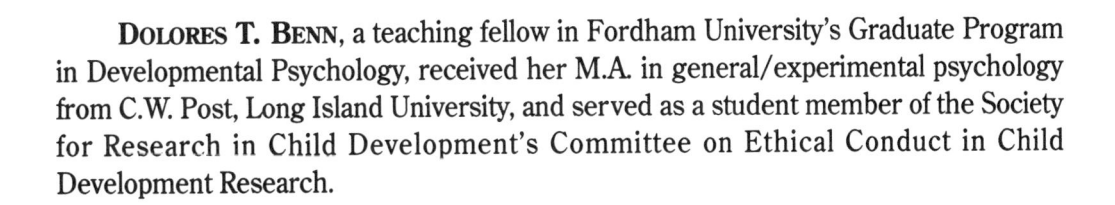

DOLORES T. BENN, a teaching fellow in Fordham University's Graduate Program in Developmental Psychology, received her M.A. in general/experimental psychology from C.W. Post, Long Island University, and served as a student member of the Society for Research in Child Development's Committee on Ethical Conduct in Child Development Research.

Dr. Celia B. Fisher, professor and director of Fordham University's Graduate Program in Developmental Psychology, has served as chair of the Society for Research in Child Development's Committee on Ethical Conduct in Child Development Research and the New York State Licensing Board for Psychology. Dr. Fisher has published extensively on applied developmental psychology, ethical standards in the science and practice of psychology, family conflict, and perceptual development.

CHAPTER TEN

Career Opportunities as a Clinical Psychologist

John D. Robinson, Ed.D., MPH, ABPP(CL)

Most clinical psychologists enter this field because they found clinical work—helping patients—to be personally fulfilling and intellectually challenging. As a clinical psychologist, I have found my role with patients and other professionals to be very rewarding and fulfilling. It provides a form of professional intimacy that no other field affords. Clinical psychology is that aspect of psychological science and practice concerned with the analysis, treatment, and prevention of human psychological disabilities and with the enhancement of personal adjustment and effectiveness. This is very similar to other mental health professional fields (clinical social work, psychiatry, etc.). Clinical psychology also has emphasis on systematic research as the basis of its clinical procedures. Clinical psychologists, that is, those professional psychologists who are in clinical practice, provide services to people and may encompass the distinct disciplines of clinical, counseling, medical, and other areas of professional psychology. Therefore, clinical psychology is not just one *field* of psychology, but is considered that *area* of psychology devoted to the assessment and treatment of mental disorders.

On Becoming a Clinical Psychologist

Clinical psychology requires a doctorate in psychology with a specialization in clinical, counseling, or professional psychology. Depending on the university, this degree can be a Doctor of Philosophy (Ph.D.), Doctor of Education (Ed.D.), or Doctor of Psychology (Psy.D.) degree. In order to be admitted into a doctoral program, students typically must have a four-year undergraduate degree in psychology or a closely related field. If the undergraduate degree is not in psychology, you will be required to take the necessary *undergraduate* courses in psychology before you can take *graduate* courses in psychology. Most graduate schools have specific undergraduate entrance requirements in psychology. Getting into a graduate program in clinical psychology is very competitive and several factors are considered in a candidate's application, such as undergraduate grade point average, standardized test scores, interviews, and letters of recommendation. Any community service, volunteer, or research experience will enhance your application. Most graduate school programs in clinical, counseling, and professional psychology are approved by the American Psychological Association (APA). Graduate programs are usually three to four years of academic work, one year of a full-time internship in a healthcare setting, and one year for the doctoral dissertation or research project. Although most programs take an average of five years to complete, it is not unlikely that six or seven years are needed.

During the course work period, students gain some direct experience, under supervision, with clients. This part-time experience is called a practicum and usually lasts for nine months to one year. This gives the student an opportunity to become involved in the assessment and treatment of patients and to gain a better understanding of the work of a clinical psychologist. It is usually at this point that one decides if s/he really wants the life of a clinical psychologist. The bulk of the supervised experience is represented by the clinical internship in professional psychology.

The Clinical Psychology Internship

The internship lasts 12 months and is based at a specific hospital, medical center, counseling center, or mental health center. It usually requires 50 to 75 hours per week. This is the first time a student gets paid for performing the duties of a junior clinical psychologist-in-training under supervision. The pay is called a stipend and is only a token payment to assist in meeting expenses. The internship is usually in a different location than the academic training program at the university. Students complete their internships all over the United States. Most interns are paid between $7,000 and $17,000 for the year depending on the particular internship program. Internships in professional psychology are also accredited by the American Psychological Association and highly competitive. Your graduate grade point average, letters of recommendation, and practicum experience will enhance your application.

During the internship year, one gets a good idea of the life of a clinical psychologist. Depending on the internship setting, interns get experience in inpatient care, outpatient care, adults, adolescents, children, families, assessment, etc. The intern becomes skilled at handling a variety of psychological situations and problems. After the internship, students usually return to their home university to complete work on an area of original research called a dissertation. At the completion of this piece of original research, the student graduates.

After Graduation

Due to the expanding role of the clinical psychologist, the new graduates sometimes elect to continue their study and to specialize in an area of clinical psychology, such as medical psychology, neuropsychology, forensic psychology, etc. This requires a post-doctoral internship or residency. Oftentimes this is called a fellowship. It is similar to the graduate-level internship and typically lasts for one year and focuses on a specialized area.

Psychologists may elect to teach at a university or work in a mental health setting. The usual salary for a first-year psychologist is about $35,000. For the first year, the psychologist in a non-academic setting usually works under supervision before obtaining a license to practice. In most states, it usually takes one year of post-doctoral supervision to be eligible for a license. After you obtain a license, you can practice on your own without supervision and offer services to the public. In some states, you cannot call yourself a psychologist until you are licensed.

Career Opportunities

There is a need for psychologists in clinical practice. Nationwide, there are positions available in community mental health centers, general and psychiatric hospitals, colleges and universities, and in private practice. Psychologists are especially needed in rural and inner-city areas.

A psychologist in solo or group private practice increases his/her income by increasing productivity. Incomes range from $30,000 to $160,000 per year, depending upon location, specialty, type of practice, seniority in the field, and other factors. There is also a growing need for psychologists in Health Maintenance Organizations (HMOs) and in the area of prevention and health promotion. Psychologists in medical settings work as members of the mental health team and are a vital part of the care of patients and provide for the diagnosis, assessment, and treatment of a variety of mental disorders. There is an increased need for psychologists with an understanding of cultural diversity.

ADVICE FROM THE PRO'S

The Future Looks Bright for Clinical Psychology

Clinical psychology will continue to thrive as a profession that offers mental health services in traditional areas of need. However, health and mental health problems that did not exist previously are now affecting the nation's health, such as AIDS, smoking, heart disease, substance abuse, and cancer. Psychologists will play an important role in assisting in understanding and correcting these disorders. In short, the role of the psychologist in clinical practice is ever-expanding and the need for the general and specialized clinical psychologists will continue to increase.

The Role of Psychologists in the Future

Clinical psychologists are independent, autonomous providers of health services within psychology. Although the number of clinical psychologists is increasing, the need for their services has outgrown the number of psychologists. Examples of this include a definite need for psychologists to provide services to the underserved areas of our society. The areas of community mental health and health psychology are also growing fields where psychologists are at a shortage.

Clinical psychology will continue to thrive as a profession that offers mental health services in traditional areas of need. However, health and mental health problems that did not exist previously are now affecting the nation's health, such as AIDS, smoking, heart disease, substance abuse, and cancer. Psychologists will play an important role in assisting in understanding and correcting these disorders. In short, the role of the psychologist in clinical practice is ever-expanding and the need for the general and specialized clinical psychologists will continue to increase.

Dr. John D. Robinson received a B.A. in zoology and an M.A. in counseling psychology at the University of Texas at Austin. He then received his doctor of education degree in counseling psychology at the University of Massachusetts at Amherst and his master of public health degree in psychiatric epidemiology at the Harvard University School of Public Health. He did his residency in clinical psychology at the University of Texas Health Sciences Center at San Antonio. He currently lives in Washington, DC, and is a professor of psychiatry at Georgetown University and Howard University medical schools. Dr. Robinson is a diplomate in clinical psychology of the American Board of Professional Psychology (ABPP).

CHAPTER ELEVEN

The Study and Measurement of Brain Functions

C. Munro Cullum, Ph.D.,
Clinical Neuropsychologist and Assistant Professor,
University of Colorado Health Sciences Center

Definition and Overview

Broadly defined, **neuropsychology** is an area of specialization that deals specifically with the study of brain- behavior relationships. Quantitative methods originally derived from the fields of psychology and behavioral neurology are used in the clinical neuropsychological examination to evaluate cognitive abilities in individuals with known or suspected brain dysfunction. Most of the measures used to evaluate human brain functions are of the pencil-paper, question-answer variety, although there is an increasing reliance on computer-assisted scoring and/or administration of tests. Various animal behavior and brain function paradigms also exist, both of which have provided major contributions to our understanding of brain-behavior relationships in human and non-human animals.

Settings and Activities

Neuropsychology represents a relatively new area of specialization and is enjoying rapid growth as a discipline. Neuropsychologists are employed in a variety of settings, including universities, medical schools, general and psychiatric hospitals (state, community, private, Veterans Administration, etc.), rehabilitation settings, and private practice. There is often close collaboration in clinical and research endeavors with neurologists, psychiatrists, neurosurgeons, and other psychologists and physicians. Many neuropsychologists espouse a scientist-practitioner approach to the field and include clinical activities along with research and teaching in their work.

Within the context of this diversity, any given "job description" might differ dramatically from another. Thus, it is difficult to depict a *typical day* in the life of a neuropsychologist. Truly, as with other professionals and academicians, neuropsychologists are a rather diverse group, and a multiplicity of tasks typify their routine. For some, much of their time is spent preparing lectures and teaching classes. Others evaluate and/or treat patients clinically, either overseeing the administration of neuropsychological tests or performing them directly. Such activities are performed in a variety of settings, and neuropsychologists are often used as expert witnesses in court, where questions regarding brain dysfunction exist. Some are involved in treatment planning and providing therapeutic and rehabilitation interventions for patients, either as part of a team or more independently. Others are involved in various aspects of research, ranging from basic underlying neurobiological mechanisms of brain function to the behavioral effects of clinical disorders.

Regardless of setting, neuropsychologists are commonly involved in the investigation of brain function and dysfunction. Some of the more common areas of interest have included head injury, learning disabilities, Alzheimer's disease, psychiatric illness (e.g., schizophrenia, depression), stroke, epilepsy, and other brain disorders of childhood, adolescence, adulthood, and aging.

How to Get There

During college, recommended course work often includes various psychology classes (abnormal, experimental, physiological, neuropsychology), along with other relevant courses, such as statistics, computer methods, neuroanatomy, and biology. As with many other areas, English classes that focus on writing and composition are also useful. Obviously, many college courses have relevance to the field with its emphasis on brain-behavior relationships, and it can be argued that a relatively well-rounded liberal arts education provides an excellent background for graduate training. Students are also strongly encouraged to become involved in research as undergraduates, whether by being a teaching assistant, participating in class research projects, or by volunteering research time with faculty. The specific major in college is not critical, although this commonly is psychology. Early on, it is important to realize (and keep in mind) that one's academic record will be carefully and competitively reviewed for graduate study. Specifically, very good grades, Graduate Record Examination (GRE) scores, and letters of recommendation are critical.

After undergraduate studies, graduate training in psychology is the next step. Keep in mind that graduate school is highly competitive. Thus, anything that reflects *extra effort* or unique skills that can be documented on your application is encouraged. When applying to graduate school, be sure to take the "Statement of Goals" section very seriously—this is one area wherein writing skills and future planning abilities can be highlighted.

Many, but not all, programs throughout the country offer doctoral degrees in various areas of psychology, and it is important to identify those that offer course work and experience specifically in neuropsychology. There are a few programs that offer formal tracks or degrees in clinical neuropsychology, although at this point, most neuropsychologists hold the Ph.D. in clinical psychology. Other options include counseling, educational psychology, experimental, and biopsychology programs, but again, it is critical that the appropriate training and course work be available.

If interested in a particular school, the American Psychological Association

(APA) publishes a listing of graduate programs in psychology. Also, you can often identify those that offer particular types of training by consulting with professors, contacting individual departments, and looking at available lists of training programs published in neuropsychology journals. Furthermore, in selecting a training program, postgraduate goals must also be considered, insofar as some specialized programs may limit what students are able to accomplish during and after graduation in terms of neuropsychology. For example, consider whether teaching, research, and/or clinical work might be more important—what sorts of things do you think you might want to do as a neuropsychologist?

As part of the Ph.D., a clinical internship is typically required of those in clinically-oriented programs. Whereas a breadth of training is recommended, obviously some opportunity for involvement in neuropsychological work *per se* is desirable. The internship is often designed to be the fifth year of graduate school, although many extend the duration of training beyond this point. Programs without internship requirements typically are designed to be completed in three to four years.

Regardless of program or doctoral degree, one to two years of postdoctoral specialization in neuropsychology is also strongly recommended to become a neuropsychologist. Various postdoctoral training programs in neuropsychology exist throughout the country, and many laboratories welcome postdoctoral fellows into their research and clinical endeavors. Postdoctoral training allows for an intensive immersion into neuropsychology, typically under the tutelage of mentor neuropsychologists. Clinical and research training are common components of such fellowships, and involvement in grant writing and research publications may be possible for those interested in academic careers.

Hot Topics in Neuropsychology

Regardless of setting, neuropsychologists are commonly involved in the investigation of brain function and dysfunction. Some of the more common areas of interest have included head injury, learning disabilities, Alzheimer's disease, psychiatric illness (e.g., schizophrenia, depression), stroke, epilepsy, and other brain disorders of childhood, adolescence, adulthood, and aging.

Information Sources

Several professional organizations in neuropsychology exist, including the National Academy of Neuropsychology (NAN), the International Neuropsychological Society (INS), and Division 40 (Neuropsychology) of the American Psychological Association (APA). Each has a somewhat different focus, but most members and executive board members of these organizations would probably be happy to provide information regarding the field. Another way of learning more about neuropsychology (in addition to the numerous texts that exist) is to become a student member in one or more of these organizations. Student membership in each of the aforementioned groups includes a subscription to a journal in neuropsychology, wherein scholarly articles are published on a regular basis. These organizations also hold annual meetings throughout the country, wherein cutting edge scientific information in the field is presented. Typically, there are reduced rates for student memberships and conference attendance. Such conferences also represent a convenient forum for meeting people in the field, and most neuropsychologists are more than willing to speak with prospective students with interests in the discipline.

Career Opportunities

At this point, neuropsychologists are in relatively high demand in many of the settings mentioned above, and the field continues to grow at a rapid pace. Salaries vary widely depending on the setting, duties involved, and the level of training and experience of the individual.

Summary

Neuropsychology is a dynamic and growing field, with the opportunity to be involved in many activities in a variety of settings. As with any profession, neuropsychological study requires discipline and dedication, yet can also provide many rewards. Much of the excitement within the field is that so many questions remain regarding how the brain works, how to adequately measure the complexities of brain-behavior relationships, and how to attempt to remediate deficiencies related to brain dysfunction.

▼

DR. MUNRO CULLUM is a clinical neuropsychologist and assistant professor of psychiatry and neurology at the University of Colorado Health Sciences Center in Denver. He obtained his Ph.D. in clinical psychology from the University of Texas at Austin and completed postdoctoral training in neuropsychology at the University of California at San Diego and San Diego VA Medical Center. Dr. Cullum serves as the executive secretary of The National Academy of Neuropsychology and is associate director of the Neuropsychology Laboratory at the University of Colorado Health Sciences Center.

In addition to clinical and teaching activities, he actively conducts research, with most of his work focusing on neuropsychological functions and neuroimaging findings in aging and neurological/neuropsychiatric disorders. He has published widely, serves on a number of local and national committees, and is a fellow of the National Academy of Neuropsychology.

CHAPTER TWELVE

Forensic Psychology: Psychology in the Courtroom

**Alan M. Goldstein, Ph.D., ABPP,
Diplomate in Forensic Psychology**

When people hear that I am a **forensic psychologist**, many think of Quincy, the forensic pathologist on television, busily dissecting a body. In some ways, their reaction is not entirely incorrect. Like Quincy, forensic psychologists frequently assist courts and law enforcement agencies on legal matters. Similarly, forensic psychologists may serve as expert witnesses in court, having "dissected" a defendant's state of mind, presenting their findings to judge and jury. However, this is but one area of the practice of forensic psychology.

What Is Forensic Psychology?

The word *forensic* is taken from *forensis*, the legal forum in Rome where legal proceedings were held. Forensic psychology involves the application of psychological research, theory, methodology, and knowledge to address legal issues. Both law and psychology are involved with human behavior. Law is concerned with regulating behavior so that social norms are not violated. Psychology, on the other hand, focuses on understanding behavior and, in part, assessing the thoughts, feelings, and actions which comprise our functioning. The interface of law and psychology comprises the field of forensic psychology.

What Do We Do?

Through statutes and case law, the courts have long recognized psychologists as experts in human behavior. As a result, psychologists may be called upon to offer opinions on a wide range of legal/behavioral issues. Forensic psychologists may offer expert opinions in such areas as whether a defendant is competent to stand trial, whether the defendant could make a valid waiver of his/her Miranda rights, the mental state of a defendant at the time of an alleged offense (sanity/diminished capacity), and advising the court in cases involving the possibility of the death penalty. In civil or non-criminal cases, psychologists may serve as expert witnesses in cases involving product liability/personal injury suits, child custody and visitation disputes, assessing allegations of child abuse and neglect, and juvenile delinquency proceedings. Evaluating people for the possibility of civil or involuntary commitment to mental hospitals and assessing the potential for dangerousness are other areas of legal involvement for forensic psychologists.

While most forensic testimony is based upon an evaluation of a specific individual, other testimony may focus on a specific topic. For example, experts on such topics as the accuracy of eyewitness testimony or the validity of child sex abuse complaints or battered woman's syndrome may be called as expert witnesses to educate the jury so that they can more appropriately consider cases involving those legal/psychological issues.

The role of the forensic psychologist is not limited to that of evaluator or expert witness. Forensic psychologists may serve as consultants to law enforcement agencies performing such functions as evaluating police officer applicants, assessing the fitness for duty of police officers experiencing emotional or alcohol/drug-related difficulties on the job, or performing forensic hypnosis with crime victims and witnesses. They may work as consultants in the field of corrections or conducting treatment with inmates including those convicted of sex offenses. Others may be involved as consultants to federal, state, and local legislators, advising them on matters related to mental health and public policy. Forensic psychologists are also frequently employed in the fields of probation and parole as well as victims assistance services. Many forensic psychologists conduct research on topics related to the legal system and public policy. Forensic psychologists are frequently employed by colleges and universities conducting research and teaching in departments of psychology, law, and/or criminal justice.

Having What It Takes to Be a Forensic Psychology

Forensic psychology is not for everyone. Forensic psychologists are expected to explain the reasons for their findings and they must withstand close, often hostile, cross-examination when they serve as witnesses. Those interested in this career, in addition to possessing the appropriate academic training and experience, should be able to express themselves clearly, remain unflustered under pressure, and be willing to work under time constraints imposed by courts and attorneys.

How Do We Do It?

To reach expert opinions, forensic psychologists rely upon multiple sources of information in evaluating a case. Most likely, they will conduct clinical interviews with the defendant/plaintiff, administer a battery of psychological tests to this person, interview others familiar with this individual, and review a wide range of records including school and employment records, military records, and any and all related police, hospitalization, and court documents. Because forensic psychologists are expected to address legal matters in a relevant fashion, they must be familiar with the appropriate legal statutes and case law, since concepts and terms appearing in these documents are the specific behaviors that forensic psychologists are expected to assess.

Forensic Psychology as a Specialty

Psychology is a broad field with numerous areas of specialization. Forensic psychologists usually have their doctoral degrees (Ph.D. or Psy.D.) in clinical or counseling psychology. Others may have their doctorates in social psychology, industrial-organizational psychology, or experimental psychology. The practice of forensic psychology is guided by both the American Psychological Association's *Ethical Principles of Psychologists and Code of Conduct* and the *Specialty Guidelines for Forensic Psychologists*, an aspirational model for the practice of forensic psychology co-authored by the American Board of Forensic Psychology and Division 41 of the American Psychological Association. Division 41, the American Psychology-Law Society has approximately 1,500 members, those who have identified themselves as having specific interests in psychology and the law. The American Board of Forensic Psychology, founded in 1978, is affiliated with the American Board of Professional Psychology and administers the Diplomate in Forensic Psychology. The Diplomate of ABPP serves as the credential for the highest level of professional competence in the field and is based, in part, upon peer examination. There are approximately 150 Diplomates in Forensic Psychology in the United States.

Entering the Field of Forensic Psychology: An Overview

In psychology, the doctorate (Ph.D. or Psy.D) is the terminal degree. Yet, there is not a single forensic psychologist in the United States with a doctorate in forensic psychology. The reason for this is simple—no doctoral programs exist in forensic psychology! Most forensic psychologists have their doctorates in clinical psychology and their state license is a general or *generic* one. Psychologists must limit their area of practice to their area of professional competence.

Undergraduate Training

Since the required degree is the doctorate, those interested in forensic psychology should major in psychology in college, selecting courses to gain admission to graduate school. Courses should be taken in a wide range of areas. With the exception of John Jay College of Criminal Justice in New York City, no college offers a forensic psychology major. While some undergraduate programs may offer the opportunity for forensic placements or internships, these tend to be rare. Certainly, if you can arrange for a placement working in a correctional setting or in a state hospital forensic ward, this is perhaps the best way to find out whether you are interested in forensic psychology as a career.

Graduate Training

In the past, graduate students interested in forensic psychology had to design their own individually tailored programs. That is, they obtained permission from the psychology department to take law courses at their university's law school. Frequently, credits earned in these courses would count toward their doctorate in psychology. Over the last 15 years, however, a number of doctoral programs have been developed which have specifically addressed the interests of potential forensic psychologists. These programs tend to take one of two forms: programs offering joint degrees—a doctorate in clinical psychology and a J.D. (doctor of jurisprudence) degree; and programs which offer the Ph.D. or Psy.D. in psychology with a specific area of specialization in forensic psychology.

Joint degree programs involve a considerable investment of both time and money. A minimum of six to eight years is required to obtain both a doctorate in psychology and a J.D degree. A joint degree program requires the student to take courses at the university's graduate school of arts and sciences in psychology and at the university's school of law. Tuition for such programs may total well over $120,000. Fortunately, most universities offer financial aid in the form of scholarships, teaching and research assistanceships, or fellowships. The first law/psychology program, offered at the University of Nebraska-Lincoln, was started in 1974. Other joint degree programs include: University of Arizona in Tucson; Stanford University in California; Hahnemann University/Villanova Law School in Philadelphia; and Widener University in Chester, PA. Most of these programs offer placements in forensic settings.

A number of graduate programs offer the doctorate in psychology with an area of specialization in forensic psychology. Students are given the opportunity to complete internships in a wide range of forensic settings including correctional institutions, forensic mental health units, and at criminal justice agencies. Students take traditional psychology courses and can then select courses which integrate concepts from the law with traditional clinical research, theory, and methodology. Students may select from courses covering psychology and the law, methods of forensic assessment, and public policy and mental health.

Universities offering a specialization in forensic psychology include the University of Virginia, SUNY-Buffalo, University of Alabama, and the University of Nebraska-Lincoln. Northwestern University, through its Psycholegal Studies Program in the Department of Psychiatry, offers doctoral students the opportunity to conduct research on forensic psychology topics.

Since joint degree and specialty programs are a relatively new approach to forensic psychology education, most psychologists in the field never took law courses, nor were forensic psychology content courses offered to them. Rather, such psychologists must get their education in forensic psychology in another manner. John Jay College of Criminal Justice in New York City offers the only master of arts program in forensic psychology in the United States. The majority of students in this program are interested solely in completing an M.A. degree. Many already work for criminal justice agencies or for the courts. Others may, upon completion of the program, obtain positions working for these agencies or in such areas as probation and parole, correction, or working for psychological services units of police departments or other law enforcement agencies. Those interested in obtaining a master's degree in forensic psychology must remember that the terminal degree is the doctorate. Numerous doctoral-level psychologists have returned to graduate school to take forensic psychology courses at John Jay's forensic psychology program so that they may be competent to work in the area of forensic psychology. Others interested in graduate training in forensic psychology may enroll in master of legal studies programs (M.L.S.). The M.L.S. degree is offered at such institutions as Stanford University, University of Minnesota, and the University of Nebraska-Lincoln.

Post-Doctoral Training in Forensic Psychology

Post-doctoral programs exist for doctoral-level psychologists seeking more formal forensic training. Most programs are for one year, with some offering the option of a second year. Programs include: the Institute of Psychiatry, Law, and Behavioral Science at the University of Southern California; the Law and Psychiatry Program at the University of Massachusetts Medical Center; and programs offered at the Kirby Forensic Psychiatric Center in New York City and at St. Elizabeth Hospital in Washington, D.C. Other doctoral-level psychologists acquire forensic training through American Psychological Association-approved continuing education programs, such as those offered by the American Academy of Forensic Psychology.

Other doctoral-level psychologists may obtain individual supervision to enhance their forensic psychology skills.

Salaries

Training to be a forensic psychologist involves an investment of both time and money. A forensic psychologist typically attends college for four years, graduate school for five years, and perhaps receives two or three additional years of post-doctoral training/experience. Salaries range widely, depending upon level of training, experience, location, and the employer. Those with a master's degree in forensic psychology are most frequently employed by public agencies under supervision of a doctoral-level psychologist. They may expect to earn approximately $22,000 to $34,000 per year. Some may be employed as assistants to forensic psychologists and psychiatrists, working under close supervision. Doctoral-level psychologists employed by agencies may expect to earn $35,000 to $75,000 per year. Those forensic psychologists in independent practice usually charge $60 to as much as $200 per hour for their services.

Is Forensic Psychology for You?

Forensic psychology is not for everyone. Forensic psychologists are expected to explain the reasons for their findings and they must withstand close, often hostile, cross-examination when they serve as witnesses. Those interested in this career, in addition to possessing the appropriate academic training and experience, should be able to express themselves clearly, remain unflustered under pressure, and be willing to work under time constraints imposed by courts and attorneys.

The Future of Forensic Psychology

Over the last five years, many doctoral-level psychologists have been looking to specialize. The independent practice of clinical psychology has been greatly influenced by the economic ups-and-downs in our country. In addition, managed care and health maintenance organizations are making deep inroads into independent practice, limiting the fees charged by independent practitioners and setting limits on the number of reimbursed psychotherapy visits a patient may make. In some ways, forensic psychology is *recession proof*. The two major areas of forensic psychology practice—the assessment of criminal psycho-legal issues and evaluations for child custody determination—are relatively unaffected by economic conditions in the country. Crime and divorce are constants and psychologists frequently are asked to address these issues by attorneys and the courts. Public and political concerns about crime and criminal behavior also bodes well for the need for forensic psychologists in the future.

▼

ALAN M. GOLDSTEIN, Ph.D. received his B.A. in psychology from Hunter College, Bronx, NY. He received his master's in psychology and his Ph.D. in clinical psychology from Fordham University. An associate professor of psychology at John Jay College of Criminal Justice in New York City, Dr. Goldstein holds the Diplomate in Forensic Psychology from the American Board of Professional Psychology and serves on the Ethics Committee of the Board. He is also a member of the Board of Directors of the American Board of Forensic Psychology. Dr. Goldstein is a forensic consultant to the Westchester County Medical Center, to defense and prosecuting attorneys, and to a number of law enforcement agencies.

CHAPTER THIRTEEN

Psychiatry: An Opportunity to Ease Human Suffering

**Theresa Anna Yuschok, M.D.,
Duke University Medical Center**

Cartoons stereotype the bearded psychiatrist scribbling notes behind a couch. The field has changed a lot since Freud. Psychotherapy techniques are broader. More women have entered the field. A variety of other medical treatments are available, such as ECT and medications. A choice of practice options are open. A career in psychiatry may take many forms and appeal to many types of people.

Medical School

As in Freud's day, however, medical school is required to practice psychiatry, a medical specialty. In the four-year college degree, one may major in any art degree or science, psychology, if you'd like. But pre-medical science classes are required in chemistry, physics, and biology. (If the science classes are intimidating, other careers in the mental health fields such as psychologist, social worker, or psychiatric nurse may be more appealing).

Medical school requires another four years of study. The first two years include more science classes and laboratory work, such as anatomy, dissection of the human body, and histology—examining the cell structure of each organ. Medicine is a lot to learn—memorizing every artery, muscle, and nerve and how each works. The third year is spent out of the classroom and in the hospital wards. Students rotate through each specialty experiencing delivery rooms, as well as the psychiatric wards. This year reinforces the book learning with patient care. By the end of the third year, most medical students have chosen a specialty and apply for further training in a residency program.

Residency Training

The post-graduate residency training takes four years including neurology and medicine during the first "internship" year. Residents are paid $25,000. They work long hours with "on-call" (overnight) duties every three to six nights during the first two years. They work in the hospitals using stethoscopes and expanding skills from medical school. They also acquire new skills in psychotherapy, psychopharmacology and electroconvulsive therapy (ECT).

Psychotherapy is a complex art learned by observing senior psychiatrists interviewing patients, the resident discussing patient sessions with a supervisor, reading, or attending conferences, and sometimes experientially through a group meeting or hiring a psychotherapist for oneself. Some programs offer special training in group therapy, family therapy, substance abuse treatments, and behavioral therapy.

Psychiatrists also learn to prescribe medications for mental illnesses, such as depression and schizophrenia. Although other professionals may be licensed to do psychotherapy, the psychiatrist has the prescription pad and ECT, and the psychologist interprets tests such as Rorschach "ink blots" and personality testing.

Career Paths

After residency training, a variety of practice options are available. As a relatively young specialty, psychiatry attracts academic researchers. Funding is available to find cures or at least more effective treatment for schizophrenia, Alzheimer's disease, mood disorders, and other mental illnesses. This is an exciting time when much will be discovered during our lifetime. The research may include animals which are used for models of behaviors and diseases.

Some psychiatrists work independently or with a group. The practice may be office-based or hospital-based. Others work for salaries in State Mental Health Centers, HMOs, State Hospitals, or VAMCs. Most psychiatrists begin their practice with a variety of roles, including a part-time salaried position, a private office, and perhaps a teaching affiliation. It is easy to work part-time with a choice of hours and this appeals to those starting a family. Starting incomes range from $60,000 to $120,000 full time.

Further training choices include child psychiatry, forensics in prisons or courtroom, geriatrics, consultation-liaison with other medical specialties, or psychoanalysis. (Yes, the couch still exists). Child psychiatry may be the best choice—a scarcity of practitioners is predicted compared to expected need.

Psychiatrists are privy to a full range of human suffering, which can be quite stressful. Empathy, genuine caring for human beings and their struggles, is needed, but one must be able to also be an objective "participant observer" and not become overly involved or overwhelmed. The specialty can be fulfilling for those interested in the human condition and helping people with the tools of medication, communication, support, and insight.

THERESA ANNA YUSCHOK, M.D. practices psychiatry at Duke University Medical Center, Durham, NC. In addition to seeing patients for medication therapy and psychotherapy, she does group and family therapy, teaches residents and medical students at Durham Veterans Administration Medical Center, serves on committees, and has administrative duties. She graduated from a small town high school, enrolled in Northwestern University's Honors Program in Medical Education, and graduated from Northwestern University Medical School in Chicago in 1986. She did her residency training for four years at Duke University Medical Center and then continued on staff in 1990. She belongs to the American Psychiatric Association and the American Group Psychotherapy Association. In her free time, she enjoys playwriting and poetry.

CHAPTER FOURTEEN

Social Work: Carving Out My Own Special Piece

Sonja R. Berry, CSW-ACP

What Is This Thing Called Social Work?

During my approximately 20 years of social work practice, I have found that there is much confusion about what social work *is* and what social workers *do*. I like to define social work as a combination of art and science. It is a profession that helps people solve problems that are related to personal issues (mental illness, chemical dependency, and emotional disturbances), family issues (divorce, child abuse, homelessness, and parenting problems), and community issues (unemployment, housing, and discrimination). A social worker has a variety of options for practice through work with individuals, groups, communities, research, and administration. There are several characteristics that distinguish social work from the other helping professions. A few of them are:

- The focus on the total person in the total environment.
- The emphasis on the importance of family in molding and influencing behavior.
- The utilization of community resources in problem solving.
- The use of a supporting and accepting relationship with the client during the helping process.
- Maintaining a goal of helping the client to help him/herself.
- An educational program involving classroom work and practical field work experience.

Choosing Social Work

My decision to become a social worker was made many years ago when I realized that I was a people-person and that trying to understand and solve interpersonal problems was always much more interesting to me than some of the other subjects that I was learning. My decision to become an independent, self-employed, clinical social worker was made many years after my entrance into the profession. After 10 years as an independent practitioner, I continue to find my work challenging, rewarding, and interesting. Before I discuss what is involved in my current work, I think it is critical that I share information about what I did previously and how I and other colleagues got to the point of becoming independent practitioners.

Education, Training, and Legal Regulation of Social Workers

Being a social worker requires a degree in social work. The beginning degree is a baccalaureate degree in social work (BSW). The professional degree is called either a MSW (Master of Social Work) or MSSW (Master of Science in Social Work). It is also possible to obtain a post-graduate degree (Ph.D. or D.S.W.) in social work. The Ph.D. or D.S.W. is usually necessary if you wish to pursue a career in teaching at the university level. At both the baccalaureate and graduate level, students are required to complete classroom work as well as an internship (field placement) experience. Social workers with a BSW are considered to be prepared for entry-level positions, while those with the master's degree are frequently considered to be ready for more skilled or supervisory positions. Many social workers with a baccalaureate degree decide to return to graduate school to continue their education, and it is usually this group of professionals who return to work as supervisors and administrators. Social workers with a B.S.W. and extensive experience are also able to move into some administrative and/or other leadership positions in agencies or companies.

The graduate degree in social work is generally a two-year program, however, some schools do offer a shortened program for those students who have a B.S.W. It is also possible to gain admission to a graduate school of social work, even if you do not have an undergraduate degree in social work. A degree in one of the social sciences and some work experience in a people-oriented job can be critical elements in gaining admission to a graduate program, if you do not have a B.S.W.

Each of the 50 states now has laws defining who can call themselves a social worker and/or who can practice social work. The different classifications and eligibility requirements laid out by the states are dependent upon education and experience. The primary goal of legal regulation of social work is to provide some assurance to the public that persons providing social work services are appropriately educated and qualified to provide such services.

Opportunities for Social Workers

You will remember that I mentioned earlier that social workers have a variety of opportunities for practice. Social workers can be found working in medical and psychiatric hospitals and clinics, family service agencies, child welfare agencies, law enforcement and criminal justice agencies, schools and universities; governmental, private health, and human service agencies; child care facilities; local, state, and national government; nursing homes, business entities, and in private practice. They may work with individual clients and groups, supervise staff, manage or administer human service programs, develop public social policy, or organize community groups.

My own practice over the years allowed me to work with individuals (adoptions), develop and manage a new program (public housing), and supervise staff and administer a program (children's protective services). Once I had accomplished all this, I decided to engage in a private/independent practice. Other colleagues of mine have since entered into a private practice after working in an agency setting for many years, in order to perfect their skills in working with clients, one-on-one or in groups. Learning the business of social work, fine-tuning one's skills, and developing a network of professional relationships are necessary prerequisites for establishing a private practice.

ADVICE FROM THE PRO'S

Independence and Self-Employment as a Social Worker

My decision to leave the security of agency employment and start an independent practice occurred because I was interested in having more control over my own professional activities. I enjoyed all of the different social work jobs I previously held and believed that I had learned a lot. I place a great deal of value on those experiences. In fact, it was because of those experiences that I felt I was ready to strike out on my own and engage in those professional activities that were most meaningful to me.

Starting my own business meant that I had to carve out my own piece of social work based on my own previous experiences. Over the years, I have become quite comfortable with my business as it has developed. I have made the decision to maintain a varied practice, which includes clinical social work as well as consultation and training. My clinical work includes psychotherapy with adults and children, marital counseling, and completion of court-ordered home studies for adoption and custody disputes. My consultation and training work has provided me opportunities to consult with local agencies, to do staff development seminars with a variety of community agencies, and to conduct personal and professional development seminars. At various times, I have also had the opportunity to teach several academic courses in a social work program at a university in my community.

Best States for Women Entrepreneurs

Ranked by: Rate of business ownership among adult women in 1987
 1. Alaska, with 84.7 businesses
 2. Colorado, 72.9
 3. Vermont, 65.4
 4. Wyoming, 65.0
 5. Montana, 60.0
 6. Kansas, 56.6
 7. Oregon, 56.3
 8. Utah, 55.6
 9. New Hampshire, 55.5
 9. Hawaii, 55.5
Source: *American Demographics*

As in any other position, there are advantages and disadvantages of an independent practice. Of course, a major disadvantage is the fact that you are solely responsible for your income. If you have only a *few* clients, you have only a *little* income. When you are an employee in an agency, you get a set salary, regardless of how many clients you see, and you are not responsible for providing yourself with a place to work or supplies to use. As a self-employed person, those things become *your* responsibility. It is almost impossible to start a private practice with a full load of paying clients, so it becomes necessary to have some source of income to support yourself and your business while you get started. In time, it is possible to accomplish this by way of an independent social work practice.

Another disadvantage can be the lack of regular contact with colleagues. My own practice is a solo one. I do not have officemates or a supervisor or boss. I have solved this dilemma by making sure that I maintain contact with colleagues and by working with others on special cases or projects. I also frequently provide contract services for agencies, which provides opportunities for me to stay in touch with a variety of agency social workers. Many of my colleagues solve this dilemma by engaging in a group (rather than solo) practice, having associates, or sharing office space.

If you are not good at time management, or organizing yourself and your work, maintaining the business can become a nightmare. You must be self-directed and self-motivated to get all the necessary (even those you don't enjoy) parts of your work done. I have no one else to ask to do something that I would prefer not to do.

The major advantage to me of independent social work practice is the opportunity it provides for me to maintain a sense of control of my own work and to provide myself with more opportunities to engage in those social work activities that I enjoy most. I have been able to continue to work with individuals, couples, and families to help them find ways to solve their problems. I have also been able to continue to work with colleagues in a variety of ways.

The Future of Independent Social Work

Social work is a valuable and necessary service. Communities and individuals have demonstrated their willingness to pay for this service, whether it be through a government-offered service, a private agency funded through charitable contributions, or directly to a social work provider for a specific service delivered. As a private practitioner of social work, it has been important for me to maintain my commitment to the values of the profession. My business, along with those of other colleagues in independent practice, merely offers an additional resource for people to seek out assistance in solving their problems.

The private practice of social work is not really a new idea. Some of my colleague have been in private practice for much longer than my 10 years. There are a variety of fairly new options for social work practice in settings such as business and industry, employee assistance, and politics. I believe that in time, the private practice of social work, these other new areas, and the traditional settings will be considered by the general public, as well as those in the profession, as just another option for social work practice.

▼

SONJA R. BERRY, CSW-ACP, received her B.A. in sociology from Fisk University, Nashville, TN, and an M.S.W. from the University of Kentucky, Lexington. She has held social work jobs for the Kentucky Department of Social Services, the Lexington, Kentucky Housing Authority, and the Texas Department of Human Services.

Currently living and working in Austin, TX, she started private practice in 1983 and has enjoyed all of it, but claims that she would not be willing to trade in any of her other social work experiences.

CHAPTER FIFTEEN

Infant Mental Health: An Exciting, Emerging Field to Consider

**Marjorie Frank, LCSW,
Virginia Frank Child Developmental Center**

The field of **infant mental health** concerns itself with the physical, social, emotional, and developmental needs of children up to age six and their families. It is a field that has developed rapidly over the past several decades, as research has confirmed the primary importance of the child's experiences in early infancy on his subsequent development. Of primary importance is the infant's caregiving environment, which either promotes or detracts from his ongoing growth. Professionals interested in how babies form the initial bond and subsequent attachment to their parents have taught us that the quality of the parent-infant interaction is the single most important factor in determining how free the infant will be to thrive, develop, and learn. This knowledge has both enlightened and burdened parents, who now feel more than ever that they must strive for perfection as caregivers in order not to in some way hurt their children.

Tempering this rather awesome responsibility is an exciting new knowledge about inborn infant competencies. In addition, we now know that the newborn infant is capable of actively influencing his caregiving environment. The infant is not the passive, totally helpless creature we once though he was. Indeed, his ability to actively engage his caregiver is an incredibly powerful stimulus to his receiving good care. The success of the mother-infant pair is, in large measure, dependent on how well they fit each other temperamentally. The well-being of the infant depends on his mother also being well cared for by others, and understanding the needs of both partners in this dyad can often be a complicated business. It is in answer to the needs of both small children and parents in this new age of burgeoning knowledge and interest that infant mental health was born and has developed as a profession.

Who Is the Infant Mental Health Specialist?

The infant mental health specialist comes from a wide range of fields, including pediatrics, neonatology, psychiatry, nursing, social work, psychology, and special education. As a result, it is not possible to define a specific training program, such as one can in other professions. Therefore, I will generally describe the field and then focus on the potential career track from social work to infant mental health, since that is what I know best.

What is common to all who become interested in this field is an interest in and love for very small children and, hopefully, high regard and respect for those most intensely involved in their care—their parents. As the field is today, one must first choose one of the fields listed above for training and then later on specialize in infant mental health. How one goes about this depends on one's particular interests. For example, if your primary interest is in teaching, you would enroll in a bachelor's program in special education and then apply to either a master's or certificate program in infant mental health. Such programs now exist throughout the country. When you have completed your education on this track, you might choose to be an educational therapist in a therapeutic nursery, thus combining education and mental health training. If interested in working in a medical setting, you would follow the career course for either medicine (specializing in pediatrics or neonatology) or nursing (requesting practical training in newborn or pediatric wards). If your interest is more in the mental health aspects of this work, you would choose a degree program in either social work, psychology, or psychiatry. All of these programs, except for psychiatry which requires a medical school degree, are three to four years long. Social work and psychology both require field work placements, and one usually has a choice of placement according to one's interests. In social work, one would choose at least one field work placement, either in a child development center, a child welfare agency, a family service agency, or a hospital that provides the opportunity for work with infants and parents. The need for additional training beyond the degree would depend on the nature of the training you've already had.

A Focus on Awareness

The most important aspect of infant mental health training is clinical course work and supervised practical training. This is one reason why the training is directed to those who already have a first degree. Experience in school as well as in life adds to one's maturity. To work with infants and their families requires the practitioner to be willing to deal with very personal feelings and emotions. Having a baby and raising it is the most intensely personal and emotional experience in a parent's life, and professionals entrusted to help families with this all-important task must be as sensitive to and aware of parental and child vulnerabilities as they are of their strengths. This requires the practitioner to also have awareness of his/her own vulnerabilities, for the capacity to be sensitive to others is rooted in one's own self-awareness.

I am stressing this because the field of infant mental health is still in the process of becoming *professionalized*. Many people, professional and non-professional, work with infants and toddlers in caregiving capacities. One has only to take note of the ever-growing numbers of infants spending their days in day care as mothers return to work either out of economic need or for personal fulfillment. The debate over whether day care is good or bad for small children has raged for decades, and the experts appear to have concluded that it all depends on the quality of the care. Quality is determined by appropriate ratios of caregiver to child and by the training of the daycare staff. Yet, for decades, women provided day care to infants and toddlers with the prime qualification of being mothers themselves, working under impossible conditions and for very little salary. Day care centers were overcrowded with children and understaffed with untrained caregivers working against the odds, and the children suffered. That is changing now with increased awareness and understanding of children's needs and with improved federal laws that set guidelines for care. It is my hope that one day all day care caregivers will be trained infant mental health specialists. My point is that love for children alone is not enough to do this work. It requires the willingness to invest the necessary time and training to do it *well*.

The Infant Mental Health Specialist: Roles to Consider

There is a very wide range of services that an infant mental health specialist may provide. To illustrate, I will delineate some of the services *I* have provided over the years.

> **ADVICE FROM THE PRO'S**
>
> **Top Employee Motivators**
>
> Ranked by: Conclusions in article by Frederick Hertzbert as published in the *Harvard Business Review*.
> 1. On-the-job achievement
> 2. Recognition
> 3. Type of work done
> 4. Responsibility assigned
> 5. Advancement and growth opportunities
> 6. Salary
> 7. Relationships with other employees
> 8. Type of supervision received
> 9. Working conditions
> 10. Company policies and administration
>
> Source: *Homecare*

- Counseling new mothers in well-baby clinics on their concerns regarding their infants' eating, sleeping, training, discipline—on all of the worries that arise is the process of parenting.

- Demonstrating the competencies of newborns to their parents through neonatal behavioral assessment. This is an assessment wherein one shows the baby's behavioral abilities within the first month of life, which includes how the infant negotiates states of sleeping and waking, his reflexes, ability to self-soothe, and ability to follow both visual and auditory stimuli. Performing this assessment requires additional specific training.

- Participating in a mother-infant "get together" group where mothers meet with their babies to socialize with other mothers and to get informal advice from professional staff.

- Ongoing long-term treatment to families of children with developmental, behavioral, or emotional problems.

- Teaching courses on parenting to university students interested in studying infant mental health.

- Consulting to the staff of a transitional home for preschool children who were removed from their parental homes for reasons of abuse or neglect.

- Developing and directing an early intervention in day care program, wherein trained social workers entered day care centers and provided assistance and consultation to day care staff, direct intervention to targeted children, and reach out services to the parents of the children in care.

As can be seen from this list, the possibilities are many, and the infant mental health specialist can choose where to invest his/her energies once trained. Salaries, too, vary widely, depending on one's choice of primary profession and whether one chooses to work in a public or private agency or hospital, or whether one decides to have a private practice.

MARJORIE A. FRANK received her B.S. from Northwestern University in Evanston, IL, and her M.A. in social work from The University of Chicago. Following a period of time working as a school social worker in Illinois, Mrs. Frank moved to Israel where she lived for 14 years. It was during this period that she moved into the area of infant mental health. Mrs. Frank currently works at the Virginia Frank Child Developmental Center and is a student in the doctoral program at the Institute for Clinical Social Work, both of which are located in Chicago.

CHAPTER SIXTEEN

So You Want to Be a State Child Welfare Worker?

**S. Donna Helm Murphy,
Staff Development Supervisor,
Missouri Division of Family Services**

Working as a **child welfare worker** for a state agency can be both a rewarding and frustrating experience, one that requires reserves of experience, enthusiasm, patience, tenacity, and, most of all, the ability to see progress in small increments and to allow the credit for that progress to belong to the families with whom we work.

The Job

Many families come to a state child welfare agency for help involuntarily, usually as a result of a call to the state's child abuse/neglect reporting facility. All families want to care for their children; not all families have the all the skills needed to do so. The focus of our job is to help families stay together where possible and to find permanent homes for children when unity cannot be maintained. Knowledge of family systems and dynamics and possession of the skills needed to intervene effectively in a time of crisis is imperative.

In some of the smaller local offices, the social worker will most likely be given a generalist load, doing a little of everything there is to do in an agency: investigations of child abuse/neglect calls, family centered/protective services, and alternative care services.

In offices serving larger regions, a degree of caseload specialization may exist in which the social worker does a part of the services described above and eventually transfers the case to another specialized load within the agency, as the focus of the services changes with the family's need(s). In some instances, specialized loads are considered support loads, e.g., the study and license of prospective foster homes or adoptive homes.

In all of these situations, the worker will be assessing the need for services for the family, acting as case manager, and providing some direct services. When the

MENTAL HEALTH CAREER DIRECTORY

assessment and case plan reveal that referral to providers is necessary for specialized needs, those referrals will be made.

Time frames, set either by federal or state law or policy are built into the progress of the work being done with the family. For instance, a child abuse/neglect investigation must be completed within a defined number of days and, if appropriate, will be referred to a family-centered or protective services social worker with another set of time frames for the assessment, service plan development, and implementation. Because of these time frames, a myriad of forms, the serious problems facing families of today, and the high caseloads, workers often experience stress and burnout. Frustration is most often due to the perceived difference in what the worker had been educated to do, and what they find themselves actually doing. Often they feel more like paper pushers than social workers.

Social workers interact with various members of the community—business leaders, who are sought out for advice or resources, and law enforcement staff, especially juvenile officers, who have the authority to remove children from homes when necessary.

The Supervision/Agency Structure

The social worker is the backbone of the agency; s/he does the work required by law and good practice. The social worker reports to and has the support of a **first-line supervisor**, with one or two supervisory levels above that, depending on the size of the region being served. Beyond that, a **regional director** heads the region, which is often grouped into geographic administrative areas. Regional directors are often supervised by the **agency director**, however, there are some states with varying degrees of local autonomy in terms of administration. Finally, throughout the agency, support staff provide policy, training, and management assistance as well as clerical support.

Tough Issues, Tough Decisions

The ideal candidate should demonstrate the ability to: value persons who may not have the ability to value themselves; accept persons as they are with their problems; and want to empower persons to learn a problem-solving process applicable to many situations that they will encounter. Above all, the ideal applicant should have a strong sense of family—not strong feelings of saving children from their families. At the same time, s/he must be open and honest with families when no progress has been made and a recommendation must be made to remove the children from the home.

The Education and Preparation

Ideally, a state child welfare worker will have a minimum of a bachelor's degree in social work, counseling, psychology, or other related fields, such as education or nursing. A degree in social work gives the applicant exposure to the attitudes, knowledge, values, and skills needed. Specific course work should address family systems theory and application.

Any course that addresses the assessment and treatment of the many problems families face in today's society should be taken. Anything that covers the dynamics of abuse and neglect in families or on the developing child should be considered.

The Values

In addition to the above recommended educational background, the ideal candidate should also demonstrate the ability to: value persons who may not have the ability to value themselves; accept persons as they are with their problems; and want to empower persons to learn a problem-solving process applicable to many situations that they will encounter. Above all, the ideal applicant should have a strong sense of family—not strong feelings of saving children from their families. At the same time, s/he must be open and honest with families when no progress has been made and a recommendation must be made to remove the children from the home.

While the issues necessitating removal are addressed by the family, the social worker, and therapists, the social worker must have the ability to guide the family through this painful, but potentially, growth-producing process.

The Hiring Process

Several agencies use various behavioral interviewing profiles which provide a picture of how the applicant has handled situations in their history, not how they will handle something should it arise. Within agencies, staff develop other interviewing tools designed to find the person most suited to the job available. A person with a good sense of humor and a good sense of their own values, how those values may differ from their agency's agenda, and how they must constructively resolve this difference will be a valuable employee.

The Training

Prior to full-fledged field work, the new employee usually attends orientation training, if required by the state. This is supplemented with time spent in on-the-job training with the immediate supervisor. Training takes place soon after hiring and is usually completed within a set probationary period.

The orientation training offers an overview of the laws under which the state agency operates as well as the philosophy of the agency; the knowledge and skills needed to identify and investigate abuse and neglect, sexual abuse, and emotional maltreatment; and the fields of assessment and case planning to meet the treatment needs of the family and children. The orientation is usually based on the policy and practice manuals governing the agency approach to investigation, treatment, and alternative care. Infused throughout the training will be the agencies approach to working with families.

During their career with the agency, social workers and supervisors receive additional training in policy, practice, knowledge, and skills issues. For some job specializations, a set number of training hours are mandated; for others, minimum hours are strongly recommended.

The Opportunities

Social workers who begin their careers in a public child welfare agency often start in positions classified as **Social Services Worker I** or **Social Services Worker II**. In order to begin at the SSW II level, a candidate may be required to enter the job with several years of experience, in addition to the required undergraduate degree.

Often, a master's degree can be substituted for the desired experience. Either entry-level position will involve a probationary period, during which orientation training and some on-the-job experience might occur. At the completion of the probationary period, the worker is usually offered a permanent position and a raise. In some instances, the probationary period may be extended.

Those entering an agency in one of these entry-level positions often move laterally to other types of caseload. If required by state law or policy and if eligible, persons take merit examinations to be considered for promotional opportunities. In many public child welfare agencies, an employee must have worked a period of two or more years to be eligible for promotion to first-line supervisor. Further advancement within the state agency is often contingent upon the supervisory, administrative, or consultative experience that the child welfare worker has gained with the state agency or elsewhere, such as with a private or some other public social welfare agency.

Workers who decide to leave public child welfare often find work in private social work agencies as juvenile officers or as workers for other public agencies. After several years of experience, some persons may accept positions with the federal government at regional planning levels.

Salaries

A recent survey of current starting salaries in a 15-state area revealed that salaries for the entry-level social worker start at $1,315 to $1,902 per month. In states that give a pay raise at the completion of a successful probationary period, that amount goes up as state funding policy provides. Cost of living increases, occasional merit raises, and infrequent classification repositioning can result in additional increases.

The same survey indicated that salaries for a first-level supervisor begin at $1,588 to $2,496 per month, depending on the state. Mid-level supervisors begin at $1,957 to $2,753 per month. Upper-level supervisory or administrative personnel begin at a range of $2,045 to $3,813 per month. States outside this 15-state survey may have different varying amounts.

Travel Requirements

Depending upon the administrative structure for training, the orientation training may require travel to a stationary training facility in the state. At other times throughout the career in a public child welfare agency, travel may be required for in-service training opportunities as well as for conferences. Social workers are expected to be able to travel when required.

Social work in a public child welfare agency often requires that families are seen in their homes, although office visits by foster parents and children and adoptive parent applicants are sometimes necessary.

Unless budget constraints dictate otherwise, most public agencies reimburse social workers for expenses such as meals and mileage, while in the local area doing field work, and lodging, if overnight stays are required.

Conclusion

Over the years in various training sessions, I have heard social workers, especially those who work in public child welfare agencies, described in many ways—sometimes in an unflattering manner. But the one description that has remained with me is that the need to help others is in our genes. We can't help it! Working in a public child welfare agency gives one the opportunity to use the knowledge and skills gained in a school of social work with a clientele who may not want them to help, outwardly, but who, when they find they can use some of the skills taught, can go on to do good works in their life! It is the most challenging form of social work there is—knowing that you cannot change anyone; you can only provide them with the environment and skills needed to change themselves.

For all the frustrations you can feel when there is a setback within a family, nothing can match the glowing warmth felt when a family is able to watch their child graduate. For all the irritation felt when community persons refer to families receiving services from a public child welfare agency as *those people*, nothing can match the pride when observing a young adult express her thanks for the support given, which now enables her to work on her master's degree and teach other adolescents the skills needed to make it on their own.

I would encourage anyone who wants to perform social work to begin their career at a public child welfare agency. *This* is where the children and families are, where the need is, and where change begins!

▼

STELLA DONNA HELM MURPHY began her career as a caseworker in Joplin, MO, in 1968. After moving laterally to other caseload types in the agency, she was promoted to supervisor in 1972, supervising AFDC workers. For two years, she served as the county volunteer coordinator, seeking volunteers to provide a multitude of services not available through other resources. Later, she returned to direct supervision after substantive Missouri child abuse laws went into effect and supervised a unit of seven workers, each with a different caseload type.

In 1977, Donna was promoted to staff development specialist (trainer) and moved to Jefferson City, MO. While living in the state capitol, she obtained an M.S.W. in 1981 and left training for five months in order to take part in a refugee program. However, when the opportunity presented itself, she accepted her current position of staff development supervisor with the Missouri Division of Family Services.

Ms. Murphy is married and has two sons. Her hobbies include staying active in her church, singing acappella with a group of singers, and playing the piano.

CHAPTER SEVENTEEN

Social Work in the Schools

**Steve Turner, MSW,
School Social Worker, Gull Lake Public School System**

It's 7:30 in the morning and time for that second cup of coffee while you plan your daily appointments at the mental health clinic. It's lunch time, a time to relax with your colleagues after spending a hectic morning counseling adolescents in the drug treatment center where you work. It's 7:30 pm, and you finally get a chance to unwind after a busy day dealing with parents, children, and medical staff at the pediatric hospital unit where you are assigned. Such are the work days of many social workers in agency treatment settings. Do you know what? Such scenes could be plugged into the daily calendar of events of a social worker in the school setting, too. It is very conceivable that one or more of those time blocks could be devoted to providing school social work services.

Take the 7:30 am time slot, for instance. That second cup of coffee could just as easily be consumed while gathered around the conference table in the principal's office, participating in a crisis team meeting or planning a schedule change for a new special education student. The lunch hour could be devoted to running a support group for children of divorce that you are offering to fourth and fifth graders in an elementary school you serve. The 7:30 pm time slot might have to be reserved now and again, for instance, to lead a group of parents of preschoolers discussing effective parenting methods.

These scenarios are referenced, not to make the case for the position of **school social workers** being on call 24 hours a day, but to point out that the hours and responsibilities of the position can be flexible and varied.

What Is the Role of School Social Worker?

As a mental health professional in a school setting, the school social worker's role is defined by a variety of factors, including the articulated needs of the school district, the mandated services spelled out in state and/or federal law, and the individual building needs, coupled with the areas of expertise, that the social worker brings to the position. Other factors that go into defining the role are the age of the students, the size of the building and district, the number of other social workers on staff, the number and type of special services and programs offered, and so forth. In other words, there is no one role of a school social worker, but rather a wide variety of services that may be a part of the one position.

There may be a varied degree of flexibility in the position, but most school social workers provide a combination of preventative mental health services and crisis intervention services. Preventative mental health services include, but are not limited to, working with school staff, students, and parents to build self-esteem, make good decisions, and create a positive learning environment. Examples of crisis intervention or providing on-going treatment could include the divorce group mentioned above, meeting with a student who recently lost a parent, discussing alternatives with a student who frequently fights on the playground, or helping a single parent design an effective home discipline plan for his teenage daughter. For most school social workers, there is not a clear dichotomy between preventative and crisis treatment, since the job requires that *both* sectors be addressed.

What You'll Earn

As with teachers, a school social worker's salary is determined by the teacher's pay schedule—the number of years of work experience in education coupled with the educational degree achieved. A beginning school social worker possessing a master's degree would be paid a starting salary in the range of $22,000-$25,000, though in larger metropolitan areas, it could be higher. Yearly increments are built into the teacher's contract and could range from $500-$1,200 a year or more. At present, a school social worker at the 13th step on the teacher's pay scale could earn $40,000-$50,000 or more. Other fringe benefits may include full family health, dental, and vision care insurance, plus a retirement plan.

Preparing for Your First Job

School social work is one area of specialization within the field of graduate social work education. It is necessary to obtain a master's degree in social work (MSW or equivalent), in order to be hired as a school social worker. Master's degree programs are offered at a number of universities around the country. An undergraduate major in social work, psychology, or sociology may be extremely helpful in gaining access to a master's program. Also, social work job experience at the BA level can assist a candidate in gaining admission. With competition for admission to many MSW programs so keen, experience in the field, paid or volunteer, can mean the difference between acceptance or rejection. Gaining experience as a social worker at the BA level is not allowable in schools, but many other agencies do hire social workers with undergraduate degrees.

Some programs offered at large universities provide specific areas of specialization, enabling the candidate to graduate with the MSW degree with specialization in school social work. Other programs are more generic, and it is up to the candidate to tailor the program, so as to gain exposure to the area of interest. One way to make certain that school social work experience is part of the program is to select a field work placement in a school. All master's programs require a certain number of hours in field work training. Usually the student has some choice of placement and, by procuring a school setting, there will be opportunity to shoulder at least some of the responsibilities and experiences of a school social worker.

Landing Your First Job

With a master's degree in social work and school social work credentials, you are now ready for the job market. In making the decision to pursue employment as a school social worker, several important factors need to be considered. For one thing, the school social worker functions as a mental health professional in an educational institution. Unless hired into a large school system with a number of social workers on staff, there may be few, if any, fellow social workers with whom to interact. Colleagues may include school psychologists, teachers, principals, and other educational professionals. Again, unlike in an agency setting, many of the supports (supervision, secretarial) may or may not be readily available. Your daily schedule will be dictated by the host setting and include moving from office to classroom to student's home and back. Appointments are often set according to the teacher's schedule in terms of frequency, length, day, and time. You need, therefore, to be flexible and creative, so as to implement your social work plan, being mindful of the educational parameters.

In some school districts, there exists a large special education itinerant staff made up of a director, secretarial support, school social workers, school psychologists, speech and language pathologists, and teacher consultants. In such departments, there is collegial support, supervision, and staff to consult.

There is also the potential to advance into a supervisory position, as head of the social work department. However, in many school districts, such an opportunity does not exist. That is not to say that salary increases aren't possible. In education, such increases and other fringe benefits are tied into the teacher contract.

How Much Can You Expect to Earn

As with teachers, a school social worker's salary is determined by the teacher's pay schedule—the number of years of work experience in education coupled with the educational degree achieved. A beginning school social worker possessing a master's degree would be paid a starting salary in the range of $22,000- $25,000, though in larger metropolitan areas, it could be higher. Yearly increments are built into the teacher's contract and could range from $500-$1,200 a year or more. At present, a school social worker at the 13th step on the teacher's pay scale could earn $40,000-$50,000 or more. Other fringe benefits may include full family health, dental, and vision care insurance, plus a retirement plan.

Your Career Options

While working as a school social worker can offer many challenges and opportunities to work with America's youth and its parents, it can be wearing, and professional burnout is possible. That is why many professionals decide to try their hand at another type of social work or another area altogether. Possessing a master's degree in social work and school social work experience provides you with that option. In these cases, your skills and experience working with children and parents can be an asset. The more removed from an educational or child-oriented setting, the less some of those skills and experience may count. However, the interpersonal relationship skills many school social workers develop are invaluable in a variety of other professional situations.

A "Typical" Working Day of a School Social Worker

We have dealt with several aspects of the role and working conditions of a school social worker, but we have yet to address the nuts and bolts of the day-to-day experiences you might encounter while on the job. Be forewarned—there is no typical day in the life of a school social worker. The following examples may help to define the role, however.

Working in Special Education

Many school social workers are hired to work with the special education population in the schools. Such work includes evaluating students suspected of having a handicap, observing them in classes, interviewing them, their parents, and teachers, reviewing records, contacting other agencies that know the student, and participating along with other educational professionals and parents in meetings, where the findings are reviewed and decisions made. Once a student is determined to be eligible for special education, s/he is placed on the caseload of the social worker. Such contacts with individual or groups of students may occupy a major portion of the social worker's day.

A school social worker also consults with special education teachers in order to plan programs and, where appropriate, assists in their implementation. A third component of the job is maintaining contact with the parents, so as to coordinate the efforts of home and school. Finally, school social workers act as a liaison between school and home and various community agencies that may be dealing with that student and his/her family. While these activities comprise the major portion of your day, any or all of them may be superseded by emergencies, which from time to time occur. Examples of these emergencies include dealing with a death, suicide, bus problem, runaway situations, etc. Again, it is necessary to be flexible and creative, so as to address these diverse demands and, at the same time, maintain a level head.

Working in General Education

Some social workers are hired through general education and often their roles are much the same as the special education school social worker, except that they do not need to be concerned about certification for special education. Usually, there is a lessening of the paperwork, but in most other respects, the functions are similar. A referral for social work services can be initiated by the parents, a teacher, principal, or at the high school level by the student him/herself. Once the referral is initiated, it is the school social worker's responsibility, along with teachers, parents, student, and any other significant parties, to design a treatment plan. Such a plan may or may not include direct treatment—meeting regularly with the school social worker. It is up to the social worker to implement this plan and to assess progress toward its goals at least annually. In special education, this is accomplished at the annual review individual education planning committee meeting (I.E.P.C.). In general education, year- end reports may serve this assessment purpose.

What About Work Settings?

Some school social workers work in pre-schools and elementary school settings, while others find positions in middle, junior, or senior high school settings. Some work in specialized programs, such as drop-out prevention centers, school-age parents programs, or severely handicapped programs. Others work in combinations of the above settings. In all of these settings, there are some commonalities: the ability to work with a diverse group of people (parents, educators, students), to empathize with people while maintaining your perspective, and to be resourceful in assisting clients attain their multiplicity of goals.

So now you know something about a career as a school social worker! The hours may be varied (Remember those 7:30 meetings?) and the pay scale limited when compared with other comparably trained professionals, but you will find it both challenging and rewarding, for you are impacting the lives of a variety of people in ways you can't imagine. Good luck!

▼

STEVE TURNER has worked as a school social worker for the past 22 years. Prior to that, he worked for four years as a clinical social worker for the Michigan Department of Mental Health. He received his BA degree from Kalamazoo College and attended the University of Michigan School of Social Work, where he received is MSW degree. Despite grousing about paperwork, he continues to find his career both challenging and rewarding.

CHAPTER EIGHTEEN

Marriage and Family Therapists—Healing Wounded Families in a Changing World

**Henry C. Malone, ACSW, CSW,
Licensed Marriage and Family Therapist**

Marriage counseling, as it once was called in a simpler time, has exploded in the last decade or two, shooting specialty areas of this profession in many different directions. As marriage and family life has dramatically changed, along with almost every aspect of American life, it has become necessary for the traditional *marriage counselor* to develop new skills and broadened understanding to deal with a host of often-startling, frequently problematic new ways in which Americans establish intimacy with each other in relationships, and how they rear their offspring.

Discovering the Field of Marriage and Family Therapy

Few people know, when they pursue their undergraduate, or even graduate professional degrees (the M.S.W., L.L.P., R.N., or Ph.D.), that their motives to enter such social service professions as social work, psychology, or nursing will lead them into a specialty field where the majority of their work will be with couples or entire families.

People frequently decide on a specialty in social service professions based on complex motives. The most common being that their own personal life experiences have given them a special interest in what are otherwise very broad-based professions. Though people with postgraduate social service can, and do, move about in their professions, working perhaps with adolescent groups at one point, with hospitalized mentally ill persons at another, or in administrative work at another time, it is likely that they will, sooner or later, find a definite preference for a specialized field.

Working in marriage or couples counseling and family therapy is definitely a choice! Often, it is a choice made gradually, discovered, perhaps, after several years of pursuing social service in other areas.

Typically, the college graduate headed for social service will have spent her/his energy focused on a broad range of classes, including the general sciences, usually strong in psychology and social work, and in philosophy and the humanities. It is in professional graduate school (psychology, social work, or nursing), where some real focus generally begins to appear. The graduate student often finds her/himself drawn toward aspects of a career specialty as s/he makes choices among her/his elective classes.

The potential marriage and family therapist will likely be drawn to those courses that explore issues involving the interactions of society, culture, and the individual; specifically, how the family bridges them. The potential marriage and family therapist begins to see how profoundly the family is about the business, for better or worse, of passing along the values and beliefs of the changing culture in which they live to the next generation as best they can.

Entering the Field of Marriage and Family Therapy

As the professional enters the job market, most frequently as an entry-level caseworker (as in the case of a master's level social worker or psychologist), s/he tends to enter either a large public or private agency, such as a state department of social services or mental health or a *United Way* agency, with services often aimed at the financially indigent. In settings like these, the new professional will gather much specific experience. Typically, the caseworker will manage a caseload of between 30 to 50 cases, seeing these individual clients or couples weekly, monthly, or on a variety of *as needed* occasions.

In most cases, clients who are seen individually are presenting personal problems (such as depression, grief, anxiety, or stress) that are directly related to family issues. But because these symptoms are experienced by the individual alone, that person usually comes for therapy alone, seeking symptom-relief. Efforts are generally made to draw in other members of the family, but there is often resistance to this: "it's not my problem, it's his." Rarely does a family realize that they have a *family* problem.

In planning the ongoing treatment of the professional's caseload at the entry-level position, the caseworker will be supervised systematically (formally, for at least an hour each week) by a seasoned licensed professional who has worked in the same job specialty, often for many years.

As the caseworker-professional begins to join academic learning with the supervised day-to-day specifics of clinically dealing with real people, the therapist moving in the direction of marriage and family therapy begins to discover, practice, and refine what s/he finds to be most useful in dealing with a wide variety of situations. The more the therapist works with people, and involves family members, the more s/he will tend to be aware of the many issues that wound and sometimes destroy family function. As the potential marriage and family therapist grows in knowledge and skills, s/he will tend to *specialize* in some of the more important areas that prevent families from doing their job adequately:

1. Drug and alcohol abuse in the family setting;
2. Physical abuse and neglect issues;
3. Family trauma: sudden death, acute illness, long-term illness;
4. Sexual abuse: intra-familial sexual behavior, pregnancy;
5. Poverty and social chaos, alienated families;
6. Education and mis-education issues;
7. Lack of any spiritual organization in family life;
8. Lack of family intimacy and socialization;
9. The adult-child, the offspring of dysfunctional families;
10. Intra-generational conflicts in the family;
11. Marriage dissolution: *picking up the pieces, moving on*;
12. Sibling rivalry, love issues between children and parents;
13. Mental illness in the family;
14. Non-traditional relationships: interracial couples, homosexual couples, couples with physical disabilities.

This partial list serves to highlight only a few of the many areas that the novice professional must become aware of as a marriage and family therapist. Typically, the young graduate caseworker seeks educational enhancement in these areas by attending workshops and seminars regularly, which serve to detail up-to-date perspectives for clinical practitioners.

In the process of moving toward meeting the qualifications of a licensed marriage and family therapist, the working professional caseworker accumulates a variety of skills that allow him/her to work in many other areas of the social service profession:

1. Drug abuse;
2. Children's therapy;
3. Economic and budget education;
4. Sexuality and intimacy;
5. Employment specialization;
6. Pastoral counseling;
7. Communications enhancement;
8. Conflict resolution.

If the marriage and family therapist does not alter course, it is likely that within two to three years after receiving a graduate degree and beginning entry-level work, s/he will be working with a caseload more or less focused on families, with licensed supervision also focused on family issues.

At this point, the therapist is often *doing* marriage and family therapy, but is not yet *licensed* to do so independent of licensed supervision. This period of time and practice may be viewed as the *internship* for becoming a licensed marriage and family therapist. The next step is to meet the formal requirements of the state in which you reside to become a licensed marriage and family therapist.

Becoming a Licensed Marriage and Family Therapist

Each state's department of commerce licensing and certification office makes licensure available to individuals to become independent practitioners. This allows the therapist to pursue an independent practice, if that is the goal, or in a private clinic, with clients of one's own choosing. Many fully-licensed marriage and family therapists, however, choose to remain with public or private non-profit agencies, and so for them, the main function of licensure is to become an unsupervised practitioner in the agency setting.

In most states, licensure requires proof (written documentation, usually from the agency or agencies where the therapist has practiced) that, over a period of five years, the therapist has had a minimum of 2,000 direct client contact hours, half of which were with families, couples, or other family-related sub-systems, where the therapist was physically present in the therapy room with the clients and overseen by the licensed supervisor of the therapist. This experience with families must be acquired after the therapist has obtained his/her appropriate qualifying degree, such as an M.S.W. in social work, an R.N. in nursing, or a Ph.D. in psychology.

Typically, as part of this *package*, 200 hours of work must be completed with the training supervisor physically present, and 100 hours where the therapist is alone with the clients.

Along with documentation of performance, the licensing department of the state typically requires inclusion of transcripts of both undergraduate and graduate professional credentials. In many states, at least three courses in the following areas are required as part of one's graduate level class work: family studies; family therapy methodology; and human development, personality theory, or psychopathology. Usually, at least one course is also required in ethics, law and standards of professional practice, and formal research methodology.

Because so much is demanded to become an independent licensed marriage and family therapist, many therapists simply continue to work under licensed supervision. Often, the person who seeks licensure is looking to go into private practice for him/herself, where the independence is greater, the work hours more flexible, and the bureaucratic aspects of working within an agency setting are gone.

Crucially, the independent therapist is also able to generate his own clients, since people most often seek clinical services at clinics, rather than with the singular practitioner. The licensed therapist must have a good referral system and must be prepared to network with businesses frequently to create referral sources. Also, the independent practitioner must have good skills with insurance providers, since most people seeking marriage and family therapy will usually be in treatment for a few

Getting Started in the Field

As the professional enters the job market, most frequently as an entry-level caseworker (as in the case of a master's level social worker or psychologist), s/he tends to enter either a large public or private agency, such as a state department of social services or mental health or a *United Way* agency, with services often aimed at the financially indigent. In settings like these, the new professional will gather much specific experience. Typically, the caseworker will manage a caseload of between 30 to 50 cases, seeing these individual clients or couples weekly, monthly, or on a variety of *as needed* occasions.

months, and will almost always want to use their work-related insurance for at least partial payment of the fee for service. The independent therapist will need to deal with this matter, one way or another, since his/her success in billing is often a key to being paid appropriately and in a timely fashion.

Career Opportunities

Pursuing a career of *saving marriages* is no longer the singular specialty it once was 20 years ago. It is doubtful that one could build a serious full-time and exclusive practice of marriage and family therapy (20-40 clients) on an independent basis in the '90s.

Perhaps it is because the values of the culture have changed so much, but when a couple comes for counsel in our era, it is frequently with the intent of *making a last ditch effort* before divorcing. Among many professionals what was known as *marriage counseling* is now often referred to, half-seriously, as *divorce counseling*. The counselor quickly realizes that the couple has come for help *too late*. Often, something in the marriage has been broken irreparably, and all that remains is counsel to facilitate divorce.

It is more common to see expanding career opportunities for therapists occurring during and after a divorce in our era, where the marriage and family therapist is providing a host of *survival* services for the *victims* of the marital break-up. Often, it is then, and only then, that the issues of abuse, trauma, neglect, dysfunction, and the breakdown of communication can be addressed by the therapist. Often, the marriage and family therapist is rebuilding what remains of the former family (perhaps an ex-wife and her three children), and laying the groundwork for what might be a good *next marriage*, or at least an acceptable adaptation to the lifestyle of a single parent rearing three children. Marriage and family therapy now seems to be an ever-diversifying field of subspecialties involving focus on the special problems that *haunted* the marriage/family before it was dissolved by divorce or the abandonment of one or both parents. Nowadays, the marriage and family therapist may work with dysfunctional groups, made up of members of dysfunctional families, in an effort to build real functional adaptation for the future. It is now common to work with the *one-parent family* or the *latch-key family* (where both parents work long hours) where the children are desperately trying to raise themselves. It is also common to begin work with one child, whose symptoms are often quite severe, and then to find oneself as a therapist, gradually bringing all members of the family into regular counsel; for it is most frequent that the *problem child* is only the symptom-bearer of a deep-seated global family problem, a problem that most of the family members have fearfully tried to hide or deny.

Salaries

In the first five years, the marriage and family therapist, depending on whether s/he works in private practice, in a non-profit clinic, or for a government organization, can typically expect to earn $22,000 to $32,000, with significant regional differences.

Thereafter, if the therapist remains with the non-profit clinic, he can earn a salary with good benefit packages of up to $40,000. If the therapist decides to take on supervisory responsibilities as well as continue therapy, the salary increase can jump an additional $5,000. The marriage and family therapist who pursues his own private practice in a *for-profit* clinic, for instance, typically sees clients who are able to afford higher hourly rates to counsel with therapists with long and varied expertise.

Seasoned professionals in the private sector can usually obtain the highest dollar. It is not uncommon for a marriage and family therapist to generate from $55 to $100 per hour, and to earn in excess of $50,000 per year, seeing 20 to 30 clients per week. However, remember this: in private practice, the therapist pays his own light bills, rent, and secretarial services. The private practitioner buys his own *fringe benefits*, and does not get paid when clients don't show up for therapy sessions. There is a good deal of independence, however, in professional private practice. Some therapists, rather than spending a lot of time in the business aspects of their private practice, opt instead to work for agencies as independent contractors, where they retain much of their independence, but ease their business burdens by arranging to give a share of their income to the agency, in exchange for the agency taking care of all business matters. An increasing number of therapists are becoming independent contractors. It is often a terrific compromise.

Marriage and Family Therapy for the Future

The marriage counselor is no longer *just* the marriage counselor. Yet, as long as couples get together, get married, have children, and try to have a good family life, it is likely that the marriage and family therapist will continue to flourish in the very center of all the social service professions. It is because all things truly human—or inhuman—come from the family experience. Civilization and its cultures are little more than groups of families, regardless of how functional, that try to be happy and to realize the ideals of society. So, as long as our culture demands some level of civilized behavior, and as long as children are clearly the spearheads of the future, then whatever it is we call *a marriage* and *a family* will continue to need all the help it can get. This includes couples as well . . . more recently, same-sex couples . . . and who knows what the future brings?

▼

HENRY MALONE, ACSW, CSW, and licensed marriage and family therapist in Michigan, has been working for the last eight years as an independent contractor with a private clinic group in Livonia, MI, known as Metropolitan Transactional Analysis and Gestalt Institute, P.C. He received his B.A. at Wayne State University in Detroit with a double major in English and philosophy, and later obtained his M.S.W. at WSU. He has worked as a clinician for most of his 20-year career, has worked in clinical supervision, and as an administrator for several agencies. He has also been a part-time instructor in the graduate school of social work at Wayne State University.

CHAPTER NINETEEN

Diversity and Challenge: Social Work Careers in Employee Assistance

**Bridget Arens-Jones, ACSW,
Employee Assistance Program, Lutheran Hospital**

A career in **employee assistance** is best described as a merging of human service skills with the needs of today's workplaces, the exciting dynamics of the business world, and the continuous evolution of the healthcare industry. This professional path is for those individuals who seek diversity in their roles and clientele, as well as the constant challenge to grow as the field itself grows.

Employee Assistance Programs: An Overview

Employee Assistance Programs, or EAPs, are designed to provide assessment, counseling, and resource referral services for employees and, in most instances, their dependent family members. Just as employers offer benefits in the form of vacation, retirement plans, or healthcare coverage, so, too, is an EAP a benefit paid for by the employer and, in some instances, in conjunction with organized labor. The key intent of an EAP is to assist employees and their family members in dealing with a wide spectrum of personal or work-related problems. These problems, if gone untreated, may severely affect the individual's physical or emotional well-being, as well as their continued productivity on the job. Employers wishing to maintain a healthy, efficient workforce have recognized that offering an EAP can reduce the personal and work-related costs incurred by a troubled employee.

It has been stated, "If you've seen one EAP, you've seen one EAP," illustrating the wide variety of programs that exist. Some EAPs are located within the business or organization they serve, and are known as *internal* EAPs. These EAPs may be freestanding as a department of their own or may be affiliated with a human resource, employee health, or industrial relations department within the organization. Employee Assistance Programs known as *external* EAPs provide services under contract to businesses or organizations. The EAP vendor of external services is typically a hospital, mental health organization, or free-standing health services agency. Finally, some EAPs provide a combination of internal and external services, offering services to employees within their own facility, as well as contracting out with community businesses.

Another EAP model is that which provides telephone consultation services to employees or family members. Businesses contract with this type of EAP to provide telephone assessment, limited counseling, and resource referral. No face-to-face counselor contact occurs within this model. A modification of this model involves initial contact with a telephone EAP service, followed by referral of the employee to a local EAP provider for continued EAP services, which involves direct contact with a counselor.

Just as there are variations in the location and scope of EAPs, so, too, are there differences in the duration of services. Some models offer up to three sessions with an EAP counselor, while others offer up to five, ten, or an unlimited number of sessions. Many EAPs have contractual agreements linking them to managed care services, thus directing them to use their EAP services in lieu of accessing their mental health insurance benefits.

Finally, EAPs differ in the primary thrust of their programs. Some EAPs maintain a strong focus on assessment and treatment of chemical abuse problems. Others are firmly rooted in the "broadbrush" approach, which considers the impact of all personal or work-related problems the client may struggle with. Still others lean toward health and wellness programming as an adjunct to their assessment and counseling services.

Employee Assistance Programs are found in over 90 percent of Fortune 500 companies, and in such diverse industries as airlines, educational systems, railroads, manufacturing plants, local municipalities, hospitals, clinics, and private business. In addition to the United States, such countries as Canada, Bermuda, England, Ireland, South Africa, Australia, and Guatemala are locations of thriving EAPs.

EAP Staff Positions/Job Descriptions

The most common staff positions within an EAP are those of **program director,** or **coordinator,** and the **EAP counselors.** Some EAPs have supervising staff for areas of specialization, such as chemical dependency services, while others have staff who are designated as consultants to business and industry.

Job descriptions for EAP counselors vary according to the scope of the particular EAP model the program ascribes to. If the program is strictly a telephone consultation service, strong verbal communication and assessment skills are essential. Once the presenting psychosocial problems are assessed, the telephone counselor must have the ability to identify and link clients with appropriate community resources they may be needing. The majority of EAPs offer direct face-to-face counselor contact. These counselors must be skilled in complete psychosocial problem assessment, short-term counseling and/or brief therapy, crisis intervention, and resource referral. Many programs require counselors to be familiar with chemical dependency screening tools and the DSM-III-R, the psychiatric diagnostic manual currently recognized by the psychiatric and medical communities. Strong verbal and written communication skills are required, as are strong interpersonal skills in general. Some programs require experience in group facilitation, while most require strong public speaking and group training skills. Knowledge of case documentation and client record keeping standards are requirements of most EAPs. Finally, a keen adherence to strict confidentiality standards is an expectation for any EAP counselor.

As with any human service position, much of the program knowledge and specific skills are learned on the job and developed with the guidance of the EAP director. Such supervision typically occurs on a weekly basis for the entry-level EAP staff member.

Educational Preparation

At present, employee assistance professionals have no standardized educational preparation for their careers. Current EAP practitioners range from individuals who have advanced degrees in a variety of disciplines to those who have little formal education, but who have extensive personal histories and life experience which qualify them for their work. The latter typically have expertise in the fields of chemical dependency counseling or labor/management issues and have risen through the EAP ranks.

Master's degrees are generally required for most private sector EAPs as well as federal programs. Commonly held advanced degrees include social work, counseling, psychology, business, and health education. A bachelor's degree in a human service field may qualify someone for a position in EAP. Typical undergraduate degrees include social work, psychology, health education, and occupational health. There are currently two undergraduate programs in employee assistance in the United States, at Western Michigan University and at Franklin University in Columbus, OH. An undergraduate degree with strong mental health experience, certification in alcohol/drug assessment, or experience in an EAP may offset the requirement of an advanced degree. Some programs actually require AODA (alcohol and other drug assessment) certification, and it is highly valued by most EAPs.

Completion of the CEAP (Certified Employee Assistance Professional) exam is recommended for those who wish to solidify their career path in employee assistance. This is not an entry-level credential. A candidate for certification must have three years of experience in an EAP or 3,000 hours in the area of EAP programming.

Salary/Benefit Considerations

Many different variables enter into the amount of annual salary paid to EAP counselors. These include education, experience in EAP, other previous work experience, locale, and the type of organization offering the EAP program. As with many entry-level positions in human services, the salary range for an EAP counselor may begin as low as $15,000 or as high as $30,000 per year, depending on the variables of education and experience. In addition to annual salary considerations, other benefits may include opportunities for continued education, attendance at state or

ADVICE FROM THE PRO'S

Career Opportunities Abound!

Employee Assistance Programs are found in over 90 percent of Fortune 500 companies, and in such diverse industries as airlines, educational systems, railroads, manufacturing plants, local municipalities, hospitals, clinics, and private business. In addition to the United States, such countries as Canada, Bermuda, England, Ireland, South Africa, Australia, and Guatemala are locations of thriving EAPs.

national EAP conferences, opportunities for innovative program development, and flexibility in one's role within the program.

Challenges for the Employee Assistance Professional

One word which best sums up the work of the EAP professional is diversity. Just as the job description calls for a wide range of skills and abilities, so too does a typical day include variety and a degree of unknowns. Whether the EAP counselor provides services strictly by telephone or through direct client contact, they are assured of a mixture of presenting problems by their clients. As the personal and economic stressors of living in the '90s continue to increase, EAP counselors are seeing the intensity of client distress increasing and the physical/psychological needs being more severe. Employee assistance professionals are being called on to assess clients who may be suicidal, clients who may be of physical threat to others, and clients who may be decompensating psychologically as they attempt to maintain themselves within their jobs and families. Employee assistance counselors face the challenge of accurately assessing the client's needs, weighing their safety as well as the safety of others, and channeling the client to the appropriate help. Client problems may range from marital problems, financial concerns, chemical misuse, or sexual identity issues all in the course of a morning's work. From factory workers and assembly line technicians, to white collar professionals and CEOs, the EAP counselor must be flexible to assess, counsel, and refer a wide variety of employees as needed.

Diversity also comes in the form of flexible work schedules, depending upon the needs of the businesses served. Most EAPs offer evening hours to clients, thus requiring EAP staff to alter their work hours accordingly. Some EAPs require staff to be "on call" during evenings, weekends, or holidays, often with limited compensation for that "on call" coverage. Several EAPs have minimum or maximum requirements for numbers of client contact hours in a given day. One standard held by EASNA, a professional organization for EAPs, states that counselors should have no more than 30 client contact hours in a work week, or six hours per day. The remaining hours of the work week are then free for case documentation, program development, consultation visits to businesses, or training.

Future Career Growth

With the field of employee assistance evolving to address changes on the business and healthcare fronts, the greatest challenge to the EAP professional is staying abreast of that change. Continued education and the pursuit of specialized certifications (such as AODA certification, CEAP achievement, or Critical Incident Stress Debriefing training) serve to heighten one's opportunities within the profession. Future career growth for the EAP counselor may be through promotion within their own program or organization, progression into a larger EAP organization, transfer to or advancement within health-related organizations, advancement within one of the businesses they may provide services for, or making the transition to an alternate type of social work practice.

Diversity and challenge. For the individual wishing to be on the cutting-edge of social work practice, the field of employee assistance offers that and more.

ADVICE FROM THE PRO'S

▼

BRIDGET ARENS-JONES, ACSW, is a counselor with the Employee Assistance Program at Lutheran Hospital, La Crosse, Wisconsin. She received her B.S. in criminal justice from the University of Wisconsin-Platteville in 1978. In 1980, she received her master's degree in social work from the University of Wisconsin-Madison.

In addition to her work in the field of employee assistance, Ms. Arens-Jones has held a variety of social work positions, including that of protective services worker for a county human service agency, medical social worker for a regional medical center, social worker for a multi-disciplinary prevention and treatment program for adolescents, and as an instructor in the School of Social Work at the University of Wisconsin-La Crosse. She is currently a member of Lutheran Hospital's Critical Incident Stress Debriefing Team. She will be pursuing her Certification for Employee Assistance Professional (CEAP) in November, 1993.

CHAPTER TWENTY

Medical Social Work in a Physical Therapy Clinic: A Unique Opportunity

Jennie Petrovich, M.S.W.,
Greater Lansing Rehabilitation Agency

Social work is an exciting profession, in part because of the wide range of work settings from which to choose. Contrary to popular belief, all social workers are not connected to the welfare system. There are job opportunities in education, industry, politics, healthcare, and numerous other settings in the public and private sector. Selecting a specific career path within the field was a difficult decision for me, but I knew that I wanted to be able to utilize as many of my skills as possible. My current position as a medical social worker in a private physical therapy clinic allows me to do just that. I am pleased to have discovered this unique and challenging career.

The Social Work/Physical Therapy Connection

In order for a physical therapy clinic to be registered as a rehabilitation facility, the U.S. Department of Health and Human Services requires that one of the following be on staff: a psychologist, a vocational specialist, or a professional social worker. This adjunct service must be available to patients free of charge while they are involved in therapy. The extent to which these services are provided varies greatly among agencies. Some meet the requirement by hiring the social worker on a contractual or part-time basis to simply refer patients to community resources if problems are identified. Other clinics hire full-time social workers who are available to assess patients' needs and actually provide the appropriate interventions.

A social worker in this setting, in very simple terms, is there to assist patients and physical therapists (P.T.'s) in any way possible to make the rehabilitation process go smoothly and efficiently. People generally enter a physical therapy clinic because they are faced with an injury or disability that is impacting their daily functioning to some degree. The problem could stem from any number of sources, including auto accidents, work injuries, diseases, or athletic injuries, to name a few. The person may be unable to work, participate in usual recreational activities, maintain their homes, enjoy a sex life, or even dress themselves.

Being unable to perform everyday activities that most of us take for granted can lead to a variety of emotional reactions, including anger, depression, frustration, and interpersonal difficulties. Financial concerns also tend to be prominent, as the person may be faced with temporary or permanent unemployment, legal battles, healthcare costs, and an unsure future. If left unattended, the combination of these factors can be overwhelming and interfere with their ability to put the necessary effort into physical therapy, thus prolonging an already difficult situation. Social workers are uniquely qualified to provide the range of intervention necessary to help patients make the most of the rehabilitation process and move ahead with their lives.

The Delivery of Services

Not all patients are in *need* of—or *want*—social work services. They are able to request the services at any point during treatment, but people are often hesitant to ask for help, and/or believe that *nothing* can help (which is why simply referring them to community resources can be ineffective). To reach more patients, an intake form is generally used, which screens for the presence of the difficulties I have mentioned. If these factors are noted, either on the form, or by the attending staff, the social worker meets with the patient to further assess the situation, explain the scope of services, and intervene as appropriate.

A typical day at the clinic begins with examining new intake forms to identify patients in need of services. The clinic treatment schedule must then be reviewed so that a plan can be made as to who will be seen on that day. Physical therapy patients tend to be scheduled at very short notice, which makes it difficult to plan one's day ahead of time. New patients must be fit in as soon as possible among those already receiving services.

The type of services provided, as well as the length and frequency of sessions, can vary greatly among patients. Common services provided include community resource allocation, advocacy, serving as a liaison between various professionals, educating the patient about topics such as stress management and the psychosocial aspects of a particular physical condition, crisis intervention, and various forms of counseling. The counseling may involve allowing isolated patients to ventilate their concerns and fears, helping them to problem-solve solutions to new life problems, teaching cognitive/behavioral techniques for managing chronic pain, and supporting their self-esteem as they are faced with the inability to carry out their usual roles.

For some people, brief psychotherapy is appropriate. Injury and illness can leave people feeling emotionally vulnerable, exacerbating any pre-existing problems. I commonly see patients with marital and/or parenting difficulties, grief reactions, substance abuse issues, as well as histories of child abuse, sexual abuse, and highly

---

Top Employee Motivators

Ranked by: Conclusions in article by Frederick Hertzbert as published in the *Harvard Business Review*.
1. On-the-job achievement
2. Recognition
3. Type of work done
4. Responsibility assigned
5. Advancement and growth opportunities
6. Salary
7. Relationships with other employees
8. Type of supervision received
9. Working conditions
10. Company policies and administration

Source: *Homecare*

dysfunctional families of origin. As the old wounds come to the surface, the person can become easily overwhelmed, increasingly tense, and less likely to benefit from physical therapy. Helping patients to organize their personal issues provides them an increased feeling of control and frees them to channel their energy into physical rehabilitation. Given that some patients are not involved in physical therapy for an extended period of time, they may be referred elsewhere for long-term psychotherapy, if appropriate.

Working with patients' families can also be helpful, as they highly impact and are impacted *by* the situation. A common example would be that of an older couple comprised of one healthy spouse and one who has had a stroke. Not only must the stroke victim struggle with the loss of functioning, but the spouse must contend with a partner who may be very different from the one they had known. They may be thrust into and frightened by a range of new responsibilities, resentful of not having the retirement they had planned, and sad or frustrated that their spouse can no longer communicate with them clearly. Family members can be helped to grieve their losses, plan for the future, and achieve a balance between caring for their loved one and attending to their own needs.

Another possible area of service is group work. The type of group is limited only by one's creativity. Groups designed to teach patients to manage chronic pain have been found to be quite successful. My agency has also sponsored programs for parents of handicapped children and people who have experienced back injuries. On occasion, our social work staff has been contracted by businesses and community groups to make presentations on stress management, time management, and coping with pain. These experiences have been very rewarding and serve as good public relations and income for the clinic.

Education

To work in this setting as a social worker, there is a minimum requirement of a B.A. in social work from a college accredited by the Council on Social Work Education, plus one year experience in a healthcare setting. Job options will be quite limited if you do not continue your education beyond this point. Employers (in all settings) are increasingly requiring candidates to hold a master's degree in social work (M.S.W.). The graduate program generally involves two years of full-time education that includes internships. Some universities offer an accelerated, 12- to 15-month program for those who have an undergraduate degree in social work.

The undergraduate training tends to be quite broad-based, and specific courses in medical social work may not be offered at this level; however, electives can generally be found in a variety of departments that would provide useful background. Courses on substance abuse, grief, and race and gender issues would be beneficial. Volunteer work may not be required, but I feel that it is invaluable and should be sought out in the first two years of college. Social work is an incredibly broad field, and this exposure can help a student to focus their academic and vocational goals. It also looks good on a resume. Senior year of study does include an internship and you may be able to request or seek out a placement in a medical setting.

Graduate study for clinical social work involves more in-depth exploration of human behavior, mental disorders, and methods of intervention. Depending on individual interests, it may involve training in psychotherapy with children, adults, families, couples, and/or groups. Electives may be chosen related to special settings, including medical social work. I also did an independent study to further my knowledge in this area. In conjunction with the classroom work, an ongoing internship provides an opportunity to utilize the skills learned. Look for a placement that provides exposure to health issues, a variety of clients and concerns, and brief therapy techniques.

Finding a Job That Suits You

Investigate various health agencies in your area (and others) to get a sense of typical hiring requirements; they often vary among cities and rural areas, and in different parts of the country. Finding entry-level positions in medical social work can be quite difficult. Nursing homes, the public health department, and home health agencies are good places to start looking. Hospitals may be a possibility, but they generally look for more experience. Any job in which you work with persons with handicaps would be useful, such as vocational rehabilitation or community mental health centers. You might also get involved with organizations such as the Arthritis Foundation and the Multiple Sclerosis Society to expand your experience and knowledge base. In addition, participating in the local chapter of the National Association of Social Workers (NASW) can provide useful contacts.

Obtaining a job in a physical therapy clinic may require you to promote yourself and your profession quite heavily. I am fortunate to work in a clinic whose administration recognizes that the social worker is an integral part of the rehabilitation process, and not simply a licensure requirement. All organizations are not this enlightened. Be aware of the fact that basic social work services in a physical therapy/rehabilitation facility do not generate revenue—an important consideration in private clinics. You may need to help other professionals to understand your role and how you can be an asset to the company. Don't expect this to happen overnight, but if you are tactful, enthusiastic, and consider the economics of the situation, you may be able to win them over.

Salaries within the profession and *this* specialty can vary greatly depending on the agency and the location. The NASW has recommended minimum salaries of $20,000 per year for a person with a B.S.W. and $25,000 for one with an M.S.W. Recently, I have seen a range of M.S.W. starting salaries between $23,000 and $27,000, with medical social work jobs tending to be at the higher end of the scale.

The career ladder for this specialty can be somewhat limited; however, there are numerous opportunities for program development and professional growth. The paperwork is minimal, compared to many social work jobs, and the extent to which you are busy with patients tends to run hot and cold. Days with slow patient loads provide time to enrich the level of services by developing educational programs, supportive groups, and other methods of assisting patients as well as the company.

The position can be quite isolating because you do not work with other social workers. Our agency does have another social worker who also provides my clinical supervision, but smaller clinics may only have one social worker on staff. Be aware that you may need social work supervision in order to earn more advanced certifications within the profession. In some cases, it is possible to hire this supervision independently. Contact the local NASW for guidance in this regard.

A social worker in this setting must be able to work with other professionals assertively, cooperatively, and respectfully. Good organizational skills and a willingness to be flexible are also imperative, as the schedule for the day can change quickly. Given the level of independence on the job, a person must be highly motivated, reliable, and demonstrate sound judgement.

Helping people to successfully overcome major life hurdles can be a very challenging, rewarding experience. It requires an ability to face a barrage of intense emotions, such as anger and grief. Without letting it become intertwined with one's own issues, I continually strive to keep my work life and home life separate, which allows me to approach patients with the energy and compassion needed to serve them effectively. The job remains interesting because of the ongoing variety. There are few settings that involve working with such a wide range of people in regard to age, income level, and functioning level, and allows the opportunity to truly address the needs of the *whole person*.

Looking to the Future

It is difficult to speculate the extent to which changes in the nation's healthcare system will impact the medical social work profession. Hopefully, it will be recognized that social workers can facilitate greater efficiency in the delivery of services and the prevention of additional, costly problems. I am optimistic that social workers will havean increasingly prominent role in a variety of medical settings, including physical therapy clinics. Together withother medical professionals, social workers can make a difference in improving patients' quality of life and paving the way for a healthier future.

▼

JENNIE PETROVICH earned her bachelor of arts degree at Michigan State University, where she had a dual major in social work and psychology. She later returned to M.S.U. to complete her master's degree in social work, and is now certified as a social worker in the state of Michigan. In addition to the field of healthcare, Ms. Petrovich's experience includes work with chronically mentally ill adults, injured/handicapped workers, and the families of troubled adolescents. She currently lives in Mason, MI, and is employed by Greater Lansing Rehabilitation Agency.

CHAPTER TWENTY-ONE

Why Social Work Practice in Corrections?

**Marjorie Hammock,
Chief of Social Work Services,
South Carolina Department of Corrections**

It is doubtful that young children fantasize about growing up and becoming a **social worker** in a prison setting. Veteran correctional social workers, including this author, list any number of reasons for entering the field—everything from avoiding the draft to a curiosity about working with one of society's least appealing group of clients (known as *prisoners* or *offenders*). Once on board, many feel that corrections is important work, assisting an offender (also known as an *inmate*) in developing life skills and basic competencies to function appropriately in his or her environment.

Some social workers want to be a part of progressive programming for offenders for whom the loss of freedom and use of punishment is not enough to correct faulty-thinking and destructive behaviors that result in offender recidivism, or the recurrence of criminal activities and reincarceration. Others with a social work background come to corrections because there is growth (unfortunately) in the prison industry. Job availability and promotional opportunities in both urban and rural settings all over the country and in the United States Territories attract social workers to corrections. Diversity in the nature of the work and the clients served is appealing to job seekers. In addition, there is the opportunity to work in a setting which is overwhelmingly male for those who have selected what is stereotyped as a *female profession*.

Current students and recent social work graduates have shown increased interest in corrections as a career area because of involvement in internships and volunteer experiences. Some have started out as correctional officers, become interested in social work, returned to school, and joined the correctional social worker ranks. Some veteran social workers have come from more traditional fields of social work practice, such as work with families and children, mental health, and health-related social work. They are seeking work that is challenging, and offers the opportunity to develop and use a broad range of practice skills.

Social Work in Corrections

Social workers can be found in every aspect of criminal justice and corrections and have a long history of participation in corrections. Criminal justice professionals who are trained in social work are employed in a variety of settings, including: courts, local jails, juvenile and adult probation, and juvenile and adult corrections. Some are administrators of state systems, some are wardens, and some are judges or other officers of the court. Many are the principal planners and providers of mental health, substance abuse, family relations, case management, and social work services for the nearly 800,000 offenders who are incarcerated in prisons and jails throughout the nation.

Career Preparation

Preparation for social work practice in any setting requires the following: a substantial liberal arts foundation; knowledge and understanding of the social and human problems historically and in today's society; the biological, social/cultural, and psychological components of human development; and an understanding of the forces and influences that have shaped social welfare policies. Social work training prepares practitioners to assess client problems, develop problem-solving programs, identify and negotiate complicated service delivery systems, and implement services that meet the needs, achieve the goals, and facilitate change on behalf of clients.

Preparation also includes the ability to determine the effectiveness of existing programs and the identification of the need for new programs through evaluation and research. Students may choose to concentrate their studies on direct practice with individuals, families, and groups; or they may focus on administrative, management, and policy development. Courses in criminal justice issues and practice may be available as electives.

Social workers who are successful practitioners demonstrate effective writing, speaking, and communication skills. They exhibit an interest in and the ability to work with people and display a strong commitment to advocacy for positive change in social conditions.

Social work education at both the bachelor's (B.S.W.) and the master's level (M.S.W.) provides entry-level and advanced practice preparation for social work in adult correctional settings. In addition to the professional and personal requirements, a correctional setting compels a social work practitioner to be understanding of and sensitive to the public safety charge of all correctional staff. These systems are mandated by law to protect the public by maintaining offenders behind "bars" and away from the community for a designated period of time. Knowledge of social and criminal justice issues and a sound grounding in ethical concerns are also essential for effective work in these settings.

The Nature of the Correctional Environment

Most social work correctional staff work in a correctional facility. The role and function of the social work staff varies according to the type of facility and the kind of correctional offender client being served. Some facilities or institutions (we used to call them prisons or penitentiaries) enforce the strictest control of inmates with the use of bars, gates, fences, steel wire, restraints, restricted offender movement, and electronic surveillance. At the other extreme is a one- or two-story building with well-kept grounds; only the sign identifying the Department of Corrections setting identifies an open, less-restrictive correctional facility that can easily pass on the surface for a campus, a nursing home, or a drug treatment facility. In fact, the building might be serving offenders who are studying for basic literacy or an advanced college degree. The population may include the frail or elderly and/or house an intensive residential addiction treatment unit or a sex offender program. Most state systems also have facilities that are exclusive for the smaller population of women offenders. Under one roof, women may find education, vocational training, anti-victimization, and life skills development programs.

Social workers, like all other staff, are restricted in what they can do in a prison. The range of personal movement, and the nature of the relationship with an offender is governed by the potential danger of the clients to harm themselves or others. There is an atmosphere of constant surveillance and the prison environment does require specific behaviors which are cautious and mindful of the setting. Specialized training in security issues is available for all staff.

ADVICE FROM THE PRO'S

The Offender Client

The most-restricted facility houses offenders who are the most dangerous to others. Persons who can accurately be described as violent are those who have been convicted of crimes such as homicide, assault, armed robbery, sexual assault, and arson. Serious crimes might also include drug trafficking and driving under the influence. Fraudulent check writers, habitual gamblers, embezzlers, and those charged with small amounts of drug possession might be located in the least-restricted facilities. The security presence maintained by correctional officers is apparent everywhere.

The range of clients or offenders needing social work services in corrections is diverse. There may be offenders with substance abuse problems and other addictions; there are sexual offenders, mentally ill, mentally retarded, those who display socially inappropriate behaviors, or those who are lacking in appropriate social skills. Offender clients are disproportionately poor and persons of color. Young men not yet out of their teens are coming to prisons in increasing numbers. Geriatric and handicapped offenders are also in the correctional population. Female offenders charged with an increasing range of crimes are another fast-growing population. This diverse group of offenders provides the corrections social worker with the opportunity to work with a disparate population using a range of interventions—individual counseling, case management, group treatment, resource development, and referral. Social workers are called upon to provide intake and assessment, develop treatment plans, offer pre-release or

Where the Jobs Are

Social workers can be found in every aspect of criminal justice and corrections and have a long history of participation in corrections. Criminal justice professionals who are trained in social work are employed in a variety of settings, including: courts, local jails, juvenile and adult probation, and juvenile and adult corrections. Some are administrators of state systems, some are wardens, and some are judges or other officers of the court. Many are the principal planners and providers of mental health, substance abuse, family relations, case management, and social work services for the nearly 800,000 offenders who are incarcerated in prisons and jails throughout the nation.

discharge planning, family reunification, parenting skills, and multi-disciplinary activities.

Social Work Behind the Walls

Some systems require a master's degree to provide treatment/mental health services, or to work with specialized populations such as substance abusers or sex offenders. Entry-level bachelor practitioners more often will support the security role by assisting in processing offenders through the system, providing some counseling services, facilitating family contacts, and preparing the client to return to the community. Those social workers involved in providing therapeutic and counseling services are responsible for thorough assessment, treatment planning, and substantive individual and group work.

After the hiring process is completed, all new social work staff reports to a training academy for a week-long general orientation. *Specific* orientation to social work is conducted by the central office and institutional staff. Social workers may be located in a program services section or in the offenders' living area. Those centrally placed in a program area serve the entire facility with caseloads established and assigned for individual work with clients as well as group work in social skills, psychotherapy, and counseling.

The days of a social worker in corrections are demanding and full of activity. The routine includes seeing offender clients individually and in groups, meeting with other staff about case management, and making referrals for services available outside the facility. Managing large numbers of offenders in settings that are crowded and intense fosters crises and conflicts. Therefore, cooperation, coordination, consistency, and team work are essential, and complete understanding of the roles of all the disciplines is required. Staff teams work together in classifying and placing inmates. Behavior management or interdisciplinary teams meet to discuss problem offender clients who may require administrative segregation or transfer to other settings. There are extensive contacts with client offenders experiencing crises of a personal or institutional nature. Consultation and team meetings with other staff are ongoing tasks as are the contacts with external programs and community services. Some evening work is required, and most mental health programs in institutions have a person on-call for emergencies procedure.

What About the Money?

Salaries in state correctional systems are on par with entry-level positions in other state agencies, less than private, fee-service correctional programs, and more than private family and children services. Starting salaries are in the $20,000 range for social workers with a B.S.W. and $25,000 for those with an M.S.W. in the Southeastern part of the country. Salaries are greater in the Northeast, Far West, and major metropolitan areas. Most state systems that have a social work or mental health classification series have fixed salaries at each grade level and within grades. They are fairly rigid and are based primarily on the amount of education and years of experience.

In these times of budget shortfalls, there has been very little chance for merit, cost of living, or annual increases. As an example, the most that could be earned in a social work series would be about $50,000 in South Carolina. Opportunities for grade promotion are tied to changes in role and function and an increase in responsibility. Leaving the social work series and joining the security ranks offers greater variety in advancement and a higher salary maximum than the social work promotion ladder. Some social work staff welcome this opportunity; others prefer to stay in the treatment or counseling mode even with the obvious limitations.

Social work titles that reflect the promotional ladder include social worker, social work senior, institutional social work/mental health coordinator, and state mental health coordinator. Those titles reflect grades or levels such as line staff direct service, clinical supervision responsibilities, institutional management and coordination activities, and statewide director positions. Social workers can also become unit managers, deputy wardens, wardens, and state directors.

Life After Prison for the Social Worker

Basic social work skills are transferable. Social workers who leave adult corrections find positions in colleges and universities; police departments; local, state, and federal court settings; probation and parole; and forensic mental health settings, as well as private early intervention, family reunification, and substance abuse programs. Some former correctional social workers work for criminal justice consultant firms, which write grants for correctional programs and provide consultation in evaluation, research, policy, and program design. Former correctional social workers provide services to ex-offenders or families of offenders. Some become officials in criminal justice associations or managers of major federal departments. Some find their way to other public and private arenas of practice.

Challenges and Opportunities

In summary, social work in corrections presents many challenges. Discrepancies exist between the social work mission and the prevailing view of society that sees corrections as punishment only. In numbers and in status, corrections social workers are still viewed as only marginally important, which requires a constant struggle on our part about the definition of the social work role based on our knowledge, training, professional, and ethical standards. Salaries are not always commensurate with performance, and rewards for outstanding service often exclude the social work rank. Bureaucratic control over service delivery and management of inmates is an ongoing tug-of-war. Despite these problems, our numbers and influence continue to grow. Social work figures significantly in the management of offenders and in the future of corrections.

Social workers bring to the correctional setting a holistic perspective, specialized knowledge, and training in human behavior and ecosystems. They are competent not only in advocating on behalf of their offender client but at balancing the needs of the clients with that of the social environment. Fostering the self-esteem and dignity of clients and protecting the safety of the community are compatible tasks that we can share with our colleagues in this critical arena. Social work will continue to be a part of the corrections process.

▼

MARJORIE BRITTAIN HAMMOCK is a social work practitioner with more than 33 years of experience in direct service, program development, administration, and staff supervision and training. Areas of interest and specialty include advocacy and clinical work with families and children, college students, women, people of color, and correctional clients.

Currently serving as the chief of social work services at the South Carolina Department of Corrections, she is responsible for social work programming and staff development for some 90 social workers in 31 institutions throughout the state. Ms. Hammock is a past-president of the South Carolina chapter of the National Association of Social Workers (NASW), was named 1990 Social Worker of the Year by the South Carolina chapter, and is the recently elected Region Six representative to the NASW National Board.

A former executive director of the state chapter, she holds membership in the Academy of Certified Social Workers, is a diplomat of the American Board of Examiners in Clinical Social Work, and is licensed in South Carolina at the independent level.

She has served on the accession Committees of the Columbia Museum of Art, and the South Carolina State Museum, is the former board chairperson of the Mann Simon Cottage of African American Culture and History, former board member of the Rape Crisis Network, and is a member of the American Correctional Association and the National Association of Blacks in Criminal Justice. She is a 1992 member of the South Carolina Department of Health and Environmental Control, Office of Minority Health, Advisory Task-Force, 1992, and the Mental Health Association, State Plan Children's Association.

A 1984 participant in Leadership South Carolina, she received the 1992 Ernest E. Just Award, University of South Carolina for Research at the Doctoral Level. Ms. Hammock received a BA and MSW from Howard University, Washington, DC, and is currently a student in the Ph.D. program at the University of South Carolina. She is the mother of two daughters.

CHAPTER TWENTY-TWO

Career Opportunities in Aging/Gerontology: Expanding Opportunities

Dr. Wilma L. Greenfield-Moore,
Chairperson, Department of Social Work,
Florida Atlantic University

America is no longer a country of youth. In 1983, the number of Americans over 65 surpassed the number of teenagers. Projections estimate that by the year 2020, those over 65 will outnumber teens two to one (Dychtwald). This massive demographic shift has already begun to impact the personal, professional, social, and political lives of all Americans. The impact of this age boom on the social work and psychological service professions has already been felt, creating an area of practices that is rapidly expanding and will continue to do so for the foreseeable future. There are ample entry-level opportunities for those with a bachelor's degree in social work (BSW) and an internship or work experience in the field of gerontology; these opportunities are also available with a B.A. degree in psychology or human services with a specialization or experience in the field.

One of the most pervasive myths about the aging population is that most people over 65 years of age are in poor health. In reality, 65 was an arbitrary age for retirement that was selected during the framing of the first Social Security Act in Germany in 1889. In fact, gerontologists currently define old age as 80+ years. The majority of folks in the 65 to 79 age category live active and independent lifestyles and are interested in social, health, and leisure activities. In addition, this group expresses growing concern over the limitations a serious illness could cause, over the need for assistance with the tasks of daily living, and their increasing unsettled feelings over the death of close friends and loved ones. It is in these areas of health and well-being that many jobs are beginning to emerge and will continue to be created for social work and human service workers.

Career Opportunities Are Numerous

Geriatric Care Management—It is estimated that more than 2,000 care management agencies offering comprehensive care management services exist across the country, a number that is growing rapidly. Many are private operations that belong to larger referral networks such as Aging Network Services out of Bethesda, MD; some are affiliated with nonprofit social service organizations and hospitals; and still others are under local government auspices. In most cases, the care managers are social workers, but some are nurses and graduates of mental health and human service programs. The private organizations are generally headed by people with a master's of social work degree, M.S.W.'s, with the assistance of B.S.W.'s. The public and nonprofit operations frequently hire B.S.W.'s and graduates from related disciplines to do the care management.

A typical geriatric care case referral comes from a working daughter who lives a long distance from her aging parents and is unable to just pick up and go to take care of them. With the right services from a geriatric care manager, the parents can stay in their own home for an indefinite period of time. The care manager will do whatever is necessary for the parents, including acting as an advocate, providing counseling, arranging and monitoring home health care, assisting with daily living chores, and serving as a liaison between the doctor and family members. Unique tasks often arise, including moving the client, arranging for long term care, closing bank accounts, accompanying the client to the doctor, etc.

Salaries in these entry-level positions range from part-time hourly wages at $10 to $15 an hour, to salaried positions in the $18,000 to 20,000 range for full-time bachelor's-level graduates. Those with M.S.W.'s and experience managing such agencies can command considerably more on both a salary and hourly basis. For a new M.S.W., salaries start at $25,000. On an hourly basis, experienced geriatric care managers who are licensed as clinical social workers make up to $100 an hour for case management services and counseling. It should be noted that many of these jobs require evening and weekend work and access to an automobile. Mileage is frequently reimbursed. For those who aspire to move beyond an entry-level position, it is advisable to seek an M.S.W. degree. If one already has a B.S.W., this can be done in one year in an advanced standing program. Licensure requires an M.S.W. degree and two years of clinical experience depending upon state law.

Long-Term Care—Opportunities abound for B.S.W. graduates in nursing homes and life care communities. All nursing homes over a certain size have a social service department. Many states require that these departments be staffed by personnel with at least a bachelor's degree in social work. When this is not possible, the homes are required to periodically consult with an M.S.W. The majority of these jobs, therefore, *do* go to B.S.W.'s. Responsibilities include counseling residents and their families, doing admissions and discharge planning, and arranging for all manner of services. In many cases, it is also up to the social work department to keep beds filled and do marketing for the facility. Documentation is a particularly important and time-consuming part of the job of the social worker in long-term care, which means that good writing skills that articulate problem solving and goal oriented results are crucial. Records are periodically reviewed by state licensing agencies, so their importance is obvious. Jobs of this type start at approximately $18,000, although salaries are generally higher for those with experience.

Nursing homes are increasingly becoming a part of life care communities that provide more than one level of care. In these communities, there are often three levels of care—independent living, assisted living, and skilled nursing care. Although not required by law, social work departments are often established to counsel those who live independently or in assisted living and to help them with problem solving the activities of daily living. Frequently, counseling is centered around the issues of loss and change. In addition, social workers often conduct group and social activities for residents. Examples of such groups may include a "reminisce group," or a theme group on "how a current news event may impact me." The goal of these activities is to always have a positive impact on the mental health of residents. Jobs of this type also start at around $18,000, and experience is often more important than the particular degree a person holds. A degree in psychology or human services may be acceptable.

Senior Centers—Senior centers usually have programs for both the physically able and impaired senior citizens. Helping professionals are frequently hired to work in a recreational capacity or in case management. Depending on the size of a center, a job of this type will often combine counseling, group work, and social activities. Many people enter this field via the internship route. Starting salaries average $18,000.

> **ADVICE FROM THE PRO'S**
>
> **Top Reasons for Relocating Employees**
>
> Ranked by: Conclusions drawn by Runzheimer International, by percent.
> 1. Career-pathing, with 68%
> 2. Reorganization or restructuring, 62%
> 3. Open new territories, 43%
> 4. Training, 29%
> 5. Buyout/merger, 12%
> 6. Others, total 17%
>
> Source: *Business Facilities*

The Future In Gerontology

There is little doubt to those of us in the field that opportunities for employment can only expand in the coming years. As the baby boomers become age boomers at the turn of the century, we can expect a proliferation of jobs to meet the needs of an aging America. If you are challenged by the idea of working with a population whose wisdom, experience, and gratitude is unmatched by any population that the helping professions serve, then get ready for a very satisfying career. The possibilities for employment in this area are only limited by your imagination!

Bibliography and Recommended Reading

Dychtwald, Ken (1989). *Age Wave*. Jeremy P. Tarcher, Inc., Los Angeles.

DR. WILMA GREENFIELD-MOORE is chair of the Department of Social Work at Florida Atlantic University. She received her MSW and doctorate from the University of California, Berkeley. As a social work educator, she firmly believes faculty must stay actively involved in practice. To this end, she has a small part-time practice in geriatric care management, counseling, and consultation. She is affiliated with Aging Network Services in Bethesda, MD. She has a variety of publications to her credit in the social work field.

CHAPTER TWENTY-THREE

Social Work Researchers: Studying Ways to Better Help People

**Cynthia A. Loveland Cook, Ph.D., ACSW,
Senior Research Health Scientist,
Richard L. Roudebush VA Medical Center**

Social work researchers are scientists who study ways to provide better assistance to clients, help agencies provide services more effectively, and facilitate efforts to promote social change in this country. Some social work researchers study the problems experienced by individuals and families, such as marital problems, alcoholism, and the psychological trauma of child sexual abuse. Other researchers study how well social service agencies operate to help clients with their problems. Determining the effectiveness of different treatment approaches, such as behavioral therapy, self-help groups, and case management, is another area of scientific inquiry. Social work researchers also study important areas of concern to the larger society, including gang violence, healthcare reform, AIDS, and homelessness.

Research is important because it helps the social work profession develop a scientific basis for practice, providing information to better plan and implement treatment at an individual, organizational, and societal level. Social work research often focuses on ways to solve problems. It is an important foundation upon which the profession is built. In addition, this kind of research is helpful to members of other professions, including psychologists, psychiatrists, and nurses.

What Is Social Work Research?

Social work research is a creative process that involves a variety of quantitative and qualitative techniques. It relies heavily on the systematic collection of data to arrive at scientific conclusions. These data are collected using methods of inquiry such as surveys, natural field studies, laboratory experiments, case study designs, and other approaches. Statistics and mathematical models are often used to analyze data and draw conclusions.

A typical day in the life of a full-time social work researcher is seldom boring and often includes a variety of activities. For example, you might find yourself preparing slides for a research presentation you will be giving at a major conference in another city. Because social work researchers need to inform others on their research findings, they often need to travel to interesting places to present their findings at conferences and workshops. In a typical day, you might also meet with your project staff to discuss and organize the next step in conducting one of your research projects. The focus of these meetings often includes overcoming obstacles in collecting data, developing a new questionnaire, and planning the approach to data analysis. Some of your day might also be spent analyzing data for an article to be submitted for publication.

Other professionals often call upon social work researchers for consultation. In a hospital setting, for example, hospital administrators may consult with you to determine whether or not research is needed to provide information to help make an important policy decision.

Preparation for the Field of Social Work Research

Nearly all social work researchers have a doctoral degree in social work or a related field. First, you should go to a four-year college for a bachelor's degree in either social work or a similar field, such as sociology, psychology, human growth and development, political science, economics, or education. In high school, involvement in a college preparatory program is important. You also might take courses in science to learn about the scientific method of inquiry, and computer science to learn about the role of computers in research. After a bachelor's degree, you will then need to get a master's degree, usually in social work. The master's program in social work involves two years of training, with nearly half of the time being spent in the field. Although most social work researchers get their master's degree before entering a doctoral program, some are able to complete this degree while they are doctoral students.

It is important to choose a doctoral program in social work that will provide you with extensive training in research. Most schools require that you complete doctoral course work that trains you in the foundations of social work research, research methods, and statistics. You will get actual experience conducting research by completing a doctoral dissertation. Your dissertation is your original research on a topic that you are interested in studying. Selected faculty help guide you through this process. Some doctoral students choose topics for their dissertation that they intend to pursue later as social work researchers. To gain even more experience in research, many doctoral students choose to work as research assistants on projects with experienced researchers. For example, as a research assistant, you could learn how to design a questionnaire, train interviewers, collect data, and enter data on the computer. It usually takes three to five years to complete a doctoral program, depending on the program and your ability and commitment to finish in a timely manner.

Entering the Field of Social Work Research

The employment opportunities for social work researchers are excellent. Most social work researchers begin in jobs that involve teaching in a college or university. In addition to their teaching, they conduct research or direct the research efforts of other people. Some social work researchers may find themselves employed in large agencies and organizations, particularly the federal government. In these cases, they predominantly conduct research, but also may be responsible for consulting with key individuals in the organization of research-related issues.

For college or university positions, a social work researcher can advance from the rank of assistant professor to full professor. In 1991, the Council on Social Work Education reported that the median salary for an assistant professor was $34,290 for a nine-month appointment. For a full professor, the median salary was nearly $55,000 for the same type of appointment. Advancing through the academic ranks from assistant to full professor is usually based on demonstrated excellence in research, teaching, and community service, as well as involvement in the academic community itself. Depending on the school, research excellence is often determined by the ability to get funding for research by writing grant proposals, the publication of research articles in major journals, the demonstrated ability to successfully run a research project, and the ability to critically review the research of other investigators for scientific rigor.

There is usually competition for the full-time research positions available in large organizations. Often, these positions are part of the federal government, such as the Department of Veterans Affairs and Agency for Health Care Policy Research, or are part of private industry, such as Ford Motor Company and private research organizations. The expected salary for an entry-level position can be as high as $40,000, with substantial increases over time. Most often, these positions require a full-time involvement in research activities, including collecting data that enhances the operation of the host organization. The social work researcher may also be involved in helping clinical and administrative social workers use existing research to better plan, implement, and administer their programs. At the same time, one may consult or serve as an advisor on selected research issues.

ADVICE FROM THE PRO'S

Gaining Valuable Hands-On Experience

It is often helpful to become involved in research *before* making the final decision to become a social work researcher. One way to get experience is to work as a research assistant while you are pursuing your bachelor's or master's degree. Some master's programs in social work also have a specialization or major in research that includes courses and an opportunity to do a master's thesis. In both cases, you would get some *hands on* experience conducting research before entering a doctoral program.

Characteristics of a Good Social Work Researcher

Many types of research require strong analytic and quantitative skills, so an aptitude for math is helpful. Interest in working with computers is essential. Because social work researchers work closely with other people to conduct studies and get research funding, it is important to have good interpersonal skills. Prospective researchers should have an inquiring mind and enjoy learning about issues related to the profession of social work. The ability to pay attention to details and maintain a sense of organization is particularly helpful in conducting research. Good writing and public speaking skills will take you far in disseminating your research findings and developing research grants.

Deciding upon a Career in Social Work Research

It is often helpful to become involved in research *before* making the final decision to become a social work researcher. One way to get experience is to work as a research assistant while you are pursuing your bachelor's or master's degree. Some master's programs in social work also have a specialization or major in research that includes courses and an opportunity to do a master's thesis. In both cases, you would get some *hands on* experience conducting research before entering a doctoral program. Another suggestion is to talk directly to people in the field. Don't be hesitant or shy. Contact the school of social work at a nearby college or university and ask to speak with faculty who are actively engaged in research.

The Future of Social Work Research

More and more social work researchers are needed in the profession as we are further developing our scientific basis of practice. Employment opportunities are excellent, particularly for social work researchers who pursue jobs in academic settings. Advertisements for available faculty positions in schools of social work throughout the country are common, and active recruitment efforts are a part of each school's mission. More and more people are being trained to enter the field; evident in the growing number of students who are pursuing doctoral education in social work. In 1991, over 2000 students were enrolled in these programs.

In sum, social work researchers study issues that are important to the profession and to society in general. In the profession's effort to alleviate and prevent social problems, social work researchers are studying poverty, physical illness, substance abuse, unemployment, family problems, violence, mental illness, antisocial behavior, physical handicaps, and other important issues. As these problems continue to escalate, this branch of our profession will continue its efforts to systematically determine what can be done to alleviate them.

▼

DR. CYNTHIA A. LOVELAND COOK received a B.S. in nursing at the University of Arizona, Tucson, AZ. She later received a master's degree in social work at the University of Washington, Seattle, WA. After doing a master's thesis and conducting several small studies as a clinical social worker at the Seattle VA Medical Center, she entered the doctoral program in social work and social psychology at the University of

Michigan, Ann Arbor. She is currently a senior research health scientist at the Richard L. Roudebush VA Medical Center in Indianapolis, IN, where she conducts research on social work issues, including discharge planning, quality assurance, treatment outcomes, and comorbid mental health problems in the medically ill. She also holds an adjunct faculty position in the George Warren Brown School of Social Work at Washington University, St. Louis, MO.

CHAPTER TWENTY-FOUR

Improving Our Society through Policy and Planning

**Sunny Harris Rome, M.S.W., J.D.,
Lobbyist, National Association of Social Workers**

One of the most fundamental concepts of social work practice is that all entities—individuals, families, organizations, communities, even society—are capable of change. Social workers in the fields of policy and planning devote themselves to social change. They develop and promote laws and programs aimed at solving social problems, such as child abuse, homelessness, substance abuse, poverty, mental illness, domestic violence, unemployment, illiteracy, and discrimination.

Policy practitioners perform a variety of functions including: policy analysis (examining existing or proposed solutions to determine what their intended and unintended consequences might be); social planning/policy development (identifying what people need and developing policies or programs to provide it); and advocacy (persuading those in positions of power to enact desirable proposals into law).

Preparing to Enter the Field

Although policy and planning are widely recognized areas of specialization within the social work field, not all professionals in policy and planning are social workers. Many enter the field with backgrounds in law, public policy, or political science.

In my experience, however, social workers bring unique strengths to policy and planning work: they are conversant with the social systems and programs that exist in the community, they understand the dynamics of human behavior, and they are professionally committed to improving the quality of life.

Entry-level positions in policy and planning typically require a master's degree—though some employers hire individuals with a bachelor's degree and substantial experience.

All accredited baccalaureate (B.S.W.) degree programs in social work require a two-semester course in social policy, typically taken during the junior year. Also required is a senior-year practicum that involves 400 hours of work in a supervised employment setting. Most schools offer practicums in policy and planning, as well as advanced course work and special electives for those with a particular interest in the policy field. In many schools, qualified graduates with a BSW degree can enter an MSW program with advanced standing.

Applicants to master's (M.S.W.) degree programs in social work are generally asked to indicate, at the time of application, whether they are interested in a micro (direct service) or macro (community organization, administration, policy and planning, or evaluation) concentration. The first year of MSW study is dominated by a generic curriculum that includes, for all students, a two- semester course in social policy. Students also participate in a part-time (2 to 3 days per week) field practicum. At the beginning of their second year, students are asked to declare an area of specialization. Policy and planning is one of the possibilities. Course work in the second year is largely devoted to one's area of concentration, including electives and a theory and practice course designed to complement the second-year field placement. Some M.S.W. programs offer a *block* field placement (full time, for one semester) rather than two separate part-time placements.

The importance of field placements or practicums, at both the B.S.W. and M.S.W. levels, cannot be overstated. This is your best opportunity to gain experience, learn valuable skills, and get a taste of what a career in any particular setting might be like. Likewise, summer jobs, volunteer work, and internships provide important opportunities for experience. It is advisable to have at least one such foray into the policy arena under your belt before seeking professional employment in a policy setting.

Finding a Policy Job

Entry-level jobs in policy and planning can be difficult to obtain because they tend to carry considerable prestige. Many people, in fact, turn to policy later in their careers, after years of direct service, administrative, or supervisory experience.

The most likely settings for policy practice include: legislatures (both federal and state), government agencies (federal, state, and local), trade associations, membership organizations, think tanks, public interest groups, and advocacy organizations. Washington, D.C. and the various state capitals offer particularly good opportunities because of the proximity to government.

While established professionals tend to move easily from job to job within the policy arena, new professionals often find that getting a foot in the door can be tricky. Employers generally look for excellent writing and analytic skills, good interpersonal skills, some familiarity with current social issues and with the way government works, and personal maturity. Prior work experience in a policy setting—even a student internship or practicum—is a definite plus. I often advise those who can afford it to volunteer their time initially, in the hope of being kept on as a full-fledged employee.

Networking is an important job search tool. Agencies that deal with particular social issues tend to maintain frequent contact with each other and, thus, may be aware of job openings before they are officially announced.

It is important to note that many human service agencies and organizations hire on very short notice; that is, they don't start interviewing until their need to add staff is acute, then they expect someone to start almost immediately. This poses a particular problem for students who may have to abandon hopes of having a job lined up in advance of graduation.

Entry-level salaries vary considerably, depending upon the specific employment setting. Social workers in policy and planning, however, are invariably paid more than their counterparts in direct service.

In most settings, entry-level policy professionals perform the same tasks as experienced professionals, but are given fewer assignments and are more closely supervised.

Making It a Career

There is no question that the social policy arena is one in which a social worker could remain content for many years. The burnout factor is comparatively low, salaries are comparatively high, and opportunities for advancement abound.

What is a typical work day like? As an advocate, my time is split fairly evenly between the office (where I keep informed about the issues I lobby on, prepare written materials, and consult with my colleagues on strategy) and Capitol Hill and the federal government agencies (where I actually meet with policymakers to try to persuade them to enact constructive social policies). I also attend meetings with other advocates to plan joint strategies and share key information.

Policy analysts typically spend more time in the office, though many have the opportunity to travel and examine actual programs in operation. Policy analysis, policy development, and advocacy are intellectually rigorous careers. They are also dynamic, in that, they thrust one into the pressing issues of the day. Often, policy careers involve long work hours, but they also offer the amenities of an office environment.

Although social work in policy and planning does not offer the fulfillment of direct contact with clients, it offers the equally fulfilling opportunity to affect the well-being of large numbers of people by being an active participant in the political process.

More and more social workers are assuming important policy positions. There are currently three social workers in the U.S. Congress and over 100 more who have been elected to state and local office. President Clinton has already appointed four social workers to top posts in the Administration, and more may be forthcoming. In addition, a sizeable number of staff in Congress and the Administration—not to mention in state and local government—have social work degrees.

The Future

Opportunities for social workers in policy and planning will continue to grow.

ADVICE FROM THE PRO'S

What Employers Seek in a Job Candidate

Employers generally look for excellent writing and analytic skills, good interpersonal skills, some familiarity with current social issues and with the way government works, and personal maturity. Prior work experience in a policy setting—even a student internship or practicum—is a definite plus. I often advise those who can afford it to volunteer their time initially, in the hope of being kept on as a full-fledged employee.

MENTAL HEALTH CAREER DIRECTORY

The social problems that beset our citizenry demand attention from the best and the brightest. Social workers who are trained in policy and planning are uniquely situated to foster humane and constructive policies that will improve the quality of life for all.

▼

SUNNY HARRIS ROME has an M.S.W. degree from the University of Michigan and a J.D. degree from Georgetown University. Since 1986, she has been a lobbyist for the National Association of Social Workers, promoting policy improvements in welfare, social services, education, child welfare, and civil rights. She is also an adjunct instructor of policy analysis and advocacy in the social work programs at George Mason University in Fairfax, VA, and the Catholic University of America, Washington, DC.

CHAPTER TWENTY-FIVE

Community Organizers: For a Change

**Terry Mizrahi, Ph.D.,
Hunter College, School of Social Work**

Community organizers are everywhere. Thousands—indeed millions—of people in this country are involved in *community work*. They are active in civic organizations, tenant and block associations, neighborhood improvement committees, parent associations, church outreach to the poor, citizen mobilization, school-based projects, and countless other local action groups. Indeed, active grassroots groups are a necessary and vital part of a democratic form of government.

Yet, organizing is not a well-known career choice for several reasons. First, the term *community organizer* is not listed as an occupation by the Department of Labor. As a result, many young people who may want to get involved in community life don't necessarily know that they can do this *for a living*. Additionally, some people don't pursue jobs as organizers because they assume that the skills involved are *natural* ones. The term organizer may be perceived as being synonymous with *leader*, and people may wrongly believe that they just don't *have the knack*. As a result, training in order to work in the field is not considered. Also, some people may not identify community organizing as a career because it is often invisible; that is, organizers are getting things done *behind the scenes*, while the president or leader of the organization gets the credit. Finally, since organizing has been identified with social change and social reform, these issues or causes taken up by organizers are controversial. There are often obstacles and opposition to change which may make some people feel uncomfortable.

Community organizing as a career is alive and well, comprising a variety of job titles, educational qualifications, and functions. There are knowledge and skills to acquire, and competent organizers with a social commitment to the common good are needed in many settings.

Community organizing is about working collectively with people to solve problems—joining or forming organizations to address issues that concern people in their neighborhood, workplace, or community of interest (eg., senior citizens, health care, housing, environment, education, economic development). Community organizers work with others to: improve the social conditions of a community, enhance the quality of life of people, and bring people into the political process. Sometimes, they work directly with oppressed and disadvantaged groups in the society, e.g. the homeless, the poor, immigrants and refugees, and people of color.

Organizers' jobs have many facets to them. Depending upon the agency or organization for whom they work, they could be involved in: stopping a toxic waste incinerator from being placed in a community, planning an alternative school or health center, developing a housing plan for the neighborhood, getting the drug dealers off the block, bringing in funds to develop a senior citizen program, changing a law to prevent banks from discriminating against poor districts, organizing a campaign to clean up the environment, coordinating services for the mentally retarded, recruiting volunteers to work at a battered women's shelter, promoting public awareness of benefits and entitlements, organizing stockholders to promote corporate responsibility, advocating human rights and social justice, or engaging in international solidarity work.

History Of Organizing

Organizing has a long, noble, and at times, controversial tradition. It has developed during the social reform movements of the various historical periods, especially the 1930s and 1960s. Organizing—taking collective action—is one of the reasons for the growth of the labor, civil rights, women, peace, consumer, environment, gay and lesbian, AIDS, and other movements throughout this century. Some of the most visible organizers—Ralph Nader, Saul Alinsky, Walter Reuther, Caesar Chavez, Jesse Jackson, Eleanor Smeal, Heather Booth, Faye Wattleton, Marion Wright Edelman, Ada Dear, Wilma Mankiller, Gary Delgado, Wade Rathke, George Wiley, Si Kahn—have all influenced our country's laws and systems. These well-known activists have been affiliated with causes for which there are countless other organizers also working at the local, state, and regional levels.

Values Are Essential to the Job

While the knowledge and skills an organizer brings to the process can be used for any goals, it is the values of social work that helps shape what people do, where, with whom, and why. These humanistic values include: social and economic justice, equality, democracy, and peace.

Community organizing within social work has contributed its knowledge, skills, and leaders to these causes, and also has its own tradition. The early social workers were leaders in the social reform struggles of their day and also helped build community institutions, such as settlement houses and social services to meet people's needs. While community organizers have always been a minority in number within the social work profession, their impact has been significantly felt. Beginning with Jane Addams who founded one of the first settlement houses in Chicago (Hull House), they have been among the leaders of the movements for social security, labor reform, and health care, as well as shapers of the social programs in the 1960s and 1970s through the Economic Opportunity Act, Model Cities, Community Block Grants, and a myriad of other social service initiatives. The 1990s under President Clinton seem to be ushering in a new commitment to community work and community service, as well as expanded opportunities to revitalize and develop communities—in urban and rural areas—across the country. The time is ripe for new jobs in this field.

Roles and Goals

Organizers wear many hats and are called many things—enablers, advocates, brokers, facilitators, leaders, planners, resource and program developers, coordinators, reformers, and social change agents. The terms associated with the field of community organization include community development and social planning. Within social work and other human service disciplines, it is also called community work or community practice.

Successful organizers work toward the goal of empowerment—helping people mobilize, obtain resources, and develop strategies that promote their interests or causes. While the knowledge and skills an organizer brings to the process can be used for any goals, it is the values of social work that helps shape what people do, where, with whom, and why. These humanistic values include: social and economic justice, equality, democracy, and peace.

Getting Started

Individuals usually get started in this field because of personal commitments, volunteer experiences, or beginning jobs. For example, they may have a passion for social cause, or they may feel deeply about local problems that have surfaced in their community, be it in their school, on their block, in their region, or a problem related to their racial, ethnic, or social group. "What are people doing about it?" is the question that gets young people and adults involved. This path is the *natural*, spontaneous way in.

There are also more structured ways of *testing the waters* through volunteer work. In the past, people have joined the federal government-supported VISTA or Peace Corps. Volunteer bureaus operated by local governments and private organizations such as United Way often offer a range of opportunities that go beyond traditional social services.

Additionally, entry-level jobs are offered by such groups as ACORN, Public Interest Research Group, Center for Third World Organizing, Grassroots Leadership, as well as with the thousands of membership organizations, social service agencies, and associations working on a particular issue. Every *cause* has its leadership organizations—sometimes more than one, and sometimes competing ones. Those interested in organizing can find their *niche* according to their political and social beliefs.

Educational Opportunities

Many of the groups listed welcome committed people who may not have a college education, but who are willing to be trained on the job. More typically, most organizations seek persons who have college degrees, preferably in the social sciences or human services, where they have had an opportunity to do some *field work* or an internship. Sometimes they encourage and even support a staff person in returning to school on a part-time basis.

For those beginning at the college level, majoring in the social and human sciences is the usual area of concentration. However, it is important to note that some of the best organizers enter the career from other liberal arts and specialized backgrounds.

Selecting a social work major at the undergraduate level is a direct route into the field. All accredited social work degree programs require course instruction and field work in communities as a part of a general curriculum. Students who typically enter a BSW program in their junior year are required to do a part-time internship, which usually includes understanding community life and institutions, analyzing communities—their people, institutions, culture—and working on community projects. Depending upon the interest of the student, faculty, and agencies affiliated with a particular BSW program, community work can have different degrees of emphasis.

At the graduate level, there are several ways to enter professional organizing life. While it is not necessary to have a master's degree, many effective leaders of advocacy organizations and coalition and human service campaigns have one. Within MSW programs, some schools still offer a concentration or major in community organizing or community development. Unfortunately, during the 1980s, some schools eliminated the major in community organizing or else incorporated it into what has become known as *macro* practice or policy, planning, and administration (PPA). Nevertheless, all accredited graduate schools of social work expose students to methods of working with people that includes working with communities, as they do in BSW programs. However, the ability to acquire a specialization in the area will vary from school to school.

Courses at the graduate level cover such topics as: knowledge of community and social systems, organization and groups, inter-organizational and political arenas, skills-building in program planning and evaluation, collaborations and coalition-building, lobbying, community assessment, leadership development, grant writing and fundraising, public relations, service-coordination, and case and class advocacy.

During a typical two-year MSW program, students will have an internship for one or both years in which they have a supervised practicum to develop their competencies in community practice. If the program has a two-year major, the initial year might be spend in a grassroots setting with a neighborhood group or community center, while the second year might be served in a politician's office getting experience as a legislative aide.

Other graduate degree programs outside of social work offer some aspects of community organizing, each with their own perspective. Among them are: urban planning, community health education, human service and public administration, international studies, and labor studies. There are also a few independent, non-academic schools for organizers. These include the MidWest Academy and the Industrial Areas Foundation, both in Chicago.

Career Paths

Career paths in community organizing are vast and varied. Experience has demonstrated that, regardless of the job title, the community organizing approach to problem-solving and the involvement of people always exists. Here are just a few of the job titles held by graduates of MSW programs: settlement house director, advocate for the homeless, commissioner of the Department of Youth and Juvenile Justice and other departments, youth program coordinator, health coalition director, family policy analyst, tenant organizer, housing specialist, drug prevention program director, AIDS program developer, legislative aide to elected public officials, and politician. The community organizing specialization in social work allows for a diversity of career opportunities.

Caveats and Challenges

While the revitalization of community organizing within social work is occurring, it is not in the mainstream of the profession. Those interested in pursuing careers in organizing within social work will have to find or establish their own support group and seek comfort in the social missions grounding their work.

Organizers are few in number relative to the need and did not have a professional association until recently. A National Organizers' Association, begun in 1993, is designed to help obtain job benefits, security, and advancement. The Association on Community Organization and Social Administration (ACOSA) has existed since 1988 to promote these areas in social work education and practice. There are also centers affiliated with schools of social work that support community organizing research, training, and program development: the Education Center for Community Organizing (ECCO) at the Hunter College School of Social Work and the Center for Community Education at the Rutgers School of Social Work, are two examples.

Salaries

Grassroots organizers and even leaders of advocacy and policy organizations are paid relatively low wages. To gain more pay, organizers usually have to move away from the front line. The hours can be long: there are often night meetings and weekend events, since those are the times when people come most conveniently together as citizens.

The process of change is sometimes a slow one and not without its frustrations. Organizers need tenacity and determination as well as good interpersonal and analytical skills. They must interact with and influence diverse groups of people, not all of whom share the same values, goals, and strategies. The payoffs and victories may be slow, so satisfaction must often be derived from the process of engaging and educating people. Ultimately, though, an organizer's investment of time, energy, and resources will have an impact on society and seem worth it—for a change.

ADVICE FROM THE PRO'S

Dr. Terry Mizrahi is a professor at the Hunter College, School of Social Work and director of the Education Center for Community Organizing. Her research expertise is in the areas of professional socialization, interdisciplinary collaboration, and coalition-building. Dr. Mizrahi has also worked as a consultant with organizations in both rural and urban low-income communities including Appalachia, New York City, and Virginia. She has been the recipient of several research and program grants from public and private sources to further her work.

Dr. Mizrahi is co-editor of a new book entitled *Community Organization and Social Administration: Advance, Trends and Emerging Principles* and also co-editor of *Computers for Social Change and Community Organizing* (1991, The Haworth Press). She has also written articles and books on health advocacy, patients' rights, housing, and community development.

The Job Search Process

CHAPTER TWENTY-SIX

Getting Started: Self-Evaluation and Career Objectives

Getting a job may be a relatively simple one-step or couple of weeks process or a complex, months-long operation.

Starting, nurturing and developing a career (or even a series of careers) is a lifelong process.

What we'll be talking about in the five chapters that together form our Job Search Process are those basic steps to take, assumptions to make, things to think about if you want a job—especially a first job in some area of psychology or mental health. But when these steps—this process—are applied and expanded over a lifetime, most if not all of them are the same procedures, carried out over and over again, that are necessary to develop a successful, lifelong, professional career.

What does all this have to do with putting together a resume, writing a cover letter, heading off for interviews and the other "traditional" steps necessary to get a job? Whether your college graduation is just around the corner or a far distant memory, you will continuously need to focus, evaluate and re-evaluate your response to the ever-changing challenge of your future: Just what do you want to do with the rest of your life? Whether you like it or not, you're all looking for that "entry-level opportunity."

You're already one or two steps ahead of the competition—you're sure you want to pursue a career in psychology or mental health. By heeding the advice of the many professionals who have written chapters for this *Career Directory*—and utilizing the extensive entry-level job, organization, and career resource listings we've included—you're well on your way to fulfilling that dream. But there are some key decisions and time-consuming preparations to make if you want to transform that hopeful dream into a real, live job.

The actual process of finding the right company, right career path and, most importantly, the right first job, begins long before you start mailing out resumes to potential employers. The choices and decisions you make now are not irrevocable, but this first job will have a definite impact on the career options you leave yourself. To help you make some of the right decisions and choices along the way (and avoid some of the most notable traps and pitfalls), the following chapters will lead you through a series of organized steps. If the entire job search process we are recommending here is properly executed, it will undoubtedly help you land exactly the job you want.

If you're currently in high school and hope, after college, to land a job in the mental health industry, then attending the right college, choosing the right major, and getting the summer work experience many companies look for are all important steps. Read the section of this *Career Directory* that covers the particular field and/or job specialty in which you're interested—many of the contributors have recommended colleges or graduate programs they favor.

If you're hoping to jump right into any of these fields without a college degree or other professional training, our best and only advice is—don't do it. As you'll soon see in the detailed information included in the **Job Opportunities Databank,** there are not that many job openings for students without a college degree or training. Those that do exist are generally clerical and will only rarely lead to promising careers.

The Concept of a Job Search Process

As we've explained, a job search is not a series of random events. Rather, it is a series of connected events that together form the job search process. It is important to know the eight steps that go into that process:

1. Evaluating yourself

Know thyself. What skills and abilities can you offer a prospective employer? What do you enjoy doing? What are your strengths and weaknesses? What do you want to do?

2. Establishing your career objectives

Where do you want to be next year, three years, five years from now? What do you ultimately want to accomplish in your career and your life?

3. Creating a company target list

How to prepare a "Hit List" of potential employers—researching them, matching their needs with your skills and starting your job search assault. Preparing company information sheets and evaluating your chances.

4. Networking for success

Learning how to utilize every contact, every friend, every relative, and anyone else you can think of to break down the barriers facing any would-be psychology or mental health professional. How to organize your home office to keep track of your communications and stay on top of your job campaign.

5. Preparing your resume

How to encapsulate years of school and little actual work experience into a professional, selling resume. Learning when and how to use it.

6. Preparing cover letters

The many ordinary and the all-too-few extraordinary cover letters, the kind that land interviews and jobs.

7. Interviewing

How to make the interview process work for you—from the first "hello" to the first day on the job.

8. Following up

Often overlooked, it's perhaps the most important part of the job search process.

We won't try to kid you—it is a lot of work. To do it right, you have to get started early, probably quite a bit earlier than you'd planned. Frankly, we recommend beginning this process one full year prior to the day you plan to start work.

So if you're in college, the end of your junior year is the right time to begin your research and preparations. That should give you enough time during summer vacation to set up your files and begin your library research.

Whether you're in college or graduate school, one item may need to be planned even earlier—allowing enough free time in your schedule of classes for interview preparations and appointments. Waiting until your senior year to "make some time" is already too late. Searching for a full-time job is itself a full-time job! Though you're naturally restricted by your schedule, it's not difficult to plan ahead and prepare for your upcoming job search. Try to leave at least a couple of free mornings or afternoons a week. A day or even two without classes is even better.

Otherwise, you'll find yourself, crazed and distracted, trying to prepare for an interview in the ten-minute period between classes. Not the best way to make a first impression and certainly not the way you want to approach an important meeting.

The Self-Evaluation Process

Learning about who you are, what you want to be, what you can be, are critical first steps in the job search process and, unfortunately, the ones most often ignored by job seekers everywhere, especially students eager to leave the ivy behind and plunge into the "real world." But avoiding this crucial self-evaluation can hinder your progress and even damage some decent prospects.

Why? Because in order to land a job with a company at which you'll actually be happy, you need to be able to identify those firms and/or job descriptions that best match your own skills, likes, and strengths. The more you know about yourself, the more you'll bring to this process and the more accurate the "match-ups." You'll be able to structure your presentation (resume, cover letter, interviews, follow up) to stress your most marketable skills and talents (and, dare we say it, conveniently avoid your weaknesses?). Later, you'll be able to evaluate potential employers and job offers on the basis of your own needs and desires. This spells the difference between waking up in the morning ready to enthusiastically tackle a new day of challenges and shutting off the alarm in the hopes the day (and your job) will just disappear.

Creating Your Self-Evaluation Form

If your self-evaluation is to have any meaning, you must first be honest with yourself. This self-evaluation form should help you achieve that goal by providing a structured environment to answer these tough questions.

Take a sheet of lined notebook paper. Set up eight columns across the top—Strengths, Weaknesses, Skills, Hobbies, Courses, Experience, Likes, Dislikes.

Now, fill in each of these columns according to these guidelines:

Strengths: Describe personality traits you consider your strengths (and try to look at them as an employer would)—e.g., persistence, organization, ambition, intelligence, logic, assertiveness, aggression, leadership, etc.

Weaknesses: The traits you consider glaring weaknesses—e.g., impatience, conceit, etc. Remember: Look at these as a potential employer would. Don't assume that the personal traits you consider weaknesses will necessarily be considered negatives in the business world. You may be "easily bored," a trait that led to lousy grades early on because teachers couldn't keep you interested in the subjects they were teaching. Well, many entrepreneurs need ever-changing challenges. Strength or weakness?

Skills: Any skill you have, whether you think it's marketable or not. Everything from basic business skills—like typing and word processing—to computer or teaching experience and foreign language literacy. Don't forget possibly obscure but marketable skills like "good telephone voice."

Hobbies: The things you enjoy doing that, more than likely, have no overt connection to career objectives. These should be distinct from the skills listed above, and may include activities such as reading, games, travel, sports, and the like. While these may not be marketable in any general sense, they may well be useful in specific circumstances.

Courses: All the general subject areas (history, literature, etc.) and/or specific courses you've taken which may be marketable, you really enjoyed, or both.

Experience: Just the specific functions you performed at any part-time (school year) or full-time (summer) jobs. Entries may include "General Office" (typing, filing, answering phones, etc.), "Research Assistant," "Retail Clerk" etc.

Likes: List all your "likes," those important considerations that you haven't listed anywhere else yet. These might include the types of people you like to be with, the kind of environment you prefer (city, country, large places, small places, quiet, loud, fast-paced, slow-paced) and anything else which hasn't shown up somewhere on this form. Try to think of "likes" that you have that are related to the job you are applying for. For example, if you're applying for a job at a major corporation, mention that you enjoy reading the Wall St. Journal. However, try not to include entries which refer to specific jobs or companies. We'll list those on another form.

Dislikes: All the people, places and things you can easily live without.

Now assess the "marketability" of each item you've listed. (In other words, are some of your likes, skills or courses easier to match to a psychology or mental health job description, or do they have little to do with a specific job or company?) Mark highly marketable skills with an "H." Use "M" to characterize those skills which may be marketable in a particular set of circumstances, "L" for those with minimal potential application to any job.

Referring back to the same list, decide if you'd enjoy using your marketable skills or talents as part of your everyday job—"Y" for yes, "N" for no. You may type 80 words a minute but truly despise typing or worry that stressing it too much will land you on the permanent clerical staff. If so, mark typing with an "N." (Keep one thing in mind—just because you dislike typing shouldn't mean you absolutely won't accept a job that requires it. Almost every professional job today requires computer-based work that make typing a plus.)

Now, go over the entire form carefully and look for inconsistencies.

To help you with your own form, consult the sample form on the next page that a job-hunter might complete.

The Value of a Second Opinion

There is a familiar misconception about the self-evaluation process that gets in the way of many new job applicants—the belief that it is a process which must be accomplished in isolation. Nothing could be further from the truth. Just because the family doctor tells you you need an operation doesn't mean you run right off to the hospital. Prudence dictates that you check out the opinion with another physician. Getting such a "second opinion"—someone else's, not just your own—is a valuable practice throughout the job search process, as well.

So after you've completed the various exercises in this chapter, review them with a friend, relative, or parent—just be sure it's someone who knows you well and cares about you. These second opinions may reveal some aspects of your self-description on which you and the rest of the world differ. If so, discuss them, learn from them and, if necessary, change some conclusions. Should everyone concur with your self-evaluation, you will be reassured that your choices are on target.

Establishing Your Career Objective(s)

For better or worse, you now know something more of who and what you are. But we've yet to establish and evaluate another important area—your overall needs, desires and goals. Where are you going? What do you want to accomplish?

If you're getting ready to graduate from college or graduate school, the next five years are the most critical period of your whole career. You need to make the initial transition from college to the workplace, establish yourself in a new and completely unfamiliar company environment, and begin to build the professional credentials necessary to achieve your career goals.

If that strikes you as a pretty tall order, well, it is. Unless you've narrowly prepared yourself for a specific profession, you're probably most ill-prepared for any

MENTAL HEALTH CAREER DIRECTORY

Strength	Weakness	Skill	Hobby	Course	Experience	Like	Dislike
Marketable?							
Enjoy?							
Marketable?							
Enjoy?							
Marketable?							
Enjoy?							

real job. Instead, you've (hopefully) learned some basic principles—research and analytical skills that are necessary for success at almost any level—and, more or less, how to think.

It's tough to face, but face it you must: No matter what your college, major, or degree, all you represent right now is potential. How you package that potential and what you eventually make of it is completely up to you. It's an unfortunate fact that many companies will take a professional with barely a year or two experience over any newcomer, no matter how promising. Smaller firms, especially, can rarely afford to hire someone who can't begin contributing immediately.

So you have to be prepared to take your comparatively modest skills and experience and package them in a way that will get you interviewed and hired. Quite a challenge.

There are a number of different ways to approach such a task. If you find yourself confused or unable to list such goals, you might want to check a few books in your local library that have more time to spend on the topic of "goal-oriented planning."

But Is the Psychology and Mental Health Industry Right for You?

Presuming you now have a much better idea of yourself and where you'd like to be, let's make sure some of your basic assumptions are right. We presume you purchased this *Career Directory* because you're considering a career in some area of psychology or mental health. Are you sure? Do you know enough about the industry as a whole and the particular part you're heading for to decide whether it's right for you? Probably not. So start your research now—learn as much about your potential career field as you now know about yourself.

Start with the essays in the Advice for the Pro's section—these will give you an excellent overview of the psychology and mental health industry, some very specialized (and growing) areas, and some things to keep in mind as you start on your career search. They will also give you a relatively simplified, though very necessary, understanding of just what people who work in all these areas of healthcare actually do.

Other sources you should consider consulting to learn more about this business are listed in the Career Resources section of this book.

In that section, we've listed trade associations and publications associated with psychology and mental health and therapy professions (together with many other resources that will help your job search. (Consult the front of this directory for a complete description of the Career Resource section.) Where possible in the association entries, we've included details on educational information they make available, but you should certainly consider writing each of the pertinent associations, letting them know you're interested in a career in their area of specialization and would appreciate whatever help and advice they're willing to impart. You'll find many sponsor seminars and conferences throughout the country, some of which you may be able to attend.

The trade publications are dedicated to the highly specific interests of mental health professionals. These magazines are generally not available at newsstands, but you may be able to obtain back issues at your local library (most major libraries have extensive collections of such journals) or by writing to the magazines' circulation/subscription departments. We've also included regional and local magazines.

You may also try writing to the publishers and/or editors of these publications. State in your cover letter what area of psychology or mental health you're considering and ask them for whatever help and advice they can offer. But be specific. These are busy professionals and they do not have the time or the inclination to simply "tell me everything you can about working at a clinic."

If you can afford it now, we strongly suggest subscribing to whichever trade magazines are applicable to the specialty you're considering. If you can't subscribe to all of them, make it a point to regularly read the copies that arrive at your local public or college library.

These publications may well provide the most imaginative and far-reaching information for your job search. Even a quick perusal of an issue or two will give you an excellent feel for the industry. After reading only a few articles, you'll already get a handle on what's happening in the field and some of the industry's peculiar and particular jargon. Later, more detailed study will aid you in your search for a specific job.

Authors of the articles themselves may well turn out to be important resources. If an article is directly related to your chosen specialty, why not call the author and ask some questions? You'd be amazed how willing many of these professionals will be to talk to you and answer your questions, and the worst they can do is say no. (But *do* use common sense—authors will not *always* respond graciously to your invitation to "chat about the business." And don't be *too* aggressive here.)

You'll find such research to be a double-edged sword. In addition to helping you get a handle on whether the area you've chosen is really right for you, you'll slowly learn enough about particular specialties, companies, the industry, etc., to actually sound like you know what you're talking about when you hit the pavement looking for your first job. And nothing is better than sounding like a pro—except being one.

Mental Health Is It. Now What?

After all this research, we're going to assume you've reached that final decision—you really do want a career in some aspect of psychology or mental health. It is with this vague certainty that all too many of you will race off, hunting for any firm willing to give you a job. You'll manage to get interviews at a couple and, smiling brightly, tell everyone you meet, "I want a career in mental health." The interviewers, unfortunately, will all ask the same awkward question—"What *exactly* do you want to do at our company?"—and that will be the end of that.

It is simply not enough to narrow your job search to a specific industry. And so far, that's all you've done. You must now establish a specific career objective—the job you want to start, the career you want to pursue. Just knowing that you "want to get into psychology or mental health" doesn't mean anything to anybody. If that's all you can tell an interviewer, it demonstrates a lack of research into the industry itself and your failure to think ahead.

Interviewers will *not* welcome you with open arms if you're still vague about your career goals. If you've managed to get an "informational interview" with an executive whose company currently has no job openings, what is he or she supposed to do with your resume after you leave? Who should he or she send it to for future consideration? Since *you* don't seem to know exactly what you want to do, how's he or she going to figure it out? Worse, that person will probably resent your asking him or her to function as your personal career counselor.

Remember, the more specific your career objective, the better your chances of finding a job. It's that simple and that important. Naturally, before you declare your objective to the world, check once again to make sure your specific job target matches the skills and interests you defined in your self- evaluation. Eventually, you may want to state such an objective on your resume, and "To obtain an entry-level position as a staff psychologist at a mid-sized hospital," is quite a bit better than "I want a career in mental health." Do not consider this step final until you can summarize your job/career objective in a single, short, accurate sentence.

CHAPTER TWENTY-SEVEN

Targeting Prospective Employers and Networking For Success

As you move along the job search path, one fact will quickly become crystal clear—it is primarily a process of **elimination**: your task is to consider and research as many options as possible, then—for good reasons—**eliminate** as many as possible, attempting to continually narrow your focus.

Your Ideal Company Profile

Let's establish some criteria to evaluate potential employers. This will enable you to identify your target companies, the places you'd really like to work. (This process, as we've pointed out, is not specific to any industry or field; the same steps, with perhaps some research resource variations, are applicable to any job, any company, any industry.)

Take a sheet of blank paper and divide it into three vertical columns. Title it "Target Company—Ideal Profile." Call the lefthand column "Musts," the middle column "Preferences," and the righthand column "Nevers."

We've listed a series of questions below. After considering each question, decide whether a particular criteria *must* be met, whether you would simply *prefer* it or *never* would consider it at all. If there are other criteria you consider important, feel free to add them to the list below and mark them accordingly on your Profile.

1. What are your geographical preferences? (Possible answers: U.S., Canada, International, Anywhere). If you only want to work in the U.S., then "Work in United States" would be the entry in the "Must" column. "Work in Canada or Foreign Country" might be the first entry in your "Never" column. There would be no applicable entry for this question in the "Preference" column. If, however, you will consider working in two of the three, then your "Must" column entry might read "Work in U.S. or Canada," your "Preference"

entry—if you preferred one over the other—could read "Work in U.S.," and the "Never" column, "Work Overseas."

2. If you prefer to work in the U.S. or Canada, what area, state(s) or province(s)? If overseas, what area or countries?

3. Do you prefer a large city, small city, town, or somewhere as far away from civilization as possible?

4. In regard to question three, any specific preferences?

5. Do you prefer a warm or cold climate?

6. Do you prefer a large or small company? Define your terms (by sales, income, employees, offices, etc.).

7. Do you mind relocating right now? Do you want to work for a firm with a reputation for *frequently* relocating top people?

8. Do you mind travelling frequently? What percent do you consider reasonable? (Make sure this matches the normal requirements of the job specialization you're considering.)

9. What salary would you *like* to receive (put in the "Preference" column)? What's the *lowest* salary you'll accept (in the "Must" column)?

10. Are there any benefits (such as an expense account, medical and/or dental insurance, company car, etc.) you must or would like to have?

11. Are you planning to attend graduate school at some point in the future and, if so, is a tuition reimbursement plan important to you?

12. Do you feel that a formal training program is necessary?

13. If applicable, what kinds of specific accounts would you prefer to work with? What specific products?

It's important to keep revising this new form, just as you should continue to update your Self-Evaluation Form. After all, it contains the criteria by which you will judge every potential employer. Armed with a complete list of such criteria, you're now ready to find all the companies that match them.

Targeting Individual Companies

To begin creating your initial list of targeted companies, start with the **Job Opportunities Databank** in this directory. We've listed many major psychiatric hospitals, counseling centers, and state government social services agencies, most of which were contacted by telephone for this edition. These listings provide a plethora of data concerning the companies' overall operations, hiring practices, and other important information on entry-level job opportunities. This latter information includes key contacts (names), the average number of entry-level people they hire each year, along with complete job descriptions and requirements.

One word of advice. You'll notice that some of the companies list "0" under average entry-level hiring. This is more a reflection of the current economic times than a long-range projection. In the past, these companies did have new hires, and they will again in the future. We have listed these companies for three reasons: 1) to present you with the overall view of prospective employers; 2) because even companies that don't plan to do any hiring will experience unexpected job openings; and 3) things change, so as soon as the economy begins to pick up, expect entry-level hiring to increase again.

We have attempted to include information on those major firms that represent many of the entry-level jobs out there. But there are, of course, many other companies of all sizes and shapes that you may also wish to research. In the Career Resources section, we have listed other reference tools you can use to obtain more information on the companies we've listed, as well as those we haven't.

The Other Side of the Iceberg

You are now better prepared to choose those companies that meet your own list of criteria. But a word of caution about these now-"obvious" requirements—they are not the only ones you need to take into consideration. And you probably won't be able to find all or many of the answers to this second set of questions in any reference book—they are known, however, by those persons already at work in the industry. Here is the list you will want to follow:

Promotion

If you are aggressive about your career plans, you'll want to know if you have a shot at the top. Look for companies that traditionally promote from within.

Training

Look for companies in which your early tenure will actually be a period of on-the-job training, hopefully ones in which training remains part of the long-term process. As new techniques and technologies enter the workplace, you must make sure you are updated on these skills. Most importantly, look for training that is craft- or function-oriented—these are the so-called **transferable skills**, ones you can easily bring along with you from job-to-job, company-to-company, sometimes industry-to-industry.

Salary

Some industries are generally high paying, some not. But even an industry with a tradition of paying abnormally low salaries may have particular companies or job functions (like sales) within companies that command high remuneration. But it's important you know what the industry standard is.

THE JOB SEARCH PROCESS

Ask the Person Who Owns One

Some years ago, this advice was used as the theme for a highly successful automobile advertising campaign. The prospective car buyer was encouraged to find out about the product by asking the (supposedly) most trustworthy judge of all—someone who was already an owner.

You can use the same approach in your job search. You all have relatives or friends already out in the workplace—these are your best sources of information about those industries. Cast your net in as wide a circle as possible. Contact these valuable resources. You'll be amazed at how readily they will answer your questions. I suggest you check the criteria list at the beginning of this chapter to formulate your own list of pertinent questions. Ideally and minimally you will want to learn: how the industry is doing, what its long-term prospects are, the kinds of personalities they favor (aggressive, low key), rate of employee turnover, and the availability of training.

Benefits

Look for companies in which health insurance, vacation pay, retirement plans, 401K accounts, stock purchase opportunities, and other important employee benefits are extensive—and company paid. If you have to pay for basic benefits like medical coverage yourself, you'll be surprised at how expensive they are. An exceptional benefit package may even lead you to accept a lower- than-usual salary.

Unions

Make sure you know about the union situation in each industry you research. Periodic, union-mandated salary increases are one benefit nonunion workers may find hard to match.

Making Friends and Influencing People

Networking is a term you have probably heard; it is definitely a key aspect of any successful job search and a process you must master.

Informational interviews and **job interviews** are the two primary outgrowths of successful networking.

Referrals, an aspect of the networking process, entail using someone else's name, credentials and recommendation to set up a receptive environment when seeking a job interview.

All of these terms have one thing in common: Each depends on the actions of other people to put them in motion. Don't let this idea of "dependency" slow you down, however. A job search *must* be a very pro-active process—*you* have to initiate the action. When networking, this means contacting as many people as you can. The more you contact, the better the chances of getting one of those people you are "depending" on to take action and help you out.

So what *is* networking? How do you build your own network? And why do you need one in the first place? The balance of this chapter answers all of those questions and more.

Get your telephone ready. It's time to make some friends.

Not the World's Oldest Profession, But...

Networking is the process of creating your own group of relatives, friends, and acquaintances who can feed you the information you need to find a job—identifying where the jobs are and giving you the personal introductions and background data necessary to pursue them.

If the job market were so well-organized that details on all employment opportunities were immediately available to all applicants, there would be no need for such a process. Rest assured the job market is *not* such a smooth-running machine—most applicants are left very much to their own devices. Build and use your own network wisely and you'll be amazed at the amount of useful job intelligence you will turn up.

While the term networking didn't gain prominence until the 1970s, it is by no means a new phenomenon. A selection process that connects people of similar skills, backgrounds, and/or attitudes—in other words, networking—has been in existence in a variety of forms for centuries. Attend any Ivy League school and you're automatically part of its very special centuries-old network.

And it works. Remember your own reaction when you were asked to recommend someone for a job, club or school office? You certainly didn't want to look foolish, so you gave it some thought and tried to recommend the best-qualified person that you thought would "fit in" with the rest of the group. It's a built-in screening process.

Creating the Ideal Network

As in most endeavors, there's a wrong way and a right way to network. The following tips will help you construct your own wide- ranging, information-gathering, interview-generating group—*your* network.

Diversify

Unlike the Harvard or Princeton network—confined to former graduates of each school—your network should be as diversified and wide-ranging as possible. You never know who might be in a position to help, so don't limit your group of friends. The more diverse they are, the greater the variety of information they may supply you with.

Don't Forget...

...to include everyone you know in your initial networking list: friends, relatives, social acquaintances, classmates, college alumni, professors, teachers, your dentist, doctor, family lawyer, insurance agent, banker, travel agent, elected officials in your community, ministers, fellow church members, local tradesmen, and local business or social club officers. And everybody they know!

Be Specific

Make a list of the kinds of assistance you will require from those in your network, then make specific requests of each. Do they know of jobs at their company? Can they introduce you to the proper executives? Have they heard something about or know someone at the company you're planning to interview with next week?

The more organized you are, the easier it will be to target the information you need and figure out who might have it. Begin to keep a business card file or case so you can keep track of all your contacts. A small plastic case for file cards that is available at any discount store will do nicely. One system you can use is to staple the card to a 3 x 5 index card. On the card, write down any information about that contact that you might need later—when you talked to them, job leads they provided, specific job search advice, etc. You will then have all the information you need about each company or contact in one easily accessible location.

Learn the Difference...

...between an **informational** interview and a **job** interview. The former requires you to cast yourself in the role of information gatherer; *you* are the interviewer and knowledge is your goal—about an industry, company, job function, key executive, etc. Such a meeting with someone already doing what you soon hope to be doing is by far the best way to find out everything you need to know—before you walk through the door and sit down for a formal job interview, at which time your purpose is more sharply defined: to get the job you're interviewing for.

If you learn of a specific job opening during an informational interview, you are in a position to find out details about the job, identify the interviewer and, possibly, even learn some things about him or her. In addition, presuming you get your contact's permission, you may be able to use his or her name as a referral. Calling up the interviewer and saying, "Joan Smith in your human resources department suggested I contact you regarding openings for case workers," is far superior to "Hello. Do you have any job openings at your agency?"

(In such a case, be careful about referring to a specific job opening, even if your contact told you about it. It may not be something you're supposed to know about. By presenting your query as an open-ended question, you give your prospective employer the option of exploring your background without further commitment. If there is a job there and you're qualified for it, you'll find out soon enough.)

Don't Waste a Contact

Not everyone you call on your highly-diversified networking list will know about a job opening. It would be surprising if each one did. But what about *their* friends and colleagues? It's amazing how everyone knows someone who knows someone. Ask—you'll find that someone.

Value Your Contacts

If someone has provided you with helpful information or an introduction to a friend or colleague, keep him or her informed about how it all turns out. A referral that's panned out should be reported to the person who opened the door for you in the first place. Such courtesy will be appreciated—and may lead to more contacts. If someone has nothing to offer today, a call back in the future is still appropriate and may pay off.

The lesson is clear: Keep your options open, your contact list alive. Detailed records of your network—whom you spoke with, when, what transpired, etc.—will help you keep track of your overall progress and organize what can be a complicated and involved process.

Informational Interviews

So now you've done your homework, built your network, and begun using your contacts. It's time to go on your first informational interview.

A Typical Interview

You were, of course, smart enough to include John Fredericks, the bank officer who handled your dad's mortgage, on your original contact list. He knew you as a bright and conscientious college senior; in fact, your perfect three-year repayment record on the loan you took out to buy that '67 Plymouth impressed him. When you called him, he was happy to refer you to his friend, Carol Jones, a substance abuse counselor at New Horizons, Inc. Armed with permission to use Fredericks' name and recommendation, you wrote a letter to Carol Jones, the gist of which went something like this:

I am writing at the suggestion of Mr. John Fredericks at Fidelity National Bank. He knows of my interest in a counseling career and, given your position at New Horizons, Inc., thought you might be able to help me gain a better understanding of this specialized field and the career opportunities it presents.

While I am majoring in psychology, I know I need to speak with professionals such as yourself to learn how to apply my studies to a work environment. If you could spare a half hour to meet with me, I'm certain I would be able to get enough information about this specialty to give me the direction I need.

I'll call your office next week in the hope that we can schedule a meeting.

Send a copy of this letter to Mr. Fredericks at the bank—it will refresh his memory should Ms. Jones call to inquire about you. Next step: the follow-up phone call. After you get Ms. Jones' secretary on the line, it will, with luck, go something like this:

"Hello, I'm Paul Smith. I'm calling in reference to a letter I wrote to Ms. Jones requesting an appointment."

"Oh, yes. You're the young man interested in magazines. Ms. Jones can see you on June 23rd. Will 10 A.M. be satisfactory?"

"That's fine. I'll be there."

Well, the appointed day arrives. Well-scrubbed and dressed in your best (and most conservative) suit, you are ushered into Ms. Jones' office. She offers you coffee (you decline) and says that it is okay to light up if you wish to smoke (you decline). The conversation might go something like this:

You: "Thank you for seeing me, Ms. Jones. I know you are busy and appreciate your taking the time to talk with me."

Jones: "Well it's my pleasure since you come so highly recommended. I'm always pleased to meet someone interested in my field."

MENTAL HEALTH CAREER DIRECTORY

You: "As I stated in my letter, my interest in substance abuse counseling is very real, but I'm having trouble seeing how all of my studies will adapt to the work environment. I think I'll be much better prepared to evaluate future job offers if I can learn more about your experiences. May I ask you a few questions about New Horizons?"

Jones: "Fire away, Paul".

Ms. Jones relaxes. She realizes this is a knowledge hunt you are on, not a thinly-veiled job interview. Your approach has kept her off the spot—she doesn't have to be concerned with making a hiring decision. You've already gotten high marks for not putting her on the defensive.

You: "I have a few specific questions I'd like to ask. First, at a company such as yours, where does an entry-level person start?"

Jones: "In this company, you would be assigned to an experienced counselor to work as that person's assistant for the first month of your employment. This gives you a chance to see the way we work and to become comfortable with our facilities and patients. After that, if you had progressed well, you would begin seeing patients on your own."

You: "Where and how fast does someone progress after that?"

Jones: "Obviously, that depends on the person, but given the proper aptitude and ability, that person would simply get more responsibilities to handle. How well you do all along the way will determine how far and how fast you progress."

You: "What is the work environment like—is it pretty hectic?"

Jones: "We try to keep the work load at an even keel. The comfort of our workers is of prime importance to us. Excessive turnover is costly, you know. But this is an exciting business, and things change sometimes minute-to-minute. It's not a profession for the faint-hearted!"

You: "If I may shift to another area, I'd be interested in your opinion about counseling in general and what you see as the most likely areas of opportunity in the foreseeable future. Do you think this is a growth career area, despite the many changes that have occurred in the last 18 months?"

Jones: "Well, judging by the hiring record of our company, I think you'll find it's an area worth making a commitment to. At the entry level, we've hired a number of new people in the past three or four years. There always seems to be opportunities, though it's gotten far more competitive."

You: "Do you think someone with my qualifications and background could get started in substance abuse counseling? Perhaps a look at my resume. would be helpful to you." *(Give it to Ms. Jones.)*

Jones: "Your course work looks appropriate. I especially like the internships you've held every summer. I think you have a real chance to break into this field. I don't think we're hiring right now, but I know a couple of centers that are looking for bright young people with qualifications like yours. Let me give you a couple of phone numbers." (Write down names and phone numbers.)

You: "You have been very generous with your time, but I can see from those flashing buttons on your phone that you have other things to do. Thank you again for taking the time to talk with me."

Jones: "You're welcome."

After the Interview

The next step should be obvious: **Two** thank-you letters are required, one to Ms. Jones, the second to Mr. Fredericks. Get them both out immediately. (And see the chapter on writing letters if you need help writing them.)

Keeping Track of the Interview Trail

Let's talk about record keeping again. If your networking works the way it's supposed to, this was only the first of many such interviews. Experts have estimated that the average person could develop a contact list of 250 people. Even if we limit your initial list to only 100, if each of them gave you one referral, your list would suddenly have 200 names. Presuming that it will not be necessary or helpful to see all of them, it's certainly possible that such a list could lead to 100 informational and/or job interviews! Unless you keep accurate records, by the time you're on No. 50, you won't even remember the first dozen!

So get the results of each interview down on paper. Use whatever format with which you're comfortable. You should create some kind of file, folder, or note card that is an "Interview Recap Record." If you have access to a personal computer, take advantage of it. It will be much easier to keep you information stored in one place and well-organized. Your record should be set up and contain something like the following:

Name: New Horizons, Inc.
Address: 333 E. 54th St., Rochester, NY 10000
Phone: (212) 555-4000
Contact: Carol Jones
Type of Business: Substance abuse counseling
Referral Contact: Mr. Fredericks, Fidelity National Bank
Date: June 23, 1993

At this point, you should add a one- or two-paragraph summary of what you found out at the meeting. Since these comments are for your eyes only, you should be both objective and subjective. State the facts—what you found out in response to your specific questions—but include your impressions—your estimate of the opportunities for further discussions, your chances for future consideration for employment.

"I Was Just Calling To..."

Find any logical opportunity to stay in touch with Ms. Jones. You may, for example, let her know when you graduate and tell her your grade point average, copy her in on any letters you write to Mr. Fredericks, even send a congratulatory note if her company's year-end financial results are positive or if you read something in the local paper about her department. This type of follow up has the all-important effect of keeping you and your name in the forefront of others' minds. Out of sight *is* out of mind. No matter how talented you may be or how good an impression you made, you'll have to work hard to "stay visible."

There Are Rules, Just Like Any Game

It should already be obvious that the networking process is not only effective, but also quite deliberate in its objectives. There are two specific groups of people you must attempt to target: those who can give you information about an industry or career area and those who are potential employers. The line between these groups may often blur. Don't be concerned—you'll soon learn when (and how) to shift the focus from interviewer to interviewee.

To simplify this process, follow a single rule: Show interest in the field or job area under discussion, but wait to be asked about actually working for that company. During your informational interviews, you will be surprised at the number of times the person you're interviewing turns to you and asks, "Would you be interested in...?" Consider carefully what's being asked and, if you *would* be interested in the position under discussion, make your feelings known.

If the Process Scares You

Some of you will undoubtedly be hesitant about, even fear, the networking process. It is not an unusual response—it is very human to want to accomplish things "on your own," without anyone's help. Understandable and commendable as such independence might seem, it is, in reality, an impediment if it limits your involvement in this important process. Networking has such universal application because **there is no other effective way to bridge the gap between job applicant and job.** Employers are grateful for its existence. You should be, too.

Why Should You Network?

- To unearth current information about the industry, company and pertinent job functions. Remember: Your knowledge and understanding of broad industry trends, financial health, hiring opportunities, and the competitive picture are key.
- To investigate each company's hiring policies—who makes the decisions, who the key players are (personnel, staff managers), whether there's a hiring season, whether they prefer applicants going direct or through recruiters, etc.
- To sell yourself—discuss your interests and research activities—and leave your calling card, your resume.
- To seek out advice on refining your job search process.
- To obtain the names of other persons (referrals) who can give you additional information on where the jobs are and what the market conditions are like.
- To develop a list of follow-up activities that will keep you visible to key contacts.

Whether you are a first-time applicant or reentering the work force now that the children are grown, the networking process will more than likely be your point of entry. Sending out mass mailings of your resume and answering the help-wanted ads may well be less personal (and, therefore, "easier") approaches, but they will also be far less effective. The natural selection process of the networking phenomenon is your assurance that water does indeed seek its own level—you will be matched up with companies and job opportunities in which there is a mutual fit.

Six Good Reasons to Network

Many people fear the networking process because they think they are "bothering" others with their own selfish demands. Nonsense! There are good reasons—six of them, at least—why the people on your networking list will be happy to help you:

1. **Some day you will get to return the favor.** An ace insurance salesman built a successful business by offering low-cost coverage to first-year medical students. Ten years later, these now-successful practitioners remembered the company (and person) that helped them when they were just getting started. He gets new referrals every day.

2. **They, too, are seeking information.** An employer who has been out of school for several years might be interested in what the latest developments in the classroom are. He or she may be hoping to learn as much from you as you are from them, so be forthcoming in offering information. This desire for new information may be the reason he or she agreed to see you in the first place.

3. **Internal politics.** Some people will see you simply to make themselves appear powerful, implying to others in their organization that they have the authority to hire (they may or may not), an envied prerogative.

4. **They're "saving for a rainy day".** Executives know that it never hurts to look and that maintaining a backlog of qualified candidates is a big asset when the floodgates open and supervisors are forced to hire quickly.

5. **They're just plain nice.** Some people will see you simply because they feel it's the decent thing to do or because they just can't say "no."

6. **They are looking themselves.** Some people will see you because they are anxious to do a friend (whoever referred you) a favor. Or because they have another friend seeking new talent, in which case you represent a referral they can make (part of their own continuing network process). You see, networking never does stop—it helps them and it helps you.

Before you proceed to the next chapter, begin making your contact list. You may wish to keep a separate sheet of paper or note card on each person (especially the dozen or so you think are most important), even a separate telephone list to make your communications easier and more efficient. However you set up your list, be sure to keep it up to date—it won't be long before you'll be calling each and every name on the list.

CHAPTER TWENTY-EIGHT

Preparing Your Resume

Your resume is a one-page summary of you—your education, skills, employment experience and career objective(s). It is not a biography, but a "quick and dirty" way to identify and describe you to potential employers. Most importantly, its real purpose is to sell you to the company you want to work for. It must set you apart from all the other applicants (those competitors) out there.

So, as you sit down to formulate your resume, remember you're trying to present the pertinent information in a format and manner that will convince an executive to grant you an interview, the prelude to any job offer. All resumes must follow two basic rules—excellent visual presentation and honesty—but it's important to realize that different career markets require different resumes. The resume you are compiling for your career in psychology and mental health is different than one you would prepare for a finance career. As more and more resume "training" services become available, employers are becoming increasingly choosy about the resumes they receive. They expect to view a professional presentation, one that sets a candidate apart from the crowd. Your resume has to be perfect and it has to be specialized—clearly demonstrating the relationship between your qualifications and the job you are applying for.

An Overview of Resume Preparation

- **Know what you're doing**—your resume is a personal billboard of accomplishments. It must communicate your worth to a prospective employer in specific terms.
- **Your language should be action-oriented,** full of "doing"-type words. And less is better than more—be concise and direct. Don't worry about using complete sentences.

- **Be persuasive.** In those sections that allow you the freedom to do so, don't hesitate to communicate your worth in the strongest language. This does not mean a numbing list of self-congratulatory superlatives; it does mean truthful claims about your abilities and the evidence (educational, experiential) that supports them.

- **Don't be cheap or gaudy.** Don't hesitate to spend the few extra dollars necessary to present a professional-looking resume. Do avoid outlandish (and generally ineffective) gimmicks like oversized or brightly-colored paper.

- **Find an editor.** Every good writer needs one, and you are writing your resume. At the very least, it will offer you a second set of eyes proofreading for embarrassing typos. But if you are fortunate enough to have a professional in the field—a recruiter or personnel executive—critique a draft, grab the opportunity and be immensely grateful.

- **If you're the next Michelangelo,** so multitalented that you can easily qualify for jobs in different career areas, don't hesitate to prepare two or more completely different resumes. This will enable you to change the emphasis on your education and skills according to the specific career objective on each resume, a necessary alteration that will correctly target each one.

- **Choose the proper format.** There are only three we recommend—chronological, functional, and targeted format—and it's important you use the one that's right for you.

Considerations in the Electronic Age

Like most other areas of everyday life, computers have left their mark in the resume business. There are the obvious changes—the increased number of personal computers has made it easier to produce a professional-looking resume at home—and the not so obvious changes, such as the development of resume databases.

There are two kinds of resume databases: 1) An internal file maintained by a large corporation to keep track of the flood of resumes it gets each day (*U.S. News and World Report* stated that Fortune 50 companies receive more than 1,000 unsolicited resumes a day and that four out of every five are thrown away after a quick review). 2) Commercial databases that solicit resumes from job-seekers around the United States and make them available to corporations, who pay a fee to search the database.

Internal Databases Mean Some of the Old Rules Don't Apply

The internal databases maintained by large companies are changing some of the time-honored traditions of resume preparation. In the past, it was acceptable, even desirable, to use italic type and other eye-catching formats to make a resume more visually appealing. Not so today. Most of the companies that have a database enter resumes into it by using an optical scanner that reads the resume character by character and automatically enters it into the database. While these scanners are becoming more and more sophisticated, there are still significant limits as to what they can recognize and interpret.

What does this mean to you? It means that in addition to the normal screening process that all resumes go through, there is now one more screening step that determines if the scanner will be able to read your resume. If it can't, chances are your resume is going to be one of the four that is thrown away, instead of the one that is kept. To enhance the chances of your resume making it past this scanner test, here are some simple guidelines you can follow:

- Use larger typefaces (nothing smaller than 12 point), and avoid all but the most basic typefaces. Among the most common are Times Roman and Helvetica.
- No italics or underlining, and definitely no graphic images or boxes.
- Do not send copies. Either print a fresh copy out on your own printer, or take the resume to a print shop and have it professionally copied onto high-quality paper. Avoid dot matrix printers.
- Use 8 1/2 x 11 paper, unfolded. Any words that end up in a crease will not be scannable.
- Use only white or beige paper. Any other color will lessen the contrast between the paper and the letters and make it harder for the scanner to read.
- Use only a single column format. Scanners read from right to left on a page, so two- or three-columns formats lead to nonsensical information when the document is scanned.
- While it is still appropriate to use action words to detail your accomplishments (initiated, planned, implemented, etc.), it is also important to include precise technical terms whenever possible as well. That's because databases are searched by key words, and only resumes that match those key words will be looked at. For example, if a publishing company was seeking someone who was experienced in a desktop publishing, they might search the database for all occurrences of "PageMaker" or "Ventura," two common desktop publishing software packages. If your resume only said "Successfully implemented and oversaw in-house desktop publishing program," it would be overlooked, and you wouldn't get the job!

National Databases: Spreading Your Good Name Around

Commercial resume databases are also having an impact on the job search process in the 1990s, so much so that anyone about to enter the job market should seriously consider utilizing one of these services.

Most of these new services work this way: Job-seekers send the database company a copy of their resume, or they fill out a lengthy application provided by the company. The information is then loaded into the company's computer, along with hundreds of other resumes from other job-seekers. The cost of this listing is usually nominal—$20 to $50 for a six- to 12-month listing. Some colleges operate systems for their graduates that are free of charge, so check with your placement office before utilizing a commercial service.

Once in the system, the resumes are available for viewing by corporate clients who have openings to fill. This is where the database companies really make their money—depending on the skill-level of the listees and the professions covered, companies can pay thousands of dollars for annual subscriptions to the service or for custom searches of the database.

Worried that your current employer might just pull up *your* resume when it goes searching for new employees? No need to be—most services allow listees to designate companies that their resume should not be released to, thus allowing you to conduct a job search with the peace of mind that your boss won't find out!

One warning about these services—most of them are new, so do as much research as you can before paying to have your resume listed. If you hear about a database you think you might want to be listed in, call the company and ask some questions:

- How long have they been in business?
- What has their placement rate been?
- What fields do they specialize in? (In other words, will the right people even *see* your resume?)
- Can you block certain companies from seeing your resume?
- How many other resumes are listed in the database? How many in your specialty?
- Is your experience level similar to that of other listees in the database?

The right answers to these questions should let you know if you have found the right database for you.

To help you locate these resume databases, we have listed many of them in the **Career Resources** chapter of this book.

The Records You Need

Well, now that you've heard all the dos and don'ts and rules about preparing a resume, it's time to put those rules to work. The resume-writing process begins with the assembly and organization of all the personal, educational, and employment data from which you will choose the pieces that actually end up on paper. If this information is properly organized, writing your resume will be a relatively easy task, essentially a simple process of just shifting data from a set of the worksheets to another, to your actual resume. At the end of this chapter, you'll find all the forms you need to prepare your resume, including worksheets, fill-in-the-blanks resume forms, and sample resumes.

As you will soon see, there is a great deal of information you'll need to keep track of. In order to avoid a fevered search for important information, take the time right now to designate a single location in which to store all your records. My recommendation is either a filing cabinet or an expandable pocket portfolio. The latter is less expensive, yet it will still enable you to sort your records into an unlimited number of more-manageable categories.

Losing important report cards, citations, letters, etc., is easy to do if your life's history is scattered throughout your room or, even worse, your house! While copies of many of these items may be obtainable, why put yourself through all that extra work? Making good organization a habit will ensure that all the records you need to prepare your resume will be right where you need them when you need them.

For each of the categories summarized below, designate a separate file folder in which pertinent records can be kept. Your own notes are important, but keeping actual report cards, award citations, letters, etc. is even more so. Here's what your record-keeping system should include:

Transcripts (Including GPA and Class Rank Information)

Transcripts are your school's official record of your academic history, usually available, on request, from your high school's guidance office or college registrar's office. Your college may charge you for copies and "on request" doesn't mean "whenever you want"—you may have to wait some time for your request to be processed (so **don't** wait until the last minute!).

Your school-calculated GPA (Grade Point Average) is on the transcript. Most schools calculate this by multiplying the credit hours assigned to each course times a numerical grade equivalent (e.g., "A" = 4.0, "B" = 3.0, etc.), then dividing by total credits/courses taken. Class rank is simply a listing of GPAs, from highest to lowest.

Employment Records

Details on every part-time or full-time job you've held, including:

- Each employer's name, address and telephone number
- Name of supervisor
- Exact dates worked
- Approximate numbers of hours per week
- Specific duties and responsibilities
- Specific skills utilized and developed
- Accomplishments, honors
- Copies of awards, letters of recommendation

Volunteer Activities

Just because you weren't paid for a specific job—stuffing envelopes for the local Democratic candidate, running a car wash to raise money for the homeless, manning a drug hotline—doesn't mean that it wasn't significant or that you shouldn't include it on your resume.

So keep the same detailed notes on these volunteer activities as you have on the jobs you've held:

- Each organization's name, address and telephone number
- Name of supervisor
- Exact dates worked

- Approximate numbers of hours per week
- Specific duties and responsibilities
- Specific skills utilized
- Accomplishments, honors
- Copies of awards, letters of recommendation

Extracurricular Activities

List all sports, clubs, or other activities in which you've participated, either inside or outside school. For each, you should include:

- Name of activity/club/group
- Office(s) held
- Purpose of club/activity
- Specific duties/responsibilities
- Achievements, accomplishments, awards

If you were a long-standing member of a group or club, also include the dates that you were a member. This could demonstrate a high-level of commitment that could be used as a selling point.

Honors and Awards

Even if some of these honors are previously listed, specific data on every honor or award you receive should be kept, including, of course, the award itself! Keep the following information in your awards folder:

- Award name
- Date and from whom received
- What it was for
- Any pertinent details

Military Records

Complete military history, if pertinent, including:

- Dates of service
- Final rank awarded
- Duties and responsibilities
- All citations and awards
- Details on specific training and/or special schooling
- Skills developed
- Specific accomplishments

At the end of this chapter are seven **Data Input Sheets**. The first five cover employment, volunteer work, education, activities, and awards and are essential to any resume. The last two—covering military service and language skills—are important if, of course, they apply to you. I've only included one copy of each but, if you need to, you can copy the forms you need or simply write up your own using these as models.

Here are some pointers on how to fill out these all-important Data Sheets:

Employment Data Input Sheet: You will need to record the basic information—employer's name, address, and phone number; dates of employment; and supervisor's name—for your own files anyway. It may be an important addition to your networking list and will be necessary should you be asked to supply a reference list.

Duties should be a series of brief action statements describing what you did on this job. For example, if you worked as a hostess in a restaurant, this section might read: "Responsible for the delivery of 250 meals at dinner time and the supervision of 20 waiters and busboys. Coordinated reservations. Responsible for check and payment verification."

Skills should enumerate specific capabilities either necessary for the job or developed through it.

If you achieved *specific results*—e.g., "developed new filing system," "collected over $5,000 in previously-assumed bad debt," "instituted award-winning art program," etc.—or *received any award, citation or other honor*—"named Employee of the Month three times," "received Mayor's Citation for Innovation," etc.—make sure you list these.

Prepare one employment data sheet for each of the last three positions you have held; this is a basic guideline, but you can include more if relevant. Do not include sheets for short-term jobs (i.e., those that lasted one month or less).

Volunteer Work Data Input Sheet: Treat any volunteer work, no matter how basic or short (one day counts!), as if it were a job and record the same information. In both cases, it is especially important to note specific duties and responsibilities, skills required or developed and any accomplishments or achievements you can point to as evidence of your success.

Educational Data Input Sheet: If you're in college, omit details on high school. If you're a graduate student, list details on both graduate and undergraduate coursework. If you have not yet graduated, list your anticipated date of graduation. If more than a year away, indicate the numbers of credits earned through the most recent semester to be completed.

Activities Data Input Sheet: List your participation in the Student Government, Winter Carnival Committee, Math Club, Ski Patrol, etc., plus sports teams and/or any participation in community or church groups. Make sure you indicate if you were elected to any positions in clubs, groups, or on teams.

Awards And Honors Data Input Sheet: List awards and honors from your school (prestigious high school awards can still be included here, even if you're in graduate school), community groups, church groups, clubs, etc.

Military Service Data Input Sheet: Many useful skills are learned in the armed forces. A military stint often hastens the maturation process, making you a more attractive candidate. So if you have served in the military, make sure you include details in your resume. Again, include any computer skills you gained while in the service.

Language Data Input Sheet: An extremely important section for those of you with a real proficiency in a second language. And do make sure you have at least conversational fluency in the language(s) you list. One year of college French doesn't count, but if you've studied abroad, you probably are fluent or proficient. Such a talent could be invaluable, especially in today's increasingly international business climate.

While you should use the Data Input Sheets to summarize all of the data you have collected, do not throw away any of the specific information—report cards, transcripts, citations, etc.—just because it is recorded on these sheets. Keep all records in your files; you'll never know when you'll need them again!

Creating Your First Resume

There are many options that you can include or leave out. In general, we suggest you always include the following data:

1. Your name, address and telephone number
2. Pertinent educational history (grades, class rank, activities, etc.) Follow the grade point "rule of thumb"—mention it only if it is above 3.0.
3. Pertinent work history
4. Academic honors
5. Memberships in organizations
6. Military service history (if applicable)

You have the option of including the following:

1. Your career objective
2. Personal data
3. Hobbies
4. Summary of qualifications
5. Feelings about travel and relocation (Include this if you know in advance that the job you are applying for requires it. Often times, for future promotion, job seekers **must** be willing to relocate.

And you should never include the following:

1. Photographs or illustrations (of yourself or anything else) unless they are required by your profession—e.g., actors' composites
2. Why you left past jobs
3. References
4. Salary history or present salary objectives/requirements (if salary history is specifically requested in an ad, it may be included in your cover letter)

Special note: There is definitely a school of thought that discourages any mention of personal data—marital status, health, etc.—on a resume. While I am not vehemently opposed to including such information, I am not convinced it is particularly necessary, either.

As far as hobbies go, I would only include such information if it were in some way pertinent to the job/career you're targeting, or if it shows how well-rounded you are. Your love of reading is pertinent if, for example, you are applying for a part-time job at a library. But including details on the joys of "hiking, long walks with my dog and Isaac Asimov short stories" is nothing but filler and should be left out.

Maximizing Form and Substance

Your resume should be limited to a single page if possible. A two-page resume should be used **only** if you have an extensive work background related to a future goal. When you're laying out the resume, try to leave a reasonable amount of "white space"—generous margins all around and spacing between entries. It should be typed or printed (not Xeroxed) on 8 1/2" x 11" white, cream, or ivory stock. The ink should be black. Don't scrimp on the paper quality—use the best bond you can afford. And since printing 100 or even 200 copies will cost only a little more than 50, if you do decide to print your resume, *over*estimate your needs and opt for the highest quantity you think you may need. Prices at various "quick print" shops are not exorbitant and the quality look printing affords will leave the impression you want.

Use Power Words for Impact

Be brief. Use phrases rather than complete sentences. Your resume is a summary of your talents, not a term paper. Choose your words carefully and use "power words" whenever possible. "Organized" is more powerful than "put together;" "supervised" better than "oversaw;" "formulated" better than "thought up." Strong words like these can make the most mundane clerical work sound like a series of responsible, professional positions. And, of course, they will tend to make your resume stand out. Here's a starter list of words that you may want to use in your resume:

accomplished	budgeted	critiqued	expanded
achieved	built	defined	fixed
acted	calculated	delegated	forecast
adapted	chaired	delivered	formulated
addressed	changed	demonstrated	gathered
administered	classified	designed	gave
advised	collected	determined	generated
allocated	communicated	developed	guided
analyzed	compiled	devised	implemented
applied	completed	directed	improved
approved	composed	discovered	initiated
arranged	computed	drafted	installed
assembled	conceptualized	edited	instituted
assessed	conducted	established	instructed
assigned	consolidated	estimated	introduced
assisted	contributed	evaluated	invented
attained	coordinated	executed	issued

launched	oversaw	remodeled	streamlined
learned	participated	renovated	studied
lectured	planned	reorganized	suggested
led	prepared	researched	supervised
litigated	presented	restored	systematized
lobbied	presided	reviewed	taught
made	produced	revised	tested
managed	programmed	rewrote	trained
marketed	promoted	saved	updated
mediated	proposed	scheduled	upgraded
negotiated	publicized	selected	utilized
obtained	ran	served	won
operated	recommended	sold	wrote
organized	recruited	solved	
overhauled	regulated	started	

Choose the Right Format

There is not much mystery here—your background will generally lead you to the right format. For an entry-level job applicant with limited work experience, the chronological format, which organizes your educational and employment history by date (most recent first) is the obvious choice. For older or more experienced applicants, the functional—which emphasizes the duties and responsibilities of all your jobs over the course of your career, may be more suitable. If you are applying for a specific position in one field, the targeted format is for you. While I have tended to emphasize the chronological format in this chapter, one of the other two may well be the right one for you.

A List of Do's and Don't's

In case we didn't stress them enough, here are some rules to follow:

- **Do** be brief and to the point—Two pages if absolutely necessary, one page if at all possible. Never longer!
- **Don't** be fancy. Multicolored paper and all-italic type won't impress employers, just make your resume harder to read (and easier to discard). Use plain white or ivory paper, black ink and an easy-to-read standard typeface.
- **Do** forget rules about sentences. Say what you need to say in the fewest words possible; use phrases, not drawn-out sentences.
- **Do** stick to the facts. Don't talk about your dog, vacation, etc.
- **Don't** ever send a resume blind. A cover letter should always accompany a resume and that letter should always be directed to a specific person.
- **Don't** have any typos. Your resume must be perfect—proofread everything as many times as necessary to catch any misspellings, grammatical errors, strange hyphenations, or typos.

- **Do** use the spell check feature on your personal computer to find errors, and also try reading the resume backwards—you'll be surprised at how errors jump out at you when you do this. Finally, have a friend proof your resume.
- **Do** use your resume as your sales tool. It is, in many cases, as close to you as an employer will ever get. Make sure it includes the information necessary to sell yourself the way you want to be sold!
- **Do** spend the money for good printing. Soiled, tattered or poorly reproduced copies speak poorly of your own self-image. Spend the money and take the time to make sure your resume is the best presentation you've ever made.
- **Do** help the reader, by organizing your resume in a clear-cut manner so key points are easily gleaned.
- **Don't** have a cluttered resume. Leave plenty of white space, especially around headings and all four margins.
- **Do** use bullets, asterisks, or other symbols as "stop signs" that the reader's eye will be naturally drawn to.

On the following pages, I've included a "fill-in-the-blanks" resume form so you can construct your own resume right away, plus one example each of a chronological, functional, and targeted resume.

MENTAL HEALTH CAREER DIRECTORY

EMPLOYMENT DATA INPUT SHEET

Employer name: _____

Address: _____

Phone: _____ Dates of employment: _____

Hours per week: _____ Salary/Pay: _____

Supervisor's name and title: _____

Duties: _____

_____

_____

Skills utilized: _____

_____

_____

_____

Accomplishments/Honors/Awards: _____

_____

_____

_____

Other important information: _____

_____

_____

_____

VOLUNTEER WORK DATA INPUT SHEET

Organization name: _____

Address: _____

Phone: _____ Dates of activity: _____

Hours per week: _____

Supervisor's name and title: _____

Duties: _____

_____

_____

Skills utilized: _____

_____

_____

_____

Accomplishments/Honors/Awards: _____

_____

_____

_____

Other important information: _____

_____

_____

_____

MENTAL HEALTH CAREER DIRECTORY

HIGH SCHOOL DATA INPUT SHEET

School name: _____

Address: _____

Phone: _____ Years attended: _____

Major studies: _____

GPA/Class rank: _____

Honors: _____

Important courses: _____

_____

_____

_____

OTHER SCHOOL DATA INPUT SHEET

School name: _____

Address: _____

Phone: _____ Years attended: _____

Major studies: _____

GPA/Class rank: _____

Honors: _____

Important courses _____

_____

_____

_____

COLLEGE DATA INPUT SHEET

College: _____

Address: _____

Phone: _____ Years attended: _____

Degrees earned: _____ Major: _____ Minor: _____

Honors: _____

Important courses: _____

_____

_____

_____

_____

GRADUATE SCHOOL DATA INPUT SHEET

College: _____

Address: _____

Phone: _____ Years attended: _____

Degrees earned: _____ Major: _____ Minor: _____

Honors: _____

Important courses: _____

_____

_____

_____

_____

MENTAL HEALTH CAREER DIRECTORY

MILITARY SERVICE DATA INPUT SHEET

Branch: _____

Rank (at discharge): _____

Dates of service: _____

Duties and responsibilities: _____

_____

_____

_____

Special training and/or school attended: _____

_____

_____

_____

Citations or awards: _____

_____

_____

_____

Specific accomplishments: _____

_____

_____

_____

_____

ACTIVITIES DATA INPUT SHEET

Club/activity: _____ Office(s) held: _____

Description of participation: _____

_____

_____

Duties/responsibilities: _____

_____

Club/activity: _____ Office(s) held: _____

Description of participation: _____

_____

_____

Duties/responsibilities: _____

_____

Club/activity: _____ Office(s) held: _____

Description of participation: _____

_____

_____

Duties/responsibilities: _____

_____

_____

MENTAL HEALTH CAREER DIRECTORY

AWARDS AND HONORS DATA INPUT SHEET

Name of Award or Citation: _____

From Whom Received: _____ Date: _____

Significance: _____

_____

Other pertinent information: _____

_____

Name of Award or Citation: _____

From Whom Received: _____ Date: _____

Significance: _____

_____

Other pertinent information: _____

_____

Name of Award or Citation: _____

From Whom Received: _____ Date: _____

Significance: _____

_____

Other pertinent information: _____

_____

LANGUAGE DATA INPUT SHEET

Language: _____

___Read   ___Write   ___Converse

Background (number of years studied, travel, etc.) _____

_____

_____

_____

Language: _____

___Read   ___Write   ___Converse

Background (number of years studied, travel, etc.) _____

_____

_____

_____

Language: _____

___Read   ___Write   ___Converse

Background (number of years studied, travel, etc.) _____

_____

_____

_____

FILL-IN-THE-BLANKS RESUME OUTLINE

Name: _____

Address: _____

City, state, ZIP Code: _____

Telephone number: _____

OBJECTIVE: _____

_____

_____

_____

_____

SUMMARY OF QUALIFICATIONS: _____

_____

_____

_____

EDUCATION

GRADUATE SCHOOL: _____

Address: _____

City, state, ZIP Code: _____

Expected graduation date: _____ Grade Point Average: _____

Degree earned (expected): _____ Class Rank: _____

Important classes, especially those related to your career: _____

_____

_____

_____

_____

_____

_____

_____

The Job Search Process

COLLEGE: _____

Address: _____

City, state, ZIP Code: _____

Expected graduation date:_____ Grade Point Average: _____

Class rank:_____ Major:_____ Minor:_____

Important classes, especially those related to your career: _____

_____

_____

_____

_____

_____

_____

_____

_____

MENTAL HEALTH CAREER DIRECTORY

HIGH SCHOOL: _____

Address: _____

City, state, ZIP Code: _____

Expected graduation date: _____ Grade Point Average: _____

Class rank: _____

Important classes, especially those related to your career: _____
_____
_____
_____
_____
_____
_____
_____

HOBBIES AND OTHER INTERESTS (OPTIONAL) _____
_____
_____
_____
_____
_____
_____
_____
_____

EXTRACURRICULAR ACTIVITIES (Activity name, dates participated, duties and responsibilities, offices held, accomplishments): _____

_____
_____
_____
_____
_____
_____
_____
_____
_____

AWARDS AND HONORS (Award name, from whom and date received, significance of the award and any other pertinent details): _____

_____
_____
_____
_____
_____
_____
_____
_____
_____
_____

MENTAL HEALTH CAREER DIRECTORY

WORK EXPERIENCE. Include job title, name of business, address and telephone number, dates of employment, supervisor's name and title, your major responsibilities, accomplishments, and any awards won. Include volunteer experience in this category. List your experiences with the most recent dates first, even if you later decide not to use a chronological format.

_____

_____

_____

_____

_____

_____

_____

_____

_____

_____

_____

_____

_____

_____

_____

_____

_____

_____

_____

REFERENCES. Though you should *not* include references in your resume, you do need to prepare a separate list of at least three people who know you fairly well and will recommend you highly to prospective employers. For each, include job title, company name, address, and telephone number. Before you include anyone on this list, make sure you have their permission to use their name as a reference and confirm what they intend to say about you to a potential employer.

1. _____

_____

_____

2. _____

_____

_____

3. _____

_____

_____

4. _____

_____

_____

5. _____

_____

_____

SAMPLE RESUME - CHRONOLOGICAL

ANGELA N. JETT

Local	Permanent
N. Quad # 367	852 Brittany Ct.
Los Angeles, CA 90078	Novato, CA 94947
(415) 002-5940	(415) 039-4930

EDUCATION

Bachelor of Arts in **Social Work**
University of Southern California
Los Angeles, CA
May, 1994
Cum Laude

PROFESSIONAL EXPERIENCE

Summer, 1993

Intern, Hospice of Southern California   San Francisco, CA
- Trained in group grief counseling; accompanied counselor during visits to client homes and AIDS shelter.

Summer, 1992

Intern, Kingswood Mental Hospital   Novato, CA
- Learned intake procedures for patients including case write-up.

EMPLOYMENT

University of Southern California   Los Angeles, CA

9/93 - Present
9/92 - 5/93
9/91 - 5/92

Placement Department Receptionist
Duties include answering phone system for staff of seven; greeting students and employers; handling difficult situations; typing correspondence and tracking postings for student employment service. Excellent working knowledge of WordPerfect 5.1, Paradox, Quattro Pro.

5/89 - 8/91

Andrew Cleaning Marin, CA Counter/Cashier

HONORS

Donald Hunt Scholarship Award
Social Work Honor Society, Secretary
National Honor Society

ACTIVITIES

All Star Soccer Team, Captain
Downhill skiing, camping, and fishing.
Enjoy home computing.

SAMPLE RESUME - FUNCTIONAL

ROBERT P. STACEY
1424 Lorene Ct.
Lindsey, OH 34615
(216) 993-1017

OBJECTIVE Entry level position in the Counseling Field. Special Area of Interest: **Substance Abuse Counseling.**

EDUCATION Bachelor of Arts   Major: Psychology
Cleveland State   Cleveland, OH
May, 1994   Overall GPA: 2.8   Major: 3.6
Certificate in Addiction Studies

Technical Expertise
Senior Project: *Peer Pressure: Reality or Excuse?*
Clear understanding and application of the 12 Step Process.
Computer knowledge: WP5.1, Quattro Pro.

Communications Ability
Resident Advisor for floor of 150 students; accompanied 50
first-year-students on wilderness trip.
Problem-solved difficult situations regarding dorm governance policies.
English tutor for International Students from countries such as Saudia Arabia and Thailand.

Counseling Knowledge
Participation in group counseling sessions.
Trained in hospital intake procedures.

EMPLOYMENT Cleveland State   9/92 - Present
Cleveland, OH
Residence Life Office
Resident Advisor

Barnes and Noble Bookstore   9/91 - 8/92
Cleveland, OH
Cashier/Stocker

Grace Hospital   Summer, 1991
Lindsey, OH
Intern in Patient Relations

EXTRA- Sigma Pi Social Fraternity
CURRICULAR Red Cross Donor
University Student AA Program, Facilitator

MENTAL HEALTH CAREER DIRECTORY

SAMPLE RESUME - TARGETED

VERONICA P. JONES
123 Forester Rd.
Detroit, MI 48221
(313) 793-1923

GOAL Caseworker

EDUCATION Bachelor of Arts in **Social Work**
University of Detroit Mercy
December, 1994
Honors: **Cum Laude**

ACCOMPLISHMENTS

First hand knowledge of government system and paperwork procedures.
Apprised of local area referral contacts including mental
health, medical, and child/parent resources.
Adept at treatment planning and monitoring medications.
Able to handle confidential information.

PROFESSIONAL EXPERIENCE

9/92 - Present   Moore Day Care Center   Ferndale, MI
Organized activities and schedules for group field trips.
Key Results: Dealt effectively with both children and parents.
Handled difficult situations as needed.

9/91 - 8/92   Social Security Administration Co-op   Detroit, MI
Key Results: Learned all aspects of federal regulations and practiced counseling techniques.

Summer, 1990-91   Interdependence Intern   Detroit, MI
Key Results: As residential advisor, assisted clients in daily living. Set realistic goals with clients and assisted them in successful achievement methods.

HONORS Dean's List
Academic Scholarship
National Honor Society

PERSONAL INTERESTS
- Student Association of Social Workers
- Afro American Association
- Focus Hope Walk
- March of Dimes Volunteer
- State Fair Community Theater

REFERENCES   Furnished Upon Request

CHAPTER TWENTY-NINE

Writing Better Letters

Stop for a moment and review your resume draft. It is undoubtedly (by now) a near-perfect document that instantly tells the reader the kind of job you want and why you are qualified. But does it say anything personal about you? Any amplification of your talents? Any words that are ideally "you?" Any hint of the kind of person who stands behind that resume?

If you've prepared it properly, the answers should be a series of ringing "no's"—your resume should be a mere sketch of your life, a bare-bones summary of your skills, education, and experience.

To the general we must add the specific. That's what your letters must accomplish—adding the lines, colors, and shading that will help fill out your self-portrait. This chapter will cover the kinds of letters you will most often be called upon to prepare in your job search. There are essentially nine different types you will utilize again and again, based primarily on what each is trying to accomplish. One well-written example of each is included at the end of this chapter.

Answer these Questions

Before you put pencil to paper to compose any letter, there are five key questions you must ask yourself:

- **Why** are you writing it?
- To **Whom**?
- **What** are you trying to accomplish?
- **Which** lead will get the reader's attention?
- **How** do you organize the letter to best accomplish your objectives?

Why?

There should be a single, easily definable reason you are writing any letter. This reason will often dictate what and how you write—the tone and flavor of the letter—as well as what you include or leave out.

Have you been asked in an ad to amplify your qualifications for a job and provide a salary history and college transcripts? Then that (minimally) is your objective in writing. Limit yourself to following instructions and do a little personal selling—but very little. Including everything asked for and a simple, adequate cover letter is better than writing a "knock 'em, sock 'em" letter and omitting the one piece of information the ad specifically asked for.

If, however, you are on a networking search, the objective of your letter is to seek out contacts who will refer you for possible informational or job interviews. In this case, getting a name and address—a referral—is your stated purpose for writing. You have to be specific and ask for this action.

You will no doubt follow up with a phone call, but be certain the letter conveys what you are after. Being vague or oblique won't help you. You are after a definite yes or no when it comes to contact assistance. The recipient of your letter should know this. As they say in the world of selling, at some point you have to ask for the order.

Who?

Using the proper "tone" in a letter is as important as the content—you wouldn't write to the owner of the local meat market using the same words and style as you would employ in a letter to the director of personnel of a major company. Properly addressing the person or persons you are writing to is as important as what you say to them.

Always utilize the recipient's job title and level (correct title and spelling are a **must**). If you know what kind of person they are (based on your knowledge of their area of involvement) use that knowledge to your advantage as well. It also helps if you know his or her hiring clout, but even if you know the letter is going through a screening stage instead of to the actual person you need to contact, don't take the easy way out. You have to sell the person doing the screening just as convincingly as you would the actual contact, or else you might get passed over instead of passed along! Don't underestimate the power of the person doing the screening.

For example, it pays to sound technical with technical people—in other words, use the kinds of words and language which they use on the job. If you have had the opportunity to speak with them, it will be easy for you. If not, and you have formed some opinions as to their types then use these as the basis of the language you employ. The cardinal rule is to say it in words you think the recipient will be comfortable hearing, not in the words you might otherwise personally choose.

What?

What do you have to offer that company? What do you have to contribute to the job, process or work situation that is unique and/or of particular benefit to the recipient of your letter.

For example, if you were applying for a sales position and recently ranked number one in a summer sales job, then conveying this benefit is logical and desirable. It is a factor you may have left off your resume. Even if it was listed in the skills/accomplishment section of the resume, you can underscore and call attention to it in your letter. Repetition, when it is properly focused, can be a good thing.

Which?

Of all the opening sentences you can compose, which will immediately get the reader's attention? If your opening sentence is dynamic, you are already 50 percent of the way to your end objective—having your entire letter read. Don't slide into it. Know the point you are trying to make and come right to it. One word of caution: your first sentence **must** make mention of what led you to write—was it an ad, someone at the company, a story you saw on television? Be sure to give this point of reference.

How?

While a good opening is essential, how do you organize your letter so that it is easy for the recipient to read in its entirety? This is a question of *flow*—the way the words and sentences naturally lead one to another, holding the reader's interest until he or she reaches your signature.

If you have your objective clearly in mind, this task is easier than it sounds: Simply convey your message(s) in a logical sequence. End your letter by stating what the next steps are—yours and/or the reader's.

One More Time

Pay attention to the small things. Neatness still counts. Have your letters typed. Spend a few extra dollars and have some personal stationery printed.

And most important, make certain that your correspondence goes out quickly. The general rule is to get a letter in the mail during the week in which the project comes to your attention or in which you have had some contact with the organization. I personally attempt to mail follow-up letters the same day as the contact; at worst, within 24 hours.

When to Write

- To answer an ad
- To prospect (many companies)
- To inquire about specific openings (single company)
- To obtain a referral
- To obtain an informational interview
- To obtain a job interview
- To say "thank you"
- To accept or reject a job offer
- To withdraw from consideration for a job

In some cases, the letter will accompany your resume; in others, it will need to stand alone. Each of the above circumstance is described in the pages that follow. I have included at least one sample of each type of letter at the end of this chapter.

Answering an Ad

Your eye catches an ad in the Positions Available section of the Sunday paper for a substance abuse counselor. It tells you that the position is in a private facility and that, though some experience would be desirable, it is not required. Well, you possess *those* skills. The ad asks that you send a letter and resume to a Post Office Box. No salary is indicated, no phone number given. You decide to reply.

Your purpose in writing—the objective (why?)—is to secure a job interview. Since no person is singled out for receipt of the ad, and since it is a large company, you assume it will be screened by Human Resources.

Adopt a professional, formal tone. You are answering a "blind" ad, so you have to play it safe. In your first sentence, refer to the ad, including the place and date of publication and the position outlined. (There is a chance that the company is running more than one ad on the same date and in the same paper, so you need to identify the one to which you are replying.) Tell the reader what (specifically) you have to offer that company. Include your resume, phone number, and the times it is easiest to reach you. Ask for the order—tell them you'd like to have an appointment.

Blanket Prospecting Letter

In June of this year you will graduate from a four-year college with a degree in psychology. You seek a position (internship or full-time employment) at a substance abuse facility. You have decided to write to 50 private and government facilities, sending each a copy of your resume. You don't know which, if any, have job openings.

Such blanket mailings are effective given two circumstances: 1) You must have an exemplary record and a resume which reflects it; and 2) You must send out a goodly number of packages, since the response rate to such mailings is very low.

A blanket mailing doesn't mean an impersonal one—you should always be writing to a specific executive. If you have a referral, send a personalized letter to that person. If not, do not simply mail a package to the Human Resources department; identify the department head and *then* send a personalized letter. And make sure you get on the phone and follow up each letter within about ten days. Don't just sit back and wait for everyone to call you. They won't.

Just Inquiring

The inquiry letter is a step above the blanket prospecting letter; it's a "cold-calling" device with a twist. You have earmarked a company (and a person) as a possibility in your job search based on something you have read about them. Your general research tells you that it is a good place to work. Although you are not aware of any specific openings, you know that they employ entry-level personnel with your credentials.

While ostensibly inquiring about any openings, you are really just "referring yourself" to them in order to place your resume in front of the right person. This is what I would call a "why not?" attempt at securing a job interview. Its effectiveness depends on their actually having been in the news. This, after all, is your "excuse" for writing.

Networking

It's time to get out that folder marked "Contacts" and prepare a draft networking letter. The lead sentence should be very specific, referring immediately to the friend, colleague, etc. "who suggested I write you about..." Remember: Your objective is to secure an informational interview, pave the way for a job interview, and/or get referred to still other contacts.

This type of letter should not place the recipient in a position where a decision is necessary; rather, the request should be couched in terms of "career advice." The second paragraph can then inform the reader of your level of experience. Finally, be specific about seeking an appointment.

Unless you have been specifically asked by the referring person to do so, you will probably not be including a resume with such letters. So the letter itself must highlight your credentials, enabling the reader to gauge your relative level of experience. For entry-level personnel, education, of course, will be most important.

For an Informational Interview

Though the objectives of this letter are similar to those of the networking letter, they are not as personal. These are "knowledge quests" on your part and the recipient will most likely not be someone you have been referred to. The idea is to convince the reader of the sincerity of your research effort. Whatever selling you do, if you do any at all, will arise as a consequence of the meeting, not beforehand. A positive response to this type of request is in itself a good step forward. It is, after all, exposure, and amazing things can develop when people in authority agree to see you.

Thank-You Letters

Although it may not always seem so, manners do count in the job world. But what counts even more are the simple gestures that show you actually care—like writing a thank-you letter. A well-executed, timely thank-you note tells more about your personality than anything else you may have sent, and it also demonstrates excellent follow-through skills. It says something about the way you were brought up—whatever else your resume tells them, you are, at least, polite, courteous and thoughtful.

Thank-you letters may well become the beginning of an all-important dialogue that leads directly to a job. So be extra careful in composing them, and make certain that they are custom made for each occasion and person.

The following are the primary situations in which you will be called upon to write some variation of a thank-you letter:

1. After a job interview
2. After an informational interview

3. Accepting a job offer
4. Responding to rejection: While optional, such a letter is appropriate if you have been among the finalists in a job search or were rejected due to limited experience. Remember: Some day you'll *have* enough experience; make the interviewer want to stay in touch.
5. Withdrawing from consideration: Used when you decide you are no longer interested in a particular position. (A variation is usable for declining an actual job offer.) Whatever the reason for writing such a letter, it's wise to do so and thus keep future lines of communication open.

IN RESPONSE TO AN AD

10 E. 89th Street
New York, NY 10028
October 22, 1993

The New York Times
PO Box 7520
New York, NY 10128

Dear Sir or Madam:

This letter is in response to your advertisement for a clinical psychologist which appeared in the October 18th issue of the *New York Times*.

I have the qualifications you are seeking. I graduated from American University with a B.S. in psychology and an M.A. in counseling psychology. I then received a doctor of psychology degree from Thomas Jefferson University.

I did my internship at Maryville Mental Health Center last year and then finished my dissertation. For the past year, I have been completing my residency at the Johnson University Hospital's Mental Health Center. I am a member of the National Society of Clinical Psychologists and the American Psychological Association.

My resume is enclosed. I would like to have the opportunity to meet with you personally to discuss your requirements for the position. I can be reached at (212) 785-1225 between 8:00 a.m. and 5:00 p.m. and at (212) 785-4221 after 5:00 p.m. I look forward to hearing from you.

Sincerely,

Karen Weber, Psy.D.

Enclosure: Resume

MENTAL HEALTH CAREER DIRECTORY

PROSPECTING LETTER

>Kim Kerr
>8 Robutuck Hwy.
>Hammond, IN 54054
>555-875-2392

October 22, 1993

Mr. Fred Jones
Personnel Director
Alcott Community Hospital
Family Therapy Clinic
Chicago, Illinois 91221

Dear Mr. Jones:

The name of Alcott Hospital's Family Therapy Clinic continually pops up in our classroom discussions of outstanding mental health facilities. Given my interest in psychology as a career and family therapy as a specialty, I've taken the liberty of enclosing my resume.

As you can see, I have just completed a very comprehensive educational program at Warren University, majoring in clinical psychology with a minor in counseling. Though my resume does not indicate it, I will be graduating in the top 10% of my class, with honors.

I will be in the Chicago area on November 29 and will call your office to see when it is convenient to arrange an appointment.

Sincerely yours,

Kim Kerr

INQUIRY LETTER

42 7th Street
Ski City, Vermont 85722

October 22, 1993

Dr. Michael Maniaci
Executive Director
Pinnacle Art Therapy Center
521 West Elm Street
Indianapolis, IN 83230

Dear Dr. Maniaci:

I just completed reading the article in the January issue of *Psychology Today* on your company's ground-breaking new techniques. Congratulations!

Your innovative approach to recruiting minorities is of particular interest to me because of my background in psychology and minority recruitment.

I am interested in learning more about your work as well as the possibilities of joining your company. My qualifications include:

- M.A. in Art Therapy
- Research on minority recruitment
- Art Therapy Seminar participation (Univ. of Virginia)
- Reports preparation on art therapy, imagery, and minorities

I will be in Indiana during the week of November 22 and hope your schedule will permit us to meet briefly to discuss our mutual interests. I will call your office next week to see if such a meeting can be arranged.

I appreciate your consideration.

Sincerely yours,

Ronald W. Sommerville

MENTAL HEALTH CAREER DIRECTORY

NETWORKING LETTER

Rochelle A. Starky
42 Bach St.
Musical City, IN 20202
317-555-1515

October 22, 1993

Dr. Michelle Fleming
Executive Director
Heights Community Hospital
42 Jenkins Avenue
Fulton, Missouri 23232

Dear Dr. Fleming:

Sam Kinney suggested I write you. I am interested in a school social worker position in a high school setting, and Sam felt it would be mutually beneficial for us to meet and talk.

I have an B.S. from Musical City University in psychology and an M.S.W. from the University of Kettering School of Social Work. While working on my postgraduate degree, I worked as a social worker in the Missouri Department of Social Services. I also worked for a year as an intern at the Parnell Pediatric facility in Jefferson City.

I know from Sam how similar our backgrounds are—the same training, the same interests. And, of course, I am aware of how successful you have managed your career—three promotions in four years!

As I begin my job search during the next few months, I am certain your advice would help me. Would it be possible for us to meet briefly? My resume is enclosed.

I will call your office next week to see when your schedule would permit such a meeting.

Sincerely,

Rochelle A. Starky

TO OBTAIN AN INFORMATIONAL INTERVIEW

16 NW 128th Street
Raleigh, NC 757755
October 22, 1992

Ms. Jackie B. McClure
General Manager
Golden County Social Services
484 Smithers Road
Awkmont, North Carolina 76857

Dear Ms. McClure:

I'm sure a good deal of the credit for your facility's success last year is attributable to the highly-motivated and knowledgeable staff you have recruited during the last three years. I hope to obtain a social services position with a facility just as committed to growth.

I have two years of social work experience, which I acquired while working as an intern at the Gullway Mental Health Center. I graduated from Gresham University with a B.S. in psychology and an M.S.W. from their School of Social Work. I believe my experience as well as my education have properly prepared me for a career in social work.

As I begin my job search, I am trying to gather as much information and advice as possible before applying for positions. Could I take a few minutes of your time next week to discuss my career plans? I will call your office on Monday, October 29, to see if such a meeting can be arranged.

I appreciate your consideration and look forward to meeting you.

Sincerely,

Karen R. Burns

MENTAL HEALTH CAREER DIRECTORY

AFTER AN INFORMATIONAL INTERVIEW

Lazelle Wright
921 West Fourth Street
Steamboat, Colorado 72105
303-310-3303

November 22, 1993

Dr. James R. Payne
Managing Director
Bradley Finch Mental Health Clinic
241 Snowridge
Ogden, Utah 72108

Dear Dr. Payne:

Jinny Bastienelli was right when she said you would be most helpful in advising me on a career in psychology.

I appreciated your taking the time from your busy schedule to meet with me. Your advice was most helpful and I have incorporated your suggestions into my resume. I will send you a copy next week.

Again, thanks so much for your assistance. As you suggested, I will contact Joe Simmons at Cregskill County Hospital next week in regard to a possible opening with his facility.

Sincerely,

Lazelle Wright

AFTER A JOB INTERVIEW

1497 Lilac Street
Old Adams, MA 01281
November 22, 1993

Mr. Rudy Delacort
Director of Personnel
Ann Grace Hospital
175 Boylston Avenue
Ribbit, Massachusetts 02857

Dear Mr. Delacort:

Thank you for the opportunity to interview yesterday for the staff psychologist position. I enjoyed meeting with you and Dr. Cliff Stoudt and learning more about Ann Grace.

Your facility appears to be growing in a direction which parallels my interests and goals. The interview with you and your staff confirmed my initial positive impressions of Ann Grace, and I want to reiterate my strong interest in working for you.

I am convinced that my prior experience as an intern with the Fellowes Pediatric Center in Old Adams, fellowship with the Prattsville County Hospital, and M.S.W. from the University of Adams School of Social Work would enable me to progress steadily through your training program and become a productive member of your staff.

Again, thank you for your consideration. If you need any additional information from me, please feel free to call.

Yours truly,

Harold Beaumont

cc: Dr. Cliff Stoudt

MENTAL HEALTH CAREER DIRECTORY

ACCEPTING A JOB OFFER

1497 Lilac Street
Old Adams, MA 01281
November 22, 1993

Mr. Rudy Delacort
Director of Personnel
Ann Grace Hospital
175 Boylston Avenue
Ribbit, Massachusetts 01281

Dear Mr. Delacort:

I want to thank you and Dr. Stoudt for giving me the opportunity to work for Ann Grace. I am very pleased to accept the position as a staff social worker with your substance abuse ward. The position entails exactly the kind of work I want to do, and I know that I will do a good job for you.

As we discussed, I shall begin work on January 5, 1994. In the interim, I shall complete all the necessary employment forms, obtain the required physical examination, and locate housing.

I plan to be in Ribbit within the next two weeks and would like to deliver the paperwork to you personally. At that time, we could handle any remaining items pertaining to my employment. I'll call next week to schedule an appointment with you.

Sincerely yours,

Harold Beaumont

cc: Dr. Cliff Stoudt

WITHDRAWING FROM CONSIDERATION

1497 Lilac Street
Old Adams, MA 01281
October 22, 1993

Mr. Rudy Delacort
Director of Personnel
Ann Grace Hospital
175 Boylston Avenue
Ribbit, Massachusetts 01281

Dear Mr. Delacort:

It was indeed a pleasure meeting with you and Dr. Stoudt last week to discuss your needs for a staff social worker. Our time together was most enjoyable and informative.

As I discussed with you during our meetings, I believe one purpose of preliminary interviews is to explore areas of mutual interest and to assess the fit between the individual and the position. After careful consideration, I have decided to withdraw from consideration for the position.

I want to thank you for interviewing me and giving me the opportunity to learn about your needs. You have a fine staff and I would have enjoyed working with them.

Yours truly,

Harold Beaumont

cc: Dr. Cliff Stoudt

IN RESPONSE TO REJECTION

1497 Lilac Street
Old Adams, MA 01281
November 22, 1993

Mr. Rudy Delacort
Director of Personnel
Ann Grace Hospital
175 Boylston Avenue
Ribbit, Massachusetts 01281

Dear Mr. Delacort:

Thank you for giving me the opportunity to interview for the staff social worker position. I appreciate your consideration and interest in me.

Although I am disappointed in not being selected for your current vacancy, I want you to know that I appreciated the courtesy and professionalism shown to me during the entire selection process. I enjoyed meeting you, Dr. Cliff Stoudt, and the other members of your staff. My meetings confirmed that Ann Grace would be an exciting place to work and build a career.

I want to reiterate my strong interest in working for you. Please keep me in mind if a similar position becomes available in the near future.

Again, thank you for the opportunity to interview and best wishes to you and your staff.

Sincerely yours,

Harold Beaumont

cc: Dr. Cliff Stoudt

CHAPTER THIRTY

Questions for You, Questions for Them

You've finished your exhaustive research, contacted everyone you've known since kindergarten, compiled a professional-looking and sounding resume, and written brilliant letters to the dozens of companies your research has revealed are perfect matches for your own strengths, interests, and abilities. Unfortunately, all of this preparatory work will be meaningless if you are unable to successfully convince one of those firms to hire you.

If you were able set up an initial meeting at one of these companies, your resume and cover letter obviously piqued someone's interest. Now you have to traverse the last minefield—the job interview itself. It's time to make all that preparation pay off.

This chapter will attempt to put the interview process in perspective, giving you the "inside story" on what to expect and how to handle the questions and circumstances that arise during the course of a normal interview—and even many of those that surface in the bizarre interview situations we have all experienced at some point.

Why Interviews Shouldn't Scare You

Interviews shouldn't scare you. The concept of two (or more) persons meeting to determine if they are right for each other is a relatively logical idea. As important as research, resumes, letters, and phone calls are, they are inherently impersonal. The interview is your chance to really see and feel the company firsthand, so think of it as a positive opportunity, your chance to succeed.

That said, many of you will still be put off by the inherently inquisitive nature of the process. Though many questions *will* be asked, interviews are essentially experiments in chemistry. Are you right for the company? Is the company right for you? Not just on paper—*in the flesh*.

If you decide the company is right for you, your purpose is simple and clear-cut—to convince the interviewer that you are the right person for the job, that you will fit in, and that you will be an asset to the company now and in the future. The interviewer's purpose is equally simple—to decide whether he or she should buy what you're selling.

This chapter will focus on the kinds of questions you are likely to be asked, how to answer them, and the questions you should be ready to ask of the interviewer. By removing the workings of the interview process from the "unknown" category, you will reduce the fear it engenders.

But all the preparation in the world won't completely eliminate your sweaty palms, unless you can convince yourself that the interview is an important, positive life experience from which you will benefit—even if you don't get the job. Approach it with enthusiasm, calm yourself, and let your personality do the rest. You will undoubtedly spend an interesting hour, one that will teach you more about yourself. It's just another step in the learning process you've undertaken.

What to Do First

Start by setting up a calendar on which you can enter and track all your scheduled appointments. When you schedule an interview with a company, ask them how much time you should allow for the appointment. Some require all new applicants to fill out numerous forms and/or complete a battery of intelligence or psychological tests—all before the first interview. If you've only allowed an hour for the interview—and scheduled another at a nearby firm 10 minutes later—the first time you confront a three-hour test series will effectively destroy any schedule.

Some companies, especially if the first interview is very positive, like to keep applicants around to talk to other executives. This process may be planned or, in a lot of cases, a spontaneous decision by an interviewer who likes you and wants you to meet some other key decision makers. Other companies will tend to schedule such a series of second interviews on a separate day. Find out, if you can, how the company you're planning to visit generally operates. Otherwise, a schedule that's too tight will fall apart in no time at all, especially if you've traveled to another city to interview with a number of firms in a short period of time.

If you need to travel out-of-state to interview with a company, be sure to ask if they will be paying some or all of your travel expenses. (It's generally expected that you'll be paying your own way to firms within your home state.) If they don't offer—and you don't ask—presume you're paying the freight.

Even if the company agrees to reimburse you, make sure you have enough money to pay all the expenses yourself. While some may reimburse you immediately, the majority of firms may take from a week to a month to send you an expense check.

Research, Research, and More Research

The research you did to find these companies is nothing compared to the research you need to do now that you're beginning to narrow your search. If you followed our detailed suggestions when you started targeting these firms in the first place, you've already amassed a great deal of information about them. If you didn't do the research *then,* you sure better decide to do it *now.* Study each company as if you were going to be tested on your detailed knowledge of their organization and operations. Here's a complete checklist of the facts you should try to know about each company you plan to visit for a job interview:

The Basics

1. The address of (and directions to) the office you're visiting
2. Headquarters location (if different)
3. Some idea of domestic and international branches
4. Relative size (compared to other similar companies)
5. Annual billings, sales, and/or income (last two years)
6. Subsidiary companies and/or specialized divisions
7. Departments (overall structure)
8. Major accounts, products, or services

The Subtleties

1. History of the firm (specialties, honors, awards, famous names)
2. Names, titles, and backgrounds of top management
3. Existence (and type) of training program
4. Relocation policy
5. Relative salaries (compared to other companies in field or by size)
6. Recent developments concerning the company and its products or services (from your trade magazine and newspaper reading)
7. Everything you can learn about the career, likes, and dislikes of the person(s) interviewing you

The amount of time and work necessary to be this well prepared for an interview is considerable. It will not be accomplished the day before the interview. You may even find some of the information you need is unavailable on short notice.

Is it really so important to do all this? Well, somebody out there is going to. And if you happen to be interviewing for the same job as that other, well-prepared, knowledgeable candidate, who do you think will impress the interviewer more?

As we've already discussed, if you give yourself enough time, most of this information is surprisingly easy to obtain. In addition to the reference sources covered in the Career Resources chapter, the company itself can probably supply you with a great deal of data. A firm's annual report—which all publicly-owned companies must publish yearly for their stockholders—is a virtual treasure trove of information. Write each company and request copies of their last two annual reports. A comparison of sales, income, and other data over this period may enable you to discover some interesting things about their overall financial health and growth potential. Many libraries also have collections of annual reports from major corporations.

Attempting to learn about your interviewer is hard work, the importance of which is underestimated by most applicants (who then, of course, don't bother to do it). Being one of the exceptions may get you a job. Find out if he or she has written any articles that have appeared in the trade press or, even better, books on his or her area(s) of expertise. Referring to these writings during the course of an interview, without making it too obvious a compliment, can be very effective. We all have egos and we all like people to talk about us. The interviewer is no different from the rest of us. You might also check to see if any of your networking contacts worked with him or her at his current (or a previous) company and can help fill you in.

Selection vs. Screening Interviews

The process to which the majority of this chapter is devoted is the actual **selection interview,** usually conducted by the person to whom the new hire will be reporting. But there is another process—the **screening interview**—which many of you may have to survive first.

Screening interviews are usually conducted by a member of the human resources department. Though they may not be empowered to hire, they are in a position to screen out or eliminate those candidates they feel (based on the facts) are not qualified to handle the job. These decisions are not usually made on the basis of personality, appearance, eloquence, persuasiveness, or any other subjective criteria, but rather by clicking off yes or no answers against a checklist of skills. If you don't have the requisite number, you will be eliminated from further consideration. This may seem arbitrary, but it is a realistic and often necessary way for corporations to minimize the time and dollars involved in filling even the lowest jobs on the corporate ladder.

Remember, screening personnel are not looking for reasons to *hire* you; they're trying to find ways to *eliminate* you from the job search pack. Resumes sent blindly to the personnel department will usually be subjected to such screening; you will be eliminated without any personal contact (an excellent reason to construct a superior resume and not send out blind mailings).

If you are contacted, it will most likely be by telephone. When you are responding to such a call, keep these four things in mind: 1) It is an interview, be on your guard; 2) Answer all questions honestly; 3) Be enthusiastic; and 4) Don't offer any more information than you are asked for. Remember, this is another screening step, so don't say anything that will get you screened out before you even get in. You will get the standard questions from the interviewer—his or her attempts to "flesh out" the information included on your resume and/or cover letter. Strictly speaking, they are seeking out any negatives which may exist. If your resume is honest and factual (and it should be), you have no reason to be anxious, because you have nothing to hide.

Don't be nervous—be glad you were called and remember your objective: to get past this screening phase so you can get on to the real interview.

The Day of the Interview

On the day of the interview, wear a conservative (not funereal) business suit—*not* a sports coat, *not* a "nice" blouse and skirt. Shoes should be shined, nails cleaned, hair cut and in place. And no low-cut or tight-fitting clothes.

It's not unusual for resumes and cover letters to head in different directions when a company starts passing them around to a number of executives. If you sent them, both may even be long gone. So bring along extra copies of your resume and your own copy of the cover letter that originally accompanied it.

Whether or not you make them available, we suggest you prepare a neatly-typed list of references (including the name, title, company, address, and phone number of each person). You may want to bring along a copy of your high school or college transcript, especially if it's something to brag about. (Once you get your first job, you'll probably never use it—or be asked for it—again, so enjoy it while you can!)

On Time Means Fifteen Minutes Early

Plan to arrive fifteen minutes before your scheduled appointment. If you're in an unfamiliar city or have a long drive to their offices, allow extra time for the unexpected delays that seem to occur with mind-numbing regularity on important days.

Arriving early will give you some time to check your appearance, catch your breath, check in with the receptionist, learn how to correctly pronounce the interviewer's name, and get yourself organized and battle ready.

Arriving late does not make a sterling first impression. If you are only a few minutes late, it's probably best not to mention it or even excuse yourself. With a little luck, everybody else is behind schedule and no one will notice. However, if you're more than fifteen minutes late, have an honest (or at least serviceable) explanation ready and offer it at your first opportunity. Then drop the subject as quickly as possible and move on to the interview.

The Eyes Have It

When you meet the interviewer, shake hands firmly. People notice handshakes and often form a first impression based solely on them.

Try to maintain eye contact with the interviewer as you talk. This will indicate you're interested in what he or she has to say. Eye contact is important for another reason—it demonstrates to the interviewer that you are confident about yourself and your job skills. That's an important message to send.

Sit straight. Body language is also another important means of conveying confidence.

Should coffee or a soft drink be offered, you may accept (but should do so only if the interviewer is joining you).

Keep your voice at a comfortable level, and try to sound enthusiastic (without

---

You Don't Have to Say a Word

"Eighty percent of the initial impression you make is nonverbal," asserts Jennifer Maxwell Morris, a New York-based image consultant, quoting a University of Minnesota study. Some tips: walk tall, enter the room briskly while making eye contact with the person you're going to speak to, keep your head up, square your shoulders and keep your hand ready for a firm handshake that involves the whole hand but does not pump.

Source: *Working Woman*

imitating Charleen Cheerleader). Be confident and poised and provide direct, accurate, and honest answers to the trickiest questions.

And, as you try to remember all this, just be yourself, and try to act like you're comfortable and almost enjoying this whole process!

Don't Name Drop...Conspicuously

A friendly relationship with other company employees may have provided you with valuable information prior to the interview, but don't flaunt such relationships. The interviewer is interested only in how you will relate to him or her and how well he or she surmises you will fit in with the rest of the staff. Name dropping may smack of favoritism. And you are in no position to know who the interviewer's favorite (or least favorite) people are.

On the other hand, if you have established a complex network of professionals through informational interviews, attending trade shows, reading trade magazines, etc., it is perfectly permissible to refer to these people, their companies, conversations you've had, whatever. It may even impress the interviewer with the extensiveness of your preparation.

Fork on the Left, Knife on the Right

Interviews are sometimes conducted over lunch, though this is not usually the case with entry-level people. If it does happen to you, though, try to order something in the middle price range, neither filet mignon nor a cheeseburger.

Do not order alcohol—ever! If your interviewer orders a carafe of wine, politely decline. You may meet another interviewer later who smells the alcohol on your breath, or your interviewer may have a drinking problem. It's just too big a risk to take after you've come so far. Just do your best to maintain your poise, and you'll do fine.

The Importance of Last Impressions

There are some things interviewers will always view with displeasure: street language, complete lack of eye contact, insufficient or vague explanations or answers, a noticeable lack of energy, poor interpersonal skills (i.e., not listening or the basic inability to carry on an intelligent conversation), and a demonstrable lack of motivation.

Every impression may count. And the very *last* impression an interviewer has may outweigh everything else. So, before you allow an interview to end, summarize why you want the job, why you are qualified, and what, in particular, you can offer their company.

Then, take some action. If the interviewer hasn't told you about the rest of the interview process and/or where you stand, ask him or her. Will you be seeing other people that day? If so, ask for some background on anyone else with whom you'll be interviewing. If there are no other meetings that day, what's the next step? When can you expect to hear from them about coming back?

Ask for a business card. This will make sure you get the person's name and title right when you write your follow-up letter. You can staple it to the company file for easy reference as you continue networking. When you return home, file all the business cards, copies of correspondence, and notes from the interview(s) with each company in the appropriate files. Finally, but most importantly, ask yourself which firms you really want to work for and which you are no longer interested in. This will quickly determine how far you want the process at each to develop before you politely tell them to stop considering you for the job.

Immediately send a thank-you letter to each executive you met. These should, of course, be neatly typed business letters, not handwritten notes (unless you are most friendly, indeed, with the interviewer and want to stress the "informal" nature of your note). If you are still interested in pursuing a position at their company, tell them in no uncertain terms. Reiterate why you feel you're the best candidate and tell each of the executives when you hope (expect?) to hear from them.

On the Eighth Day God Created Interviewers

Though most interviews will follow a relatively standard format, there will undoubtedly be a wide disparity in the skills of the interviewers you meet. Many of these executives (with the exception of the human resources staff) will most likely not have extensive interviewing experience, have limited knowledge of interviewing techniques, use them infrequently, be hurried by the other duties, or not even view your interview as critically important.

Rather than studying standardized test results or utilizing professional evaluation skills developed over many years of practice, these nonprofessionals react intuitively—their initial (first five minutes) impressions are often the lasting and over-riding factors they remember. So you must sell yourself—fast.

> A new style of interview called the "situational interview," or low-fidelity simulation, asks prospective employees what they would do in hypothetical situations, presenting illustrations that are important in the job opening. Recent research is encouraging employers to use this type of interview approach, because studies show that what people say they would do is pretty much what they will do when the real-life situation arises.
> Source: *Working Woman*

The best way to do this is to try to achieve a comfort level with your interviewer. Isn't establishing rapport—through words, gestures, appearance common interests, etc.—what you try to do in *any* social situation? It's just trying to know one another better. Against this backdrop, the questions and answers will flow in a more natural way.

The Set Sequence

Irrespective of the competence levels of the interviewer, you can anticipate an interview sequence roughly as follows:

- Greetings
- Social niceties (small talk)
- Purpose of meeting (let's get down to business)
- Broad questions/answers
- Specific questions/answers

- In-depth discussion of company, job, and opportunity
- Summarizing information given & received
- Possible salary probe (this should only be brought up at a second interview)
- Summary/indication as to next steps

When you look at this sequence closely, it is obvious that once you have gotten past the greeting, social niceties and some explanation of the job (in the "getting down to business" section), the bulk of the interview will be questions—yours and the interviewer's. In this question and answer session, there are not necessarily any right or wrong answers, only good and bad ones.

Be forewarned, however. This sequence is not written in stone, and some interviewers will deliberately **not** follow it. Some interviewers will try to fluster you by asking off-the-wall questions, while others are just eccentric by nature. Be prepared for anything once the interview has started.

It's Time to Play Q & A

You can't control the "chemistry" between you and the interviewer—do you seem to "hit it off" right from the start or never connect at all? Since you can't control such a subjective problem, it pays to focus on what you *can* control—the questions you will be asked, your answers and the questions you had better be prepared to ask.

Not surprisingly, many of the same questions pop up in interview after interview, regardless of company size, type, or location. I have chosen the 14 most common—along with appropriate hints and answers for each—for inclusion in this chapter. Remember: There are no right or wrong answers to these questions, only good and bad ones.

Substance counts more than speed when answering questions. Take your time and make sure that you listen to each question—there is nothing quite as disquieting as a lengthy, intelligent answer that is completely irrelevant to the question asked. You wind up looking like a programmed clone with stock answers to dozens of questions who has, unfortunately, pulled the wrong one out of the grab bag.

Once you have adequately answered a specific question, it is permissible to go beyond it and add more information if doing so adds something to the discussion and/or highlights a particular strength, skill, course, etc. But avoid making lengthy speeches just for the sake of sounding off. Even if the interviewer asks a question that is right up your "power alley", one you could talk about for weeks, keep your answers short. Under two minutes for any answer is a good rule of thumb.

Study the list of questions (and hints) that follow, and prepare at least one solid, concise answer for each. Practice with a friend until your answers to these most-asked questions sound intelligent, professional and, most important, unmemorized and unrehearsed.

"Why do you want to be in this field?"

Using your knowledge and understanding of the particular field, explain why you find the business exciting and where and what role you see yourself playing in it.

"Why do you think you will be successful in this business?"

Using the information from your self-evaluation and the research you did on that particular company, formulate an answer which marries your strengths to their's and to the characteristics of the position for which you're applying.

"Why did you choose our company?"

This is an excellent opportunity to explain the extensive process of education and research you've undertaken. Tell them about your strengths and how you match up with their firm. Emphasize specific things about their company that led you to seek an interview. Be a salesperson—be convincing.

"What can you do for us?"

Construct an answer that essentially lists your strengths, the experience you have which will contribute to your job performance, and any other unique qualifications that will place you at the head of the applicant pack. Use action-oriented words to tell exactly what you think you can do for the company—all your skills mean nothing if you can't use them to benefit the company you are interviewing with. Be careful: This is a question specifically designed to *eliminate* some of that pack. Sell yourself. Be one of the few called back for a second interview.

"What position here interests you?"

If you're interviewing for a specific position, answer accordingly. If you want to make sure you don't close the door on other opportunities of which you might be unaware, you can follow up with your own question: "I'm here to apply for your substance abuse counselor opening. Is there another position open for which you feel I'm qualified?"

If you've arranged an interview with a company without knowing of any specific openings, use the answer to this question to describe the kind of work you'd like to do and why you're qualified to do it. Avoid a specific job title, since they will tend to vary from firm to firm.

If you're on a first interview with the human resources department, just answer the question. They only want to figure out where to send you.

"What jobs have you held and why did you leave them?"

Or the direct approach: "Have you ever been fired?" Take this opportunity to expand on your resume, rather than precisely answering the question by merely recapping your job experiences. In discussing each job, point out what you liked about it, what factors led to your leaving, and how the next job added to your continuing professional education. If you have been fired, say so. It's very easy to check.

"What are your strengths and weaknesses?"

Or **"What are your hobbies (or outside interests)?"** Both questions can be easily answered using the data you gathered to complete the self-evaluation process. Be wary of being too forthcoming about your glaring faults (nobody expects you to volunteer every weakness and mistake), but do not reply, "I don't have any." They won't believe you and, what's worse, you won't believe you. After all, you did the evaluation—you know it's a lie!

Good answers to these questions are those in which the interviewer can identify benefits for him or herself. For example: "I consider myself to be an excellent planner. I am seldom caught by surprise and I prize myself on being able to anticipate problems and schedule my time to be ahead of the game. I devote a prescribed number of hours each week to this activity. I've noticed that many people just react. If you plan ahead, you should be able to cut off most problems before they arise."

You may consider disarming the interviewer by admitting a weakness, but doing it in such a way as to make it relatively unimportant to the job function. For example: "Higher mathematics has never been my strong suit. Though I am competent enough, I've always envied my friends with a more mathematical bent. In this industry, though, I haven't found this a liability."

"Do you think your extracurricular activities were worth the time you devoted to them?"

This is a question often asked of entry-level candidates. One possible answer: "Very definitely. As you see from my resume, I have been quite active in the Student Government and French Club. My language fluency allowed me to spend my junior year abroad as an exchange student, and working in a functioning government gave me firsthand knowledge of what can be accomplished with people in the real world. I suspect my marks would have been somewhat higher had I not taken on so many activities outside of school, but I feel the balance they gave me contributed significantly to my overall growth as a person."

"What are your career goals?"

Interviewers are always seeking to probe the motivations of prospective employees. Nowhere is this more apparent than when the area of ambition is discussed. The key answer to this question might be; "Given hard work, company growth, and personal initiative, I'd look forward to being in a top executive position by the time I'm 35. I believe in effort and the risk/reward system—my research on this company has shown me that it operates on the same principles. I would hope it would select its future leaders from those people who display such characteristics."

"At some future date would you be willing to relocate?"

Pulling up one's roots is not the easiest thing in the world to do, but it is often a fact of life in the corporate world. If you're serious about your career (and such a move often represents a step up the career ladder), you will probably not mind such a move. Tell the interviewer. If you really *don't* want to move, you may want to say so, too—though I would find out how probable or frequent such relocations would be before closing the door while still in the interview stage.

Keep in mind that as you get older, establish ties in a particular community, marry, have children, etc., you will inevitably feel less jubilation at the thought of moving once a year or even "being out on the road." So take the opportunity to experience new places and experiences while you're young. If you don't, you may never get the chance.

"How did you get along with your last supervisor?"

This question is designed to understand your relationship with (and reaction to) authority. Remember: Companies look for team players, people who will fit in with their hierarchy, their rules, their ways of doing things. An answer might be: "I prefer to work with smart, strong people who know what they want and can express themselves. I learned in the military that in order to accomplish the mission, someone has to be the leader and that person has to be given the authority to lead. Someday I aim to be that leader. I hope then my subordinates will follow me as much and as competently as I'm ready to follow now."

"What are your salary requirements?"

If they are at all interested in you, this question will probably come up, though it is more likely at a second interview. The danger, of course, is that you may price yourself too low or, even worse, right out of a job you want. Since you will have a general idea of industry figures for that position (and may even have an idea of what that company tends to pay new people for the position), why not refer to a range of salaries, such as $25,000 - $30,000?

If the interviewer doesn't bring up salary at all, it's doubtful you're being seriously considered, so you probably don't need to even bring the subject up. (If you know you aren't getting the job or aren't interested in it if offered, you may try to nail down a salary figure in order to be better prepared for the next interview.)

"Tell me about yourself"

Watch out for this one! It's often one of the first questions asked. If you falter here, the rest of the interview could quickly become a downward slide to nowhere. Be prepared, and consider it an opportunity to combine your answers to many of the previous questions into one concise description of who you are, what you want to be, and why that company should take a chance on you. Summarize your resume—briefly—and expand on particular courses or experiences relevant to the firm or position. Do not go on about your hobbies or personal life, where you spent your summer vacation, or anything that is not relevant to securing that job. You may explain how that particular job fits in with your long-range career goals and talk specifically about what attracted you to their company in the first place.

"Do you have any questions?"

It's the last fatal question on our list, often the last one an interviewer throws at you after an hour or two of grilling. Even if the interview has been very long and unusually thorough, you *should* have questions—about the job, the company, even the industry. Unfortunately, by the time this question off-handedly hits the floor, you are already looking forward to leaving and may have absolutely nothing to say.

Preparing yourself for an interview means more than having answers for some of the questions an interviewer may ask. It means having your own set of questions—at least five or six—for the interviewer. The interviewer is trying to find the right person for the job. You're trying to find the right job. So you should be just as curious about him or her and the company as he or she is about you. Be careful with any list of questions prepared ahead of time. Some of them were probably answered during the course of the interview, so to ask that same question at this stage would demonstrate poor listening skills. Listening well is becoming a lost art, and its importance cannot be stressed enough. (See the box on this page for a short list of questions you may consider asking on any interview).

> **Your Turn to Ask the Questions**
>
> 1. What will my typical day be like?
> 2. What happened to the last person who had this job?
> 3. Given my attitude and qualifications, how would you estimate my chances for career advancement at your company?
> 4. Why did you come to work here? What keeps you here?
> 5. If you were I, would you start here again?
> 6. How would you characterize the management philosophy of your company?
> 7. What characteristics do the successful employees at your company have in common?
> 8. What's the best (and worst) thing about working here?

The Not-So-Obvious Questions

Every interviewer is different and, unfortunately, there are no rules saying he or she has to use all or any of the "basic" questions covered above. But we think the odds are against his or her avoiding all of them. Whichever of these he or she includes, be assured most interviewers do like to come up with questions that are "uniquely theirs." It may be just one or a whole series—questions developed over the years that he or she feels help separate the wheat from the chaff.

You can't exactly prepare yourself for questions like, "What would you do if...(fill in the blank with some obscure occurrence)?," "What do you remember about kindergarten?," or "What's your favorite ice cream flavor?" Every interviewer we know has his or her favorites and all of these questions seem to come out of left field. Just stay relaxed, grit your teeth (quietly), and take a few seconds to frame a reasonably intelligent reply.

The Downright Illegal Questions

Some questions are more than inappropriate—they are illegal. The Civil Rights Act of 1964 makes it illegal for a company to discriminate in its hiring on the basis of race, color, religion, sex, or national origin. It also means that any interview questions covering these topics are strictly off-limits. In addition to questions about race and color, what other types of questions can't be asked? Some might surprise you:

- Any questions about marital status, number and ages of dependents, or marriage or child-bearing plans.
- Any questions about your relatives, their addresses, or their place of origin.
- Any questions about your arrest record. If security clearance is required, it can be done after hiring but before you start the job.

A Quick Quiz to Test Your Instincts

After reading the above paragraphs, read through the 10 questions below. Which ones do you think would be legal to ask at a job interview? Answers provided below.

1. Confidentially, what is your race?
2. What kind of work does your spouse do?
3. Are you single, married, or divorced?
4. What is your native language?
5. Who should we notify in case of an emergency?
6. What clubs, societies, or organizations do you belong to?
7. Do you plan to have a family?
8. Do you have any disability?
9. Do you have a good credit record?
10. What is your height and weight?

The answer? Not a single question out of the 10 is legal at a job interview, because all could lead to a discrimination suit. Some of the questions would become legal once you were hired (obviously a company would need to know who to notify in an emergency), but none belong at an interview.

Now that you know what an interviewer can't ask you, what if he or she does? Well, don't lose your cool, and don't point out that the question may be outside the law—the nonprofessional interviewer may not realize such questions are illegal, and such a response might confuse, even anger, him or her.

Instead, whenever any questions are raised that you feel are outside legal boundaries, politely state that you don't understand how the question has bearing on the job opening and ask the interviewer to clarify his or herself. If the interviewer persists, you may be forced to state that you do not feel comfortable answering questions of that nature. Bring up the legal issue as a last resort, but if things reach that stage, you probably don't want to work for that company after all.

Testing and Applications

Though not part of the selection interview itself, job applications, skill tests, and psychological testing are often part of the pre-interview process. You should know something about them.

The job application is essentially a record-keeping exercise—simply the transfer of work experience and educational data from your resume to a printed application forms. Though taking the time to recopy data may seem like a waste of time, some companies simply want the information in a particular order on a standard form. One difference: Applications often require the listing of references and salary levels achieved. Be sure to bring your list of references with you to any interview (so you can transfer the pertinent information), and don't lie about salary history; it's easily checked.

Many companies now use a variety of psychological tests as additional mechanisms to screen out undesirable candidates. Although their accuracy is subject to question, the companies that use them obviously believe they are effective at identifying applicants whose personality makeups would preclude their participating positively in a given work situation, especially those at the extreme ends of the behavior spectrum.

Their usefulness in predicting job accomplishment is considered limited. If you are normal (like the rest of us), you'll have no trouble with these tests and may even find them amusing. Just don't try to outsmart them—you'll just wind up outsmarting yourself.

Stand Up and Be Counted

Your interview is over. Breathe a sigh of relief. Make your notes—you'll want to keep a file on the important things covered for use in your next interview. Some people consider one out of 10 (one job offer for every 10 interviews) a good score—if you're keeping score. We suggest you don't. It's virtually impossible to judge how others are judging you. Just go on to the next interview. Sooner than you think, you'll be hired. For the right job.

Job Opportunities Databank

CHAPTER THIRTY-ONE

Job Opportunities Databank

The Job Opportunities Databank contains listings for more than 350 general and psychiatric specialty hospitals, long-term care facilities, nursing homes, private counseling centers, and state human services agencies that offer entry-level hiring and/or internships. It is divided into two sections: Entry-Level Job and Internship Listings, which provides full descriptive entries for companies in the United States; and Additional Companies, which includes name, address, and telephone information only for companies that did not respond to our inquiries. For complete details on the information provided in this chapter, please consult "How to Use the Job Opportunities Databank" at the front of this directory.

Entry-Level Job and Internship Listings

Alabama Department of Human Resources
50 Ripley St.
Montgomery, AL 36130
Phone: (205)242-1160
Fax: (205)242-1086

Opportunities: Hires entry-level staff with college degrees and/or previous experience. Requirements vary depending upon the position.
Benefits: Benefits include medical insurance, life insurance, dental insurance, vision insurance.
Human Resources: Waldo Spencer.
Application Procedures: Application procedures vary depending upon the hiring agency. Typically, an applicant must complete an application form from the Alabama Personnel Department. Applications are filed in the registrar's office until openings become available. At that time, prospective files are considered.

▶ **Internships**
Type: Offers unpaid internships for college credit.

Alabama State Department of Mental Health and Mental Retardation
200 Interstate Park Dr.
PO Box 3710
Montgomery, AL 36109-0710
Phone: (205)271-9207
Fax: (205)240-3195

Opportunities: Entry-level positions require a college degree and previous experience.
Benefits: Benefits include medical insurance,

MENTAL HEALTH CAREER DIRECTORY

dental insurance, retirement plans, annual leave, and savings plan.

Human Resources: Richard Hamilton.

Application Procedures: Job seeker fills out application, then personnel contacts the applicant, if interested. Applications are kept on file for one year.

▶ **Internships**

Type: The company does not offer an internship program.

The current fashion is to think of mental illness as a biological disorder, and therefore one that responds to drugs. Medication has its place, but mending the mind is not like mending the body. It takes a vastly more human touch, and good hospitals increasingly emphasize a proper balance between drugs and psychotherapy.

Source: *U.S. News & World Report*

Alaska Division of Family and Youth Services

PO Box 110630
Juneau, AK 99811
Phone: (907)465-3191
Fax: (907)465-3397

Opportunities: Usually requires previous experience. Hires mostly residents of Alaska.

Benefits: Have an optional insurance plan. Offers life insurance and savings plan.

Application Procedures: Fill out an application form in person or send a resume.

▶ **Internships**

Contact: Jo Olsen, Human Resources Mgr.

Type: Offers paid internships to residents of Alaska. College credit can be arranged. **Number Available Annually:** 14.

Qualifications: Candidates must be enrolled in courses that are relevant to the company.

Application Procedure: Apply to Jo Olsen, Human Resources manager.

Alaska Division of Mental Health and Developmental Disabilities

PO Box 110620
Juneau, AK 99811-0620
Phone: (907)465-4470
Fax: (907)465-2668

Opportunities: Hires entry-level housekeeping staff and ward aides. A high school diploma is required.

Benefits: Benefits include medical insurance, life insurance, dental insurance, vision insurance, savings plan, tuition assistance, and profit sharing.

Human Resources: Mr. Stoneacker.

Application Procedures: Send resume and cover letter. The personnel office is located in the Department of Administration.

▶ **Internships**

Type: Offers unpaid internships for college credit to college students. Internships are awarded directly through the sponsoring university. **Number Available Annually:** 2-3.

Alaska Psychiatric Institute

2900 Providence Dr.
Anchorage, AK 99508
Phone: (907)561-1633

Opportunities: Hires psychiatric nursing assistants with at least a high school diploma and appropriately degreed and certified nurses.

Benefits: Benefits include medical insurance, life insurance, dental insurance, vision insurance, savings plan, profit sharing, and retirement plans.

Human Resources: Gale White.

Application Procedures: Those interested should apply in person.

▶ **Internships**

Contact: Jim Gordon, Administrative Assistant.

Type: Offers paid internships. College credit is available. **Number Available Annually:** 1.

Qualifications: Must be a college student.

Alta Bates-Herrick Hospital
2855 Telegraph, Ste. 614
Berkeley, CA 94131
Phone: (510)540-1584
Fax: (510)204-4852

Business Description: Services provided are for acute care, rehabilitation, and mental health, both psychiatric and rehabilitative. There are also two Sportcare outpatient facilities.

Employees: 2,600. The entry level hiring number indicates 40 nursing positions, and 50 non-nursing positions.

Average Entry-Level Hiring: 90.

Opportunities: Physical therapy, speech therapy, occupational therapy, nursing, medical social workers—B.S. degree and California license registration. Radiology technicians, respiratory therapist, radiation oncology—certification required. Clerical and support positions available in business services, accounting, admitting, administration, engineering, medical records, and other specialized areas such as the AIDS clinic.

Human Resources: Mary Martha Beaton; Linda Camezon.

Alternatives Inc.
PO Box 338
Somerville, NJ 08876
Phone: (908)685-1444

Business Description: Chain of physical therapist offices.

Officers: Nancy Good, President.

Opportunities: Hires entry-level part-time staff. Previous experience and a high school diploma are required.

Benefits: Benefits include medical insurance, life insurance, dental insurance, disability insurance, and 401(k).

Human Resources: Steve Kalucki.

Application Procedures: Send resume and cover letter to the attention of Human Resources Department.

▶ **Internships**

Contact: Steve Kalucki.

Type: Offers paid and unpaid internships.
Number Available Annually: 1.

Qualifications: College students majoring in psychology or social work.

Alton Mental Health and Developmental Center
4500 College Ave.
Alton, IL 62002
Phone: (618)465-5593

Opportunities: Hires entry-level support service workers. Prospective applicants must have a master's degree in mental health or social work and be on the civil service list.

Benefits: Benefits include medical insurance and dental insurance.

Application Procedures: Applications are available at the Stratton Office Building, Bureau of State Personnel.

▶ **Internships**

Type: The company does not offer an internship program.

American Biodyne Inc.
400 Oyster Point Blvd., Ste. 306
South San Francisco, CA 94080
Phone: (415)742-0980
Fax: (415)742-0988

Business Description: Provides comprehensive managed mental health and substance abuse treatment programs for insurance companies, employers, health maintenance organizations, and other providers of mental health benefits in Arizona, Illinois, Hawaii, Indiana, Ohio, Texas, Florida, and Michigan.

Officers: Nicholas A. Cummings, Ph.D., CEO; Shannon R. Kennedy, Ph.D., Exec. VP & General Mgr.; Albert Waxman, Ph.D., President; Kenneth Zimmerman, VP of Finance & CFO.

Benefits: Benefits include 120 hours of training in the Biodyne Model of Care and weekly clinical management activities.

Human Resources: Steven Weinberg.

Application Procedures: The company places advertisements in the newspaper for job openings. Some positions require prior testing for skill level. Interested candidates should contact the Human Resources Department. Steven Weinberg.

▶ **Internships**

Type: The company offers a summer internship program. Internships may be paid or may include college credit.

Qualifications: Must be a college student and meet company qualifications.

Application Procedure: Internship applications should be sent to the Human Resources Department.

American Medical International Inc.
AMI Brookwood Medical Center
2010 Brookwood Medical Center
Birmingham, AL 35259
Phone: (205)877-1000
Fax: (205)877-2548

Business Description: A complete health care complex. The company supports a core of medical, surgical, and emergency facilities, including a variety of specialized centers - Medical and Surgical Services, Women's Medical Center, Regional Cancer Institute, Center for Mental Health, Business Health Services, Eye Institute, Foot Care Center, DIACON - Diabetes Control Centers, The Center for Health and Fitness, The Occupational Health Center, Home Care, Home Care Plus, and Hospice, Nutrition Counseling, The Center for Rehabilitation, The Family Counseling Center, and Family Health Centers.

Officers: Gregory H. Burfitt, President; Cathy Nazeer, CFO; Paul Pretsch, Sr. VP of Mktg.

Average Entry-Level Hiring: Hiring levels are expected to remain constant over the next year.

Opportunities: Hires accountants, hospital administrators, managers, departmental directors, registered nurses, dieticians, pharmacists, physicians, respiratory therapists, radiology technologists, occupational therapists, sonographers, polysomnographic technicians, medical lab technicians, medical record administrators, product line managers, secretaries, LPNs, PBX operators, receptionists, financial assistants, insurance clerks, dietary aides, patient transporters, cooks, environmental service technicians, security officers, and plant operation maintenance workers.

Benefits: Benefits include life insurance, medical insurance, dental insurance, vision insurance, long-term disability, an employee pension plan, a 401(k) plan, child-care programs, flex time, a smoke-free environment, a cafeteria, tuition assistance, bonuses/incentives, employee assistance program, free and covered employee parking, service award plans, workers compensation, and up to 3 days paid bereavement leave.

Human Resources: Linda Foster; Patti Reese; Marsha Fields.

Application Procedures: Recruits regionally at college campuses in the southeast on college placement days. Recruits at trade shows and professional exhibits, including nursing and allied health professional associations. Recruits through employment agencies, including state employment offices and occupational rehabilitation services. Maintains a job hotline at 205-877-1910. Apply in person at AMI Brookwood Medical Center, Human Resources, 557 Brookwood Blvd., Birmingham, Alabama, Between 9:00 A.M. and 3:30 P.M., or send resume and cover letter to the attention of Linda Foster.

▶ **Internships**

Type: Offers an internship program through the individual medical schools.

American Psychology Management Inc.
Hurst Associates Inc.
21 Custom House St.
Boston, MA 02110
Phone: (617)737-8600

Business Description: Substance abuse assistance programs.

Officers: Michael W. Hurst, President; Susan Silva, CFO; William A. Roiter, Exec. VP; Regina Demillia, Contact.

Opportunities: Hires entry-level candidates with a college degree or previous experience.

Benefits: Benefits include medical insurance, savings investment plan, tuition assistance, and profit sharing.

Application Procedures: Apply in person or send a resume. No phone contact is necessary.

American Treatment Centers Inc.
PO Box 667
Lebanon, IN 46052
Phone: (317)482-0991

Business Description: Rehabilitation hospitals for alcohol and drug addiction.

Officers: Richard Shabi, President; Michael Heiniger, Controller; Jon Millan, Dir. of Mktg.; Bobbie Hennessy, VP of Admin.; Bobbie Hennessy, VP of Admin.

Arizona Division of Behavioral Health Services

411 N. 24th St.
Phoenix, AZ 85008
Phone: (602)220-6506
Fax: (602)220-6502

Opportunities: Hires entry-level staff who have either a college degree or previous experience.

Benefits: Benefits include medical insurance, life insurance, dental insurance, and long-term and short-term disability.

Human Resources: Sue Wilson; Sara King.

Application Procedures: Applications must be made through the Arizona State Department in person.

▶ **Internships**

Type: Offers paid and unpaid internships.
Number Available Annually: 4.

Qualifications: College students.

Application Procedure: Interested applicants should apply through the Arizona State Department Office of Personnel.

Arizona Division of Family Health Services

1740 W. Adams St., Ste. 307
Phoenix, AZ 85007
Phone: (602)542-1223
Fax: (602)542-2789

Opportunities: Hires entry-level staff who possess a college degree or previous experience. Positions available include health program managers.

Benefits: Benefits include medical insurance, life insurance, dental insurance, vision insurance, and child-care programs.

Human Resources: Susy Genardini.

Application Procedures: Interested candidates should apply in person at the state personnel department.

▶ **Internships**

Type: The company does not offer any internship programs.

Arizona State Hospital

2500 E. VanBuren
Phoenix, AZ 85008
Phone: (602)244-1331

Opportunities: Hires appropriately degreed and certified nurses, psychiatric staff, psychologists, and occupational therapists.

Benefits: Benefits include medical insurance, life insurance, dental insurance, vision insurance, savings plan, paid holidays, and disability insurance.

Human Resources: Sue Wilson.

Application Procedures: Those interested should apply in person. Tonya Prindall, Health Services Personnel Specialist.

▶ **Internships**

Type: The company does not offer an internship program.

Arkansas Division of Alcohol and Drug Abuse Prevention

PO Box 1437
Little Rock, AR 72203-1437
Phone: (501)682-6656
Fax: (501)682-6610

Opportunities: Hires entry-level clerical workers with previous experience, a college degree, and/or completion of some college course work.

Benefits: Benefits include medical insurance, life insurance, savings plan, tuition assistance, child-care programs, and a retirement plan.

Human Resources: Virginia Harper.

Application Procedures: The company posts their job openings. Those interested in a specific positi on should contact Virginia Harper.

▶ **Internships**

Type: The company does not offer an internship program.

Arkansas Division of Mental Health Services
Arkansas State Hospital

4313 W. Markham
Little Rock, AR 72205-4096
Phone: (501)686-9000
Fax: (501)686-9182

Opportunities: Hires appropriately degreed and certified nurses.

Benefits: Benefits include medical insurance, life insurance, dental insurance, tax deferred annuities, and a pension plan.

Human Resources: Rose Bradley, Director of Personnel.

Application Procedures: Those interested

should apply in person, call, or send resume to contact. Those interested must fill out a state application.

▶ **Internships**

Type: Offers paid internships. **Number Available Annually:** 9.

Qualifications: Must be a student at the University of Alaska College of Medicine.

Augusta Mental Health Institute
PO Box 724
Augusta, ME 04330
Phone: (207)289-7200

Opportunities: Hires laborers, custodians, and CNA certified mental health workers.

Benefits: Benefits include medical insurance, life insurance, dental insurance, vision insurance, savings plan, and tuition assistance.

Human Resources: Shirley Bartlett.

Application Procedures: Apply in person to Human Resources.

▶ **Internships**

Type: Offers unpaid internships to college students. **Number Available Annually:** 50.

Application Procedure: Contact department directors for internship information.

Bangor Mental Health Institute
656 State St.
Bangor, ME 04402
Phone: (207)941-4000

Opportunities: Hires professional staff, nurses, and housekeeping staff. Applicants must have a college degree for certain positions.

Benefits: Benefits include medical insurance, life insurance, dental insurance, a credit union, and savings bonds.

Application Procedures: The company does not accept resumes. Candidates should apply through state applications only.

▶ **Internships**

Type: Offers unpaid internships to college students.

Application Procedure: Interested candidates should contact department heads.

Baptist Rehabilitation Institute of Arkansas
9601 Interstate 630, Exit 7
Little Rock, AR 72205-7249
Phone: (501)223-7578

Benefits: Benefits include medical insurance, life insurance, dental insurance, vision insurance, a savings plan, and child or elder care.

▶ **Internships**

Type: The company offers paid internships to students for college credit in physical therapy, pharmacy, human resources, administration, occupational therapy, and social work areas.

Application Procedure: Send applications to the Vice President of Human Resources.

Bay Area Recovery Centers Inc.
2733 Woolsey Ave.
Berkley, CA 94705
Phone: (510)654-9906

Business Description: Services, Manufacturing: Medical research and development of measuring and control devices.

Officers: N. Haber, Pres. & Chairman of the Board.

Opportunities: The company hires entry-level counseling staff.

Benefits: Provides medical and dental benefits.

Human Resources: Dennis Gallegos.

Application Procedures: Can contact by phone. Does not accept unsolicited resumes.

Bristol Hospital, Inc.
Brewster Rd.
Bristol, CT 06010
Phone: (203)585-3211
Fax: (203)585-3028

Employees: 1,500.

Average Entry-Level Hiring: Unknown.

Human Resources: Mark Rouleau; Sharon Osenkonski.

Application Procedures: Call for current vacancies and requirements.

Butler Hospital
345 Blackstone Blvd.
Providence, RI 02906
Phone: (401)455-6200

Business Description: Operator of psychiatric

hospitals. Engaged in the operation of establishments providing home health care services.

Officers: Frank Delmonico, CEO; Ronald Giguere, Systems Mgr.; J. Hallan Jr., Mgr. of Relations; David L. Terry, CFO.

Benefits: Offers full medical benefits, dental insurance, and 2 weeks vacation.

Human Resources: Roberta Neumann.

Application Procedures: Send resume and cover letter to the attention of the Human Resource Department.

▶ **Internships**

Type: The company does not offer an internship program.

California Department of Alcohol and Drug Programs
111 Capitol Mall, Ste. 450
Sacramento, CA 95814
Phone: (916)445-1943
Fax: (916)323-5873

Opportunities: Hires entry-level personnel in clerical and analytical capacities. A college degree or some college course work is required. The company is currently in a hiring freeze, however.

Benefits: Benefits include medical insurance, life insurance, dental insurance, vision insurance, savings plan, tuition assistance, and 401(k).

Application Procedures: Interested applicants must first take a standard state test.

▶ **Internships**

Type: The company does not offer an internship program.

California Department of Developmental Services
1600 9th St., Ste. 240
Sacramento, CA 95814
Phone: (916)654-1690
Fax: (916)654-1897

Officers: Cindy Liondakis, Contact.

Opportunities: Hires entry-level staff with clerical and analytical skills. Requires a college degree and previous experience.

Benefits: Benefits include medical insurance, life insurance, dental insurance, vision insurance, and tuition assistance.

Application Procedures: Applicants must take a State test.

California Department of Social Services
744 P St.
MS 17-11
Sacramento, CA 95814
Phone: (916)732-3072
Fax: (916)445-4846

Benefits: Benefits include medical insurance, life insurance, dental insurance and a 401(k) plan.

Application Procedures: All hiring is done through Civil Service.

> Whether you are using file cards or a computer, the trick to your job search is developing a discipline to your efforts. As you begin to send out your resume, you should automatically assign yourself a follow-up date. The idea is to realize that you are now marketing a product that you know very well: yourself.
>
> Source: H&MM

California Health and Welfare Agency
Office of the Secretary
1600 9th St., Ste. 460
Sacramento, CA 95814
Phone: (916)654-3454
Fax: (916)654-3343

Opportunities: The company is not currently hiring entry-level staff.

Benefits: Benefits include medical insurance, dental insurance, vision insurance, and savings plan.

Application Procedures: Company hires by referral only. Unsolicited resumes are not accepted.

▶ **Internships**

Type: The company does not offer an internship program.

Camargo Manor Inc.
7625 Camargo Rd.
Madeira, OH 45243
Phone: (513)561-6210

Business Description: Intermediate care nursing home.

JOB OPPORTUNITIES DATABANK

Officers: Tom Cunningham, Dir. of Admin.; Jerry Stanislaw, Controller.

Human Resources: Carol Ochnelle.

▶ **Internships**

Type: The company does not offer an internship program.

To make yourself more attractive to international employers, you might start with simple things: brushing up on your foreign languages or even learning a new one; seizing opportunities to travel abroad, whether for business or pleasure; cultivating overseas friends; or just reading widely about other cultures.

Source: *Money*

Camarillo State Hospital and Center
Box 6022
Camarillo, CA 93011
Phone: (805)484-3661

Opportunities: Hires degreed and licensed M.D.s, Ph.D.s, and M.S.W.s.

Benefits: Benefits include medical insurance, life insurance, dental insurance, and vision insurance.

Application Procedures: Openings are posted internally. Applicants can come in to review the listings, then send resume and cover letter to the Test Office. Does not accept unsolicited resumes.

▶ **Internships**

Contact: Ed Ray, Ph.D.

Type: Offers stipend internships to Ph.D.'s in clinical psychology. To apply, contact the psychology internship department at (805)389-2735.

Camelot Care Center, Inc.
1502 N. Northwest Hwy.
Palatine, IL 60067
Phone: (708)359-5600
Fax: (708)359-2759

Opportunities: Hires therapists. Requires a B.A. or B.S.

Benefits: Benefits include medical insurance, dental insurance, and a 401(k) plan.

Human Resources: Mike Bentle.

Application Procedures: Contact by phone or send resume to Mike Bentle.

Caretenders HealthCorp
9200 Shelbyville Rd.
Louisville, KY 40222
Phone: (502)425-4701

Business Description: Nursing, personal and adult day care.

Officers: Kenneth Hamlet, CEO; Richard D. Malloy, CFO; John Yarmouth, Sr. VP; William B. Yarmuth, Pres. & Chairman of the Board; Tim Luckett, Human Resources Dir.

Opportunities: Hires paraprofessionals, administrative staff, and accounting staff at entry-level. Depending on the position, previous experience and/or a college degree may be required. All accounting positions require a college degree.

Benefits: Benefits include medical insurance, life insurance, dental insurance, profit sharing, and 401(k).

Human Resources: Tim Lockhead.

Application Procedures: Send resume and cover letter or apply in person at the Personnel Department Tuesdays and Thursdays from 9:00 a.m. to 4:00 p.m.

CareUnit Clinics of Washington
10322 NE 132nd
Kirkland, WA 98034
Phone: (206)821-1122

Business Description: Chemical dependency out-patient clinic.

Officers: Don Mullen, Manager; Lois Tomplins, Finance Officer.

Opportunities: Hires entry-level dietary and finance staff. Previous experience is required.

Benefits: Benefits include medical insurance, life insurance, dental insurance, vision insurance, savings plan, 401(k), and long-term disability insurance.

Human Resources: Jean Morris, Contact.

Application Procedures: Fill out an application and send resume and cover letter to the Personnel Director.

▶ **Internships**

Type: The company does not offer any internship programs.

CareUnit Hospital of Cincinnati

3156 Glenmore Ave.
Cincinnati, OH 45211
Phone: (513)481-8822
Fax: (513)481-7317

Opportunities: The hospital hires personnel at all levels. Some positions require previous experience, others require some college course work or college degrees.

Benefits: Benefits include 401(k), medical insurance, life insurance, dental insurance, and vision insurance.

Human Resources: Marcia Hahn.

Application Procedures: Send resume to the administration office or contact in person to answer ads placed in local papers. Marcia Hahn.

CareUnit of Colorado

1290 S. Potomac St.
Aurora, CO 80012
Phone: (303)745-2273
Fax: (303)369-9556

Opportunities: Hires entry-level staff in all areas. Requirements vary depending on the position.

Benefits: Benefits include HML insurance plan, 401(k), and vacation days.

Human Resources: Julie Hansberry, Contact.

Application Procedures: Send resume and cover letter to the attention of Personnel or apply in person and fill out an application.

▶ **Internships**

Type: Offers unpaid internships for college credit. **Number Available Annually:** 3.

Qualifications: College students.

Application Procedure: Applications should be sent to the Personnel Department.

CareUnit of South Florida Inc.

12220 Bruce B. Downs
Tampa, FL 33612
Phone: (813)978-0879

Business Description: Drug dependency treatment center.

Officers: James Carmany, President; Steve Munroe, VP of Finance.

Carpenter HealthCare Systems

1 City Place
Creve Coeur, MO 63141
Phone: (314)569-2662
Fax: (314)569-2170

Business Description: A marketing and management company specializing in the development and implementation of treatment programs for behavioral related illnesses.

Officers: John Carpenter, President; Robert Coerver, VP of Project Development; Jerry Gianopulos, Dir. of Operations; David Ritchey, Dir. of Communications; Joanne Vollmer, Dir. of Programs; Oscar Watts, Exec. VP.

Opportunities: Hires counselors, interventionists, and marketing representatives.

Human Resources: John Gillespie.

Application Procedures: Send resume and cover letter to the attention of Victoria Akins.

▶ **Internships**

Type: The company does not offer any internship programs.

Catlett Corp.

807 W. 3rd St.
Little Rock, AR 72201
Phone: (501)372-7249

Business Description: Operator of nursing homes.

Officers: Leon Catlett, President.

CENAPS Corp.

18650 Dixie Hwy.
Homewood, IL 60430
Phone: (708)799-5000

Business Description: Training and consulting firm for substance abuse.

Officers: Terence T. Gorski, President; Janet Voss, Dir. of Mktg.

Opportunities: The company fills clerical positions with entry level staff. Minimum requirements vary but include previous experience in a related field.

Benefits: Benefits include medical insurance and a life insurance plan.

Human Resources: Janet Voss.

Application Procedures: Interested candidates should contact the company to fulfill the company training requirements.

MENTAL HEALTH CAREER DIRECTORY

▶ **Internships**

Type: The company offers paid internships to college students who have two years experience in rehabilitation work. All interns must go through company training.

Center of Behavioral Therapy P.C.
24453 Grand River
Detroit, MI 48219
Phone: (313)592-1765

Officers: Hollis Evans, Contact.

What is underway in the 1990s is more than a massive corporate restructuring or a one-time adjustment. It's an overhaul of the U.S. labor force, a sea change in the kinds of jobs and the type of work that will be available. Workers in this new era will have to be more flexible, more willing to move cross-country for a job, more willing to go back to school. Today's college graduate can expect 12 to 13 jobs in three to four different careers over her or his lifetime.

Source: USA Today

Centrac - Care Inc.
12401 Olive Sreet Rd., Ste. 103
St. Louis, MO 63141
Phone: (816)333-3440

Business Description: Market research and telemarketing.

Officers: Ronald Leeds, President.

Central State Hospital
3000 W. Washington St.
Indianapolis, IN 46222
Phone: (317)639-3600

Opportunities: Psychiatric attendants are required to have previous experience; there are openings for general and registered nurses.

Benefits: Benefits include medical insurance, life insurance, dental insurance, vision insurance, tuition assistance, vacation and sick days.

Human Resources: Joyce Crull.

Application Procedures: Call Indiana Job Bank (317)232-3105.

▶ **Internships**

Type: Paid internships are available through the governor's office.

Champions Psychiatric Treatment Center
14320 Walters Rd.
Houston, TX 77014
Phone: (713)537-5050
Fax: (713)537-2726

Opportunities: Hires entry-level staff in several areas, including housekeeping, direct care, maintenance, and psychology. Requirements vary depending upon the positions, but previous experience and/or a college degree is required in most positions. Applicants for psychologist positions must have a Ph.D.

Benefits: Benefits include medical insurance, life insurance, dental insurance, vision insurance, savings plan, and 401(k).

Human Resources: Steven Daniell.

Application Procedures: Apply in person, call, or send resume and cover letter to Steven Daniell.

▶ **Internships**

Type: This company does not offer any internship programs.

Charter Hospital of the East Valley
2190 N. Grace Blvd.
Chandler, AZ 85224
Phone: (602)899-8989

Business Description: Psychiatric hospital.

Officers: Edward Lamb, Dir. of Admin.; Brent Kaminsky, Controller.

Opportunities: Requires a college degree, previous experience, or at least some college course work.

Benefits: Benefits include medical insurance, life insurance, dental insurance, and vision insurance. Also offers savings plan, tuition assistance, and profit sharing.

Application Procedures: Applications will be mailed to those requesting them by phone or send a resume.

▶ **Internships**

Contact: Nancy Piclar, Internship Contact.

Type: Offers unpaid internships to college students.

Charter Medical Corp.
577 Mulberry St.
PO Box 209
Macon, GA 31298
Phone: (912)742-1161
Fax: (912)751-2335

Business Description: An international hospital management company.

Officers: C. Michael Ford, VP of Finance; William McAfee, Jr., President; Don Serfass, Dir. of Info. Systems.

Benefits: Benefits include health care programs, dental insurance, and a 401(k) plan.

Human Resources: Al Joyner, Employment.

Application Procedures: Places newspaper advertisements for certain openings. Accepts unsolicited resumes; send resume and cover letter to the attention of Al Joyner, Employment.

▶ **Internships**

Contact: Laura Pugh.

Type: Offers internships.

Qualifications: College students.

Application Procedure: For more information, contact Laura Pugh.

Chicago-Read Mental Health Center
4200 N. Oak Park Ave.
Chicago, IL 60634
Phone: (312)794-4000

Opportunities: Hires entry-level mental health technician training staff and support service workers. Previous experience and/or college course work required depending on the position desired. Psychology positions require a Ph.D. and social workers must have a master's degree.

Benefits: Benefits include medical insurance, life insurance, dental insurance, savings plan, tuition assistance, and child-care programs.

Application Procedures: Send resume, call, or apply at the Downtown State of Illinois Center.

▶ **Internships**

Type: Offers paid internships in psychology and college credit internships in nursing. **Number Available Annually:** 3 psychology, nursing varies.

Qualifications: College students. Psychology interns must be enrolled in a PhD program.

Application Procedure: Send in application and schedule an interview with the Personnel Department.

Children's Home of Detroit
900 Cook Rd.
Grosse Pointe Woods, MI 48080
Phone: (313)886-0800

Benefits: Benefits include life insurance, dental insurance, vision insurance, profit sharing, and vacation time.

Human Resources: Andy Windonski.

Application Procedures: Fill out application in person or send resume to the attention of Andy Windonski.

▶ **Internships**

Type: Offers unpaid internships for college credit in social work. **Number Available Annually:** 2.

Thirty years after the Equal Pay Act was passed, women are still earning only 70 cents for every dollar a man makes.

Source: *Working Woman*

Children's Hospital of Orange County
455 S. Main St.
Orange, CA 92668
Phone: (714)997-3000

Opportunities: The company hires entry level staff for clerical positions who have previous experience.

Benefits: Benefits include medical insurance, dental insurance, vision insurance, and a retirement plan.

Human Resources: Nora Rodriguez.

Application Procedures: Applicants should go to the personnel department in person to apply.

▶ **Internships**

Type: The company offers paid internships and internships for college credit. The application

Choate Mental Health and Developmental Center
1000 N. Main St.
Anna, IL 62906
Phone: (618)833-5161

Opportunities: May require a college degree, previous experience, or some college course work depending on position.

Benefits: Benefits include medical insurance, life insurance, dental insurance, vision insurance, savings plan, and tuition assistance.

Human Resources: Alice Kerns.

Application Procedures: Send in resume to the attention of Alice Kerns. Must receive a civil service grade to apply.

▶ **Internships**

Type: Offers internships for college credit.

Qualifications: Must have junior or senior status for most internships, although high school graduates are accepted for certain positions.

Application Procedure: Must contact department heads for internship information.

CMG Health Inc.
25 Crossroads Dr.
Owings Mills, MD 21117
Phone: (410)581-5000

Business Description: Nationally managed mental healthcare, employee assistance programs and substance abuse programs.

Officers: Alan Shusterman, President; Henry Boyd, COO; Wayne Feest, VP of Mktg.; Henry Boyd, COO; Diana Woltereck, VP of Business Development.

Human Resources: Lisa Hamburger, Human Resource Generalist.

Colmery-O'Neil Department of Veterans Affairs Medical Center
2200 Gage Blvd.
Topeka, KS 66622
Phone: (913)272-3111
Fax: (913)271-4309

Employees: 1,120.

Average Entry-Level Hiring: 20.

Opportunities: The following positions require procedures vary according to positions. Contact the company for more information.

a college degree: medical technologist, vocational rehabilitation specialist, pharmacist, physical therapist, occupational therapist, dietician, physician assistant, and social work associate. Psychologist—Ph.D. required. Social worker—M.S.W. required. Registered nurse—must be a graduate of a professional nursing program or have a bachelor's degree. Nurse anesthetist—must be a graduate of a school of professional nursing and anesthesia. LPN, PTA, OTA—specialized education required.

Human Resources: Christine Myers; Wanda Lyon.

Colorado State Hospital
1600 W. 24th St.
Pueblo, CO 81003
Phone: (719)546-4000

Officers: Jack Ford, Contact.

Opportunities: Hires entry-level nurses, technicians, and janitorial and clerical staff.

Benefits: Benefits include medical insurance, life insurance, and dental insurance.

Application Procedures: Those interested should fill out a state employee application. No unsolicited resumes.

▶ **Internships**

Type: Offers paid psychiatric internships.
Number Available Annually: 1.

Qualifications: Graduate students.

Application Procedure: Contact the hospital for information.

Columbia Health Systems Inc.
2025 E. Newport Rd.
Milwaukee, WI 53211
Phone: (414)961-3300

Business Description: Operators of medical clinics and nursing homes.

Officers: John Sculler, President.

Columbia Health Systems, Inc.
5401 College Blvd., Ste. 204
Leawood, KS 66211
Phone: (913)451-1111

Officers: Bob Reed, Contact.

Opportunities: Entry-level positions require a college degree, previous experience, or at least some college course work.

Benefits: Provides medical benefits.

Application Procedures: Apply in person, contact by phone, or send a resume.

Community Lifecare Enterprises

PO Box 20130
Springfield, IL 62708-0130
Phone: (217)523-9368

Business Description: Operator of skilled nursing care facilities other than hospitals. Operator of nursing or personal care facilities that require a lesser degree of care than skilled or intermediate care facilities.

Human Resources: Gary Engelmann.

Application Procedures: Send resume and cover letter to the attention of Gary Engelmann.

Community Psychiatric Centers

24502 Pacific Park Dr.
Laguna Hills, CA 92656
Phone: (714)831-1166

Business Description: Community Psychiatric Centers' principal line of business is the ownership and operation of acute psychiatric hospitals. The company operated 45 acute psychiatric hospitals and one 32 bed alcohol treatment facility. Each hospital in the United States is accredited by the Joint Commission on Accreditation of Healthcare Organizations (JCAHO).

Officers: James W. Conte, Pres. & Chairman of the Board; Richard L. Conte, Exec. VP, Chief Admin. Officer, General Counsel & Sec.; Barry Dyches, Sr. VP; Theodore Johson, Vice Pres.; Patrick Kelly, Vice Pres.; Sharon Kurz, Vice Pres.; Kay E. Seim, Vice Pres.; Loren B. Shook, Exec. VP; James P. Smith, Sr. VP, Sec. & Treasurer; David Wakefield, Sr. VP; Ronald Yates, Vice Pres.

Benefits: Benefits include health care programs, dental insurance, a 401(k) plan, an employee pension plan and profit sharing.

Application Procedures: Hiring is done through individual divisions. Send resume and cover letter to the attention of the Human Resources Department.

▶ **Internships**

Type: The company does not offer an internship program.

Comprehensive Aging Services Inc.

19100 W. 7 Mile Rd.
Detroit, MI 48219
Phone: (313)532-7112

Business Description: Private or government establishment engaged in providing social, counseling, welfare and/or referral services.

Officers: Robert Flynn, Finance Officer; Alan S. Funk, Exec. VP; Patricia G. Liss, Dir. of Mktg.

Human Resources: Sylvia Serwin.

According to the Bureau of Labor Statistics, the rapid growth of women entering the workforce—about 2.3% per year from 1975 to 1990—is expected to slow, growing at a rate of 1.6% per year in the next fifteen years. By 2005, minorities are expected to account for more than 25% of all working people in the US, with the fastest growth occurring among Hispanics, who will make up over 11% of the workforce by 2005.

Source: *Forbes*

Connecticut State Department of Mental Health

90 Washington St.
Hartford, CT 06106
Phone: (203)566-3650

Opportunities: Hires entry-level mental health staff with previous experience and some college course work.

Benefits: Benefits include medical insurance, life insurance, dental insurance, vision insurance, tuition assistance, and child-care programs.

Human Resources: Mary Kotiadis.

Application Procedures: Apply in person or send resume and cover letter to the attention of the personnel department.

▶ **Internships**

Type: The company does not offer an internship program.

Mental Health Career Directory

Connecticut Valley Hospital
Silver St.
Middletown, CT 06457
Phone: (203)344-2666

Officers: Regina Jones, Contact.

Opportunities: Hires nurses with training, psychologists with a bachelor's degree, and social workers with a bachelor's degree who have passed the social work examination.

Benefits: Benefits include medical insurance, life insurance, dental insurance, tuition assistance, child-care programs, elder-care programs, personal and vacation leave, and deferred compensation.

Application Procedures: Positions advertised in classifieds. Send resume and cover letter to the attention of Regina Jones.

▶ **Internships**

Type: Offers paid and unpaid internships to college students of rehabilitative services, psychology, and social work. **Number Available Annually:** 6.

Application Procedure: Psychology internships are listed in the American Psychological Association Journal. Can apply to the Director of Psychology.

To gain more control over your career, develop strong communications skills, both listening and talking. This means understanding and being able to translate what corporate goals are, and being able to talk to management. Actively solicit feedback.

Source: *Dallas Morning News*

Contact Inc.
1400 E. Southern Ave.
Tempe, AZ 85282
Phone: (602)730-5528

Business Description: Employee assistance program provider.

Officers: Larry Frazier, CEO; Anna Schwartz, Dir. of Mktg.

Coral Ridge Psychiatric Hospital
4545 N. Federal Hwy.
Fort Lauderdale, FL 33308
Phone: (305)771-2711

Opportunities: Hires the following entry-level personnel: nursing assistants; secretaries; psychiatrists; unit leaders; physicians; and social workers. Depending on the position, previous experience and/or a college degree is required.

Benefits: Benefits include medical insurance, life insurance, dental insurance, vision insurance, and tuition assistance.

Application Procedures: Apply in person for a direct interview and to fill out an application. Bring references.

▶ **Internships**

Type: The company does not offer any internship programs.

Coreance Inc.
350 Broadway
Boulder, CO 80303
Phone: (303)494-3108

Business Description: Rehabilitation center.

Officers: Joe Costello, President.

CPC St. Johns River Hospital
6300 Beach Blvd.
Jacksonville, FL 32216
Phone: (904)724-9202

Opportunities: Hires entry-level personnel in all areas. Requirements vary depending on the position.

Benefits: Benefits include medical insurance, life insurance, dental insurance, and 401(k).

Human Resources: Priscilla McReynolds.

Application Procedures: Apply in person or send resume and cover letter to the attention of Priscilla McReynolds.

▶ **Internships**

Contact: Priscilla McReynolds.

Type: Offers unpaid internships for college credit.

Application Procedure: Send resume and cover to contact person.

Day Treatment Center of Dallas
1326 Stemmons Ave.
Dallas, TX 75208
Phone: (214)943-1878

Opportunities: Hires entry-level clerical and clinical staff. Previous experience and a college degree are required.

Benefits: Benefits include medical insurance.

Human Resources: Jane Baggett.

Application Procedures: Send resume and cover letter to the attention of Jane Baggett.

▶ **Internships**

Type: The company does not offer an internship program.

De Paul Hospital

4143 S. 13th St.
Milwaukee, WI 53221
Phone: (414)281-4400

Business Description: Operator of specialized outpatient facilities.

Officers: Thomas Bozewicz, President; David Oines, CFO; Aenone M. Rosario, Dir. of Mktg.

Benefits: Benefits include dental insurance, medical insurance, long-term disability, short-term disability, and pension plan.

Human Resources: Herbert Steffes.

Application Procedures: Interested candidates should forward applications to the human resources department. Advertises in classified section of newspaper.

▶ **Internships**

Type: The company does not offer an internship program.

Delaware Curative Workshop

1600 Washington St.
Wilmington, DE 19802
Phone: (302)656-2521

Opportunities: Hires entry-level custodial staff, clerical staff, and clinical technicians. Requirements vary depending upon the position.

Benefits: Benefits include medical insurance, life insurance, savings plan, disability insurance, and 401(k).

Human Resources: Mr. Andreola.

Application Procedures: Send resume and cover letter.

▶ **Internships**

Type: Offers unpaid internships for college credit. **Number Available Annually:** 6.

Qualifications: College students.

Application Procedure: Internships are arranged through the universities.

Delaware Department of Health and Social Services

1901 N. DuPont Hwy.
New Castle, DE 19720
Phone: (302)577-4500
Fax: (302)421-8251

Opportunities: Hires at the entry level in many areas, including clerical, direct service, and social work. Requirements vary with positions. Previous experience is helpful and most social workers have a bachelor's degree.

Benefits: Benefits include medical insurance, life insurance, dental insurance, and vision insurance.

Human Resources: Wayne Bergner.

Application Procedures: Available positions are announced. Apply in person and fill out an application for a specific position.

▶ **Internships**

Contact: Dana Jefferson.

Type: Offers paid and unpaid internships. College credit is available. **Number Available Annually:** 5.

Qualifications: College students.

Application Procedure: Send letters or resumes to Dana Jefferson.

Delaware State Hospital Division of Alcoholism, Drug Abuse and Mental Health

1901 N. DuPont Hwy.
New Castle, DE 19720
Phone: (302)577-4000

Opportunities: Hires entry-level staff in most areas. May require a college degree or previous experience.

Benefits: Benefits include life insurance, dental insurance, vision insurance, savings plan, and a credit union. Sick time and vacation time are accumulated.

Application Procedures: Apply in person or send a resume.

▶ **Internships**

Type: Offers psychiatric residencies.

JOB OPPORTUNITIES DATABANK

MENTAL HEALTH CAREER DIRECTORY

Devereux Center in Arizona
6436 E. Sweetwater Ave.
Scottsdale, AZ 85254
Phone: (602)998-2920
Fax: (602)443-5589

Officers: Kay Niki, Contact.

Top Traits of Superior Leaders

1. Honest
2. Competent
3. Forward-looking
4. Inspiring
5. Intelligent
6. Fair-minded
7. Broad-minded
8. Courageous
9. Straightforward
10. Imaginative

Source: *Business Credit*

District of Columbia Alcohol and Drug Abuse Services
1300 1st St., NE
Washington, DC 20001
Phone: (202)727-1762
Fax: (202)727-1653

Officers: Beatrice Smith, Contact.

Opportunities: Entry-level openings available to those with clerical skills. Positions require a college degree or previous experience.

Benefits: Benefits include medical insurance, life insurance, dental insurance, vision insurance, and savings plan.

Application Procedures: Must submit a completed 171 State application. Does not accept unsolicited resumes.

District of Columbia Commission on Mental Health Services
St. Elizabeth's Campus
2700 Martin Luther King Jr. Ave., SE
A Bldg., Ste. 105
Washington, DC 20032
Phone: (202)373-7166
Fax: (202)373-6484

Opportunities: Hires entry-level staff with previous experience and a college degree.

Benefits: Benefits include medical insurance, life insurance, and dental insurance.

Human Resources: Morris Vines Chf. Admin. Off., Personnel.

Application Procedures: All applications must be processed through civil service procedures.

▶ **Internships**

Type: Offers paid internships for psychiatrists and social workers. **Number Available Annually:** 100.

Qualifications: College graduates.

Application Procedure: Apply through the Civil Service Department.

District of Columbia Commission on Social Services
609 H St., NE, 5th Fl.
Washington, DC 20002
Phone: (202)727-5930
Fax: (202)727-1687

Benefits: Benefits include medical insurance, life insurance, dental insurance, vision insurance, deferred compensation, workman's compensation, and paid holidays.

Human Resources: Mrs. Young.

Application Procedures: The Company requires college degrees or previous experience for all positions. Clerical candidates must also pass a typing test. Other positions include technicians, teachers, doctors, police officers, and fire fighters. Applicants must submit a completed 171 Application and show proof of training.

Diversion Associates
PO Box 16338
Portland, OR 97216
Phone: (503)253-5954

Business Description: Alcohol treatment center.

Officers: Richard Drandoff, Dir. of Admin.

Opportunities: Hires candidates with previous experience or a college degree to fill positions in the professional and counseling staffs.

Benefits: Benefits include a contributory health plan.

Human Resources: Richard Drandoff.

Application Procedures: Places newspaper advertisements for certain openings. Send resume with samples or contact by phone.

▶ **Internships**

Contact: Richard Drandoff, Human Resource Contact.

Type: Offers unpaid internships for college credit.

Application Procedure: Applications should be sent to Richard Drandoff.

East Louisiana State Hospital
PO Box 498
Jackson, LA 70748
Phone: (504)634-2651

Opportunities: Hires entry-level janitorial staff, laundry workers, and psychiatric aids with no experience (hospital will train). Also hires social workers, psychologists, and psychiatrists. These positions require a BSW, PhD, and MD, respectively.

Benefits: Benefits include medical insurance, life insurance, and dental insurance.

Human Resources: Vanessa Dunn.

Application Procedures: Applicants should fill out a civil service application with any state agency and send resume and cover letter.

▶ **Internships**

Type: The company does not offer an internship program.

Eastwood Clinic
20811 Kelly Rd., Ste. 1
East Detroit, MI 48021
Phone: (313)773-2300
Fax: (313)773-0857

Human Resources: Kay Riepe.

▶ **Internships**

Type: The company does not offer an internship program.

Edgewood Children's Center
1801 Vicente St.
San Francisco, CA 94116
Phone: (415)681-3211

Officers: Edi Hoffman, Contact.

Opportunities: Hires entry-level kitchen and maintenance staff, clerical staff, and counseling staff. Counseling positions required a bachelor's degree and some previous experience.

Benefits: Benefits include medical insurance, dental insurance, and 401(k).

Application Procedures: Send resume and cover letter to the attention of Edi Hoffman.

▶ **Internships**

Contact: Edi Hoffman.

Type: Offers unpaid internships for college credit. **Number Available Annually:** 10.

Qualifications: College students.

Application Procedure: Contact Edi Hoffman for application information.

Elgin Mental Health Center
750 S. State St.
Elgin, IL 60123
Phone: (708)742-1040

Opportunities: Hires mental health technician trainees and support service workers. Requires a college degree.

Benefits: Benefits include medical insurance, life insurance, dental insurance, and deferred compensation.

Human Resources: Russel E. Lake.

Application Procedures: Send resume to Russel E. Lake, Personnel Director.

Englewood Hospital
350 Engle St.
Englewood, NJ 07631
Phone: (201)894-3490
Fax: (201)894-4791

Employees: 2,500.

Average Entry-Level Hiring: Unknown.

Opportunities: No information on specific opportunities available.

Evansville State Hospital
3400 Lincoln Ave.
Evansville, IN 47714
Phone: (812)473-2222

Opportunities: Hires social workers. Requires a college degree.

Benefits: Benefits include medical insurance, life insurance, dental insurance, vision insurance, and deferred compensation.

Human Resources: Bruce Miller.

Application Procedures: Apply in person or

MENTAL HEALTH CAREER DIRECTORY

send resume to Bruce Miller, Personnel Director.

Ewing Residential Treatment Center

1610 Stuyvesant Ave.
Trenton, NJ 08618
Phone: (609)530-3350

Opportunities: The company is currently engaged in a hiring freeze for all levels except head nurses and repairmen. Typically, the company hires entry-level staff in all areas. Requirements vary depending on the position.

Benefits: Benefits include medical insurance, life insurance, dental insurance, vision insurance, child-care programs, tuition assistance, and deferred annuity.

Application Procedures: Applicants should return completed Civil Service applications to the company or submit a resume. Resumes will be kept on file during the job freeze.

▶ **Internships**

Type: The company does not offer any internship programs.

Social workers in general are motivated by a desire to help, to enable those they serve to enjoy a measure of health and well-being, and to be productive members of the community. While other considerations surely enter into a decision to choose a career, the decision to become a social worker is usually predicated on a belief that doing so will contribute to the greater good.

Source: National Association of Social Workers

Fairbanks Hospital, Inc.

8102 Clearvista Pkwy.
Indianapolis, IN 46256
Phone: (317)849-8222

Opportunities: Entry-level positions available for secretarial, accounting, dietary, and housekeeping staff. All positions require at least a high school degree. Dietary and housekeeping positions require previous experience. Accounting positions require related college course work.

Benefits: Benefits include medical insurance, dental insurance, pension plan, flexible spending plan, and tuition assistance.

Human Resources: Sharon Baker.

Application Procedures: Send resume and cover letter or apply in person to Sharon Baker.

Fairfield Hills Hospital

PO Box 5525
Newtown, CT 06470
Phone: (203)426-2531

Opportunities: Hires entry-level staff in all areas. Depending on the position, previous experience, college course work, and/or a college degree may be required.

Benefits: Benefits include medical insurance, life insurance, dental insurance, savings plan, and child-care programs.

Application Procedures: Send resume and cover letter and an application to the director or head of the department of interest.

▶ **Internships**

Contact: Robin Plamondon.

Type: Offers paid and unpaid internships in psychology. **Number Available Annually:** 8.

Application Procedure: Students must be referred from their school. Applications should be sent to contact.

Fairfield Hospital for Psychiatric and Addictive Disease Medicine

3000 Fairfield Ave.
Shreveport, LA 71104
Phone: (318)222-2700

Opportunities: Hires secretaries and receptionists with previous experience for entry-level work.

Benefits: Benefits include medical insurance, life insurance, dental insurance, and a retirement plan.

Human Resources: Marsha Middleton; Carol Sutton.

Application Procedures: Apply in person to Carol Sutton.

▶ **Internships**

Type: Offers unpaid internships for credit for students working towards certification. **Number Available Annually:** 2.

Application Procedure: Apply directly to unit clinical supervisors.

Florida Department of Health and Rehabilitative Services
1317 Winewood Blvd.
Tallahassee, FL 32399-0700
Phone: (904)488-7721
Fax: (904)922-2993

Opportunities: Hires entry-level clerks and senior clerks. Previous experience, high school diploma, and college degree required.

Benefits: Benefits include medical insurance, life insurance, dental insurance, vision insurance, savings plan, and child-care programs.

Application Procedures: Job listings are posted. Send resume and cover letter and application to the person named in the job listing.

▶ **Internships**

Type: The company does not offer an internship program.

Florida Department of Health and Rehabilitative Services Alcohol, Drug Abuse and Mental Health Program Office
1317 Winewood Blvd., Bldg. 6, Rm. 18
Tallahassee, FL 32399-0700
Phone: (904)488-8304
Fax: (904)487-2239

Opportunities: Hires entry-level clerical workers.

Benefits: Benefits include medical insurance, life insurance, dental insurance, supplemental insurance, retirement plans, and deferred compensation.

Human Resources: Karen Dalton, Personnel Services Specialist.

Application Procedures: Those interested can either apply in person, by phone, or by sending in a resume (for a specific position only) to any state personnel office.

▶ **Internships**

Type: Unpaid internships are available.

Florida State Hospital
PO Box 156
Chattahoochee, FL 32324
Phone: (904)663-7536

Opportunities: Hires social workers with a B.S. and psychiatrists with an M.D.

Benefits: Benefits include medical insurance, life insurance, dental insurance, and vision insurance.

Human Resources: Katherine Chandler.

Application Procedures: Fill out a state application and turn it in with copies of all degrees to any agency or the hospital.

▶ **Internships**

Contact: Katherine Chandler.

Type: Offers paid internships. **Number Available Annually:** 5-10.

Your next job need not be at another company. Pay attention to the special skills of people newly hired or recently promoted by your current employer. That will give you an indication of what talents are valued so you can upgrade your skills and re-invent your job to make sure it stays relevant to your company's needs.

Source: *Money*

Forsythe-Stokes Mental Health Center
725 N. Highland Ave.
Winston-Salem, NC 27101
Phone: (919)725-7777

Human Resources: Lanore Pless.

Fort Logan Mental Health Center
3520 W. Oxford Ave.
Denver, CO 80236
Phone: (303)761-0220

Officers: Martha Gnam, Contact.

Opportunities: Hires clerical staff, grounds workers, and maintenance workers in entry-level positions. Also offers opportunities for RNs and psychologists with a Ph.D. in clinical psychology.

Benefits: Benefits include medical insurance, life insurance, dental insurance, and vision insurance. Also offers savings plan, tuition assistance, and a nursery.

Application Procedures: Apply at any State agency office.

▶ **Internships**

Type: Offers paid internships for college credit to psychology and social work students. **Number Available Annually:** 3-4.

Application Procedure: Apply through the school. Applications will be sent to the discipline chiefs in each area.

Four Winds Chicago LP
40 Timberline Dr.
Lemont, IL 60439
Phone: (708)257-3636

Business Description: Psychiatric hospital.

Officers: Ian Aitken, CEO; Karen K. Lemaster, CFO.

Opportunities: Hires entry-level staff in all areas. Previous experience is required.

Benefits: Benefits include medical insurance, life insurance, dental insurance, vision insurance, savings plan, and tuition assistance.

Human Resources: Karen Litner, Employment.

Application Procedures: Call or send send resume and cover letter with samples to Karen Litner.

▶ **Internships**

Contact: Karen Litner.

Type: Offers programs for college credit.

Qualifications: Student nurses.

Application Procedure: Send resume and samples to contact.

Friends Recovery Center
520 N. Delaware Ave., Ste. 302
Riverview Place Bldg.
Philadelphia, PA 19123
Phone: (215)627-4278
Fax: (215)627-4058

Officers: Keith Classic.

Opportunities: Hires entry-level personnel in all service areas. A high school diploma or the equivalent is required.

Benefits: Benefits include medical insurance, life insurance, and short- and long-term disability insurance.

Application Procedures: Apply in person, call, or send resume and cover letter to the attention of Human Resources.

▶ **Internships**

Type: Offers unpaid internships for college credit. **Number Available Annually:** 4.

Qualifications: Students working on their Ph.D.

Application Procedure: Call the psychology department and request a brochure for the internship.

The Gables
604 5th St., SW
Rochester, MN 55902-3256
Phone: (507)282-2500

Officers: Nancy Jean, Contact.

Benefits: Offers paid vacations.

Application Procedures: Send resume to the attention of the CEO.

▶ **Internships**

Type: The company does not offer an internship program.

Genesis Health Ventures
148 W. State St.
Kennett Square, PA 19348
Phone: (215)444-6350

Business Description: Operator of skilled nursing care facilities other than hospitals.

Application Procedures: Interested candidates should forward resumes to Mary Ann in the Human Resource Department.

▶ **Internships**

Type: The company does not offer any internship programs.

Georgia Division of Mental Health, Mental Retardation and Substance Abuse
278 Peachtree St.
Atlanta, GA 30303
Phone: (404)894-6300
Fax: (404)853-9058

Opportunities: Hires entry-level staff in all areas. Previous experience and/or college degree required.

Benefits: Benefits include medical insurance, life insurance, dental insurance, and savings plan.

Application Procedures: For job listings, call (404) 894-4592. Apply in person.

▶ **Internships**

Type: Offers paid and unpaid internships and co-op programs. Number Available Annually: 1-10 (varies).

Qualifications: College students.

Application Procedure: Send resume to department of interest.

Georgia Mental Health Institute

1256 Briarcliff Rd., NE
Atlanta, GA 30306
Phone: (404)894-5911

Opportunities: Hires entry-level personnel in direct care and housekeeping. Previous experience and some college course work is required to work in direct care.

Benefits: Benefits include medical insurance, life insurance, dental insurance, defined contribution, and savings plan.

Human Resources: Fay Childs.

Application Procedures: Apply in person or send resume and cover letter to the attention of Fay Childs.

▶ **Internships**

Type: The company does not offer any internship programs.

Geriatric and Medical Centers Inc.

5601 Chestnut St.
Philadelphia, PA 19139
Phone: (215)476-2250

Business Description: Engaged in providing such miscellaneous local transportation as ambulances, vanpools or chauffeured limousines. Wholesaler of medical, dental, surgical, X-ray or hospital equipment and supplies. Operator of skilled nursing care facilities other than hospitals. Operator of intermediate care facilities.

Officers: Robert F. Carfagno, Sr. VP & CFO; Daniel Veloric, Pres. & Chairman of the Board.

Human Resources: James J. Wankmiller.

Application Procedures: Interested candidates should submit completed applications and resumes to the Human Resources Department.

▶ **Internships**

Type: The company does not offer any internship programs.

Glenbeigh Hospital of Cleveland

18120 Puritas Ave.
Cleveland, OH 44135
Phone: (216)476-0222

Opportunities: Hires for openings in housekeeping, dietary, and counseling departments. Some positions require previous experience, others require some college course work or college degree.

Benefits: Benefits include medical insurance, life insurance, vision insurance, savings plan, tuition assistance, and profit sharing.

Human Resources: Chris Mohnickey.

Application Procedures: Apply in person or send resume and cover letter to the attention of Chris Mohnickey.

▶ **Internships**

Type: The hospital offers unpaid internships. Number Available Annually: 3.

Qualifications: Applicants must be college juniors or seniors.

Application Procedure: Apply in person or contact the personnel department by phone.

> If complacency is bad for your career, thinking into the future will keep you ahead of change. To others, it will seem as if you are moving effortlessly into the better jobs in the successful department or company. In fact, it will be because you worked hard, planned well and prepared yourself.
>
> Source: *Business Monday/Detroit Free Press*

Glenbeigh Inc.

1001 N. US Hwy. 1
Jupiter, FL 33477
Phone: (407)747-6588

Business Description: Psychiatric hospital holding company.

Officers: Norman McCann, President.

Opportunities: All hiring levels require a college degree and previous experience.

Benefits: Offers some benefits including vision insurance and a 401(k) plan.

Application Procedures: Apply in person or send resume and samples to the attention of the Personnel Department.

▶ **Internships**

Type: Offers unpaid internships for college credit to students of junior and senior status.

Good Neighbor Services Inc.
2177 Youngman Ave.
St. Paul, MN 55116
Phone: (612)698-6544

Opportunities: Hires entry-level staff in nursing, housekeeping, social work, therapeutic recreation, and dietary aides. Previous experience required; college degree required for therapeutic recreation and social work staff.

Benefits: Benefits include medical insurance, dental insurance, vision insurance, and 401(k).

Application Procedures: Apply in person or send resume and cover letter.

▶ **Internships**

Type: The company does not offer an internship program.

Gracie Square Hospital
420 E. 76th St.
New York, NY 10021
Phone: (212)988-4400
Fax: (212)879-8249

Business Description: Psychiatric hospital with the following inpatient services: general, geriatric, eating disorders, detoxification, and drug/alcohol rehabilitation.

▶ **Internships**

Contact: Dr. Fran Luckom-Nurnberg, Dir., Dept. Psychological Services.

Type: Offers two unpaid psychology internships and four paid psychology externships. **Applications Received:** 25.

Duties: Psychology interns serve as research assistants who screen patients and attend workshops and staff meetings. Psychology externs do psychodiagnostic testing, psychotherapy, and also attend workshops and staff meetings.

Qualifications: College students, college graduates, and graduate students. Psychology externs should be enrolled in a clinical psychology Ph.D. program.

Application Procedure: Call or write the contact; personal interviews are required.

Application Deadline: March 31.

Grady Memorial Hospital
PO Box 26208
Atlanta, GA 30035-3801
Phone: (404)616-1900
Fax: (404)616-6033

Human Resources: Carolyn Hughes.

Greater Bridgeport Community Mental Health Center
1635 Central Ave.
Bridgeport, CT 06610
Phone: (203)579-6646

Opportunities: Hires nurses, doctors, and housekeepers. Requirements depend on qualifications.

Benefits: Benefits include medical insurance, life insurance, dental insurance, some optical coverage, and a savings plan.

Human Resources: Cindy Schilcowski; Carol Wallace.

Application Procedures: Apply in person or send resume to the Personnel Department.

Greenleaf Health Systems
2 Northgate Pk., Ste. 201
Chattanooga, TN 37415
Phone: (615)870-5110
Toll-free: 800-982-9922
Fax: (615)870-5545

Business Description: Operator of psychiatric hospitals.

Officers: Dan Page, President.

Application Procedures: The corporate office only recruits M.D.'s and Ph.D.'s. Other applicants should go to individual hospital's human resource department for independent employment procedures.

▶ **Internships**

Type: Many individual hospital branches offer internships. For more information, please contact the company.

Greenville Health Corp. Pain Therapy Centers
100 Mallard St.
Greenville, SC 29601
Phone: (803)455-8257

Opportunities: Entry-level positions offered in all areas. Requires a master's degree for social therapy and certification for occupational therapy.

Benefits: Benefits include medical insurance, life insurance, dental insurance, a savings plan, tuition assistance, a 401(k) plan, child or elder care.

Application Procedures: Apply in person or send resume to the Personnel Department.

▶ **Internships**

Type: Offers paid internships for college credit to graduate students.

Application Procedure: Apply in person to the Personnel Department.

Hamot Health Systems Inc.
100 State St.
Erie, PA 16507
Phone: (814)870-7000

Opportunities: May require some previous experience, a college degree, or some college coursework depending on position.

Benefits: Benefits include medical insurance, life insurance, dental insurance, vision insurance, savings investment plan, tuition assistance, and profit sharing.

Application Procedures: Apply in person.

▶ **Internships**

Type: Offers unpaid internships to college students. **Number Available Annually:** 200.

Application Procedure: Apply through school.

Hawaii Adult Mental Health Division
PO Box 3378
Honolulu, HI 96801-9984
Phone: (808)586-4686
Fax: (808)586-4016

Benefits: Benefits include medical insurance, life insurance, dental insurance, vision insurance, child-care programs, and deferred compensation.

Human Resources: Mrs. Koyame.

Application Procedures: Hires entry-level staff in clerical (high school diploma required) and professional (college degree required) areas. Openings are listed in state agencies. Applications accepted for openings only. Send resume and cover letter to the Department of Personnel. Does not accept unsolicited resumes.

▶ **Internships**

Type: The company does not offer an internship program.

Students with the luxury of a couple of years until graduation should start plotting for that first job and snagging some experience *now*. But with many employers reluctant to pay even the modest salary of an internship, getting actual business experience is increasingly difficult. One strategy: Try a so-called externship, typically a one-week, unpaid stint at a company that provides a snapshot of various careers and a chance to network with insiders. Externships can be particularly useful for liberal-arts majors without a clear career track.

Source: *U.S. News and World Report*

Hawaii Department of Human Services, Health Care Administration Division, Medicaid
820 Mililani St., Ste. 817
Box 339
Honolulu, HI 96813
Phone: (808)586-5391
Fax: (808)586-5389

Opportunities: Hires clerical and some professional applicants with a college degree.

Benefits: Benefits include medical insurance, life insurance, dental insurance, vision insurance, savings plan, tuition assistance, and child-care programs.

Human Resources: Sharon Uracleo.

Application Procedures: Those interested should contact the state personnel office.

▶ **Internships**

Type: The company does not offer an internship program.

MENTAL HEALTH CAREER DIRECTORY

HCA Psychiatric Co.
1 Park Pl.
Nashville, TN 37203
Phone: (615)327-9551

Opportunities: Hires entry-level staff who have previous experience in data processing, clerical work, and accounting.

Benefits: Benefits include medical insurance, life insurance, dental insurance, vision insurance, and a 401(k).

Human Resources: Jenny Colliard.

Application Procedures: Resumes can be forwarded to the company, but the company prefers candidates to fill out job applications in their office.

▶ **Internships**

Type: Offers paid internships.

Qualifications: College students.

HCA Rockford Center
100 Rockford Dr.
Newark, DE 19713
Phone: (302)996-5480

Officers: Mary Schaffer, Contact.

Health Care and Retirement Corp.
1 SeaGate Ave.
Toledo, OH 43604
Phone: (419)247-5023

Benefits: Benefits include medical insurance, life insurance, dental insurance, and 401(k).

Human Resources: Chuck Hall.

Application Procedures: Send resume and cover letter.

▶ **Internships**

Type: Offers internships of various types depending on the department.

Application Procedure: Contact Human Resources, if interested.

Health Management Associates Inc.
5811 Pelican Bay Blvd., Suite 500
Naples, FL 33963
Phone: (813)598-3175
Fax: (813)597-5794

Business Description: Operator of general medical and surgical hospitals. Operator of psychiatric hospitals.

Officers: Kelly Curry, Sr. VP & Finance Officer; Earl Holland, Exec. VP of Mktg.; Jim Jordan, Dir. of Info. Systems; William J. Schoen, CEO & Pres.

Benefits: Benefits include 401(k), dental insurance, tuition assistance, health insurance, paid vacation days, sick days, and holidays.

Human Resources: Fred Drow.

Application Procedures: Send resume and cover letter to the attention of Fred Drow.

▶ **Internships**

Type: The company does not offer any internship programs.

Healthcare International Inc.
912 S. Capital of Texas Hwy., 4th Fl.
Austin, TX 78746
Phone: (512)346-4300

Business Description: Operator of general medical and surgical hospitals. Operator of psychiatric hospitals.

Officers: James L. Fariss Jr., CEO & Chairman of the Board; Michael Heeley, VP of Mktg.; Elliott H. Weir, Exec. VP of Finance.

Application Procedures: Contact the company for more information.

▶ **Internships**

Type: Offers an internship program. Contact the company for more information.

Helian Health Group Inc.
9600 Blue Larkspur
Monterey, CA 93940
Phone: (408)646-9000

Business Description: Provides outpatient related medical services.

Officers: Thomas D. Wilson, CEO; Donald C. Blanding, Treasurer; J. Spencer Davis, VP of Intl. Sales; Andrew W. Miller, VP of Operations.

Highland Ridge Hospital
4578 Highland Dr.
Salt Lake City, UT 84117
Phone: (801)272-9851
Fax: (801)272-9857

Opportunities: Hires counselors, registered nurses, and licensed practical nurses. Previous experience and a college degree are required.

Benefits: Benefits include medical insurance,

life insurance, dental insurance, personal/sick days, and vacation days.

Human Resources: Janey Mryer.

Application Procedures: Call or send resume and cover letter.

▶ **Internships**

Type: The company does not offer an internship program.

Horizon Healthcare Corp.
6001 Indian School Rd. NE, Ste. 530
Albuquerque, NM 87110
Phone: (505)881-4961

Business Description: Provides long-term health care. The company has 52 long-term care centers and retirement facilities in eight states.

Officers: Klemett L. Belt, Exec. VP & CFO; Neal M. Elliott, CEO, Pres. & Chairman of the Board; Charles H. Gonzales, VP of Government Programs; Michael A. Jeffries, Sr. VP of Operations; William C. Mitchell, VP of Operations Western Div.; Randi S. Nathanson, VP, General Counsel & Sec.; Mark W. Ohlendorf, VP of Finance; Ernest A. Schofield, VP & Controller; Jeffrey A. Shepard, VP of Operations Eastern Div.

Human Resources: Rod Panyek.

▶ **Internships**

Type: Offers an internship program.

Qualifications: Administrators-in-training.

Hospital Corporation of America
1 Park Plaza
Nashville, TN 37202
Phone: (615)327-9551

Business Description: A Nashville-based health care company that either owns or manages hospitals, psychiatric units, and other medical facilities in the United States. In 1989, the company and Doheny Development Corp. embarked on a joint venture to produce a 200,000 square-foot medical mart facility in Dallas, Texas.

Officers: Thomas F. Frist, Jr., CEO, Pres. & Chairman of the Board; Roger E. Mick, Exec. VP & CFO.

Benefits: Offers a full benefits package to full-time employees.

Application Procedures: Accepts walk-in applicants between 8:30 and 4:00. Send resume and cover letter to the attention of the Staffing Assistant, Human Resources, PO Box 550, 1 Park Plaza, Nashville, TN 37202.

▶ **Internships**

Contact: Judy Collier.

Type: Offers paid internships in legal, clerical, and data-processing areas.

Qualifications: Internship applicants must be at least through their second year of college.

Application Procedure: Send applications to the attention of Judy Collier or to Human Resources.

Every resume should pass the "so what?" test. It's not enough to simply list your accomplishments. You need to demonstrate the impact of your actions on your department or the company at large. Beverly Robsham, president of Robsham & Associates, an outplacement firm in Boston, MA, advocates the "PAR" approach when delineating accomplishments: "Specify the *problem*, the *actions* you took, and the *results* for the company."

Source: *Working Woman*

Howard University Hospital
400 Byrant St.
Washington, DC 20059
Phone: (202)806-7714
Fax: (202)483-6693

Employees: 2,000.

Average Entry-Level Hiring: Unknown.

Opportunities: Nurses, M.S.W.s, respiratory therapists, physical and occupational therapists—requirements not specified.

Application Procedures: Contact Employment Services for information.

Idaho Department of Health and Welfare
Division of Health
450 W. State
Boise, ID 83720
Phone: (208)334-5945
Fax: (208)334-6581

Opportunities: The company hires entry-level

staff as receptionists and office clerks. Requirements vary depending upon the position.

Benefits: Benefits include medical insurance, life insurance, dental insurance, vision insurance, savings plan, home insurance, car insurance, and boat insurance.

Human Resources: Jennifer Ballard.

Application Procedures: Interested candidates should apply through the state.

▶ **Internships**

Type: The company does not offer any internship programs.

The US Congress's Office of Technology Assessment estimated in 1990 that US companies spent $30 billion to $40 billion annually on training, mostly in programs for executives, salespeople, and technical workers.

Source: *Business Week*

Idaho Division of Family and Children's Services, Substance Abuse Program
450 W. State
Boise, ID 83720
Phone: (208)334-5700
Fax: (208)334-6699

Opportunities: Hires entry-level office personnel. Requirements depend upon the position desired.

Benefits: Benefits include medical insurance, life insurance, vacation days, personal/sick days, and paid holidays.

Application Procedures: Posts announcements and advertises through mail listings. All responses should be directed to Personnel.

▶ **Internships**

Type: Offers paid and college credit internships in accounting and environmental quality. **Number Available Annually:** Varies.

Qualifications: College students.

Application Procedure: Send application and resume to Personnel Analyst.

Illinois Department of Mental Health and Developmental Disabilities
William G. Stratton Bldg., Ste. 401
Springfield, IL 62765
Phone: (217)782-7179
Fax: (217)524-0835

Opportunities: Hires staff for professional positions. A college degree and the passage of the state test is required.

Benefits: Benefits include medical insurance, life insurance, dental insurance, and child-care programs.

Human Resources: Norm Grimmett.

Application Procedures: Send resume and cover letter to contact.

▶ **Internships**

Type: Offers paid internships. **Number Available Annually:** 6-10.

Qualifications: College students.

Illinois Department of Public Aid
100 S. Grand Ave., E.
Springfield, IL 62762
Phone: (217)782-1200
Fax: (217)524-7979

Opportunities: Hires applicants into clerical or social service positions and requires a college degree.

Benefits: Benefits include medical insurance, life insurance, a savings plan through payroll deduction, and workers' compensation.

Application Procedures: Send samples to the attention of the Central Management Services-Testing Center.

▶ **Internships**

Type: Offer paid, unpaid, and Dunn Fellow internships to junior and senior college students, graduate students and applicants with degrees.

Application Procedure: Apply through the governor's office or send a resume.

Impact Drug and Alcohol Treatment center
1680 N. Fair Oaks Ave.
Pasadena, CA 91103
Phone: (818)798-0884

Officers: Debi Stillwell, Contact.

Indiana Department of Human Services
402 W. Washington St.
PO Box 7083
Indianapolis, IN 46207-7083
Phone: (317)232-7000
Fax: (317)232-1240

Officers: Anna Pell, Contact.

Opportunities: May require a college degree, previous experience, or some college course work.

Benefits: Benefits include medical insurance, life insurance, dental insurance, and vision insurance. Also offers savings plan, tuition assistance, and tax saver deferred compensation.

Application Procedures: The State Personnel Department maintains a job bank. Can apply for listed positions.

Indiana Department of Public Welfare
Indiana Government Center, S.
402 W. Washington, 3rd Fl.
Indianapolis, IN 46204
Phone: (317)232-4705
Fax: (317)232-4331

Opportunities: Hires entry-level applicants for clerical positions.

Benefits: Benefits include medical insurance, life insurance, dental insurance, vision insurance, a savings plan, child or elder care.

Application Procedures: Hires through State application. Apply to posted job vacancies at the central office.

▶ **Internships**

Type: Offers paid internships to college students.

Application Procedure: Apply through the State agency.

Indiana Family and Social Services Administration Division of Mental Health
Indiana Government Center, S., W341
402 W. Washington St.
Indianapolis, IN 46204
Phone: (317)232-7800
Fax: (317)233-3472

Opportunities: Hires case workers and accountants with college degrees and clerical workers with at least a high school diploma.

Benefits: Benefits include medical insurance, life insurance, dental insurance, and savings plan.

Human Resources: Mrs. Rogers.

Application Procedures: Those interested should acquire an application from the state agency and take the state exam.

▶ **Internships**

Type: Offers paid internships.

Qualifications: Must be a college student.

Integrated Health Services Inc.
11011 McCormick Rd.
Hunt Valley, MD 21031
Phone: (410)584-7050

Business Description: Operates nursing homes and retirement hotels.

Officers: Robert Elkins, CEO; Steven Drury, CFO.

Opportunities: Hires entry-level clerical, accounts payable, and administrative staff. College degree and previous experience required.

Benefits: Benefits include medical insurance, life insurance, dental insurance, vision insurance, profit sharing, and 401(k).

Application Procedures: Send resume and cover letter to the attention of Personnel.

▶ **Internships**

Type: The company does not offer an internship program.

Intercare Inc.
2575 Boyce Plaza Rd.
Pittsburgh, PA 15241
Phone: (412)257-1991

Business Description: Operates psychiatric and specialty treatment hospitals.

Officers: Alan A. Axelson, President; Keith H. Morgenlander, Vice Pres.

Intermountain Health Care Inc.
36 S. State St., 20th Fl., Ste. 2200
Salt Lake City, UT 84111
Phone: (801)533-8282
Fax: (801)531-9789

Business Description: Engaged in the operation of establishments that provide general or

Mental Health Career Directory

specialized medicine or surgery by medical doctors. Operator of general medical and surgical hospitals. Operator of hospitals. Operator of psychiatric specialty hospitals.

Officers: Scott Parker, President.

Benefits: Benefits include health care and life insurance, dental insurance, a savings plan after one year, and tuition assistance after 6 months.

Human Resources: Lonnie Deet.

Application Procedures: Maintains a job hotline at (801)533-3654. Applications accepted for openings only. Send resume and cover letter to the attention of the Human Resource Specialist.

According to Mack Hanan, author of *Tomorrow's Competition: The Next Generation of Growth Strategies*, in the new order of global business, success will depend on alliances that strengthen the customer, thus securing a company's value in the marketplace. In his book Hanan offers advice on how to compete on value rather than price or performance, how to drive markets, and how to "sell without selling" by co-managing customer operations. The goal is to prosper in a new world where "competition is cooperative, and 3 suppliers are obsolete."

Interwest Medical Corp.
3221 Hulen St.
Fort Worth, TX 76107
Phone: (817)731-2743

Business Description: Operates nursing home.

Officers: Arch B. Gilbert, CEO; Joseph E. Gearheart, CFO.

Benefits: Benefits include medical insurance.

▶ **Internships**

Type: The company does not offer an internship program.

Iowa Department of Human Services
Hoover State Office Bldg.
Des Moines, IA 50319
Phone: (515)281-5452
Fax: (515)281-4597

Officers: Tom Maudsley, Employment Services Contact.

Opportunities: Hires resident treatment workers and data entry operators with high school diplomas.

Benefits: Benefits include medical insurance, life insurance, and dental insurance.

Application Procedures: Accepts applications only.

Iowa Division of Mental Health/Mental Retardation/Mental Disabilities
Hoover State Office Bldg.
Des Moines, IA 50319
Phone: (515)281-5874

Opportunities: Hires entry-level staff into clerical and mailroom positions. Requires a college degree or previous experience.

Benefits: Benefits include medical insurance, life insurance, dental insurance, vision insurance, child-care programs, and deferred compensation.

Application Procedures: Advertises and maintains a job line at (515)281-5820.

▶ **Internships**

Type: Offers paid and unpaid internships for college credit.

Application Procedure: Interested candidates can obtain an internship application from the Department of Personnel.

Iowa Division of Substance Abuse and Health Promotion
Lucas State Office Bldg., 3rd Fl.
Des Moines, IA 50319-0075
Phone: (515)281-3641
Fax: (515)281-4958

Opportunities: Hires entry-level candidates in about 50 different areas including mail clerks and clerical staff. Requirements for employment vary according to position.

Benefits: Benefits include life insurance, dental insurance, health and dependent care, deferred compensation, and a retirement plan.

Human Resources: Evelyn Munoz; Leslie Strayer.

Application Procedures: Completed application will be held on file for 2 years and applicants can phone in any new or additional information.

▶ **Internships**

Contact: Evelyn Munoz, Human Resource Contact.

Type: Paid and unpaid internships offered by the State of Iowa.

Application Procedure: Submit a completed application with a letter from an advisor or counselor to Evelyn Munoz.

J and Company Inc.
1366 E. Morehead Rd.
Charlotte, NC 28204
Phone: (704)332-3031

Business Description: Provides psychotherapy services.

Officers: Susan Jordan, President.

Jackson Recovery Center
5354 I-55 S. Frontage Rd.
Jackson, MS 39284
Phone: (601)372-9788

Benefits: Benefits include medical insurance, life insurance, and dental insurance.

Application Procedures: Apply in person. Applications can be filled out on site.

▶ **Internships**

Contact: Doug Wills.

Type: Offers paid and college credit internships.
Number Available Annually: 30.

Qualifications: College students.

Application Procedure: Application should be sent through the applicant's school.

Jewish Board of Family and Children's Services, Inc.
120 W. 57th St.
New York, NY 10019
Phone: (212)582-9100

Opportunities: Hires social workers, childcare workers, and management. May require a college degree or previous experience.

Benefits: Benefits include medical insurance, life insurance, dental insurance, child-care programs, and elder-care programs.

Application Procedures: Apply in person or send resume to Personnel.

▶ **Internships**

Type: Offers paid internships for college credit.
Number Available Annually: 5.

Application Procedure: Recommended by other companies.

Justice Resource Institute, Inc.
132 Boylston St.
Boston, MA 02116
Phone: (617)482-0006
Fax: (617)482-2471

Officers: Sally Wannamaker, Contact.

▶ **Internships**

Type: The company does not offer an internship program.

Kalamazoo Regional Psychiatric Hospital
1312 Oakland Dr.
Kalamazoo, MI 49008
Phone: (616)337-3000

Opportunities: Hires entry-level staff with a college degree. Depending on the position, a master's degree may be required.

Benefits: Benefits include medical insurance, life insurance, dental insurance, vision insurance, income protection, and deferred compensation.

Application Procedures: File a civil service application. Write to the Michigan Department of Civil Service for information.

▶ **Internships**

Type: The company does not offer an internship program.

Kansas Mental Health and Retardation Services
915 SW Harrison
Topeka, KS 66612
Phone: (913)296-3773
Fax: (913)296-3774

Application Procedures: To apply, contact the Social and Rehabilitation Services personnel department at (913)296-2502.

JOB OPPORTUNITIES DATABANK

Mental Health Career Directory

Kansas State Department of Social and Rehabilitation Services
Docking State Office Bldg, Rm. 6255
Topeka, KS 66612
Phone: (913)296-6750
Fax: (913)296-4813

Opportunities: Hires staff for custodial and food service areas. Also hires laborers, service attendants, and homecare workers. May require a college degree, previous experience, or some college course work.

Benefits: Benefits include medical insurance, life insurance, and dental insurance. Also offers savings plan, tuition assistance, child-care programs, and elder-care programs.

Human Resources: Barbara Mardy; Sally Vandervile.

Application Procedures: Can apply by phone or send a resume. Must pass a Civil Service exam. Entry-level positions do not require the Civil Service testing.

▶ **Internships**

Type: Offers unpaid internships for college credit to students of social work. **Number Available Annually:** 120.

Application Procedure: Must apply to the State Division of Personnel and take a Civil Service test.

The optimum time for follow-up calls after job interviews is from 9 to 11 am, Tuesday through Friday, according to Jeffrey G. Allen, author of *The Perfect Follow-Up Method to Get the Job*. The book provides a suggested script for follow-up calls or letters, gives tips on handling an interview while dining, and covers typical questions raised in a follow-up interview.

Source: *Career Opportunities News*

Kendall Healthcare Properties Inc.
11355 SW 84th St.
Miami, FL 33173
Phone: (305)596-3288

Business Description: Provides assisted living and nursing care services.

Officers: Avi Bittan, President; Nancy Grab, Dir. of Mktg. & Sales.

Human Resources: Nancy Grab.

▶ **Internships**

Type: The company does not offer an internship program.

Kentucky Department for Mental Health/Mental Retardation Services
275 E. Main St.
Frankfort, KY 40621
Phone: (502)564-4527
Fax: (502)564-3844

Opportunities: Hires entry-level administrative and executive staff and case workers. A college degree is required.

Benefits: Benefits include medical insurance, life insurance, savings plan, personal/sick days, and paid holidays.

Human Resources: Mary Greenwell.

Application Procedures: Must fill out an application.

▶ **Internships**

Type: Offers paid internships. College credit may be granted depending upon the internship.

Qualifications: Must meet minimum requirements of the desired position.

Application Procedure: Fill out state application.

Kentucky Department for Social Insurance
275 E. Main St.
Frankfort, KY 40621
Phone: (502)564-3703
Fax: (502)564-6907

Benefits: Benefits include medical insurance, life insurance, dental insurance, savings plan, and personal/sick days.

Human Resources: Daryl Hyatt.

Application Procedures: Hires entry-level staff for case work. Prospective employees should have at least two years of college or previous experience. Applicants will be given an exam, and those with the top five scores will be considered for employment.

▶ **Internships**

Type: Offers paid and college credit internships.

Number Available Annually: 20.

Qualifications: College seniors.

Application Procedure: Students should apply through their school.

Koala Hospital
1404 S. State Ave.
Indianapolis, IN 46203
Phone: (317)783-4084

Application Procedures: Applications available on-site or send resume and cover letter to the attention of Personnel and specify department. The company does not accept phone calls.

Larned State Hospital
Rural Rte. 3
PO Box 89
Larned, KS 67550
Phone: (316)285-2131

Opportunities: Social workers must have a bachelor's degree in social work; a master's degree in psychology is required to be considered for the position of psychologist.

Benefits: Benefits include medical insurance, dental insurance, and life insurance.

Human Resources: Maryann Perez.

Application Procedures: State application is required.

Life Care Centers of America Inc.
PO Box 3480
Cleveland, TN 37320
Phone: (615)472-9585

Business Description: Owner and operater of nursing homes.

Officers: Forrest L. Preston, CEO.

Opportunities: Hires nurse's aides with a high school diploma and previous experience. Eventually requires certification.

Benefits: Benefits include medical insurance, life insurance, dental insurance, and a 401(k) plan.

Human Resources: Rosemary Yates.

Application Procedures: Apply to Personnel Department. Will be placed by Director of Nursing.

▶ **Internships**

Type: Offers unpaid internships for credit to college students. **Number Available Annually:** 2-3.

Application Procedure: Apply to the Personnel Department.

Living Centers of America
15415 Katy Fwy.
Houston, TX 77094
Phone: (713)578-4700

Business Description: Operator of skilled nursing care facilities other than hospitals.

Officers: Stan Brezenk, Controller; Floyd Rhoades, President; Dorthy Wiley, Dir. of Mktg.; Lee Williams, VP of Finance.

Benefits: Benefits include medical insurance, dental insurance, 401(k), life insurance, traveler's insurance, three days bereavement, one half sick day a month, two weeks vacation after first year, three weeks vacation after five years, and free parking.

Human Resources: K. Muthu Muthuswamy.

Application Procedures: The center advertises in local papers. Send a resume to the attention of Theresa Tucker.

▶ **Internships**

Type: Offers an internship program.

Regardless of the approach he or she takes, a treating or consulting psychologist must have a broad understanding of the psychological principles that govern human behavior and an ability to establish rapport with patients that is based on trust.

Source: American Psychological Association

Logansport State Hospital
Rural Rte. 2
Box 38
Logansport, IN 46947
Phone: (219)722-4141

Opportunities: Hires at entry-level for most positions. Requirements vary depending on position.

Benefits: Benefits include medical insurance,

life insurance, dental insurance, vision insurance, retirement plans, and tuition assistance.

▶ **Internships**

Type: The company does not offer an internship program.

Louisiana Office for Prevention and Recovery from Alcohol and Drug Abuse

1201 Capital Rd.
PO Box 3868
Baton Rouge, LA 70821-3868
Phone: (504)342-9352

Opportunities: Hires entry-level staff in many areas and is interested in candidates who have previous experience. Requirements for positions vary depending upon the position.

Benefits: Benefits include a savings plan, an HMO, and group benefits.

Application Procedures: Applicants must pass the Civil Service Exam. The company hires most of its employees through the State.

▶ **Internships**

Type: The company offers unpaid internships. College credit is available. Typically, the number of internships awarded is dependent upon how many applications are received.

Qualifications: College students.

Application Procedure: Interested candidates should forward their applications to the CEO of the department for which they want to work.

Louisiana Office of Human Services

PO Box 2790, Bin No. 18
Baton Rouge, LA 70821-2790
Phone: (504)342-6717
Fax: (504)342-1384

Opportunities: Hires entry-level clerks and professional staff. Previous experience and college degree required.

Benefits: Benefits include medical insurance, life insurance, dental insurance, vision insurance, and savings plan.

Application Procedures: Call or send application to the Civil Service Department.

▶ **Internships**

Type: The company does not offer an internship program.

Lutheran Social Services of Iowa

1323 Northwestern
Ames, IA 50010
Phone: (515)232-7262

Opportunities: Hires residence counselors and social workers with a B.S. or B.A. Other positions require a high school degree and 18 months post high school education.

Benefits: Benefits offered to full-time employees or those at 1,000 hours per year. Include medical insurance, life insurance, retirement, sick leave, paid vacation, accidental death, and disability insurance.

Human Resources: Vivian Khan.

Application Procedures: Residence counselors must come in and fill out an application and questionnaire. Social workers should send a resume or apply in person.

▶ **Internships**

Contact: Mary Bernard, Contact for Master's level or Mary Tharp, Contact for Bachelor's level.

Type: Offers unpaid internships for college credit to bachelor's and master's students.
Number Available Annually: 1-6.

Application Procedure: Send in resume and requirements for practicum or contact by phone.

Madison State Hospital

711 Green Rd.
Madison, IN 47250
Phone: (812)265-2611

Opportunities: Nursing applicants are sought on a regular basis. Psychiatric and social work positions usually do not have a high turn over rate so those positions are rare. Specific job qualifications and minimum requirement information is available at the state personnel "Job Bank."

Benefits: Benefits include medical insurance, life insurance, retirement plan, vacation, sick, and personal days, and a credit union.

Human Resources: Vera Hummel.

Application Procedures: All applicants must directly contact the state personnel "Job Bank."

▶ **Internships**

Type: The Company does not offer internships.

Maine Department of Human Services
State House, Station 11
Augusta, ME 04333
Phone: (207)289-2736
Fax: (207)626-5555

Opportunities: Hires entry-level staff for the central office: clerical, professional, technical, nursing, data entry, and case workers.

Benefits: Benefits include medical insurance, life insurance, and dental insurance.

Application Procedures: Applications can be filled out in person. Contact the Bureau of Human Resources, Maine State Personnel Office.

▶ **Internships**

Type: The company does not offer an internship program.

Manhattan Alcoholism Treatment Center
600 E. 125th St.
Ward's Island
New York, NY 10035
Phone: (212)473-5026

Benefits: Benefits include health insurance and savings plan.

Human Resources: Carry Micheles.

Application Procedures: Hires counselors with previous experience and some college course work. Places newspaper advertisements for certain openings. Apply in person or send resume and cover letter to the attention of Carry Micheles.

▶ **Internships**

Type: The company does not offer an internship program.

Manhattan Children's Psychiatric Center
600 E. 125th St.
Ward's Island
New York, NY 10035
Phone: (212)876-8000

Officers: Barbara Barrett, Contact.

Opportunities: Hires keyboard specialists with professional experience and a college degree.

Benefits: Benefits include medical insurance, life insurance, dental insurance, and vision insurance.

Application Procedures: Interested applicants should send resumes to the Personnel Department.

Manor Care Inc.
10750 Columbia Pike
Silver Spring, MD 20901
Phone: (301)681-9400

Business Description: Holding company with interests in the healthcare and hospitality industries.

Officers: Stewart Bainnum, Jr., CEO, Pres. & Chairman of the Board; Joseph Buckley, Sr. VP Information Resources and Development; James A. MacCutcheon, Sr. VP of Finance & Treasurer.

Human Resources: Roberta McCall; Charles A. Shields.

Application Procedures: The company publicizes job vacancies through its Job Hotline, 1-800-648-2041. Interested applicants should forward resumes to the Employment Office. Roberta McCall.

Like your appearance, your attitude can deteriorate from bad habits you develop. Just as you can let the heels of your shoes run down, you can let your attitude run down. And, like your shoes, your attitude can reach a point of where it is so run down that you might as well throw it away and start fresh.

Source: *Business Monday/Detroit Free Press*

Maryland Alcohol and Drug Abuse Administration
201 W. Preston St.
Baltimore, MD 21201
Phone: (410)225-6925
Fax: (410)333-7206

Opportunities: All positions require the appropriate license or certification. Contact the company for more information.

Benefits: Benefits include medical insurance, life insurance, dental insurance, and 401(k).

Human Resources: Joe Elliot.

Application Procedures: Applicants can apply for positions by sending resumes, telephoning the company, or inquiring in person.

▶ **Internships**

Type: The company offers paid internships to college students. Approximately 50 internships are awarded each year.

Maryland Developmental Disabilities Administration
201 W. Preston St.
Baltimore, MD 21201
Phone: (410)225-5600
Fax: (410)225-5850

Opportunities: The company offers entry level positions in various departments. Candidates need at least a license or appropriate certification to qualify.

Benefits: Benefits include medical insurance, life insurance, dental insurance, and a 401(k).

Human Resources: Joe Elliot.

Application Procedures: Contact by telephone or send resume and cover letter to the attention of Joe Elliot.

▶ **Internships**

Contact: Joe Elliot, Contact.

Type: The company offers a paid internship program.

Application Procedure: Interested candidates should contact Joe Elliot.

Maryland Mental Hygiene Administration
201 W. Preston St.
Baltimore, MD 21201
Phone: (410)225-6611
Fax: (410)333-5402

Benefits: Benefits include medical insurance, life insurance, dental insurance, savings plan, and tuition assistance.

Human Resources: Peter Jedrzejczak.

Application Procedures: Hires entry-level psychiatry staff (college degree required). Phone contact and fill out an application or send resume and cover letter.

▶ **Internships**

Type: The company does not offer an internship program.

Maryland Social Services Administration
311 W. Saratoga St., 5th Fl.
Baltimore, MD 21201
Phone: (410)333-0102
Fax: (410)333-0099

Human Resources: Marie Havak.

Application Procedures: File an application with the Personnel Department. Required to take test.

Massachusetts Bureau of Substance Abuse Services
150 Tremont St., 6th Fl.
Boston, MA 02111
Phone: (617)727-1960
Fax: (617)727-9288

Human Resources: Richard Newhall; Heather Guerare.

▶ **Internships**

Type: The company does not offer an internship program.

Massachusetts Department of Mental Health
Central Office
25 Stanford St.
Boston, MA 02114
Phone: (617)727-5500

Opportunities: Offers positions in mental health work, psychiatric work, social work, and opportunities for case managers. Requirements depend on the position.

Benefits: The company offers a benefits plan.

Human Resources: Mary Ellen Masala.

Application Procedures: Apply in person to the head of the specific department. Requires police clearance.

MCC Managed Behavioral Care Inc.
11095 Viking Dr.
Eden Prairie, MN 55344
Phone: (612)943-9500

Business Description: Psychiatric, drug and alcohol rehabilitation hospitals.

Officers: Terry Travers, President; Jean Walker, CFO; James Higgins, VP of Sales; Chris Pearson, VP of Intl. Sales; Gene Gannon, Human Resources Dir.

Opportunities: The company offers many positions. Previous experience is necessary.

Benefits: Benefits include medical insurance, dental insurance, life insurance, elder-care programs, child-care programs, savings plan, and tuition assistance.

Human Resources: Mary Endrizzi.

Application Procedures: Advertisements are placed in local papers for job openings. Call personnel department and send resume. Mary Endrizzi.

McLean Hospital
115 Mill St.
Belmont, MA 02178
Phone: (617)855-2118
Fax: (617)855-3299

Business Description: A center for psychiatric care, teaching, and research. The hospital is affiliated with Massachusetts General Hospital, and a teaching hospital of Harvard Medical School.

▶ Internships

Contact: Anne Fallon, Dir. of Volunteer Services.

Type: Offers community residences, patient education, rehabilitation programs, clinical research, and basic research internships. All internships are unpaid. **Applications Received:** 200.

Duties: Community residences interns attend meetings and initiate and organize activities; patient education interns attend meetings and assist patients in the classroom; rehabilitation program interns work with patients in music therapy, in the greenhouse, and in the thrift shop program; clinical research interns conduct library searches and gather and process data; and basic research interns assist investigators in the laboratory.

Qualifications: All candidates should have a background in psychology.

Application Procedure: Call or write the contact; a personal interview is required.

Medfield Center Corp.
12891 Seminole Blvd.
Largo, FL 34648
Phone: (813)581-8757

Business Description: Psychiatric hospital.

Officers: Stephen Wilensky, Dir. of Industrial Relations.

Benefits: Benefits include medical insurance, life insurance, dental insurance, vision insurance, savings plan, child-care programs, elder-care programs, and a 401(k) plan.

Application Procedures: Interested applicants should submit an application in person.

Trade and professional associations are good sources of information about jobs in your target field. Look for associations in *The Encyclopedia of Associations*.

Source: *Executive Female*

Medical University of South Carolina
State Institution
171 Ashley Ave.
Charleston, SC 29425-1035
Phone: (803)792-2071
Fax: (816)792-9533

Business Description: The MUSC Medical Center is made up of the Medical University Hospital, the Children's Hospital, the Storm Eye Institute, the Institute of Psychiatry, all outpatient clinics, and the Charleston Memorial Hospital. The mission of the MUSC Medical Center includes teaching students and physicians, the provision of tertiary care, and human research. Research programs are ongoing and staff is needed to support the research projects. There are 572 beds in the teaching hospital, which will soon have 600 beds. All patients will soon be in single bedrooms and there will be 50 intensive care beds.

Employees: 7,700.

Average Entry-Level Hiring: 800-1000.

Opportunities: There is a job vacancy listing published annually which identifies hard-to-fill vacancies, these are always available. Another listing, published weekly, includes clerical openings, some patient care aide, and administrative and managerial openings. Call for listing(s).

Human Resources: Jean W. Turner; Kathy Leitch; Nancy Adams, Nursing.

Mediplex Rehab-Camden Institute of Brain Injury Rehabilitation Research and Training

3 Cooper Plaza, Ste. 518
Camden, NJ 08103
Phone: (609)342-7600

Business Description: A rehabilitation treatment center that includes vocational training and special education programs. The facility serves those who have survived a traumatic brain injury.

▶ **Internships**

Contact: Peter Dunn, Training Coordinator.

Type: Offers paid programs for preprofessional research aides, allied health trainees, graduate interns, and postdoctoral fellows.

Duties: Preprofessional research aides assist in experiential work-study programs; allied health trainees get supervised experience in physical therapy, occupational therapy, respiratory care, speech-language pathology, therapeutic recreation, and nursing. Graduate interns work with school counseling, vocational services, and job placement; and postdoctoral fellows get supervised experience in psychotherapy, neuropsychology, and rehabilitation practices.

Qualifications: Preprofessional research aides should be college seniors or recent college graduates; allied health trainees should be enrolled in allied health programs; graduate internships should be advanced graduate students; and postdoctoral fellows should be licensed psychologists, have a doctorate in a field of psychology, and have finished a predoctoral clinical internship.

Memorial Medical Center

3625 University Blvd.
Jacksonville, FL 32216
Phone: (904)399-6666

Opportunities: Hires entry-level staff for medical records work, dietary work, and clerical positions.

Benefits: Benefits include medical insurance, life insurance, dental insurance, optional life insurance, long-term disability, and flexible spending accounts.

Application Procedures: Fill out application at the Human Resources Department. The department can be reached at (904) 399-6700.

▶ **Internships**

Type: Offers internships for college credit in occupational therapy areas.

Application Procedure: Apply to the Human Resources Department.

Mental Health Center of Jacksonville Inc.

PO Box 9010
Jacksonville, FL 32208
Phone: (904)695-9145

Opportunities: The center hires personnel with previous experience for clerical positions. Registered nurses must have a college degree.

Benefits: Benefits include profit sharing, medical insurance, life insurance, dental insurance, and vision insurance.

Human Resources: Glenda Dupont.

Application Procedures: Job openings are posted, or ads are placed in local papers. To apply for these openings you may apply in person or mail a resume. Glenda Dupont.

▶ **Internships**

Type: The company offers unpaid internships.

Qualifications: Internships are available to college students.

Mental Health Institute

PO Box 111
Independence, IA 50644
Phone: (319)334-2583

Opportunities: Hires entry-level staff for various positions. Requirements vary depending on the position, but at least a high school degree is required. A Ph.D. is required for psychologist positions.

Benefits: Benefits include medical insurance, life insurance, dental insurance, savings plan, and tuition assistance.

Human Resources: Connie Davis.

Application Procedures: Call or send resume and cover letter to the attention of Connie Davis.

▶ **Internships**

Type: This company does not offer any internship programs.

Mercy Hospital Medical Center
6th & University
Des Moines, IA 50314
Phone: (515)247-3100
Fax: (515)298-8831

Employees: 4,200.

Average Entry-Level Hiring: Unknown.

Opportunities: RN—associate or bachelor's degree. Social workers—M.S.W. required. Occupational therapists—bachelor's degree required. Physician assistants—state licensure required.

Application Procedures: Contact personnel for more information.

Psychiatric Institute
3339 McClure Ave.
Pittsburgh, PA 15212
Phone: (412)734-7501

Benefits: Benefits include medical insurance, life insurance, and dental insurance.

Human Resources: David Hultleson, Benefits Director.

Application Procedures: Apply in person to the Human Resources Department.

▶ **Internships**

Type: Offers unpaid internships for college credit to senior students. **Number Available Annually:** 10-20.

Application Procedure: Apply through the university.

Mercy Services for Aging
34605 12 Mile Rd.
Farmington Hills, MI 48331
Phone: (313)489-6180

Opportunities: Hires entry-level secretarial, clerical, accounting, and human resources staff.

Benefits: Benefits include medical insurance, life insurance, dental insurance, child-care programs, and 401(k).

Application Procedures: Apply in person or send resume and cover letter to the attention of Employment Manager.

▶ **Internships**

Type: Offers paid internships. **Number Available Annually:** 6.

Qualifications: College students.

Application Procedure: Apply in person.

Metropolitan State Hospital
11400 Norwalk Blvd.
Norwalk, CA 90650
Phone: (310)863-7011

Opportunities: The company hires entry-level staff in different areas. Requirements for positions vary but may include psychiatric practitioner license and nurse registration. The company is currently experiencing a hiring freeze.

Benefits: Benefits include medical insurance, life insurance, dental insurance, vision insurance, and a retirement plan.

Application Procedures: Interested candidates should forward resumes to the company.

▶ **Internships**

Type: The company does not offer any internship programs.

Meyer Rehabilitation Institute University of Nebraska Medical Center
600 S. 42nd St.
Omaha, NE 68198-5450
Phone: (402)559-6430
Fax: (402)559-5737

Business Description: The facility works with people with developmental disabilities or other chronic handicaps.

▶ **Internships**

Contact: Erlene Steele, Education Coordinator.

Type: Offers five paid traineeships and three paid postdoctoral fellowships. **Applications Received:** 20.

Duties: Trainees participate in meetings and treatment sessions with such departments as occupational therapy, physical therapy, special education, psychology, speech pathology, nutrition, and nursing. Postdoctoral fellows perform various duties in such departments as nursing, nutrition, psychology, speech pathology, and rehabilitative and genetic medicine.

JOB OPPORTUNITIES DATABANK

Qualifications: Trainees should either have or be working toward a master's degree.

> A myriad of possibilities for volunteer service are available in the United States and abroad, ranging from community service to education to development projects... In addition to the personal rewards volunteer service offers, volunteering can actually be a step toward a future career goal.
>
> Source: *Journal of Career Planning & Employment*

Michigan Department of Mental Health

Lewis Cass Bldg.
320 S. Walnut
Lansing, MI 48909
Phone: (517)373-3500
Fax: (517)373-8074

Officers: Tom Adams, Contact.

Opportunities: Hires entry-level staff in technical and human services areas. Depending on the positions, requirements may include previous experience, college course work, and/or a college degree. Administrators must have experience and a college degree.

Benefits: Benefits include medical insurance, life insurance, dental insurance, vision insurance, savings plan, and tuition assistance.

Application Procedures: Applications are processed through the Civil Service Department. Applicants must take the civil service exam. The Department will provide the company with a list of qualified applicants. Qualified applicants should call or send resume and cover letter.

▶ **Internships**

Type: Offers paid and unpaid internships for college credit. **Number Available Annually:** 40-50.

Qualifications: College students.

Application Procedure: Applicants will be processed through the Civil Service Department. Students must also be recommended by their university.

Michigan Department of Social Services

235 S. Grand Ave.
PO Box 30037
Lansing, MI 48909
Phone: (517)373-2035
Fax: (517)373-8471

Opportunities: Hires entry-level clerical staff. Depending on the position, previous experience, college course work, and/or a college degree may be required.

Benefits: Benefits for full-time, permanent employees include medical insurance, dental insurance, life insurance, vision insurance, savings plan, and tuition assistance.

Human Resources: Dee Langinfield.

Application Procedures: Applicants are required to take a civil service exam and then fill out an application after the exam has been posted.

▶ **Internships**

Contact: Peggy Price.

Type: Offers internships.

Michigan Health Care Corp.

7430 2nd Ave.
Detroit, MI 48202
Phone: (313)874-9100

Opportunities: Require previous experience.

Benefits: Benefits include medical insurance, life insurance, dental insurance, vision insurance, savings investment plan, and tuition assistance.

Human Resources: Linda Wheeler.

Application Procedures: Applications can be filled out on site between 9:30 and 4:30. Interested applicants should send a resume and any other additional information or contact the Personnel Department by phone.

Michigan Office of Substance Abuse Services
Michigan Department of Public Health

2150 Apollo Dr.
PO Box 30206
Lansing, MI 48909
Phone: (517)335-8809
Fax: (517)335-8837

Opportunities: Hires entry-level lab assistants

and clerical staff. Requirements vary with positions, but previous experience and/or a college degree may be required.

Benefits: Benefits include medical insurance, life insurance, dental insurance, vision insurance, savings plan, deferred compensation, and savings bonds.

Application Procedures: Those interested should take the civil service exam and fill out an application.

▶ **Internships**

Type: Offers unpaid internships for college credit. **Number Available Annually:** 4.

Qualifications: Full-time college students.

Application Procedure: Applicants should fill out a student application at the Civil Service Department and send it to the Personnel Department.

Miller Medical Group PC
1633 Church St.
Nashville, TN 37206
Phone: (615)340-8500

Business Description: Outpatient clinic.

Officers: Mike Law, Dir. of Industrial Relations; Larry Lance, CFO; Patty Czarnik, Dir. of Mktg.; Suzanne Brinkley, Dir. of Info. Systems.

Opportunities: Hires entry-level clerical staff with previous experience.

Benefits: Benefits include medical insurance, life insurance, dental insurance, and retirement plans.

Human Resources: Martha Underwood.

Application Procedures: Send resume and cover letter to the attention of Martha Underwood.

▶ **Internships**

Type: This company does not offer an internship program.

Minnesota Department of Human Services
444 Lafayette Rd.
St. Paul, MN 55155-3815
Phone: (612)296-6117
Fax: (612)296-5868

Opportunities: The company hires entry-level staff with some college course work, previous experience, or a college degree. Requirements vary depending upon the position. Available positions include those in human services and finance, and technical areas.

Benefits: Benefits include medical insurance.

Human Resources: Robert Cooley.

Application Procedures: Interested candidates should apply for available positions and take a required exam.

▶ **Internships**

Type: The company offers paid and unpaid internships. College credit is available.

Application Procedure: Interested candidates should contact the agency or administrative services.

Mississippi Department of Human Services
421 W. Pascagoula St.
PO Box 352
Jackson, MS 39203
Phone: (601)960-4250
Fax: (601)352-5982

Benefits: Benefits include medical insurance, life insurance, dental insurance, and disability insurance.

Human Resources: Gloria Jackson.

Application Procedures: Company places employees once they have been hired by the state personnel board. Applicants must have a certificate of eligibility from the state.

▶ **Internships**

Type: Offers summer internships.

Mississippi Department of Mental Health
1101 Robert E. Lee Bldg.
Jackson, MS 39201
Phone: (601)359-1288

Officers: Linda Patton, Contact.

Application Procedures: Contact the State Personnel Board.

Missouri Department of Mental Health
1706 E. Elm St.
PO Box 687
Jefferson City, MO 65102
Phone: (314)751-4122
Fax: (314)751-8224

Opportunities: Hires entry-level staff in many

JOB OPPORTUNITIES DATABANK

areas. Requirements vary with the position but may include previous experience, college course work, and/or a college degree.

Benefits: Benefits include medical insurance, life insurance, vacation days, personal/sick days, and deferred compensation.

Human Resources: Rebecca Halliway.

Application Procedures: Applicants should go through the state Merit System Registrar, request a certificate provided by them, and verify the certificate by calling the office.

▶ Internships

Type: The company does not offer any internship programs.

> "Eighty percent of the initial impression you make is nonverbal," asserts Jennifer Maxwell Morris, a New York-based image consultant, quoting a University of Minnesota study. Some interview tips: walk tall, enter the room briskly while making eye contact with the person you're going to speak to, keep your head up, square your shoulders and keep your hand ready for a firm handshake that involves the whole hand but does not pump.
>
> Source: *Working Woman*

Missouri Division of Maternal, Child and Family Health

1730 E. Elm
Box 570
Jefferson City, MO 65102
Phone: (314)751-6174
Fax: (314)751-8224

Opportunities: Hires entry-level health representatives, laboratory workers, programmers, and clerical staff. Depending on the position, previous experience, college course work, and/or a college degree may be required.

Benefits: Benefits include medical insurance, life insurance, dental insurance, savings plan, and tuition assistance.

Human Resources: Pat Reagan, Division of Personnel.

Application Procedures: Applications are processed through the state Merit System Registrar. Contact Pat Reagan of the Office of Personnel in the Office of Administration for further information.

▶ Internships

Type: Offers internships for college credit in the nutritionist field. **Number Available Annually:** 1-2.

Qualifications: College juniors and seniors.

Application Procedure: Send resume to Pat Reagan, Division of Personnel.

Mobile Mental Health Center, Inc.

2400 Gordon Smith Dr.
Mobile, AL 36617
Phone: (205)473-4423
Fax: (205)450-2213

Officers: Julie Bellsase, Contact.

Montana Department of Family Services

PO Box 8005
Helena, MT 59604
Phone: (406)444-5902
Fax: (406)444-5956

Benefits: Benefits include medical insurance, life insurance, dental insurance, savings plan, personal/sick days, paid holidays, retirement plans, and paid military leave.

Application Procedures: Hires entry-level staff in clerical (bachelor's degree required) and professional (master's degree required) areas. Posts job announcements. Apply in person or send resume and cover letter to the attention of Virgil Dixon, Job Placement.

▶ Internships

Type: Offers unpaid internships for college credit.

Qualifications: College students actively working on a degree.

Application Procedure: Personal interview required.

Montana Department of Social and Rehabilitation Services

111 Sanders St.
PO Box 4210
Helena, MT 59604
Phone: (406)444-5622
Fax: (406)444-1970

Opportunities: Hires disability claims representatives, examiners, rehabilitation counselors, and child support technicians. Most positions require a college degree.

Benefits: Benefits include medical insurance, life insurance, dental insurance, and a savings plan.

Human Resources: Patti Smith, Personnel contact.

Application Procedures: All hiring is done through the State Job Service.

Mount Rogers Community Service Board

770 W. Ridge Rd.
Wytheville, VA 24382
Phone: (703)228-2158

Business Description: Mental health and drug rehabilitation center.

Officers: Ralph Burnop, Dir. of Industrial Relations.

Opportunities: Hires in all areas, requirements differ with each position.

Benefits: Benefits include retirement plans, medical insurance, dental insurance, and life insurance.

Human Resources: Anne Hall.

Application Procedures: Send resume and cover letter to the attention of Anne Hall.

▶ **Internships**

Type: Internships are unpaid but may be taken for college credit. **Number Available Annually:** 8.

Qualifications: College students.

Application Procedure: Contact the mental health director in the area in which you are interested.

Mount Sinai Hospital

500 Blue Hills Ave.
Hartford, CT 06112
Phone: (203)242-4431
Toll-free: 800-882-6602
Fax: (203)286-4629

Human Resources: Colette Austin.

In a crowded job market, employers become more selective. With more applicants to choose from, they're not just looking for those who do what's expected. They look for those who take the initiative to exceed designated objectives or to improve the status quo in some way. Any instances you can point to in which you've reduced expenditures or staffing requirements, customer complaints, or product defects will tend to improve your chances. Examples of enhanced revenue, productivity, or customer satisfaction you've managed to produce will also tend to impress employers looking for ways to compete and survive.

Source: *Newark Star-Ledger*

Mountainview Hospital

628 S. Cowley
Spokane, WA 99202
Phone: (509)624-3226

Opportunities: Hires entry-level counselors, nurses, and housekeeping staff. Nursing staff must meet R.N. or L.P.N. requirements.

Benefits: Benefits include medical insurance, life insurance, dental insurance, and disability insurance.

Human Resources: Paula Brennan.

Application Procedures: Apply in person or send resume and cover letter.

▶ **Internships**

Contact: Paula Brennan, Director of Counseling.

Type: Offers paid and college credit internships. **Number Available Annually:** 2.

Qualifications: College students.

Application Procedure: Send resume and cover letter with an application.

JOB OPPORTUNITIES DATABANK

Muscatatuck State Developmental Center
PO Box 77
Butlerville, IN 47223
Phone: (812)346-4401
Fax: (812)346-6308

Employees: 1,350.

Average Entry-Level Hiring: Unknown.

Opportunities: Nurse IV—possession of a valid license to practice nursing in the state of Indiana as an RN. Charge nurse—one year of full-time paid professional experience in psychiatric, developmental disability, or geriatric nursing; possession of a valid license to practice nursing in the state of Indiana as an RN; an accredited bachelor's degree in nursing may substitute for the required experience. Behavior clinician III—one year of full-time paid professional experience in the performance of psychological services, which includes diagnostic interviewing, report preparation, interpretation of test results, and/or treatment of emotional disorders; a master's degree in psychology, educational psychology, guidance and counseling, tests and measurements, or psychometry required; internship training at the doctoral level or doctoral coursework in any of the above areas may substitute for the required experience with a maximum substitution of one year. Mental Health Administrator III— two years of full-time paid professional work experience in the provision of therapeutic patient services for the mentally ill or mentally retarded; a bachelor's degree in business administration, nursing, mental health technology, psychology, social work, education, vocational rehabilitation, speech pathology and audiology, or one of the adjunctive therapies (music, recreation, physical, occupational, or industrial) required; accredited graduate training in any of the above areas may substitute for the required experience with a maximum substitution of two years. Audiologist III—licensure as an audiologist by the Indiana Board of Examiners on Speech Pathology and Audiology required. Dietitian IV—registration as a dietitian or proof of eligibility for admission to the Dietitian Registration Examination; must successfully pass the Dietitian's Registration Examination of the Commission on Dietetic Registration prior to the granting of permanent status. Psychologist I—current certification as a psychologist by the Indiana State Psychology Board, proof must accompany application. Psychiatric attendant V—two years of full-time paid work experience; a high school diploma may substitute for the required experience.

Human Resources: Julie Broome, Nursing; Patricia Spanagel, Dietitians.

Application Procedures: All applicants must be certified to an eligible list by filing a State Application PD/100 with Indiana State Personnel Department, Indianapolis, IN; and be available for Jennings County, #40.

Napa State Hospital
2100 Napa-Vallejo Hwy.
Napa, CA 94558
Phone: (707)253-5454

Opportunities: Hires nursing, clerical and administrative positions. Also hires foodservice and maintenance positions. Must take the Civil Service Exam.

Benefits: Benefits include medical insurance, life insurance, and a retirement plan.

Application Procedures: Send a resume to the Personnel Department for an application.

▶ **Internships**

Type: Offers paid internships and college credit to students currently in a college student teaching program.

Application Procedure: Colleges submit candidates or apply through the Civil Service department.

National Expert Care Consultants, Inc.
444 W. 50th St.
New York, NY 10019
Phone: (212)262-6000

Business Description: Manager and operator of long-term care facilities and provider of accounting services to these facilities.

Officers: Robert M. Galecke, CEO; James D. Shelton, VP of Finance; Stanley C. Rippel, VP of Business Development.

Opportunities: Entry-level staff are required to have a college degree and previous experience.

Benefits: Benefits include medical insurance, life insurance, and dental insurance.

Human Resources: Jose' Juan.

Application Procedures: Those interested

should apply in person, by phone, or send resume and cover letter.

▶ **Internships**

Type: The company does not offer an internship program.

National Medical Enterprises Inc.
2700 Colorado Ave.
Santa Monica, CA 90404
Phone: (310)998-8000

Business Description: One of the largest health care service companies in the United States, owning and operating over 500 acute-care, psychiatric, and rehabilitation hospitals, and long-term care and substance abuse treatment facilities. Also operates internationally.

Officers: Richard K. Eamer, CEO & Chairman of the Board; Taylor R. Jenson, Exec. VP & CFO.

Benefits: Benefits include medical insurance, dental insurance, vision insurance, and a retirement plan.

Human Resources: Alan R. Ewalt.

Application Procedures: Send resume and cover letter to the attention of Human Resources Department.

▶ **Internships**

Type: The company offers clerical, office, and administrative internships.

Qualifications: Requirements vary but may include previous experience or a college degree.

National Medical Enterprises Psychiatric Institutes of America
3060 Williams Dr.
Fairfax, VA 22031
Phone: (703)205-7500

Business Description: Owns, operates and manages psychiatric hospitals.

Officers: Norman Zober, President; Ronald Bernstein, COO.

Nebraska State Department of Social Services
301 Centennial Mall, S.
PO Box 95026
Lincoln, NE 68509-5026
Phone: (402)471-3121
Fax: (402)471-9449

Opportunities: Hires entry-level staff with 24 completed hours of post-high school experience. The positions include client referral positions, social/protective services, and child protective services.

Benefits: Benefits include medical insurance, life insurance, dental insurance, disability leave, credit union, and retirement plans.

Human Resources: Lynn Foster.

Application Procedures: Applications can be made through the personnel department. Applications are held on file in the registrar's office.

▶ **Internships**

Type: Offers unpaid internships for college credit.

Qualifications: High school graduates.

NeuroCare Inc.
1001 Galaxy Way
Concord, CA 94520
Phone: (510)686-5500

Business Description: Acute head injury rehabilitation hospital.

Officers: Michael Grishman, President.

Opportunities: Hires entry-level clinicians and physical therapists with college degrees.

Benefits: Benefits include medical insurance, 401(k), and paid vacation.

Human Resources: Erin Krajewski; Sharon Schofield.

Application Procedures: Call to schedule an appointment. Marci Auerbach. Phone: (510)682-9000.

▶ **Internships**

Contact: James Cole, Personnel Dept.

Type: Paid internships are available for college credit. **Number Available Annually:** 2.

Qualifications: Internships are available to college graduates.

Application Procedure: Call to schedule an appointment between 8:00 and 12:00 am.

Mental Health Career Directory

Nevada Mental Hygiene and Mental Retardation Division
Kinkead Bldg., Ste. 403
505 E. King St.
Carson City, NV 89710
Phone: (702)687-5943
Fax: (702)687-4773

Opportunities: Hires entry-level mental health technicians and food service personnel. Some experience is helpful. Those applying for professional positions must have previous experience.

Benefits: Benefits include medical insurance, life insurance, dental insurance, vision insurance, savings plan, and child-care programs.

Human Resources: Diane Dempsey, State Personnel Office.

Application Procedures: Fill out a state application. Does not accept unsolicited resumes.

▶ **Internships**

Type: The company does not offer any internship programs.

Just as the aspiring musician ought to be knowledgeable about musicology or the writer about literary criticism, so should the professional social worker be well grounded in the human sciences. It is erroneous to assume, however, that theoretical excellence in itself . . . translates into virtuosity.

Source: Howard Goldstein in *Families in Society: The Journal of Contemporary Human Services*

Nevada Welfare Division
2527 N. Carson St.
Carson City, NV 89710
Phone: (702)687-4770
Fax: (702)687-5080

Opportunities: Hires in all areas statewide. Requirements depend on classification.

Benefits: Benefits include medical insurance, life insurance, dental insurance, and a deferred compensation plan.

Application Procedures: Contact the Nevada Welfare Central Office Personnel by phone to apply.

New Center Community Mental Health Services
2051 W. Grand Blvd.
Detroit, MI 48208
Phone: (313)895-4000
Fax: (313)895-9758

Human Resources: Evon Cabell.

New Dimensions, Inc.
18333 Egret Bay Blvd.
Houston, TX 77058
Phone: (713)333-2284

Human Resources: Sherry Taylor.

Application Procedures: Hires entry-level staff in the clerical area. Some college course work is required. Call or send resume to Sherry Taylor.

▶ **Internships**

Contact: Sherry Taylor.

Type: Offers paid and college credit internships.
Number Available Annually: 1.

Qualifications: Bachelor's degree.

Application Procedure: Send resume.

New Directions, Inc.
30800 Chagrin Blvd.
Cleveland, OH 44124
Phone: (216)591-0324

Officers: Dr. Nikki Babbit, Contact.

Opportunities: Hires entry-level personnel in all areas. Requirements vary depending on the position, but may include previous experience, college course work, and/or a college degree.

Benefits: Benefits include medical insurance and dental insurance.

Application Procedures: Fill out an application or send resume and cover letter to the director or program supervisor of the department of interest.

▶ **Internships**

Contact: Dr. Nikki Babbit.

Type: Offers unpaid college credit internships.
Number Available Annually: 8.

Qualifications: College students.

Application Procedure: Applicants must first be referred by the college, and will then be granted an interview.

New Hampshire Department of Health and Human Services
6 Hazen Dr.
Concord, NH 03301
Phone: (603)271-4331
Fax: (603)271-2896

Opportunities: Hires entry-level clerical staff. Previous experience and college degree are required.

Benefits: Benefits include medical insurance, life insurance, dental insurance, vision insurance, child-care programs, tuition assistance, and retirement plans.

Application Procedures: All prospective applicants must take a state exam.

▶ **Internships**

Type: Offers unpaid internships for college credit. **Number Available Annually:** Varies.

Qualifications: College juniors or seniors.

Application Procedure: Considers applicants based on referral through the student's school.

New Hampshire Division of Mental Health and Developmental Services
State Office Park, S.
105 Pleasant St.
Concord, NH 03301
Phone: (603)271-5007
Fax: (603)271-5051

Officers: Mark Swinehock, Contact.

Opportunities: Hires entry-level clerical and management personnel. Previous experience and a college degree are required.

Benefits: Benefits include medical insurance, life insurance, and dental insurance.

Application Procedures: Apply in person or send resume and cover letter.

▶ **Internships**

Type: Offers paid internships to college students. To apply, submit a letter of intent. **Number Available Annually:** 9.

New Life Treatment Centers Inc.
570 Glenneyre St.
Laguna Beach, CA 92651
Phone: (714)494-8383

Opportunities: Hires entry-level dietary and support staff. Previous experience and/or a college degree may be required.

Benefits: Benefits include medical insurance, life insurance, dental insurance, vision insurance, 401(k), and disability insurance.

Application Procedures: Call, apply in person and fill out an application, or send resume and cover letter to Human Resources.

▶ **Internships**

Type: The company does not offer any internship programs.

New Medico Associates Inc.
470 Atlantic Ave., 7th Fl.
Boston, MA 02210
Phone: (617)426-4100
Fax: (617)426-3030

Business Description: Operator of nursing or personal care facilities that require a lesser degree of care than skilled or intermediate care facilities. Operator of general medical and surgical hospitals. Operator of specialized outpatient facilities.

Officers: Jeffery Goldshine, President.

Opportunities: Hires nurses, nurses aides and therapists.

Human Resources: Paul Marsh; Steve Richelson.

Application Procedures: Send resume and cover letter to the attention of Jerry Freedman.

▶ **Internships**

Type: The company does not offer an internship program.

New Mexico Social Services Division
PO Box 45160
Santa Fe, NM 87502-5160
Phone: (505)827-8400

Opportunities: Hires entry-level staff who possess college degrees.

Benefits: Benefits include medical insurance, dental insurance, and a state sponsored HMO retirement plan.

Human Resources: Russell Ivey.

Application Procedures: Candidates who are interested in social work positions should direct their applications to Russel Ivey. Applications for

MENTAL HEALTH CAREER DIRECTORY

other positions should be directed to the New Mexico State Employment Agency. The company prefers application to be made in person.

▶ **Internships**

Type: The company does not offer an internship program.

Your future in the world of work will depend at least in part on your ability to express yourself in groups. One thing you can do in the near future is sign up for a class in public speaking. There you can get practice and guidance in speaking in front of a group.

Source: *Business Monday/Detroit Free Press*

New York Office of Mental Retardation and Developmental Disabilities
44 Holland Ave.
Albany, NY 12229
Phone: (518)473-1997
Fax: (518)473-1271

Opportunities: Hires entry-level clerical/office staff. Some college course work required. College degree required for some positions.

Benefits: Benefits include medical insurance, life insurance, dental insurance, vision insurance, tuition assistance, vacation days, and retirement plans.

Application Procedures: To apply, prospective applicants must first take the state exam.

▶ **Internships**

Contact: Tim McMullen.

Type: Offers paid internships. **Number Available Annually:** 1.

Qualifications: Master's degree required.

New York State Department of Social Services
40 N. Pearl St.
Albany, NY 12243
Phone: (518)474-9003
Fax: (518)474-9004

Opportunities: Hires entry-level staff who have either previous experience or a college degree, depending upon the position.

Benefits: Benefits include medical insurance, life insurance, dental insurance, and paid sick and vacation days.

Application Procedures: Interested candidates should forward resumes to the personnel department or apply in person. All positions require successful completion of a state regulated civil service exam.

▶ **Internships**

Type: Offers paid and unpaid internships depending upon what their budget will allow. Internships are also available for college credit. **Number Available Annually:** 3-5.

Qualifications: College students.

New York State Division of Substance Abuse
Executive Park, S.
PO Box 8200
Albany, NY 12203
Phone: (518)457-2061
Fax: (518)457-5474

Opportunities: Hires entry-level clerical and secretarial staff. Some college course work is required.

Benefits: Benefits include medical insurance, life insurance, dental insurance, vision insurance, tuition assistance, child-care programs, retirement plans, and vacation days.

Human Resources: John Debes.

Application Procedures: All prospective applicants must take a state exam.

▶ **Internships**

Type: The company does not offer an internship program.

Norrell Health Care Inc.
3535 Piedmont Rd., NE
Atlanta, GA 30305
Phone: (404)240-3000

Business Description: Intermediate care nursing homes.

Benefits: Some benefits provided depending on employment status.

Human Resources: Linda Arnold; Deborah Thomas, Director of Corporate Recruiting.

Application Procedures: Apply in person or contact by phone.

North Carolina Division of Medical Assistance

1985 Umstead Dr.
PO Box 29529
Raleigh, NC 27626-0529
Phone: (919)733-6775
Fax: (919)733-6608

Officers: Kimberly Keller, Contact.

Opportunities: Hires entry-level clerical personnel and administrative assistants. Requirements vary depending on the position.

Benefits: Benefits include medical insurance, life insurance, dental insurance, and vision insurance.

Application Procedures: Job listings are posted. Applications are accepted only for posted positions.

▶ **Internships**

Contact: Julia Hiatt.

Type: Offers paid internships.

Qualifications: College students.

North Carolina Division of Mental Health, Developmental Disabilities, and Substance Abuse Services

325 N. Salisbury St.
Raleigh, NC 27603
Phone: (919)733-7011
Fax: (919)733-9455

Opportunities: Hires entry-level clerical staff. Previous experience and college degree required.

Benefits: Benefits include medical insurance, life insurance, dental insurance, vision insurance, savings plan, tuition assistance, and childcare programs.

Application Procedures: To apply and take the state exam, contact Personnel.

▶ **Internships**

Type: The company does not offer an internship program.

North Dakota Department of Human Services

State Capitol
600 E. Boulevard Ave.
Bismarck, ND 58505-0250
Phone: (701)224-2310
Fax: (701)224-2359

Opportunities: Hires entry-level staff in all areas. A college degree is required.

Benefits: Benefits include medical insurance, life insurance, dental insurance, and vision insurance.

Human Resources: Ron Leingang.

Application Procedures: Resumes are accepted. Applications can be filled out on site.

▶ **Internships**

Type: Offers paid internships.

Qualifications: College students.

Application Procedure: Apply through the state.

North Dakota Mental Health Services Department of Human Services

Judicial Wing, 3rd Fl.
600 E. Boulevard Ave.
Bismarck, ND 58505-0271
Phone: (701)224-2766
Fax: (701)224-3000

Opportunities: Hires entry-level clerical, secretarial, and accounting staff. College degree required.

Benefits: Benefits include medical insurance, life insurance, personal/sick days, and flexible benefits.

Human Resources: Ron Leingang.

Application Procedures: Send resume and cover letter and fill out application. Submit application to centralized system.

▶ **Internships**

Type: The company does not offer an internship program.

Northern Virginia Doctors Hospital Corp.
601 S. Carling Springs
Arlington, VA 22204
Phone: (703)671-1200

Opportunities: Hires entry-level staff in many areas, including psychiatric units, pharmacy, physical therapy, dietary, housekeeping, material management, business office, and switchboard. Requirements vary depending on the position.

Benefits: Benefits include medical insurance, life insurance, dental insurance, savings plan, and 401(k).

Application Procedures: Apply in person or send resume and cover letter to the attention of Human Resources.

▶ **Internships**

Type: Offers unpaid internships for college credit in the physical therapy, laboratory, and imaging departments. **Number Available Annually:** 36-48.

Qualifications: College students.

Application Procedure: Call for application information.

A powerful combination of workers who equip themselves to be competitive and employers who provide them with challenging jobs can help businesses stay on top. But to mesh these elements managers must give employees a voice in their jobs and enable workers to develop new skills throughout their careers. Workers must get as much schooling as possible, demand broader duties on the job, and take on more responsibility for the company's success.

Source: *Business Week*

Northville Regional Psychiatric Hospital
41001 W. Seven Mile Rd.
Northville, MI 48167
Phone: (313)349-1800

Opportunities: Hires entry-level staff with a college degree.

Benefits: Benefits include medical insurance, life insurance, dental insurance, vision insurance, retirement plans, and deferred compensation.

Application Procedures: To apply, file a civil service application. The applicant's name is then put on a hiring register. For information, contact Mr. Pierson.

▶ **Internships**

Type: The company does not offer an internship program.

Nu-Med Inc.
PO Box 18260
Encino, CA 91416-8260
Phone: (818)990-2000

Business Description: Operator of psychiatric hospitals. Operator of specialty hospitals.

Officers: Stuart Bruck, VP of Mktg.; Yoram Dor, Exec. VP & CFO; Maurice Lewitt, CEO & Chairman of the Board.

Benefits: The company offers benefits to full-time employees only.

Human Resources: Carol Shardt.

Application Procedures: Interested applicants should forward resumes to the company. Resumes will remain on file for two years.

▶ **Internships**

Type: The company does not offer any internship programs.

Ohio Department of Alcohol and Drug Addiction Services
2 Nationwide Plaza
280 N. High St., 12th Fl.
Columbus, OH 43215
Phone: (614)466-3445
Fax: (614)752-8645

Benefits: Benefits include medical insurance, life insurance, dental insurance, and vision insurance.

Human Resources: Susan Weyrick.

Application Procedures: Hires entry-level clerical staff. Applicants must have previous experience. Applications are accepted for advertised positions only. Send resume and cover letter.

▶ **Internships**

Type: Offers paid internships.

Qualifications: College students.

Application Procedure: To apply, contact the governor's office.

Ohio Department of Human Services
30 E. Broad St., 32nd Fl.
Columbus, OH 43266-0423
Phone: (614)466-6282
Fax: (614)466-1504

Opportunities: Hires entry-level staff in all areas. Requirements vary depending on the position.

Benefits: Benefits include medical insurance, life insurance, dental insurance, and vision insurance.

Human Resources: Ted Dyrkek.

Application Procedures: Apply in person.

▶ **Internships**

Type: Offers paid, unpaid, and college credit internships. **Number Available Annually:** 5-12.

Qualifications: College students.

Application Procedure: Send resume to the Governor's Office or to the department of interest.

Ohio Department of Mental Health
30 E. Broad St., Ste. 1180
Columbus, OH 43266-0414
Phone: (614)466-2596
Fax: (614)752-9453

Opportunities: Hires entry-level personnel in all areas. Requirements vary depending on the position.

Benefits: Benefits include medical insurance, life insurance, dental insurance, vision insurance, and deferred compensation.

Human Resources: Ann Bonham, Contact.

▶ **Internships**

Type: The company does not offer an internship program at this time.

Oklahoma Department of Human Services
PO Box 25352
Oklahoma City, OK 73125
Phone: (405)521-3646
Fax: (405)521-6684

Opportunities: Hires entry-level staff in all areas. Requirements vary depending upon positions but include college course work, previous experience, and college degrees.

Benefits: Benefits include medical insurance, life insurance, dental insurance, vision insurance, a savings plan, and deferred compensation.

Human Resources: Karen Cothran.

Application Procedures: The company practices internal hiring, but job seekers can forward resumes to the Office of Personnel Management or contact the agency directly to fill out an application.

▶ **Internships**

Type: The company offers paid internships.

Oklahoma Department of Mental Health
PO Box 53277
Capitol Station
Oklahoma City, OK 73152
Phone: (405)271-7474

Opportunities: Various entry-level positions available in all areas.

Benefits: Benefits include medical insurance, life insurance, dental insurance, vision insurance, sick leave, annual time, and holiday pay.

Human Resources: Hank Batty; Cerelda Brown.

Application Procedures: Apply in person or send resume to Hank Batty. Best to apply as openings occur.

Omnilife Systems Inc.
1207 N. High St.
Columbus, OH 43201
Phone: (614)299-3100

Business Description: Intermediate care nursing homes.

Officers: Robert Banasik, President.

Opportunities: Hires entry-level staff with previous experience.

MENTAL HEALTH CAREER DIRECTORY

Benefits: Benefits include medical insurance and life insurance.

Human Resources: Terri Ruhwedel, Contact.

Application Procedures: Apply in person with Terri Ruhwedel. If you want to work at a specific facility, apply at that location.

▶ **Internships**

Type: This company does not offer an internship program.

Wayne Huizenga co-founded Waste Management, Inc., now the world's largest handler of waste materials, then started a bottled-water business that he sold to concentrate on creating Blockbuster Entertainment. He counsels budding entrepreneurs to plan their products around logical, foreseeable developments.

Source: *Forbes*

OptimumCare Corp.
30011 Ivy Glenn Dr.
Laguna Niguel, CA 92677
Phone: (714)495-1100

Business Description: Provides patient programs for the treatment of mental health disorders.

Officers: Edward A. Johnson, CEO; Edward A. Johnson, CEO; John Harrison, Vice Pres.; Randy Gliscan, Dir. of Data Processing; Robert Easton, Human Resources Dir.

Opportunities: Hires entry-level clerical staff. Previous experience is required.

Benefits: Benefits include medical insurance, life insurance, dental insurance, and vision insurance.

Human Resources: Rita Seok.

Application Procedures: Send resume and cover letter to the attention of Program Director.

▶ **Internships**

Type: The company does not offer an internship program.

Oregon Adult and Family Services Division
500 Summer St.
Salem, OR 97310-1013
Phone: (503)378-6142

Opportunities: No degree required for entry-level staff.

Benefits: Benefits include medical insurance, life insurance, dental insurance, and vision insurance.

Human Resources: Laurie Briles.

Application Procedures: Send resume to the Executive Department.

▶ **Internships**

Type: Offers paid internships to college students. **Number Available Annually:** 10.

Application Procedure: Apply directly to a specific agency.

Oregon Mental Health and Developmental Disability Services Division
2575 Bittern St., NE
Salem, OR 97310
Phone: (503)378-2671
Fax: (503)373-7951

Opportunities: Hires applicants for clerical and patient care positions. Previous experience is necessary.

Benefits: Benefits include medical insurance and dental insurance.

Human Resources: Cathy Cavaner.

Application Procedures: Applicants should send in resume to the state division or contact (in person or by phone):

▶ **Internships**

Type: The company does not offer an internship program.

Oregon Office of Alcohol and Drug Abuse Programs
1178 Chemtka St., NE
Salem, OR 97310
Phone: (503)378-2163
Fax: (502)378-8467

Officers: Dan Hedrick, Contact; Carol Richardson, Contact.

Parc Place

5116 E. Thomas Rd.
Phoenix, AZ 85018
Phone: (602)840-4774

Opportunities: The company requires either a college degree or two years previous experience in a related field. Positions include administration, nursing, human resources, secretarial, bachelor's degree counselors, and master's degree therapists.

Benefits: Benefits include medical insurance, profit sharing, dental insurance, paid vacations, sick days, and holidays.

Human Resources: Colleen Wilson.

Application Procedures: Applicants can send resumes to the human resources department or make contact by telephone.

▶ Internships

Contact: Mimi Rodriguez, Program Coordinator.

Type: The company does offer internships that fluctuate in compensation depending on the intern's qualifications. The company typically awards four internships per year.

Patton State Hospital

3102 E. Highland Ave.
Patton, CA 92369
Phone: (714)425-7000

Opportunities: The company hires entry-level staff in clerical and accounting positions. These positions require a typing certificate. The company also hires staff for psychologist and social work positions. These positions require PhD and master's degrees, respectively.

Benefits: Benefits include medical insurance, life insurance, dental insurance, vision insurance, savings plan.

Human Resources: Sue Silance.

Application Procedures: Interested candidates should forward resumes to the personnel department or make contact by telephone. All applicants must pass a civil service exam.

▶ Internships

Type: The company offers paid internships in psychology and social work. **Number Available Annually:** 4 psychology, 4-5 social work.

Qualifications: Psychology interns must be in the final stages of doctoral studies. Social work interns must be in a master's degree program.

Application Procedure: Psychology interns should direct their applications to Dr. Sutton. Social work interns should direct their applications to Sue Kingsley.

Membership in a cross-departmental problem-solving group provides a greater understanding of other business units and a broader perspective on issues. You'll need this broader perspective, because lateral moves will be increasingly common in any organization, and may play a part in your job search. "Middle managers must look sideways—not just up—if they want to increase their marketability in the 1990s," notes Beverly Robsham, president of Robsham & Associates, an outplacement firm in Boston, MA. On your resume be sure to mention any cross-departmental activities you've undertaken.

Source: *Working Woman*

Penn Recovery Systems, Inc.

39th and Market Sts./Mutch 4
Philadelphia, PA 19104
Phone: (215)386-4280

Opportunities: Hires entry-level staff with previous experience and a college degree.

Benefits: Benefits include medical insurance, life insurance, dental insurance, and 401(k).

Application Procedures: Call or send resume and cover letter.

▶ Internships

Type: The company does not offer any internship programs.

Pennsylvania Department of Public Welfare

Health and Welfare Bldg.
PO Box 2675
Harrisburg, PA 17105-2675
Phone: (717)787-6443
Fax: (717)787-5394

Opportunities: Hires mental health specialists with a college degree and previous experience.

Benefits: Benefits include medical insurance, life insurance, dental insurance, vision insurance, a family care account, and a deferred compensation plan.

Human Resources: Cheryl Goldman.

Application Procedures: Hire all positions through the Civil Service Commission.

Pennsylvania Drug and Alcohol Programs

Health and Welfare Bldg.
Lionville, PA 19353
Phone: (717)787-9857

Officers: Debbie Hill, Contact.

Opportunities: Hires entry-level staff in many areas. Previous experience and/or some college course work required, depending on the position.

Benefits: Benefits include medical insurance, life insurance, prescription coverage, and supplemental benefits administered by Health and Welfare.

Application Procedures: Those applying for civil service positions must take a test with the Civil Service Commission to apply. Non-civil service employees should apply through the Division of State Employment.

▶ **Internships**

Contact: Betty Williams, Bureau of Personnel, Training Div.

Type: Offers paid and college credit internships. **Number Available Annually:** 70-80.

Qualifications: College students.

Application Procedure: Varies for each internship program. Contact Betty Williams about the commonwealth's Management Internship Program.

Petrie Method

619 Middle Neck Rd.
Great Neck, NY 11023
Phone: (516)482-1220

Business Description: Hypnosis clinic.

Officers: Martin Sabba, President.

G. Pierce Wood Memorial Hospital

5847 SE Hwy. 31
Arcadia, FL 33821
Phone: (813)494-3323

Opportunities: Generally hires entry-level psychiatry and social work staff. Hospital is under a hiring freeze.

▶ **Internships**

Type: The company does not offer an internship program.

Pinecrest State School

PO Box 5191
Pineville, LA 71361-5191
Phone: (318)641-2162
Fax: (318)641-2007

Employees: 20.

Average Entry-Level Hiring: 3-6.

Opportunities: Speech pathologist—must possess or be eligible to obtain a Louisiana license to practice, restricted license will be accepted. Certificate of professional competence granted by the American Speech and Hearing Association and a master's degree are required. Occupational therapist—current Louisiana Occupational Therapist license or permit. Psychological associate—master's degree in psychology required.

Human Resources: Frank La Vallie, speech pathology, occupational therapy; Don Cross, Psychological Associate.

Planned Behavioral Health Care Inc.

9535 Forest Ln.
Dallas, TX 75243
Phone: (214)680-0400

Business Description: Provides psychotherapy services.

Officers: Joyce Ramay, CEO; Steve Embree, CFO; Donna McFaul, Dir. of Mktg.; Tom Williams, Dir. of Info. Systems.

Polestar

7800 Red Rd.
South Miami, FL 33143

Business Description: Provides counseling for substance abuse and stress management.

Officers: Hal Thompson, President.

The Presbyterian Hospital
Columbia Presbyterian Medical Center
New York, NY 10032-3784
Phone: (212)305-1956
Fax: (212)305-2012

Employees: 8,000.

Average Entry-Level Hiring: 450.

Opportunities: Registered nurse—associate degree or B.S.N. eligible for New York State license. Physician assistant—B.S. degree, minimum New York State license. Laboratory technologist, pharmacist—B.S. degree, eligible for New York State license. Physical therapist, occupational therapist—B.A. or B.S. degree, eligible for New York State license. Radiation therapy technician, radiology technician, respiratory technician—associate degree, eligible for New York State license. Social worker—M.S.W. required, and CSW eligible.

Human Resources: Letty Mintz, Nursing; Jo Ann Olson.

Preventive Lifestyles Inc.
7546 14th Ave. NE
Seattle, WA 98115
Phone: (206)525-2929

Business Description: Nicotine dependency treatment programs.

Officers: Bobette S. Jones, President; Bobette S. Jones, Treasurer.

Princeton Diagnostic Laboratories of America Inc.
100 Corporate Ct.
South Plainfield, NJ 07080
Phone: (908)769-8500

Business Description: Provides specialized clinical testing services to private psychiatric and general hospitals, psychiatrists, and clinical laboratories.

Officers: Carlton E. Turner, CEO; Frank M. Thiry, CFO; Susann L. McClellan, VP of Mktg.; Warren Majek, General Mgr.

Opportunities: Hires entry-level clerical personnel. Previous experience and a college degree are required.

Benefits: Benefits include medical insurance, dental insurance, savings plan, and 401(k).

Application Procedures: Places newspaper advertisements for certain job openings. Send resume and cover letter. Mandatory drug testing is part of the application procedure.

▶ Internships

Type: The company does not offer any internship programs.

Package designers benefit from tough times, when the high cost of introducing products and the fight for shelf space at stores is encouraging many manufacturers to turn from new product development to spicing up old packaging for a boost in sales. It's less risky to put money behind known brands rather than newcomers, and some see the redesigning trend as part of a larger effort to buff up brand identities. But companies that fail to introduce new products may hurt themselves in the long run once the economy turns around and they have little in the pipeline.

Source: USA Today

Princeton Psychiatric Recovery Network
29-31 Airpark Rd.
Princeton, NJ 08540
Phone: (609)252-0035
Fax: (609)252-0154

Opportunities: Hires receptionists for entry-level positions. All other positions require a college degree.

Benefits: Benefits include medical insurance, life insurance, and dental insurance.

Application Procedures: Send a resume to Personnel.

Psychiatric Institute of Washington
4460 MacArthur Blvd. NW
Washington, DC 20007
Phone: (202)965-8200

Opportunities: Hires mailroom staff for entry-

MENTAL HEALTH CAREER DIRECTORY

level positions. Requires a college degree or previous experience.

Benefits: Benefits include medical insurance, life insurance, dental insurance, vision insurance, savings plan, tuition assistance, profit sharing, and child-care programs.

Human Resources: Gene Carry.

Application Procedures: Can contact by phone or send a resume.

▶ **Internships**

Type: Offers unpaid internships to college students.

Application Procedure: Apply through Personnel or through a referral.

Companies are forgoing the old five-year plan method of strategic planning for a new, everyday outlook: strategic thinking. This describes what a company does in becoming smart, targeted, and nimble enough to prosper in an era of constant change. The key words for the 1990s are focus and flexibility.

Source: *Fortune*

PsychWest
9712 Fair Oaks Blvd.
Fair Oaks, CA 95628
Phone: (916)966-9697

Opportunities: The company hires clerical staff and mental health workers. Requirements fluctuate and may include a college degree, previous experience, or some college course work.

Benefits: Benefits include medical insurance, life insurance, dental insurance, vision insurance, savings plan, tuition assistance, and retirement benefits.

Application Procedures: The company does not accept any unsolicited resumes, but does post available positions.

▶ **Internships**

Type: The company does not offer any internship programs.

Quincy Mental Health Center
460 Quincy Ave.
Quincy, MA 02169
Phone: (617)770-4000

Opportunities: Entry-level positions available in mental health and nursing. Applicants must be licensed.

Benefits: Benefits include medical insurance, sick time, and personal days.

Application Procedures: Those interested must submit an application. The company does not accept unsolicited resumes.

Ramsay Health Care, Inc. Cumberland Hospital
3425 Melrose Rd.
Fayetteville, NC 28304
Phone: (919)485-7181
Fax: (919)485-8465

Business Description: Cumberland Hospital is a private, 175-bed psychiatric/chemical dependency treatment hospital offering inpatient and outpatient services to all age groups.

Employees: 300. The number of entry level people reflects 25 RNs and 5 M.S.W.s hired.

Average Entry-Level Hiring: 30.

Opportunities: RNs—psychiatric background preferred but not required. Social workers—M.S.W. required. Chemical dependency counselors—state certification required. Occupational therapists, COTAs, and recreation therapists—state registration required. Physician assistant—state licensure required.

Human Resources: Robert Reylea.

Ramsey Health Care
639 Loyola Ave., Ste. 1400
New Orleans, LA 70113
Phone: (504)525-2505

Business Description: Operator of psychiatric hospitals. Operator of specialty hospitals.

Benefits: Benefits include medical insurance, dental insurance, 401(k), sick days, a stock plan, paid holidays, paid vacation, and short-term disability insurance.

Human Resources: Barbara Molyneux.

Application Procedures: Send resume and cover letter to the attention of Pamela Neil.

▶ **Internships**

Type: The company does not offer any internship programs.

Rehab Systems Co.
3607 Rosemont Ave.
Camp Hill, PA 17011
Phone: (717)761-8350

Officers: Nancy Stover, Contact.

ReLife Inc.
813 Shades Creek Pkwy., Ste. 300
Birmingham, AL 35209
Phone: (205)870-8099

Officers: Miriam Hall, Contact.

Rhode Island Department of Human Services
600 New London Ave.
Cranston, RI 02920
Phone: (401)464-3575
Fax: (401)464-1876

Officers: Ruby Fretz, Contact.

Rhode Island Department of Mental Health, Retardation and Hospitals
Aime J. Forand Bldg.
600 New London Ave.
Cranston, RI 02920
Phone: (401)464-3201

Opportunities: Hires civil servants, nurses, and doctors. Some positions require licensing and/or a college degree and previous experience.

Benefits: Benefits include tuition assistance and savings plan.

Human Resources: Bob Plant.

Application Procedures: Apply in person or send a resume to the Personnel Department.

Richmond State Hospital
498 NW 18th St.
Richmond, IN 47374
Phone: (317)966-0511

Opportunities: Applicants must apply through The State of Indiana Job Bank. Psychiatric attendant and clerical post positions require a high school degree. Other positions include substance abuse counselors, social workers, and behavioral clinicians. These positions require either college course work, previous experience, or a college degree. Contact the company for more information.

Benefits: Benefits include medical insurance, life insurance, dental insurance, vision insurance, savings plan, tuition assistance, profit sharing, sick days, deferred compensation, and a credit union.

Human Resources: Joyce Lafuse.

Application Procedures: Applicants must contact The Indiana State Personnel Office Job Bank.

▶ **Internships**

Type: The Company does not offer any internships.

Rivendell of America Inc.
3401 West End Ave., Ste. 500
Nashville, TN 37203
Phone: (615)383-0376
Fax: (615)269-7525

Business Description: Operator of psychiatric hospitals.

Officers: Tommy Bryant, CEO & Pres.; Doug Gosnell, Dir. of Info. Systems; Alice Williams, Exec. VP & CFO; Cherryl Wilson, VP of Mktg.

Human Resources: David Lassiter.

Roosevelt Warm Springs Institute for Rehabilitation
PO Box 1000
Warm Springs, GA 31830
Phone: (706)655-5001

Opportunities: Hires entry-level staff in all areas.

Benefits: Benefits include medical insurance, life insurance, dental insurance, savings plan, and legal insurance.

Human Resources: Kay Garett.

Application Procedures: Fill out Merrit System application and send resume and cover letter.

▶ **Internships**

Contact: Kay Garett, Personnel Dept.

Type: Offers unpaid internships for college

JOB OPPORTUNITIES DATABANK

MENTAL HEALTH CAREER DIRECTORY

credit in physical therapy, nursing, and counseling. **Number Available Annually:** Varies.

Qualifications: College students.

Some handy books to help you contemplate the job-change process: *Switching Gears: How to Master Career Change and Find the Work That's Right for You*, by Carole Hyatt; *Congratulations! You've Been Fired*, by Emily Knoltnow; and *How to Get the Job You Want*, by Melvin Danaho and John L. Meyer.

Source: *Better Homes and Gardens*

Rye Psychiatric Hospital Center Inc.
754 Boston Post Rd.
Rye, NY 10580
Phone: (914)967-4567

Opportunities: Hires mental health workers, RNs, doctors, social workers, and psychologists with a college degree and previous experience.

Benefits: Benefits include medical insurance, life insurance, dental insurance, savings plan, tuition assistance, and profit sharing.

Human Resources: Eddie Mae Barnes; Flo Scenna.

Application Procedures: Nursing applicants should contact the Nursing Department. All other applicants should contact the Clinical Director or send a resume.

▶ **Internships**

Contact: Carol Dolich, Internship Coordinator.

Type: Offers college internships.

Application Procedure: Contact Carol Dolich for further information and application procedures.

Safe Recovery Systems Inc.
2300 Peachford Rd.
Atlanta, GA 30338
Phone: (404)455-7233

Opportunities: Hires entry-level personnel in all areas. Requirements vary depending on the position.

Benefits: Benefits include medical insurance, life insurance, dental insurance, and 401(k).

Human Resources: Doug Brockelbank Finance Contact; Jim Seckman, Clinical Contact.

Application Procedures: Send resume and cover letter to appropriate area.

▶ **Internships**

Contact: Jim Seckman.

Type: Offers unpaid internships for college credit. Requirements vary depending on the position. **Number Available Annually:** 4.

Application Procedure: Send resume and cover letter to contact.

Saint Elizabeth's Hospital
2700 Martin Luther King Jr. Ave., SE
Washington, DC 20032
Phone: (202)373-7166

Opportunities: Hires social workers with an M.S.W. and psychiatrists with an M.D.

Benefits: Benefits include medical insurance, life insurance, dental insurance, vision insurance, and savings plan.

Human Resources: Mary Ernest.

Application Procedures: Fill out the 1071 Federal Agency application and turn it in with copies of all degrees attached.

▶ **Internships**

Contact: Mary Ernest.

Type: Offers paid internships in psychiatry.

Application Procedure: To apply, write a letter and fill out the 1071 Federal Agency application.

St. Joseph Mercy Hospitals of Macomb
17001 19 Mile Rd.
Mt. Clemens, MI 48044
Phone: (313)263-2801
Fax: (313)263-2803

Employees: 2,000.

Average Entry-Level Hiring: 20-30.

Opportunities: Registered nurse, LPN, nurse assistant, nurse technician in critical care (ER, ICU, CCU, Telemetry), neurology/family practice, oncology, psychiatric services, physical medicine and rehabilitation, orthopedics, pediatrics, surgical services, and women's health;

nursery, labor and delivery, and gynecology. Nurse assistant—six months experience in acute care. Nurse technician—completion of medical/surgical rotation in accredited nursing school. Surgical technician—LPN or completion of accredited surgical tech program. Medical technologist—bachelor's degree and ASCP certification. Histology technologist—accredited program in histology. Occupational and physical therapists—bachelor's degree. Physical therapy assistant—associate degree. Radiology technologist—approved school of radiologic technology, American Registry of Radiologic Technologists. Nuclear medicine technologist—accredited Nuclear Medicine Technology program, ARRT or NMTCB. Ultrasound technologist—registered diagnostic medical sonographer and ARRT. Computer tomography technologist—approved school of Radiologic Technology. Respiratory therapist—two-year respiratory therapist program, RRT preferred. Respiratory technician—six months training in approved respiratory therapy program, CRTT preferred.

Human Resources: Diana Palmeri; Virginia Kastner.

▶ **Internships**

Type: Internships are available in some areas.

St. Michael's Hospital
30 Bond St.
Toronto, ON, Canada M5B 1W8
Phone: (416)360-4000
Fax: (416)867-7488

Employees: 2,400.

Average Entry-Level Hiring: Unknown.

Opportunities: RN—a two-, three-, or four-year degree is required. Other positions available.

Application Procedures: Call the employment coordinator in human resources at (416)867-7401 for more information.

San Diego County Psychiatric Hospital
3851 Rosecrans St.
San Diego, CA 92138
Phone: (619)692-8211

Opportunities: Entry-level positions require some college course work.

Benefits: Benefits include medical insurance, life insurance, dental insurance, vision insurance, tuition assistance, child-care programs, elder-care programs, and deferred compensation.

Application Procedures: Can apply in person to Human Resources for current job vacancies.

▶ **Internships**

Type: Offers paid internships to graduate students.

San Pablo Treatment Center
2801 N. 31st St.
PO Box 32650
Phoenix, AZ 85064-2650
Phone: (602)956-9090
Fax: (602)956-3018

Opportunities: Entry-level positions exist in maintenance and kitchen work. Requires a high school diploma.

Benefits: Benefits include medical insurance and dental insurance.

Human Resources: Lowell Andrews.

Application Procedures: Send resume to Lowell Andrews.

More than 16 million Americans seek mental health treatment each year, but the majority of people who could benefit from therapy never seek help.

Source: *U.S. News & World Report*

Senior Living Centers Inc.
125 7th St.
Pittsburgh, PA 15222
Phone: (412)338-1000

Officers: Dave Polanack, Contact.

SHARE, Psychiatric Day Treatment Center, Inc.
608 NW 9th, Ste. 2106
Oklahoma City, OK 73102-1064
Phone: (405)236-3336
Fax: (405)236-3339

Opportunities: Hires occupational therapists, registered nurses, and social workers at the entry-level. Previous experience and a college degree are required.

Benefits: Benefits include medical insurance, dental insurance, and profit sharing.

Human Resources: Suzy Waugh; Mr. Meadows.

Application Procedures: Send resume and cover letter to the attention of Suzy Waugh.

▶ **Internships**

Contact: Suzy Waugh.

Type: Offers unpaid internships for college credit. **Number Available Annually:** 5-8.

Qualifications: Medical students.

Application Procedure: Send resume.

Sinai Health Care System
6767 W. Outer Dr.
Detroit, MI 48235
Phone: (313)493-6800

Opportunities: Hires entry-level applicants for housekeeping, dietary work, and patient transportation. Prefers previous work experience, but it is not mandatory.

Benefits: Benefits include life insurance, dental insurance, and a pension plan.

Application Procedures: Interested applicants should send resumes to the Personnel Department. The department can be reached at (313) 493-6162. All resumes will be kept on file for six months.

▶ **Internships**

Type: The company occasionally offers unpaid internships for college credit.

Application Procedure: Send resume to the attention of the Employment Office.

South Carolina Commission on Alcohol and Drug Abuse
3700 Forest Dr., Ste. 300
Columbia, SC 29204
Phone: (803)734-9520
Fax: (803)734-9663

Opportunities: Hires entry-level staff in data control and data processing positions. Requires a college degree, previous experience, or at least some college course work.

Benefits: Benefits include medical insurance, life insurance, dental insurance, vision insurance, and savings plan.

Human Resources: Kay Kimery.

Application Procedures: Submit a State application with a resume to Kay Kimery in the Personnel Department.

▶ **Internships**

Type: Offers unpaid internships to college seniors and graduate students. **Number Available Annually:** 5.

Application Procedure: Apply through Personnel or through a school referral.

South Carolina Department of Social Services
1535 Confederate Ave.
Columbia, SC 29202
Phone: (803)734-5760
Fax: (803)734-5597

Opportunities: Opportunities in the social services office require some college course work or a bachelor's degree.

Benefits: Benefits include medical insurance, dental insurance, child or elder care, sick leave, annual leave, and 11 paid holidays.

Application Procedures: Apply in person or send resume.

▶ **Internships**

Contact: Marsha Creed.

Type: Offers internships for college credit for college juniors and seniors. **Number Available Annually:** 100.

Application Procedure: Apply in person or send resume to Marsha Creed.

South Carolina State Department of Mental Health
2414 Bull St.
PO Box 485
Columbia, SC 29201
Phone: (803)734-7780
Fax: (803)734-7879

Opportunities: Hires for housekeeping positions requiring a 10th grade education.

Benefits: Benefits include medical insurance and dental insurance.

Application Procedures: Apply in person.

South Dakota Department of Social Services
700 Governor's Dr.
Pierre, SD 57501
Phone: (605)773-3165
Fax: (605)773-4855

Opportunities: Hires clerical workers for entry-level positions. Requires a college degree and previous experience.

Benefits: Benefits include medical insurance, life insurance, dental insurance, vision insurance, tuition assistance, and a retirement savings plan.

Application Procedures: Applicants must pass a State examination.

South Dakota Division of Developmental Disabilities
Hillsview Plaza
E. Highway 34
c/o 500 E. Capitol
Pierre, SD 57501-5070
Phone: (605)773-3438
Fax: (605)773-5483

Opportunities: Hires entry-level staff in all positions. Must meet minimal requirements.

Benefits: Benefits include medical insurance, life insurance, a flexible dental plan, and optional plans for dependents.

Human Resources: Ellen Zeller, Director of Classification.

Application Procedures: Send resume and cover letter to the attention of Ellen Zeller.

▶ **Internships**

Type: Offers paid internships for college credit to students of junior status. **Number Available Annually:** 60.

Application Procedure: Send an application to Human Resources within allotted time frame.

Southboro Medical Group Inc.
24 Newton St.
Southborough, MA 01772
Phone: (508)481-5500

Opportunities: Hires entry-level data entry and reception staff and file clerks. Previous experience and high school diploma required.

Benefits: Benefits include medical insurance, life insurance, tuition assistance, and disability insurance.

Human Resources: Linda Avedisian.

Application Procedures: Send resume and cover letter.

▶ **Internships**

Type: Offers unpaid internships for college credit. **Number Available Annually:** 3.

Qualifications: Medical assistant program students.

Application Procedure: Internships are awarded through training programs.

Between positions job-seekers do best when they create a daily schedule, establishing structure for what will be done each day. Setting non-job goals to attain achievements outside job-related activities helps maintain self-confidence. Flexibility is essential; a willingness to consider alternatives can lead to opportunities in new fields and offer a chance to explore something new.

Source: *Working Woman*

Stockton Developmental Center
510 E. Magnolia St.
Stockton, CA 95202
Phone: (209)948-7335
Fax: (209)948-7646

Business Description: All clients served are developmentally disabled. The majority are adults. The youngest age served is fourteen.

Employees: 900.

Average Entry-Level Hiring: Approximately 10 percent turnover annually.

Opportunities: Physician, surgeon, clinical, educational, and counseling psychologists, psychiatric social workers (M.S.W.), physical therapists, occupational therapists, recreational therapists, music therapists, registered nurses, psychiatric technicians, and pharmacists.

Human Resources: Thomas P. Thompson.

Stormont-Vail Regional Medical Center
1500 W. 10th
Topeka, KS 66604
Phone: (913)354-6153
Fax: (913)354-5889

Employees: 1,850.

Job Opportunities Databank

Average Entry-Level Hiring: 40.

Opportunities: Typically hires 40 entry-level nurses per year, two physical therapists, two occupational therapists, ten respiratory therapists, one social service worker, three radiologists, three medical technicians, and three pharmacists.

Human Resources: Laurie Florence; Betty Hadison.

Summit Health Ltd.
2600 W. Magnolia Blvd.
PO Box 2100
Burbank, CA 91505-2100
Phone: (818)841-8750

Business Description: An integrated healthcare company operating hospitals, nursing centers, and other health-related facilities in Arizona, California, Iowa, and Texas.

Officers: Donald J. Amaral, Pres. & COO; Don Freeberg, CEO, Pres. & Chairman of the Board; Frank S. Osen, Sr. VP & General Counsel; William C. Scott, Sr. VP; Randolph H. Speer, Sr. VP & CFO.

Benefits: Benefits include medical insurance, dental insurance, vision insurance, life insurance, employee pension plan, and long and short-term disability.

Human Resources: David Rubardt.

Application Procedures: The company accepts solicited and unsolicited resumes. Interested candidates should forward resumes and cover letters to Sue Heinberd.

▶ **Internships**

Type: The company does not offer any internship programs.

Tennessee Bureau of Alcohol and Drug Abuse Services
Cordell Hull Bldg., Rm. 255
Nashville, TN 37247-4401
Phone: (615)741-1921
Fax: (615)741-2491

Opportunities: Offers Civil Service positions. May require a college degree, previous experience, or some college course work.

Benefits: Benefits include medical insurance, life insurance, and a group dental plan. Also offers savings plan, tuition assistance, child-care programs, elder-care programs, and annual days.

Human Resources: Mary Rosher.

Application Procedures: Contact Personnel by phone or send a resume. May have to take a Civil Service exam.

Tennessee Social Services
400 Deaderick St.
Nashville, TN 37248-0090
Phone: (615)741-3107
Fax: (615)741-0770

Opportunities: Hires entry-level staff in all program areas. A college degree is required. A high school diploma is required for clerical positions.

Benefits: Benefits include medical insurance, life insurance, dental insurance, and savings plan.

Human Resources: Ed Bay Personnel.

Application Procedures: Fill out an application for the State of Tennessee. Contact the Department of Personnel.

▶ **Internships**

Type: Offers unpaid internships. **Number Available Annually:** 10.

Qualifications: College juniors and seniors.

Application Procedure: Contact the department of personnel.

Texas Department of Human Services
701 W. 51st St.
PO Box 149030
Austin, TX 78751
Phone: (512)450-3054
Fax: (512)450-4176

Opportunities: Minimum requirements vary depending upon the position. Nursing applicants must have a RN degree with one or two years experience. Clerical, case worker, community care worker, and case management specialists all vary but carry a minimum bachelor's degree requirement.

Benefits: Benefits include medical insurance, life insurance, dental insurance, savings plan, tuition assistance, 401(k), differed compensation, paid sick leave, and job improvement opportunities.

Human Resources: Alan Bledsloe.

Application Procedures: Interested candidates should complete either a 40-10 or a 4009 form for an agency application, submit a resume, and contact the personnel office. Applicants should apply for a specific job.

▶ **Internships**

Type: The company does not offer an internship program.

Texas Department of Mental Health and Mental Retardation
909 W. 45th St.
PO Box 12668
Capitol Station
Austin, TX 78711
Phone: (512)454-3761
Fax: (512)465-4836

Opportunities: Hires nurses aides and secretaries with 6 months previous experience.

Benefits: Benefits include medical insurance, life insurance, dental insurance, and savings plan.

Human Resources: Debbie Lannen.

Application Procedures: Interested applicants should submit resumes or completed applications to the Hiring Authority.

Tinley Park Mental Health Center
7400 W. 183rd St.
Tinley Park, IL 60477
Phone: (708)614-4000

Benefits: Benefits include medical insurance, life insurance, dental insurance, and deferred compensation.

Human Resources: Carol Cochrane; Jerry Gulli.

Application Procedures: Must pass civil service test to be eligible. Requires a college degree and previous experience. Can apply in person or by phone or send resume to Jerry Gulli.

TME Inc.
333 N. Sam Houston
Houston, TX 77056
Phone: (713)439-7511

Business Description: Outpatient diagnostic clinic.

Officers: Cherrill Farnsworth, CEO; Stephen Jackson, Exec. VP; William L. Birch, Dir. of Systems; Elizabeth Flores, Human Resources Dir.

Opportunities: Hires clerical workers for entry-level positions.

Benefits: Benefits include medical insurance, life insurance, dental insurance, a 401(k) plan, and disability benefits.

Human Resources: Pamela Castael.

Application Procedures: Send resume to apply.

Squeezed by foreign competition and a slowing economy, employers are increasingly shunning fixed raises in favor of pay plans where employees can enrich themselves only by enriching the company. From hourly workers to managers in pin stripes, those who boost earnings, productivity, or other results prosper. Those who turn in a lackluster performance take home less.

Source: *US News & World Report*

Toledo Mental Health Center
930 S. Detroit/Caller No. 10002
Toledo, OH 43699-0002
Phone: (419)381-1881
Fax: (419)389-1967

Employees: 460. Total employees count includes fifty-nine registered nurses and ten psychiatrists.

Average Entry-Level Hiring: Psychiatrists—1-3.

Opportunities: Psychiatrist—certificate to practice medicine per section 4731.13 of Revised Code, and satisfactory completion of residency training program in psychiatry.

Human Resources: Steve Hansen; Janet Conkey.

Topeka State Hospital
2700 W. 6th St.
Topeka, KS 66606
Phone: (913)296-4596

Opportunities: Bachelor's degree is required for social workers; psychologists must have their Ph.D's; psychiatrists and psychiatric residents are also hired.

Benefits: Benefits include medical insurance, life insurance, and dental insurance.

Human Resources: Brenda Kelly.

Application Procedures: Contact the job service center.

▶ **Internships**

Type: Paid or unpaid internships are available depending on field of study. Some internships offer college credit. **Number Available Annually:** Four per year.

Application Procedure: Contact the director of internships.

Tri-State Regional Rehabilitation Hospital
4100 Covert Ave.
Evansville, IN 47715
Phone: (812)476-9983

Opportunities: The company requires college degrees for all positions. The positions include nursing, social services, optical therapist, speech therapist, and must be able to prove certification when necessary.

Benefits: The company offers medical insurance, life insurance, dental insurance, savings plan, tuition assistance, profit sharing, long-term disability, paid holidays, vacation and sick days, and a 401K plan.

Human Resources: Sue Nolte.

Application Procedures: Application for a position can be made through phone contact, in person, or by forwarding a resume to human resources.

▶ **Internships**

Type: The Company does not offer internships.

UMS Corp.
27 N. 3rd St.
Philadelphia, PA 19106
Phone: (215)592-8880

Business Description: Operates nursing homes and personal care facilities.

Officers: Mark Turnbull, President; Alex Pearl, Exec. VP.

Opportunities: Hires receptionists at entry-level. Depending on the position being applied for, previous experience and/or some college course work may be required.

Benefits: Benefits include medical insurance, life insurance, dental insurance, savings plan, and child-care programs.

Human Resources: Barbara Argeros, Contact.

Application Procedures: Advertises in newspaper. Send resume and cover letter to the attention of Barbara Argeros.

▶ **Internships**

Type: The company does not offer any internship programs.

United Behavioral Systems Inc.
PO Box 1459
Minneapolis, MN 55440
Phone: (612)936-8964

Business Description: Mental health and substance abuse clinics.

Officers: John Newstrom, CEO; John D. Tadich, VP of Mktg.

Opportunities: Hires entry-level counseling and support staff. College degree and/or previous experience required.

Benefits: Benefits include medical insurance, life insurance, dental insurance, vision insurance, tuition assistance, 401(k), and a stock purchase plan.

Human Resources: Tina Murphy, Contact.

Application Procedures: Call or send resume and cover letter to human resources or fill out an application at the human relations office in the city in which you are applying for a position.

▶ **Internships**

Type: The company does not offer an internship program.

U.S. Behavioral Health
2000 Powell St.
Emeryville, CA 94608
Phone: (510)652-1402

Business Description: Substance abuse rehabilitation services.

Opportunities: The company hires entry-level staff with previous experience and/or a high school diploma. Requirements vary depending upon the position. Positions include patient services.

Benefits: Benefits include medical insurance,

life insurance, dental insurance, savings plan, 401(k), and dependent care.

Application Procedures: Interested candidates should forward resumes to the personnel department. If a candidate is asked to interview, the personnel department will provide an application.

▶ **Internships**

Type: The company does not offer any internship programs.

Universal Health Services Inc.
367 S. Gulph Rd.
King of Prussia, PA 19406
Phone: (215)768-3300

Business Description: A hospital management company for acute care and psychiatric hospitals. Operates 20 acute care hospitals and 13 psychiatric hospitals. Three hospitals are located in the United Kingdom.

Officers: Alan B. Miller, CEO & Pres.; Sidney Miller, Exec. VP.

Benefits: Benefits include medical insurance, dental insurance, 401(k), and short- and long-term disability insurance. Part-time employees must work at least 20 hours a week to receive benefits.

Human Resources: Eileen Dove.

Application Procedures: Send resume and cover letter to the attention of Eileen Dove.

▶ **Internships**

Type: The company offers an internship program.

Utah Department of Human Services
120 N. 200 West
PO Box 45500
Salt Lake City, UT 84145-0500
Phone: (801)538-4001
Fax: (801)538-4016

Opportunities: Hires family support workers, investigators, treatment workers, and youth correction counselors. Requires a college degree.

Benefits: Benefits include medical insurance, life insurance, dental insurance, and tuition assistance.

Application Procedures: Apply in person and consult provided job list for requirements and contact person.

▶ **Internships**

Type: The company has recently instituted an internship program which offers paid internships to college students.

Most Often-Cited Corporate Restructuring Goals

1. Reduce expenses
2. Increase profits
3. Improve cash flow
4. Increase productivity
5. Increase shareholder return on investment
6. Increase competitive advantage
7. Reduce bureaucracy
8. Improve decision making
8. Increase customer satisfaction
10. Increase sales

Source: *The Wall Street Journal*

Utah Division of Substance Abuse
PO Box 45500
Salt Lake City, UT 84145
Phone: (801)538-3939
Fax: (801)538-4334

Officers: Pat Barrett, Contact.

Benefits: Benefits include medical insurance, life insurance, dental insurance, vision insurance, savings plan, child-care programs, elder-care programs, and a 401(k) plan.

Application Procedures: Fill out an application in person if there is an opening.

Utah Mental Health
PO Box 45500
Salt Lake City, UT 84145-0500
Phone: (801)538-4270

Human Resources: Chrisanta Burris.

VA Medical Center
113 Holland Ave.
Albany, NY 12208
Phone: (518)462-3311
Fax: (518)462-2519

Opportunities: Not hiring at this time.

Human Resources: Carol Ann Bedford RN, Nursing; Lawrence H. Flesh MD, Chief of Staff; Alice A. Flynn.

VA Medical Center
5500 Armstrong Rd.
Battle Creek, MI 49016
Phone: (616)966-5600
Fax: (616)966-5433

Employees: 1,600.

Average Entry-Level Hiring: 200.

Opportunities: Registered nurses, physicians, and physical therapists are needed in the areas of acute psychiatry, intermediate medicine, general medicine, and gerontology. Registered nurses—license required. Physicians—requires license and either Board eligible or certified. Physical therapist—requires appropriate degree and certification.

Human Resources: Mary Lightbody; Cynthis Sipp; Ronald Kelly.

Vari-Care Inc.
277 Alexander St.
Rochester, NY 14607
Phone: (716)325-6940

Business Description: Nursing homes.

Officers: Robert H. Hurlbut, President; William F. Doud, Exec. VP.

Opportunities: Hires entry-level accounts payable, accounts receivable, and reception staff. Previous experience required; college degree is mandatory for administrative positions.

Benefits: Benefits include medical insurance, life insurance, dental insurance, and vision insurance.

Human Resources: Patricia Gardner.

Application Procedures: Apply in person or send resume and cover letter to the attention of Patricia Gardner.

▶ **Internships**

Type: The company does not offer an internship program.

Vermont Agency of Human Services

103 S. Main St.
Waterbury, VT 05676
Phone: (802)241-2220
Fax: (802)244-8103

Opportunities: Hires entry-level social workers with a college degree.

Benefits: Benefits include medical insurance, life insurance, dental insurance, vision insurance, savings plan, and tuition assistance.

Human Resources: Mary Dunster.

Application Procedures: Send resume and cover letter or fill out an application and turn it in to the department of personnel.

▶ **Internships**

Type: Offers unpaid internships.

Qualifications: College graduates.

Application Procedure: Contact the district office to apply.

Vermont Department of Mental Health and Mental Retardation

103 S. Main St.
Waterbury, VT 05671-1601
Phone: (802)241-2610

Opportunities: Hire entry-level staff in the clerical and housekeeping departments. There is a hiring freeze in other areas.

Benefits: Benefits include medical insurance, life insurance, and dental insurance.

Human Resources: Sharon Wilson.

Application Procedures: Applicants must follow civil service employment procedures, including taking a state exam.

▶ **Internships**

Type: The company does not offer an internship program.

Vermont Department of Social Welfare
103 S. Main St.
Waterbury, VT 05676
Phone: (802)241-2853
Fax: (802)241-2830

Opportunities: Hires social workers with a college degree.

Benefits: Benefits include medical insurance, life insurance, dental insurance, vision insurance, savings plan, and tuition assistance.

Human Resources: Mary Dunster.

Application Procedures: Send resume and cover letter or fill out an application and turn it in to the department of personnel.

▶ **Internships**

Type: Offers unpaid internships.

Qualifications: College graduates.

Application Procedure: Contact the district office to apply.

Vermont Office of Alcohol and Drug Abuse Programs
103 S. Main St.
Waterbury, VT 05671-1701
Phone: (802)241-2170
Fax: (802)244-8103

Opportunities: The office requires college degrees for most of its positions. Positions include state government and civil service positions. In addition, professional levels require experience and training.

Benefits: Benefits include medical insurance, life insurance, dental insurance, and sick days. The company will also provide leave referrals.

Application Procedures: Applications should be made through Vermont state civil service applications. Applicants must pass The State of Vermont Civil Service Exam.

▶ **Internships**

Type: The company offers paid internships to interns if the intern's school will then reimburse them as employers. The company does not usually have more than one intern per year.

Village at Manor Park
3023 S. 84th St.
West Allis, WI 53227
Phone: (414)545-5451

Business Description: Own and operate retirement and intermediate care nursing homes.

Officers: R. Arthur Wagner, President; Thomas E. Tomasik, Finance Officer; Theodore A. Gibbs, Vice Pres.; Lin Reading, Human Resources Dir.

Opportunities: Hires nurses and physical therapists. Depending on the position, a college degree and/or previous experience may be required.

Benefits: Benefits include medical insurance, life insurance, dental insurance, vision insurance, and 403B.

Human Resources: Lynn Redding.

Application Procedures: Does not accept unsolicited resumes. Apply in person.

▶ **Internships**

Contact: Lynn Redding, Human Resources.

Type: Offers paid and unpaid internships.

Qualifications: College students.

Techniques for winning people over to your team when you're new on the job and change is in your program: make sure those who work for you see your vision as clearly as you do; listen to your critics—if you respect their work, they probably have good advice; make it clear that you're not on a power trip—be honest and don't promise what you can't deliver; get people involved in different aspects of the business so they know how everything works.

Source: *Working Woman*

Virginia Department of Mental Health, Mental Retardation and Substance Abuse Services
PO Box 1797
Richmond, VA 23214
Phone: (804)786-3921
Fax: (804)786-4146

Opportunities: Hires developmental aides with a high school diploma.

Benefits: Benefits include medical insurance, child-care programs, elder-care programs, and personal/sick days.

Mental Health Career Directory

Human Resources: Karen Clouse.

Application Procedures: Places newspaper advertisements for specific job openings. Applicant should then send resume to contact listed in the ad.

▶ **Internships**

Contact: Golam Rabboni.

Type: Company offers paid and unpaid internships. College credit is available. **Number Available Annually:** 5.

Qualifications: College students.

Application Procedure: Send resume to Golam Rabboni.

Some personal improvement guides: *Marketing Yourself*, by Dorothy Leeds; *The Perfect Interview: How To Get the Job You Really Want*, by John D. Drake; and *The Management Skills Builder: Self-Directed Learning Strategies for Career Development.*

Source: *Library Journal*

Virginia Department of Social Services

730 E. Broad St.
Richmond, VA 23229-8699
Phone: (804)692-1500
Fax: (804)662-7022

Opportunities: Requirements for entry-level jobs depend on the specific position open.

Benefits: Benefits include medical insurance, life insurance, dental insurance, vision insurance, savings plan, tax shelters, and annuities.

Human Resources: Vivian Cook, Employment Manager.

Application Procedures: Those interested should apply through the state personnel office.

▶ **Internships**

Type: Offers paid and unpaid internships. College credit is available.

Vista Del Mar Child and Family Services

3200 Motor Ave.
Los Angeles, CA 90034
Phone: (310)836-1223
Fax: (213)204-1405

Opportunities: Hires entry-level development counselors and clerical staff. Requirements depend on the position being applied for.

Benefits: Benefits include medical insurance, life insurance, dental insurance, vacation days, long-term disability insurance, and a pension plan.

Human Resources: Leslie Askanas, Contact.

Application Procedures: Fill out an application or send resume and cover letter to Leslie Askanas.

▶ **Internships**

Type: Offers unpaid social work internships. College credit is available.

Qualifications: College students.

Application Procedure: Send applications to the director of professional services.

Walter P. Carter Community Mental Health/Retardation Center

630 W. Fayette St.
Baltimore, MD 21201
Phone: (410)328-2139
Fax: (410)328-4270

Officers: Mike Colman, Contact.

Opportunities: Hires direct care aides with at least a high school equivalency.

Benefits: Offers a medical plan and a savings bonds plan.

Application Procedures: Interested applicants should file an application with the Personnel Department.

Washington Division of Alcohol and Substance Abuse

PO Box 45330
Mail Stop 5330
Olympia, WA 98504-5330
Phone: (206)438-8200
Fax: (206)585-8200

Human Resources: Henry Govert.

▶ **Internships**

Type: The company does not offer an internship program.

Washington Hospital Center

110 Irving St., NW
Washington, DC 20010
Phone: (202)877-6048
Toll-free: 800-432-3993
Fax: (202)877-7315

Business Description: Washington Hospital Center is an acute care, level one trauma center with 907 beds.

Employees: 5,100.

Average Entry-Level Hiring: 50-75.

Opportunities: Positions available in the following areas: nursing, PT, OT, medical technology, radiology, nuclear medicine, medical social work, respiratory therapy, pharmacy, surgical technology, cardiovascular technology, and as physician assistants. For the respective occupations, graduation from an accredited program, college, or university, and licensure is required.

Human Resources: Cynthia Wolfe, RN Nursing; Terra Cox, RN; Denise Stribling, RN.

Application Procedures: Contact Terra Cox for the following positions; PT, OT, medical technology, radiology, medical social work, nuclear medicine, and respiratory therapy. Contact Denise Stribling for the following positions; pharmacy, surgical technology, physician's assistant, and cardiovascular technology.

Washington State Department of Social and Health Services

Mail Stop HB-41
Olympia, WA 98504
Phone: (206)753-1777
Fax: (206)586-7498

Opportunities: Hires for the positions of attendants, clerical workers, social workers, and workers in the accounting department. College degree is required for all positions.

Benefits: Benefits include medical insurance, life insurance, dental insurance, and vision insurance.

Human Resources: Chuck Erson.

Application Procedures: Unsolicited resumes will not be accepted. Most positions require a completed state of Washington application. Chuck Erson. Phone: (206)753-1208.

▶ **Internships**

Contact: Pauline Carlton, Human Resources.
Type: Paid internships are available for college credit. **Number Available Annually:** 2 undergrad./1 graduate level.

Qualifications: Undergraduate or graduate students are eligible for internships.

Application Procedure: Available internships are posted in the administration office on each college campus.

Wausau Hospital

333 Pine Ridge Blvd.
Wausau, WI 54401
Phone: (715)847-2800
Fax: (715)847-2017

Employees: 1,700.

Average Entry-Level Hiring: Varies with occupation.

Opportunities: RN—associate or bachelor's degree required. Also fills positions in PT, OT, medical technology, radiology, nuclear medicine, medical social work, respiratory therapy, pharmacy, surgical technology, and cardiovascular technology.

Human Resources: Cecilia R. Rudolph RN.

Application Procedures: Call for more information.

West Virginia Bureau of Human Resources

Capitol Complex
Bldg. 6
Charleston, WV 25305
Phone: (304)558-2400
Fax: (304)348-3240

Opportunities: Hires entry-level support services staff. A high school diploma or GED is required.

Benefits: Benefits include medical insurance, dental insurance, and child-care programs.

Human Resources: Gini Roberts.

Application Procedures: Send an application to the Division of Personnel.

▶ **Internships**

Type: The company does not offer an internship program.

West Virginia Division on Alcoholism and Drug Abuse
Capitol Complex
1900 Kanawha Blvd., E.
Bldg. 3, Ste. 451
Charleston, WV 25305
Phone: (304)548-2276

Opportunities: Hires service workers in the substance abuse unit with high-school diplomas; some positions require college degrees.

Benefits: Benefits include child-care programs, medical insurance, ECP, and savings plan.

Human Resources: Jack Clohan.

Application Procedures: Applicants should contact the West Virginia Department of Civil Service.

Western State Hospital
Russellville Rd.
Hopkinsville, KY 42241
Phone: (502)886-4431

Opportunities: Hires at entry-level for kitchen and housekeeping staff and in the professional areas of psychology and social work. A high school diploma or GED is required for kitchen and housekeeping staff. For psychologists and social workers, the minimum requirements are a master's degree and a bachelor of science degree, respectively.

Benefits: Benefits include medical insurance, life insurance, child-care programs, paid holidays, and personal/sick days.

Human Resources: Bill Norris.

Application Procedures: Applications are available from the personnel department.

Internships
Type: Offers paid and college credit internships.
Number Available Annually: 2.
Qualifications: College students.
Application Procedure: Applications should be sent to the Staff Development Department.

Willow Creek Hospital and Treatment Center
6411 E. Thomas Rd.
Scottsdale, AZ 85251
Phone: (602)990-2900
Fax: (602)945-0322

Opportunities: Hires entry-level clerical staff with previous experience.

Application Procedures: Send resume and cover letter to the attention of Joy Garland.

Internships
Type: The company does not offer an internship program.

Wisconsin Department of Health and Social Services
PO Box 7850
Madison, WI 53707
Phone: (608)266-1731
Fax: (608)266-7882

Officers: Brad Czerota, Contact.

Woodhull Medical & Mental Health Center
760 Broadway
Brooklyn, NY 11206
Phone: (718)963-8000
Fax: (718)963-8169

Employees: 3,000.

Average Entry-Level Hiring: Unknown.

Opportunities: RN—associate or bachelor's degree required. Social workers—M.S.W. required. Occupational and physical therapist—bachelor's degree.

Application Procedures: Contact the Human Resources Department for more information.

Wyoming Department of Family Services
1710 Capitol Ave.
Cheyenne, WY 82002
Phone: (307)777-7561
Fax: (307)777-7747

Opportunities: Hires entry-level staff in most areas, including clerical, custodial, and sigma computer storing. Depending on the position, a college degree and/or previous experience may be required.

Benefits: Benefits include health insurance and deferred compensation.

Human Resources: Darol Dyklem.

Application Procedures: Apply in person, call, or send resume and cover letter to the attention of James Philip Carney.

Internships
Type: The company does not offer an internship program.

Additional Companies

Alamo Mental Health Association
4242 Medical Dr.
San Antonio, TX 78229
Phone: (210)690-8400

Alaska Department of Health and Social Services
PO Box 110601
Juneau, AK 99811-0601
Phone: (907)465-3030
Fax: (907)465-3068

Alaska Division of Alcoholism and Drug Abuse
PO Box 110607
Juneau, AK 99811-0607
Fax: (907)465-3068

Arkansas Department of Human Services
PO Box 1437
Little Rock, AR 72203-1437
Phone: (501)682-8650
Fax: (501)682-6571

Austin State Hospital
4110 Guadalupe St.
Austin, TX 78751
Phone: (512)452-0381

Baltimore Addictions Treatment Center
16 S. Poppleton St.
Baltimore, MD 21201
Phone: (410)962-7180
Fax: (410)682-2838

Bellevue Hospital Center
1st Ave. & 27th St.
New York, NY 10016
Phone: (212)561-4141

Bradford at Birmingham for Adults
1221 Alton Dr.
Birmingham, AL 35210
Phone: (205)833-4000

Bradman Therapy Centers
7951 SW 6th St.
Plantation, FL 33324
Phone: (305)474-8727

California Department of Mental Health
1600 9th St., Rm. 151
Sacramento, CA 95814
Phone: (916)654-2309
Fax: (916)654-3198

Care Options
700 High St., NE
Albuquerque, NM 87102
Phone: (505)848-8088
Fax: (505)243-2772

Central State Hospital
Box 4030
Petersburg, VA 23803
Phone: (804)524-7000

Cherry Hospital
Caller Box 8000
Goldsboro, NC 27530
Phone: (919)731-3202

Colorado Alcohol and Drug Abuse Division
4210 E. 11th Ave.
Denver, CO 80220
Phone: (303)331-8201
Fax: (303)320-1529

Colorado Division of Mental Health
3520 W. Oxford Ave.
Denver, CO 80236
Phone: (303)762-4088
Fax: (303)762-4373

Colorado State Department of Social Services
1575 Sherman St.
Denver, CO 80203
Phone: (303)866-5901
Fax: (303)866-4214

Connecticut Department of Human Resources
1049 Asylum Ave.
Hartford, CT 06105
Phone: (203)566-3318

Cornerstone of Recovery, Inc.
1120 Topside Rd.
Louisville, TN 37777
Phone: (615)970-7747

Danville State Hospital
Danville, PA 17821
Phone: (717)275-7011

Detroit Central City Community Mental Health, Inc.
10 Peterboro
Detroit, MI 48201
Phone: (313)831-3160
Fax: (313)831-2604

East Mississippi State Hospital
Box 4128
West Station, MS 39304
Phone: (601)482-6186

Fulton State Hospital
600 E. 5th St.
Fulton, MO 65251
Phone: (314)592-4100

Georgia Department of Human Resources
47 Trinity Ave., SW, Ste. 522H
Atlanta, GA 30334
Phone: (404)656-5680
Fax: (404)651-8669

Glass Mental Health Centers Inc. Glass Substance Abuse Programs
821 N. Utah St.
Baltimore, MD 21201
Phone: (410)225-0594

Greystone Park Psychiatric Hospital
PO Box A
Greystone Park, NJ 07950
Phone: (201)538-1800

Griffin Memorial Hospital
Box 151
Norman, OK 73070
Phone: (405)321-4880

Hawaii Alcohol and Drug Abuse Division
1270 Queen Emma St., Ste. 706
Honolulu, HI 96813
Phone: (808)586-5391
Fax: (808)586-5389

Houston Day Hospital
4665 SW Freeway
Houston, TX 77027
Phone: (713)623-2979

Jefferson Alcohol and Drug Abuse Center
600 S. Preston St.
Louisville, KY 40202
Phone: (502)583-3921
Fax: (502)581-9234

John Umstead Hospital
1003 12th St.
Butner, NC 27509
Phone: (919)575-7211

Lakeshore Mental Health Institute
5908 Lyons View Dr.
Knoxville, TN 37919
Phone: (615)584-1561

Lincoln Regional Center
PO Box 94949
Lincoln, NE 68509
Phone: (402)471-4444

Maine Bureau of Mental Health
411 State Office Bldg., Station 40
Augusta, ME 04333
Phone: (207)289-4230
Fax: (207)289-4268

Marlboro Psychiatric Hospital
Sta. A
Marlboro, NJ 07746
Phone: (908)946-8100

Mayview State Hospital
1601 Mayview Rd.
Bridgeville, PA 15017
Phone: (412)257-6200

Middle Tennessee Mental Health Institute
1501 Murfreesboro Rd.
Nashville, TN 37217
Phone: (615)366-7616

Milwaukee County Mental Health Complex
9455 Watertown Plank Rd.
Milwaukee, WI 53226
Phone: (414)257-6995

Moose Lake Regional Treatment Center
1000 Lake Shore Dr.
Moose Lake, MN 55767
Phone: (218)485-4411

Nevada Mental Health Institute
480 Galletti Way
Sparks, NV 89431
Phone: (702)688-2001

New Beginnings of Northwest
600 N. 130th St.
Seattle, WA 98133
Phone: (206)362-6000

New Hampshire Hospital
105 Pleasant St.
Concord, NH 03301
Phone: (603)271-5200

New Jersey Division of Family Health Services
363 W. State St., CN-364
Trenton, NJ 08625
Phone: (609)292-4043
Fax: (609)292-3580

New Jersey Family Development
6 Quaker Plaza
Trenton, NJ 08625
Phone: (609)588-2401
Fax: (609)588-3369

New Mexico Human Services Department
PO Box 2348
Sante Fe, NM 87504-2348
Phone: (505)827-4065
Fax: (505)827-4002

New York State Office of Mental Health
44 Holland Ave.
Albany, NY 12229
Phone: (518)473-1997
Fax: (518)473-1271

Norristown State Hospital
1001 Sterigere St.
Norristown, PA 19401
Phone: (215)270-1000

Oak Hill Nursing Homes
34225 Grand River Ave.
Farmington Hills, MI 48335
Phone: (313)477-7373

Oregon State Hospital
2600 Center St., N.E.
Salem, OR 97310
Phone: (503)378-2348

Reproductive Institute Inc.
3780 Holcomb Bridge Rd.
Norcross, GA 30092
Phone: (404)416-9781

Rusk State Hospital
Box 318
Rusk, TX 75785
Phone: (903)683-3421

St. John's Hospital, Inc.
12617 River Rd.
Richmond, VA 23233
Phone: (804)784-3501

St. Joseph's Home for Children
1121 E. 46th St.
Minneapolis, MN 55407
Phone: (612)827-9366
Fax: (612)827-7954

MENTAL HEALTH CAREER DIRECTORY

St. Peter Regional Treatment Center

100 Freeman Dr.
St. Peter, MN 56082
Phone: (507)931-7100

South Carolina State Hospital

Box 119
Columbia, SC 29202
Phone: (803)734-6520

South Dakota Division of Alcohol and Drug Abuse

3800 E. Highway 34
Hillsview Plaza
Pierre, SD 57501
Phone: (605)773-3123
Fax: (605)773-5483

Spectrum Programs Inc.

11055 NE 6th Ave.
Miami, FL 33161
Phone: (305)754-1683
Fax: (305)751-8601

Talbott Recovery System, Inc.

5448 Yorktowne Dr.
Atlanta, GA 30349
Phone: (404)994-0185

Tennessee State Department of Human Services

400 Deaderick St.
Nashville, TN 37248
Phone: (615)741-3241
Fax: (615)741-4614

Terrell State Hospital

Box 70
Terrell, TX 75160
Phone: (214)563-6452

A Touch of Care

2231 S. Carmelina Ave.
Los Angeles, CA 90064
Phone: (310)473-6525
Fax: (310)479-1287

Utah State Hospital

Box 270
Provo, UT 84603
Phone: (801)373-4400

Vermont State Hospital

103 S. Main St.
Waterbury, VT 05671
Phone: (802)241-3100

Western Reserve Psychiatric Habilitation Center

Box 305
Northfield, OH 44067
Phone: (216)467-7131

Western State Hospital

Fort Steilacoom, WA 98494
Phone: (206)756-2525

Western State Hospital

Box 2500
Staunton, VA 24401
Phone: (703)332-8000

Weston Hospital

Drawer 1127
Weston, WV 26452
Phone: (304)269-1210

Wichita Falls State Hospital

Box 300
Wichita Falls, TX 76307
Phone: (817)692-1220

Wyoming State Hospital

PO Box 177
Evanston, WY 82931
Phone: (307)789-3464

Career Resources

CHAPTER THIRTY-TWO

Career Resources

The Career Resources chapter covers additional sources of job-related information that will aid you in your job search. It includes full, descriptive listings for sources of help wanted ads, professional associations, employment agencies and search firms, career guides, professional and trade periodicals, and basic reference guides and handbooks. Each of these sections is arranged alphabetically by organization, publication, or service name. For complete details on the information provided in this chapter, consult the introductory material at the front of this directory.

Sources of Help Wanted Ads

AAHA Provider News
American Association of Homes for the Aging (AAHA)
901 E. St., NW
Washington, DC 20004
Phone: (202)783-2242

Biweekly. Free to members. Association and industry newsletter. Includes job listings.

ABA Newsletter
Association for Behavior Analysis (ABA)
258 Wood Hall
Western Michigan University
Kalamazoo, MI 49008
Phone: (616)387-4494
Fax: (616)387-4457

Three times/year. Free to members; $5.00/year for nonmembers; $15.00/year for institutions.

Academic Journal: The Educators' Employment Magazine
Academic Journal
PO Box 392
Newtown, CT 06470

Monthly. $36.00/year. Lists positions in schools, colleges, and overseas.

Addiction & Recovery
International Publishing Group
4959 Commerce Pkwy.
Cleveland, OH 44128
Phone: (216)464-1210
Fax: (216)464-1835

Bimonthly. $28.00/year; $7.00/single issue.

Mental Health Career Directory

Adolescent Counselor
A/D Communications Corp.
PO Box 2079
Redmond, WA 98073-2079
Phone: (206)867-5024
Fax: (206)881-5247

Bimonthly. $26.00/year.

Advances in Nursing Science
200 Orchard Ridge Dr.
Gaithersburg, MD 20878
Phone: (301)417-7617
Fax: (301)417-7550

Quarterly. $53.00/year.

AICS Compass
Association of Independent Colleges and Schools
1 Dupont Circle, NW, Ste. 350
Washington, DC 20036

> Social work practitioners and educators (particularly teachers of human behavior) are challenged to address the social and psychological implications of the materialistic, consumption-oriented values guiding our society.
>
> Source: *Social Work*

Alcoholism, Clinical and Experimental Research
428 E. Preston St.
Baltimore, MD 21202
Phone: (301)528-4068

Bimonthly. $102.00/year; $127.00/year for foreign subscribers; $193.00/year for institutions; $30.00/single copy.

American Annals of the Deaf
800 Florida Ave., NE
Washington, DC 20002
Phone: (202)651-5340

Five times/year. $40.00/year.

American Association for Marriage Therapy Journal
1717 K St., NW, No. 407
Washington, DC 20006
(202) 452-0109

American City and County
Communication Channels, Inc.
6255 Barfield Rd.
Atlanta, GA 30328
Phone: (404)256-9800

Monthly. $48.00/year.

American Journal of Art Therapy
Vermont College of Norwich University
Montpelier, VT 05602
Phone: (802)828-8810

Quarterly. $27.00/year; $48.00/year for institutions.

American Journal of Mental Deficiency
1719 Kalorama Rd.
Washington, DC 20009

American Journal of Nursing
American Nurses' Association (ANA)
2420 Pershing Rd.
Kansas City, MO 64108
Phone: (816)474-5720
Fax: (816)471-4903

Monthly. $24.00/year for individuals; $30.00/year for institutions. Contains employment listings, advertisers' index, calendar of events, continuing education course listings, and information on new equipment.

American Journal of Psychology
University of Illinois Press
54 E. Gregory Dr.
Champaign, IL 61820
Phone: (217)244-6488
Fax: (217)244-8082

Donelson Dulany, editor. Quarterly. $24.00/year; $48.00/year for institutions. Journal dealing with experimental psychology and basic principles of psychology.

American Journal of Public Health
American Public Health Association (APHA)
1015 15th St., NW
Washington, DC 20005
Phone: (202)789-5600
Fax: (202)789-5681

Monthly. Free to members; $80.00/year for nonmembers. Includes annual membership directory and news briefs.

The American Nurse
American Nurses' Association (ANA)
2420 Pershing Rd.
Kansas City, MO 64108
Phone: (816)474-5720
Fax: (816)471-4903

Ten times/year. Free to members; $15.00/year for nonmembers; $10.00/year for full-time nursing students. Includes employment listings.

American Psychologist
American Psychological Association
1200 Seventeenth St., NW
Washington, DC 20036
Phone: (202)955-7600

Monthly. Free to members.

The APA Monitor
American Psychological Association
1200 17th St., NW
Washington, DC 20036
Phone: (202)955-7690
Fax: (703)525-5191

Monthly. Free to members; $25.00/year for U.S. nonmembers and institutions; $37.00/year for nonmembers outside the U.S.; $49.00/year for institutions outside the U.S. Newspaper reporting on the science, profession, and social responsibility of psychology, plus legislative developments affecting mental health, education, and research support; also covers APA activities.

ARCA News
American Rehabilitation Counseling Association
Louisiana State University Medical Center
100 S. Derbieny St.
New Orleans, LA 70112

ASCUS Annual: Job Search Handbook for Educators
Association for School, College and University Staffing (ASCUS)
1600 Dodge Ave., Ste. 330
Evanston, IL 60201-3451
Phone: (708)864-1999

$.35/copy for members (minimum order of 25); $8.00/copy for nonmembers. Includes employment notices from public school systems, and *Directory of State Teacher Certification Offices*.

AWP Newsletter
Association for Women in Psychology (AWP)
c/o Angela R. Gillem, Ph.D.
Haverford College
370 Lancaster Ave.
Haverford, PA 19041-1392

Quarterly.

Catalyst
North American Association of Christians in Social Work (NACSW)
Box S-90
St. Davids, PA 19087
Phone: (215)687-5777

Bimonthly. Free to members. Contains employment opportunity listings. Newsletter examining the relationship between churches and social work. Reports on association activities, and includes calendar of events and chapter news.

"Paradigm" has become the hottest new thing in business buzzwords. It means a dominant pattern, a set of rules and regulations that both establishes boundaries and dictates behavior within those boundaries. When a paradigm shifts, you suddenly face a brand new ball game, on a new playing field, with a new set of rules. Probably a whole new team, too. These are revolutionary changes, not incremental ones, and handling them successfully demands a radical break with tradition.

Source: *Working Woman*

Child Welfare: Journal of Policy, Practice, and Program
Child Welfare League of America (CWLA)
440 1st St., NW, Ste. 310
Washington, DC 20001
Phone: (202)638-2952
Fax: (202)638-4004

Bimonthly. $40.00/year; $50.00/year for institutions; $30.00/year for students; $8.00/copy. Includes employment opportunities and book reviews. Provides articles on creative ideas and problem-solving for professionals who work with children who are disabled, homeless, abused, or new U.S. citizens. Contains cumulative indexes of subjects, book reviews, and authors.

The Chronicle of Higher Education
1255 23rd St., NW, No. 700
Washington, DC 20037
Phone: (202)466-1000

Forty-eight times/year. $62.50/year; $2.75/issue. Provides listings of faculty, administrative, and library positions.

Strategies for "jump-starting" stalled job searches are included in *Parting Company: How To Survive the Loss of a Job and Find Another Successfully*, co-authored by William J. Morin, chairman of Drake Beam Morin Inc., the world's largest career-management consulting firm. Other chapters cover such timely topics as: assessing your skills and interests, making career decisions, financial planning, exploring different options such as early retirement, starting a business, consulting, targeting your job search, resumes and references, marketing strategy, job interviews, negotiating an offer, starting a new job.

Clinical Nurse Specialist
428 E. Preston St.
Baltimore, MD 21202
Phone: (301)528-4068
Fax: (301)528-8596

Quarterly. $42.00/year; $55.00/year for institutions; $57.00/year for foreign subscribers; $70.00/year for foreign institutions; $14.00/single issue; $16.00/single issue for foreign subscribers.

Cognitive Rehabilitation
NeuroScience Publication
6555 Carrollton Ave.
Indianapolis, IN 46220
Phone: (317)257-9672

Bimonthly. $35.00/year; $7.00/issue.

Community Jobs
ACCESS: Networking in the Public Interest
1601 Connecticut Ave., NW, 6th Fl.
Washington, DC 20009
Phone: (202)667-0661
Fax: (202)387-7915

Monthly. $45.00/year to institutions; $25.00/year to nonprofit organizations; $20.00/year to individuals; $3.95/issue. Covers: Jobs and internships available with nonprofit organizations active in issues such as the environment, foreign policy, consumer advocacy, housing, education, etc. Entries include: Position title, name, address, and phone of contact; description, responsibilities, requirements, salary. Arrangement: Geographical.

Community Mental Health Journal
Human Sciences Press
233 Spring St.
New York, NY 10013
Phone: (212)620-8000

Quarterly. $42.00/year; $105.00/year for institutions. Mental health journal featuring articles related to research, theory, and practice.

Contemporary Psychology
American Psychological Association
750 1st St., NE
Washington, DC 20002-4242
Phone: (202)336-5500

Monthly. $40.00/year for members; $80.00/year for nonmembers; $160.00/year for institutions.

The Counselor
National Association of Alcoholism and Drug Abuse Counselors (NAADAC)
3717 Columbia Pike, Ste. 300
Arlington, VA 22204
Phone: (703)920-4644
Fax: (703)920-4672

Biennial. Free to members. Magazine for counselors on alcohol and drug abuse. Includes notices of employment and educational opportunities; legislative updates; book, pamphlet, and film list.

CPADN Newsletter
Career Planning and Adult Development Network (CPADN)
4965 Sierra Rd.
San Jose, CA 95132
Phone: (408)559-4946
Fax: (408)559-8211

Monthly. Free to members; $3.50/single issue for nonmembers. Includes information on employment opportunities, book reviews, calendar of events, network contacts, and new materials.

The Criminologist
American Society of Criminology (ASC)
1314 Kinnear Rd., Ste. 212
Columbus, OH 43212
Phone: (614)292-9207
Fax: (614)292-6767

Bimonthly. $7.50/year. Includes employment opportunities; calendar of events; calls for papers; conference reports; new members; research reports.

Current Openings in Education in U.S.A.
Education Information Service
4523 Andes Dr.
Fairfax, VA 22030
Phone: (617)237-0887

Seven times/year. $9.00/issue. Booklet listing institutions or school systems, each with one to a dozen or more openings for teachers, librarians, counselors, administrators, and other personnel.

EAP Digest
Performance Resource Press
1863 Technology Dr., Ste. 200
Troy, MI 48083
Phone: (313)588-7733

Bimonthly. $36.00/year; $39.00/year for foreign subscribers; $6.00/issue.

Employee Assistance
Stevens Publishing Corp.
PO Box 2573
Waco, TX 76702
Phone: (817)776-9000
Fax: (817)776-9018

Monthly.

Exceptional Children
Council for Exceptional Children
1920 Association Dr.
Reston, VA 22091-1589
Phone: (703)620-3660
Fax: (703)264-9494

Six times/year. Free to members; $40.00/year for nonmembers. Research journal covering all aspects of special education.

Families in Society
Family Service America (FSA)
11700 West Lake Park Dr.
Milwaukee, WI 53224
Phone: (414)359-1040
Fax: (414)359-1074

Ten times/year. $29.00/year for individuals; $50.00/year for institutions. Contains information on employment opportunities; articles on social work theory and practice, research on current social problems and professional concerns of social workers; and book reviews.

The Family Therapy News
1100 17th St. NW, 10th Fl.
Washington, DC 20036
Phone: (202)452-0109

Bimonthly. $15.00/year.

With big corporations no longer rewarding loyalty and performance with lifetime guarantees of employment, individuals are transforming themselves into itinerant professionals who sell their human capital on the open market. "Instead of climbing up the ladder, people now have to develop a portfolio of skills and products that they can sell directly to a series of customers," explains Charles Handy, visiting professor at the London Business School and author of *The Age of Unreason*, a book about the changing nature of work. "We are all becoming people with portfolio careers."

Source: *Business Week*

Federal Career Opportunities
Federal Research Service, Inc.
243 Church St. NW
Vienna, VA 22183
Phone: (703)281-0200

Biweekly. $160.00/year; $75.00/six months; $38.00/three months; $7.50/copy. Provides information on more than 4,200 current federal job vacancies in the United States and overseas; includes permanent, part-time, and temporary positions. Entries include: Position title, location, series and grade, job requirements, special forms, announcement number, closing date, application address. Arrangement: Classified by federal agency and occupation.

Federal Jobs Digest

Federal Jobs Digest
325 Pennsylvania Ave., SE
Washington, DC 20003
Phone: (914)762-5111

Biweekly. $110.00/year; $29.00/three months; $4.50/issue. Covers over 20,000 specific job openings in the federal government in each issue. Entries include: Position name, title, General Schedule grade and Wage Grade, closing date for applications, announcement number, application address, phone, and name of contact. Arrangement: By federal department or agency, then geographical.

As much as half of the impression you make on a prospective employer may have to do with your general knowledge of issues in your profession as well as issues in the industry in which you currently work or the industry in which you want to work. Subscribe to the journals in your field and industry, and don't forget to stay on top of the broader picture of the national and world economies.

Source: *Working Woman*

Foreign Faculty and Administrative Openings

Education Information Service
Box 662D
Newton Lower Falls, MA 02161
Phone: (617)237-0887

Approximately every six weeks. $9.00. Covers about 150 specific openings in administration, counseling, library, and other disciplines for American teachers in American schools overseas and in international schools, both of which must teach English as a primary language.

Guidepost

American Association for Counseling and Development (AACD)
5999 Stevenson Ave.
Alexandria, VA 22304
Phone: (703)823-9800
Fax: (703)823-0252

Eighteen issues/year. Free to members; $30.00/year for nonmembers; $1.25/issue. Includes employment opportunities and book reviews. Features national and international counseling issues and legislative activities affecting counselors.

Health and Social Work

National Association of Social Workers
7981 Eastern Ave.
Silver Spring, MD 20910
Phone: (301)565-0333

Quarterly. $33.00/year for members; $50.00/year for nonmembers; $22.00/year for student members; $63.00/year for institutions.

Hospital & Community Psychiatry

American Psychiatric Association
1400 K St., NW
Washington, DC 20005
Phone: (202)682-6070

Monthly. $37.00/year; $55.00/year for institutions; $6.00/single issue.

Hospital Tribune

257 Park Ave. - South
New York, NY 10010

Hospitals

American Hospital Publishing, Inc.
211 E. Chicago Ave.
Chicago, IL 60611
Phone: (312)440-6800

Semimonthly. $50.00/year.

Job Search Handbook for Educators

Association for School, College and University Staffing (ASCUS)
c/o High School
1600 Dodge Ave.
No. 5-330
Evanston, IL 60204
Phone: (708)864-1999

Annual. $5.00/copy for members; $8.00/copy for nonmembers. Includes display notices from public school systems. Contains articles for educators seeking employment. Also includes *Directory of State Teacher Certification Offices*.

Journal of Applied Psychology

1200 17th St. NW
Washington, DC 20036
Phone: (202)955-7600

Six times/year. $50.00/year for members; $100.00/year for nonmembers; $200.00/year for institutions.

Journal of Behavioral Medicine

Plenum Publishing Corporation
233 Spring St.
New York, NY 10013
Phone: (212)620-8000

Bimonthly. $165.00/year.

Journal of Jewish Communal Service

3084 State Hwy. 27, Ste. 9
Kendall Park, NJ 08824-1657
Phone: (201)821-1871

Quarterly. $24.00/year.

Journal of Psychology

4000 Albemarie St. NW
Washington, DC 20016
Phone: (202)362-6445
Fax: (202)537-0287

Six times/year. $80.00/year.

Journal of Psychosocial Nursing and Mental Health Services

6900 Grove Rd.
Thorofare, NJ 08086
Phone: (609)848-1000

Monthly. $35.00/year; $7.00/issue.

Journal of the American Academy of Nurse Practitioners

E. Washington
Philadelphia, PA 19105
Phone: (215)238-4450
Fax: (215)238-4227

Quarterly. $20.00/year for residents in the U.S.; $40.00/year for foreign subscribers; $45.00/year for institutions; $55.00/year for foreign institutions; $15.00/single issue.

The Lutheran

8765 W. Higgins Rd.
Chicago, IL 60631
Phone: (312)380-2540

Seventeen times/year. $9.20/year.

Mental Retardation

American Association of Mental Retardation
1719 Kalorama Rd., NW
Washington, DC 20009

> Good negotiating skills are not just more important in times of social and economic change, they are also more difficult to master, according to Max H. Bazerman and Margaret A. Neale, authors of *Negotiating Rationally*. "Negotiation is used every day to resolve differences and allocate resources," they explain; negotiating rationally means making the best decisions to maximize your interests. It's especially important for the job seeker.
>
> Source: *Library Journal*

Modern Healthcare

Crain Communications, Inc.
740 N. Rush St.
Chicago, IL 60611
Phone: (312)649-5200

Weekly. $110.00/year.

NASW News

National Association of Social Workers (NASW)
7981 Eastern Ave.
Silver Spring, MD 20910
Phone: (301)565-0333
Fax: (301)587-1321

Ten times/year. Free to members; $20.00/year for nonmembers. Lists employment and educational opportunities; contains legislative and regulatory update. Includes updates on social policy developments in such areas as child welfare, Medicaid, AIDS, and housing.

National Employment Listing Service Bulletin

Sam Houston State University
College of Criminal Justice
Huntsville, TX 77341

Monthly. $30.00/year for individuals; $65.00/year for institutions/agencies.

National Weekly Bulletin
National Education Service Center
PO Box 1279
Riverton, WY 82501-1279

Lists positions in education, at the elementary, secondary, and post-secondary levels. Covers alternative positions as well.

Managers are turning to tried-and-true as well as innovative imperatives to boost staff performance. Among them: communicate, creatively and often, through electronic bulletin boards, multimedia presentations, videotapes, handwritten notes, and employee-generated mottoes; build role-playing into training efforts; bring problem-solving and decision-making down to as low an organizational level as possible, giving everyone the training, information, and tools they need to make the right choices; set up incentive programs that are linked to both team effort and individual performance.

Source: *Working Woman*

The Nation's Health
American Public Health Association (APHA)
1015 15th St., NW
Washington, DC 20005
Phone: (202)789-5600
Fax: (202)789-5681

Ten times/year. Free to members; $8.00/year for nonmembers. Includes employment opportunity listings and reports on current health issues, association actions, and legislative, regulatory, and policy issues affecting public health.

The NonProfit Times
The NonProfit Times
PO Box 870
Wantagh, NY 11793-0870

Monthly. $39.00/year.

NRA Newsletter: Committed to Enhancing the Lives of Persons with Disabilities
National Rehabilitation Association (NRA)
633 S. Washington St.
Alexandria, VA 22314
Phone: (703)836-0850
Fax: (703)836-2209

Eight times/year. Free to members. Includes listing of employment opportunities, calendar of events, and chapter news.

Nurse Practitioner
Vernon Publications, Inc.
3000 Northrup Way, Ste. 200
PO Box 96043
Bellevue, WA 98004
Phone: (206)827-9900

Monthly. $36.00/year; $52.00/year for institutions; $5.00/issue.

Nurse Practitioner Forum
PO Box 6467
Duluth, MN 55806-9854
Phone: 800-654-2452

Quarterly. $39.00/year; $29.00/year for students; $49.00/year for institutions; $18.00/single issue.

Nursing '92
Springhouse Corp.
1111 Bethlehem Pike
Springhouse, PA 19477
Phone: (215)646-8700
Fax: (215)646-4399

Monthly. $28.00/year.

Nursing & Health Care
National League for Nursing, Inc.
350 Hudson St.
New York, NY 10014
Phone: (212)989-9393

Monthly, September through June. $50.00/year; $5.00/single issue.

Nursing Economics
Anthony J. Janetti, Inc.
Box 56
N. Woodbury Rd.
Pitman, NJ 08071
Phone: (609)589-2319
Fax: (609)589-7463

Bimonthly.

Nursing Management
103 N. 2nd St., Ste. 200
West Dundee, IL 60118
Phone: (708)426-6100
Fax: (708)426-6416

Monthly. $25.00/year.

Nursing Outlook
555 W. 57th St.
New York, NY 10019-2961
Phone: (212)582-8820

Bimonthly. $25.00/year; $35.00/year for institutions; $5.00/issue.

Nursing Research
555 W. 57th St.
New York, NY 10019-2961
Phone: (212)582-8820

Bimonthly. $23.00/year.

Nursing World Journal
Prime National Publishing Corporation
470 Boston Post Rd.
Weston, MA 02193
Phone: (617)899-2702

Monthly. $22.00.

Opportunities in Non-Profit Organizations
ACCESS/Networking in the Public Interest
96 Mt. Auburn St.
Cambridge, MA 02138

Monthly. Lists opportunities in many fields, including public interest law.

Perspectives in Psychiatric Care
1211 Locust St.
Philadelphia, PA 19107
Phone: (215)545-7222
Fax: (215)545-8107

Quarterly.

Professional Counselor
A/D Communications Corp.
PO Box 2079
Redmond, WA 98073-2079
Phone: (206)867-5024
Fax: (206)881-5247

Bimonthly. $20.00/year.

Professional Report of the National Rehabilitation Counseling Association
National Rehabilitation Counseling Association (NRCA)
633 S. Washington St.
Alexandria, VA 22314
Phone: (703)836-7677

Bimonthly. Free to members. Membership activities newsletter, including list of employment opportunities and legislative news.

Psychiatric Annals
6900 Grove St.
Thorofare, NJ 08086
Phone: (609)848-1000

Monthly. $85.00/year; $95.00/year for institutions. Journal analyzing concepts and practices in every area of psychiatry.

Psychiatric News
American Psychiatric Association
1400 K St., NW
Washington, DC 20005
Phone: (202)682-6133

Semimonthly. $40.00/year.

Psychologists work in a wide range of settings, from private practice to clinics, in both general and specialty hospitals, in schools and university settings, and in corporate-based, industrial health clinics.

Source: American Psychological Association

Psychological Bulletin
American Psychological Association
750 1st St., NE
Washington, DC 20002-4242
Phone: (202)336-5500

Six times/year. $50.00/year for members; $100.00/year for nonmembers; $200.00/year for institutions. Presents comprehensive and integrative reviews and interpretations of critical, substantive, and methodological issues and practical problems from diversed areas of psychology.

Psychology Today
80 5th Ave.
New York, NY 10011
Phone: (212)337-6890

Monthly. $15.99/year; $1.95/single issue. Magazine covering psychology for the layperson.

Mental Health Career Directory

The Psychotherapy Bulletin
388 LydeckerSt.
Englewood, NJ 07631

Rehabilitation Today
Sportscape, Inc.
Framingham Corp. Ct.
492 Old Connecticut Path
3rd Fl.
Framingham, MA 01701
Phone: (508)872-2021
Fax: (508)872-2114

Nine times/year.

> When training is unavailable free on the job, the next cheapest way to acquire new skills may be right in the back yard. The majority of Americans live within 30 miles of one of the nation's nearly 1,200 community and technical colleges, which are rapidly gaining importance as centers of retraining.
>
> Source: *U.S. News & World Report*

Research in Nursing & Health
605 3rd Ave.
New York, NY 10158-0012
Phone: (212)850-6289

Six times/year. $60.00/year.

RNc
680 Kinderkamack Rd.
Oradell, NJ 07649
Phone: (201)262-3030

Monthly. $35.00/year; $40.00/year for subscribers in Canada; $17.50/year for students.

Social Service Jobs
Ten Angelica Dr.
Framingham, MA 01701

Biweekly. $39.00 for 3 months; $62.00 for 6 months; $118.00/year.

Social Work
7981 Eastern Ave.
Silver Spring, MD 20910
Phone: (301)565-0333
Fax: (301)587-1321

Six times/year. $51.00/year; $64.00/year for institutions.

Spotlight: On Career Planning, Placement, and Recruitment
College Placement Council
62 Highland Ave.
Bethlehem, PA 18017
Phone: (215)868-1421

Biweekly (except monthly in July, August, and December). Free to members; $65.00/year for nonmembers. Price includes subscription to the *Journal of Career Planning and Employment*.

Teaching Exceptional Children
The Council for Exceptional Children
1920 Association Dr.
Reston, VA 22091-1589
Phone: (703)620-3660
Fax: (703)264-9494

Quarterly. Free to members; $25.00/year for nonmembers. Magazine including classroom-oriented information about instructional methods, materials, and techniques for students of all ages with special needs.

Professional Associations

American Art Therapy Association (AATA)
1202 Allanson Rd.
Mundelein, IL 60006
Phone: (708)949-6064
Fax: (708)566-4580

An association made up of art therapists, students, and individuals in related fields, the AATA supports the progressive development of therapeutic uses of art, the advancement of research, and improvements in the standards of practice. It has established specific professional criteria for training art therapists. The group conducts seminars and publishes a quarterly newsletter.

American Association for Counseling and Development (AACD)
5999 Stevenson Ave.
Alexandria, VA 22304
Phone: (703)823-9800
Fax: (703)823-0252

Membership: Counseling and human development professionals in elementary and secondary schools, higher education, community agencies and organizations, rehabilitations programs, government, industry, business, and private practice. Activities: Provides placement service for members. Maintains special library of 5000 books and pamphlets. Conducts professional development institutes and provides liability insurance. Maintains AACD Foundation to fund counseling and human development projects.

American Association for Marriage and Family Therapy (AAMFT)

1100 17th St., NW, 10th Fl.
Washington, DC 20036
Phone: (202)452-0109
Fax: (202)223-2329

The association is the professional society of marriage and family therapists. It assumes a major role in maintaining and extending the highest standards of excellence in the field. AAMFT has 50 accredited training centers throughout the United States, and individuals serve as international affiliates in 13 foreign countries. It bestows awards for research, sponsors scholarships for minorities, and publishes brochures and a bimonthly journal.

American Association of Homes for the Aging (AAHA)

901 E. St., NW, Ste. 500
Washington, DC 20004-2037
Phone: (202)783-2242
Fax: (202)223-5920

Membership: Voluntary nonprofit and governmental homes, housing, and health-related facilities and services for the elderly; state associations; interested individuals. **Purpose:** Provides a unified means of identifying and solving problems in order to protect and advance the interests of the residents served. Believes that long-term care should be geared toward individual needs and provided in a spectrum ranging from nursing care to independent living and community-based care. Is committed to community involvement in the home to ensure the highest quality of care for residents. Maintains liaison with Congress and federal agencies. Provides educational programs, group purchasing program, and insurance programs. Presents awards annually. **Publication(s):** *AAHA Provider News*, periodic. • *American Association of Homes for the Aging Publications Catalog*, periodic. • *Directory of Members*, annual. • Also offers books and other publications.

American Association of Industrial Social Workers (AAISW)

781 Beta Dr., Ste. K
Cleveland, OH 44143
Phone: (216)461-4333
Fax: (216)729-9319

AAISW is made up of industrial social workers, professors, and students. Its objectives are to educate the public about the profession, to promote an understanding of industrial social work and employee assistance programs, to provide a support network for industrial social workers, and to conduct research, conferences, and seminars on industrial social work. The group maintains biographical archives and provides a listing of academic programs and resources.

A recent study by Northwestern National Life Insurance Company found that 46 percent of American workers worry about their jobs and feel more pressured to prove their value because of the recession. . . Unfortunately, the more you worry about whether you are doing a good enough job, the more likely you are to erode your efficiency, creativity and morale—and damage your health.

Source: *Business Monday/Detroit Free Press*

American Association of Mental Health Professionals in Corrections (AAMHPC)

c/o John S. Zil, M.D., J.D.
PO Box 511
Sacramento, CA 95812
Phone: (707)864-0910
Toll-free: 800-645-6337
Fax: (516)921-8743

Membership: Psychiatrists, psychologists, social workers, and other mental health professionals; individuals working in correctional settings. **Purpose:** Fosters the progress of behavioral sciences related to corrections. Goals are: to improve the treatment, rehabilitation, and

Mental Health Career Directory

care of the mentally ill, mentally retarded, and emotionally disturbed; to promote research and professional education in psychiatry and allied fields in corrections; to advance standards of correctional services and facilities; to foster cooperation between individuals concerned with the medical, psychological, social, and legal aspects of corrections; to share knowledge with other medical practitioners, scientists, and the public. Conducts scientific meetings to contribute to the advancement of the therapeutic community in all its institutional settings, including correctional institutions, hospitals, churches, schools, industry, and the family. Sponsors workshops to assist other groups with staff education and analysis of program organization and development. Presents Presidential Award for special contributions to correctional research. **Publication(s):** *Corrective and Social Psychiatry*, quarterly. • Also publishes papers. *Supervising Assessor; Supervising Auditor; Tax Auditor.*

People assume that they get better within their careers over time, that growth is a step-by-step improvement. Studies have shown that growth occurs in episodic movement, often triggered by a small event. People tend to remain at a uniform level until some change propels them toward a new level of performance.

Source: *The Canadian Nurse*

American Counseling Association (AACD)
5999 Stevenson Ave.
Alexandria, VA 22304
Phone: (703)823-9800
Toll-free: 800-347-6647
Fax: (703)823-0252

Membership: Counseling and human development professionals in elementary and secondary schools, higher education, community agencies and organizations, rehabilitation programs, government, industry, business, and private practice. **Purpose:** Maintains special library of 5000 books and pamphlets. Provides placement service for members; conducts professional development institutes and provides liability insurance. Maintains AACD Foundation to fund counseling and human development projects. **Publication(s):** *Career Development Quarterly.* • *Counseling and Values*, 3/year. • *Counselor Education and Supervision*, quarterly. • *Elementary School Guidance and Counseling Journal*, quarterly. • *Guidepost*, 14/year. • *Journal of College Student Personnel*, bimonthly. • *Journal of Counseling and Development*, bimonthly. • *Journal of Employment Counseling*, quarterly. • *Journal of Humanist Education and Development*, quarterly. • *Journal of Mental Health Counselors*, quarterly. • *Journal of Addictions and Offender Counseling*, semiannual. • *Measurement and Evaluations in Counseling and Development*, quarterly. • *Rehabilitation Counseling Bulletin*, quarterly. • *School Counselor*, 5/year. • *Specialists in Group Work*, quarterly.

American Humanics (AH)
4601 Madison Ave.
Kansas City, MO 64112
Phone: (816)561-6415
Toll-free: 800-343-6466
Fax: (816)531-3527

The organization is made up of individuals, corporations, and foundations who work in preparing young people for professional leadership in youth and human service agencies. AH provides leadership for co-curricular programs on 15 campuses, sponsors field trips, workshops, and special courses. It offers counseling and loan programs, conducts research, and bestows awards. American Humanics publishes an annual report and several periodic journals.

American Medical Association (AMA)
515 N. State St.
Chicago, IL 60610
Phone: (312)464-5000
Fax: (312)645-4184

Membership: County medical societies and physicians. **Purpose:** Disseminates scientific information to members and the public. Informs members on significant medical and health legislation on state and national levels and represents the profession before Congress and governmental agencies. Cooperates in setting standards for medical schools, hospitals, residency programs, and continuing medical education courses. Offers physician placement service and counseling on practice management problems. Operates library which lends material and provides specific medical information to physicians. Ad-hoc committees are formed for such topics as health care planning and principles of medical ethics. **Publication(s):** *American Journal of Diseases of Children*, monthly. • *American Medical News*, weekly. • *Archives of Dermatology*, monthly. • *Archives of General Psychiatry*, monthly. • *Archives of Internal Medicine*, monthly. • *Archives of Neurology*, periodic. • *Archives of Ophthalmology*, monthly. • *Archives of Otolaryngology—Head and Neck Surgery*, monthly. • *Archives of Pathology and Laboratory Medicine*, monthly. • *Archives of Surgery*, monthly. • *Journal of the American Medical Association*, weekly.

American Mental Health Counselors Association (AMHCA)

c/o Amer. Assn. for Counseling and Development
5999 Stevenson Ave.
Alexandria, VA 22304
Phone: (703)823-9800
Toll-free: 800-545-AACD
Fax: (703)823-0252

Membership: A division of the American Association for Counseling and Development. Professional counselors employed in mental health services; students. **Purpose:** Aims to: deliver quality mental health services to children, youth, adults, families, and organizations; improve the availability and quality of counseling services through licensure and certification, political and legislative action, training standards, and consumer advocacy. Supports specialty and special interest networks. Fosters communication among members. **Publication(s):** *AMHCA News*, quarterly. • *Journal of Mental Health Counseling*, quarterly.

American Psychiatric Association (APA)

1400 K St., NW
Washington, DC 20005
Phone: (202)682-6000
Fax: (202)682-6114

The association consists of psychiatrists united to further the study of the nature, treatment, and prevention of mental disorders. It assists in formulating programs to meet mental health needs, compiles and disseminates facts and figures about psychiatry, and furthers psychiatric education and research. The APA publishes a membership directory and several monthly professional journals.

American Psychological Association (APA)

750 1st St., NE
Washington, DC 20002-4242
Phone: (202)336-5500
Fax: (703)525-5191

Membership: Scientific and professional society of psychologists. Students participate as affiliates. **Purpose:** To advance psychology as a science, a profession, and as a means of promoting human welfare. Maintains 46 divisions. **Publication(s):** *American Psychologist*, monthly. • *APA Membership Register*, periodic. • *APA Monitor*, monthly. • *Behavioral Neuroscience*, bimonthly. • *Biographical Directory*, periodic. • *Contemporary Psychology*, monthly. • *Developmental Psychology*, bimonthly. • *Journal of Abnormal Psychology*, quarterly. • *Journal of Applied Psychology*, quarterly. • *Journal of Comparative Psychology*, quarterly. • *Journal of Consulting and Clinical Psychology*, bimonthly. • *Journal of Counseling Psychology*, quarterly. • *Journal of Educational Psychology*, quarterly. • *Journal of Experimental Psychology: Animal Behavior Processes*, quarterly. • *Journal of Experimental Psychology: General*, quarterly. • *Journal of Experimental Psychology: Human Perception and Performance*, quarterly. • *Journal of Experimental Psychology: Learning, Memory, and Cognition*, bimonthly. • *Journal of Personality and Social Psychology*, monthly. • *Professional Psychology: Research and Practice*, bimonthly. • *Psychological Abstracts*, monthly. • *Psychological Assessment: A Journal of Consulting and Clinical Psychology*, quarterly. • *Psychological Bulletin*, bimonthly. • *Psychological Review*, quarterly. • *Psychology and Aging*, quarterly. • *PsycSCAN: Applied Experimental and Engineering Psychology*, quarterly. • *PsycSCAN: Applied Psychology*, quarterly. • *PsycSCAN: Clinical Psychology*, quarterly. • *PsycSCAN: Developmental Psychology*, quarterly. • *PsycSCAN: LD/MR*, quarterly. • *PsycSCAN: Psychoanalysis*, quarterly.

American Public Health Association (APHA)
1015 15th St., NW
Washington, DC 20005
Phone: (202)789-5600
Fax: (202)789-5681

Membership: Professional organization of physicians, nurses, educators, academicians, environmentalists, epidemiologists, new professionals, social workers, health administrators, optometrists, podiatrists, pharmacists, pharmacy assistants, dentists, dental assistants, nutritionists, health planners, health care workers, other community and mental health specialists, and interested consumers. Activities: Sponsors job placement service. Seeks to protect and promote personal, mental, and environmental health. Services include: promulgation of standards; establishment of uniform practices and procedures; development of the etiology of communicable diseases; research in public health; exploration of medical care programs and their relationships to public health. Presents Award for Excellence to individuals for outstanding contributions to the improvement of public health; also bestows the Drotman Award to a young health professional who demonstrates potential in the health field and Sedgwick Memorial Medal to those who have advanced public health knowledge and practices. Maintains Action Board and Program Development Board.

What makes one job better than another? High pay? Prestige? Pleasant working conditions? Or, these days, might the clincher be job security? The answer is that there is no single deciding factor. Truly great jobs offer all of the above and more . . . . Jobs, after all, are a complicated mix of pluses and minuses.

Source: *Money*

American Rehabilitation Counseling Association (ARCA)
c/o American Association for Counseling and Development
5999 Stevenson Ave.
Alexandria, VA 22304
Phone: (703)823-9800
Toll-free: 800-545-AACD
Fax: (703)823-0252

Rehabilitation counselors and interested professionals and students whose purpose is to improve the rehabilitation counseling profession and its services to individuals with disabilities. The group promotes high standards in rehabilitation counseling, practice, research, and education. It encourages the exchange of information between rehabilitation professionals and consumer groups and serves as liaison among members and public and private rehabilitation counselors. ARCA publishes a quarterly newsletter.

American School Counselor Association (ASCA)
c/o Amer. Assn. for Counseling and Development
5999 Stevenson Ave.
Alexandria, VA 22304
Phone: (703)823-9800
Toll-free: 800-545-AACD
Fax: (703)823-0252

Membership: A division of the American Association for Counseling and Development. School counselors; professionals engaged in school counseling or related activities at least 50% of the time; students; other interested individuals. **Purpose:** Promotes human rights, children's welfare, healthy learning environments, and positive interpersonal relationships; fosters academic, occupational, personal, and social growth among members. Works to improve professional standards in school counseling and in other student personnel services; seeks to further public awareness of such services. Develops and promotes career development programs; sponsors interprofessional activities and leadership development programs. Represents members' interests in governmental and public relations. Serves as liaison among members and counselors in other settings; disseminates educational, professional, and scientific materials. Maintains 19 committees. **Publication(s):** *ASCA Counselor*, 5/year. • *ASCA Newsletter*. • *Elementary School Guidance and Counseling*, quarterly. • *The School Counselor*, 5/year. • Also issues books, mongraphs, and manuals.

American School Health Association (ASHA)
7263 State, Rte. 43
PO Box 708
Kent, OH 44240
Phone: (216)678-1601
Fax: (216)678-4526

Membership: School physicians, dentists, nurses, nutritionists, health educators, dental hygienists, and public health workers. Activities: Maintains placement service. Formed to promote comprehensive and constructive school health programs including the teaching of health, health services, and promotion of a healthful school environment. Offers a professional referral service, classroom teaching aids, and professional reference materials. Conducts research programs; compiles statistics. Sponsors annual foreign travel study tour. Bestows William A. How Award annually for distinguished service in school health.

American Society of Criminology (ASC)
1314 Kinnear Rd., Ste. 212
Columbus, OH 43212
Phone: (614)292-9207
Fax: (614)292-6767

Membership: Professional and academic criminologists; students of criminology in accredited universities; psychiatrists, psychologists, and sociologists. Activities: Provides placement service at annual convention. ASC is organized to develop criminology as a science and academic discipline; to aid in the construction of criminologic curricula in accredited universities; to upgrade the practitioner in criminological fields (police, prisons, probation, parole, delinquency workers). Presents Vollmer, Bloch, Sutherland, and Sellin-Glueck Awards annually. Conducts research programs; sponsors three student paper competitions. Affiliated With: American Association for the Advancement of Science.

Asian American Psychological Association (AAPA)
c/o Dr. David S. Goh
Queens College/CUNY
School of Education
Flushing, NY 11367
Phone: (718)997-5236

Membership: Psychologists and graduate students in psychology. Activities: Operates placement service. Formed to advance the welfare of Asian-Americans and others through the use and development of psychology. Assists in and encourages research and services that affect Asian-Americans. Makes known psychological issues facing Asian-Americans. Bestows award for distinguished service.

Association for Behavior Analysis (ABA)
258 Wood Hall
Western Michigan University
Kalamazoo, MI 49008
Phone: (616)387-4494
Fax: (616)387-4457

Membership: Professionals, paraprofessionals, and students interested in the applied, experimental, and theoretical analysis of behavior. Activities: Offers placement service. Promotes the development of behavior analysis as a profession and science. Provides a forum for the discussion of issues; disseminates information on behavior analysis. Conducts workshops and seminars in 16 specialty areas including: Behavioral Pharmacology and Toxicology; Developmental Disabilities; Organizational Behavior Analysis. Offers continuing education credits for psychologists. Maintains archives of the association's publications.

One thousand unsolicited resumes typically arrive in the daily mail at Fortune 50 companies. Four out of five are tossed after a quick perusal.

Source: *U.S. News & World Report*

Association for Chemoreception Sciences (AChemS)
c/o Panacer Associates
229 Westridge Dr.
Tallahassee, FL 32304
Phone: (215)898-2084

Membership: Research scientists, experimental psychologists, and industrial researchers. Activities: Maintains placement service. Purpose is to study chemoreception (the physiological reception of chemical stimuli) by the senses of taste and smell. Offers seminars, fellowships, and workshops. Bestows annual award for Best Student Presentation at conference.

Association for Holistic Health (AHH)
PO Box 1122
Del Mar, CA 92014
Phone: (619)535-0101

Membership: Registered nurses, medical doctors, osteopathic physicians, chiropractors, dentists, social workers, psychologists, therapists, ministers, and healers. Activities: Maintains placement service. Formed to promote and support holistic health and to build a bridge between traditional and alternative health care methods. Informs holistic health operations of successful methods of traditional and alternative healing and health programs; provides a forum for individuals and organizations dedicated to promotion of holistic health; attempts to set standards for responsible practitioners and centers. Conducts workshops, seminars, and correspondence courses. Bestows awards; maintains speakers' bureau.

Association for Humanistic Education and Development (AHEAD)
c/o American Association for Counseling and Development
5999 Stevenson Ave.
Alexandria, VA 22304
Phone: (703)823-9800

Membership: Teachers, educational administrators, community agency workers, counselors, school social workers, and psychologists; others interested in the area of human development. Activities: Offers placement service. Stresses humanism in all phases of education by exchanging information about humanistically-oriented administrative and instructional practices. Supports humanistic practices; encourages research on instructional and organizational methods for facilitating humanistic education. Maintains archives; bestows awards. A division of the American Association for Counseling and Development.

Association for Media Psychology (AMP)
228 Santa Monica Blvd., Ste. 4
Santa Monica, CA 90401
Phone: (213)394-4546
Fax: (213)394-4546

Membership: Psychologists, psychiatrists, social workers, psychiatric nurses, and graduate students studying mental health or behavioral science; members of the communications media. Activities: Offers placement services. Seeks to publicize scientific psychology. Promotes research on the influence of the media on attitude, behavior, and well-being. Encourages innovative use of the media in the prevention of physical and mental disorders. Assists mental health professionals in developing program ideas and finding ways to effectively communicate to the public through the media. Conducts seminars and workshops to train psychologists in effective use of the media. Cosponsors educational films and conferences with similar organizations. Maintains speakers' bureau; bestows awards.

Association for Multicultural Counseling and Development (AMCD)
c/o American Association for Counseling and Development
5999 Stevenson Ave.
Alexandria, VA 22304
Phone: (703)823-9800
Fax: (703)823-0252

Membership: Professionals involved in personnel and guidance careers in educational settings, social services, and community agencies; interested individuals; students. Activities: Offers placement service. Works to enhance members' ability to serve as behavioral change agents. Bestows awards. A division of the American Association for Counseling and Development.

Association for Specialists in Group Work (ASGW)
c/o American Association for Counseling and Development
5999 Stevenson Ave.
Alexandria, VA 22304
Phone: (703)823-9800
Fax: (703)823-0252

Membership: Individuals interested in group counseling holding master's or doctoral degrees, and engaged in practice, teaching, or research in group work; persons holding undergraduate degrees who are interested in group work, but not actively engaged in practice, teaching, or research; students. Activities: Conducts placement service. Sponsors programs to advance group work in schools, clinics, universities, private practice, and mental health institutions. Bestows awards.

Association for Women in Psychology (AWP)
c/o Angela R. Gillem, Ph.D.
Haverford College
370 Lancaster Ave.
Haverford, PA 19041-1392
Phone: (215)789-9301

Purpose: Seeks to end the role that the association feels psychology has had in perpetuating unscientific and unquestioned assumptions about the "natures" of women and men; encourages unbiased psychological research on sex and gender in order to establish facts and expose myths; encourage research and theory directed toward alternative sex-role socialization, child rearing practices, life-styles, and language use; educate and sensitize the science and psychology professions as well as the public to the psychological, social, political, and economic rights of women; combat the oppression of women of color; encourage research on issues of concern to women of color; achieve equality of opportunity for women and men within the profession and science of psychology. Conducts business and professional sessions at meetings of regional psychology associations. Maintains hall of fame, archives, and speakers' bureau; bestows Distinguished Publication, Women of Color Psychologies, Lesbian Psychologies Unpublished Manuscript Awards annually, and a student prize for research on women and gender. Monitors sexism in APA. **Publication(s):** *AWP Membership Directory*, annual. • *Newsletter*, quarterly. • Also publishes *A Feminist Mental Health Agenda for the Year 2,000*.

Association of Black Psychologists (ABPsi)
PO Box 55999
Washington, DC 20040-5999
Phone: (202)722-0808
Fax: (202)722-5941

Membership: Professional psychologists and others in associated disciplines. **Purpose:** Aims to: enhance the psychological well-being of black people in America; define mental health in consonance with newly established psychological concepts and standards; develop policies for local, state, and national decision-making which have impact on the mental health of the black community; support established black sister organizations and aid in the development of new, independent black institutions to enhance the psychological, educational, cultural, and economic situation. Offers training and information on AIDS. Conducts seminars, workshops, and research. Bestows awards. **Publication(s):** *Association of Black Psychologists—Newsletter*, quarterly. • *Journal of Black Psychology*, semiannual. • *Monographs from the Journal of Black Psychology*, biennial. • *Proceedings of Annual Convention*. • *Psych Discourse*, bimonthly. • Also publishes *Sourcebook on the Teaching of Black Psychology*, *Resource Manual for Black Psychology Students*, *Association of Black Psychologists Publications Manual*, brochures, bulletin, and research projects; distributes videotapes on issues in black psychology.

> Growth in employment is only one source of job openings. In fact, most openings arise because of the need to replace workers who transfer to other occupations or leave the labor force.
>
> Source: *Occupational Outlook Quarterly*

Association of Mental Health Administrators (AMHA)
60 Revere Dr., Ste. 500
Northbrook, IL 60062
Phone: (708)480-9626

The group is made up of administrators of services for the emotionally disturbed, mentally ill, mentally retarded, developmentally disabled, and those with problems of alcohol and substance abuse. Its objectives are to further the education of administrators, develop criteria for and certify the competence of administrators, and promote adherence to a code of ethics. The AMHA publishes a semiannual professional journal and a bimonthly newsletter.

Association of Mental Health Practitioners With Disabilities (AMHPD)
3 E. 10th St., Ste. 48
New York, NY 10003
Phone: (212)673-4284

Membership: Disabled psychiatrists, social workers, psychologists, psychiatric nurses, other mental health practitioners, and students. **Activities:** Offers job information and referral services. Formed in response to complaints of discrimination by disabled colleagues who have been rejected by training institutes and in career opportunities. Devoted to the education, research, training, and advocacy of all areas affecting the clinical practice and professional advancement of members. Offers peer supervision, consultation, and education on the impact of the practitioner's disability on training and patient treatment. Explores how the patient's reaction to a disability can be used in treatment. Works with mental health agencies and educational and training institutes. Sponsors conferences, workshops, and seminars.

> When we consciously choose to do the work that we enjoy, not only can we get things done, but we can get them done well and be intrinsically rewarded for our effort, according to organizational psychologist Marsha Sinetar.
>
> Source: *The Detroit News*

Association on Handicapped Student Service Programs in Postsecondary Education (AHSSPPE)
PO Box 21192
Columbus, OH 43221
Phone: (614)488-4972

Membership: Individuals interested in promoting the equal rights and opportunities of handicapped postsecondary students and graduates. Activities: Offers employment exchange for positions in handicapped student services, and resource referral system. Facilitates communication among those professionally involved with handicapped students; encourages and supports legislation for the benefit of handicapped students. Conducts surveys and research programs; bestows awards; compiles statistics.

Child Life Council (CLC)
7910 Woodmont Ave., Ste. 300
Bethesda, MD 20895

Membership: Professional organization representing child life personnel, patient activities specialists, recreational therapists, and students in the field. Activities: Offers a job bank service listing employment openings. Promotes psychological well-being and optimum development of children, adolescents, and their families in health care settings. Works to minimize the stress and anxiety of illness and hospitalization. Addresses professional issues such as program standards, competencies, and core curriculum. Provides resources and conducts research and educational programs. Bestows awards.

Child Welfare League of America (CWLA)
440 1st St., NW, Ste. 310
Washington, DC 20001
Phone: (202)638-2952
Fax: (202)638-4004

Activities: Maintains placement service. Privately and publicly supported membership organization devoted to the improvement of care and services for deprived, dependent, or neglected children, youth, and their families. Maintains the Child Welfare League of America Children's Campaign, a grass roots advocacy network of individuals committed to speaking out on behalf of children. Provides consultation; conducts research; maintains 3000 volume reference library and information service; conducts agency and community surveys; develops standards for services; administers special projects.

Christian Medical Foundation International (CMF)
7522 N. Hines Ave.
Tampa, FL 33614
Phone: (813)932-3688

Membership: Physicians, nurses, clergy, and laity. Activities: Offers placement service. Seeks to: investigate and promote the Christian spiritual care of those who are ill; educate doctors, nurses, and medical students regarding Christian medical and ethical principles. Bestows awards. Maintains speakers' bureau, biographical archives, and 2500 volume library.

College for Human Services
345 Hudson St.
New York, NY 10014
Phone: (212)989-2002

Membership: Collegians preparing for careers as human service professionals in public and private human service agencies and businesses.

Activities: Provides placement service. Association is devoted to operating a new theory-practice performance-based professional curriculum in the human services, emphasizing close relationships between classroom and field work. Graduates who receive bachelor's degrees enter careers in public and private service sectors. Presented Academy for Educational Development Award for innovative educational program and Chase Bank Award for outstanding service in education. Compiles statistics; maintains library of 25,000 volumes.

Consortium of Social Science Associations (COSSA)
1522 K St. NW, Ste. 836
Washington, DC 20005
Phone: (202)842-3525
Fax: (202)842-2788

Membership: National organizations representing professionals in the social and behavioral sciences; affiliates are smaller and/or regional associations; contributors are research universities and scholarly organizations. **Purpose:** Purpose is to inform and educate members of Congress, congressional staff, and officials in the administration and in federal agencies about recent research in the social and behavioral sciences. Stresses the importance of such research and the need for maintaining adequate financial support. Monitors the research budgets and research policy issues of federal agencies; disseminates information on legislative actions and federal policies to social and behavioral scientists. Conducts seminars and briefings on current and emerging research, particularly in areas of congressional interest and responsibility. **Publication(s):** *COSSA Washington Update*, biweekly.

Council for Health and Human Services Ministries (CHHSM)
700 Prospect Ave., E.
Cleveland, OH 44115
Phone: (216)736-2250
Fax: (216)736-2251

Membership: Health and human service institutions related to the United Church of Christ. Activities: Maintains placement service. Seeks to promote the development of health and human service programs and ministries, both institutional and noninstitutional. Operates hall of fame; bestows awards; compiles statistics. Provides specialized education programs; offers fellowship in hospital administration for UCC ordained clergy.

Council on Social Work Education (CSWE)
1600 Duke St.
Alexandria, VA 22314
Phone: (703)683-8080
Fax: (703)683-8099

Membership: Graduate and undergraduate programs of social work education; national, regional, and local social welfare agencies; libraries and individuals. **Purpose:** Formulates criteria and standards for all levels of social work education; accredits graduate and undergraduate social work programs; provides consulting to social work educators on curriculum, faculty recruitment and development, students and admissions, and teaching methods and materials; conducts research and compiles data on social work education. **Publication(s):** *Directory of Colleges and Universities with Accredited Social Work Degree Programs*, annual. • *Journal of Social Work Education*, 3/year. • *Social Work Education Reporter*, 3/year. • *Statistics on Social Work Education*, annual. • *Summary Information on Masters of Social Work Programs*, annual. • Also publishes books, monographs, pamphlets, teaching materials, reports on special subjects, and catalog of publications.

Networking isn't talking about yourself. You can get information only if the other party is talking about himself or herself, his or her company and associates. If you find networking is your-sided, you'd better rethink your approach.

Source: *Business Monday/Detroit Free Press*

Employment Support Center (ESC)
900 Massachusetts Ave. NW, Ste. 444
Washington, DC 20001
Phone: (202)783-4747

Activities: Operates job bank. Trains individuals to lead support groups for job-seekers; helps people learn to network for job contacts. Conducts seminars.

MENTAL HEALTH CAREER DIRECTORY

Family Service America (FSA)
11700 West Lake Park Dr.
Milwaukee, WI 53224
Phone: (414)359-1040
Fax: (414)359-1074

Membership: Federation of local agencies in over 200 communities providing family counseling, family life education and family advocacy services, and other programs to help families with parent-child, marital, mental health, and other problems of family living. Activities: Offers placement service to members only. Works with the media, government, and corporations to promote strong family life. Compiles statistics; conducts research. Sponsors competitions; bestows awards. Maintains a 2000 volume library on social work, family life, psychology, and nonprofit agency management; also maintains extensive files of unpublished materials from member agencies.

Much faster than average employment growth is anticipated for psychologists due to increased attention being paid to the expanding elderly population, the maintenance of mental health, and the testing and counseling of children.

Source: *Occupational Outlook Quarterly*

Gerontological Society of America (GSA)
1275 K St., NW, Ste. 350
Washington, DC 20005
Phone: (202)842-1275

GSA is made up of physicians, physiologists, psychologists, biochemists, sociologists, social workers, botanists, psychiatrists, pharmacologists, nurses, geneticists, zoologists, endocrinologists, economists, administrators, and other professionals interested in improving the well-being of older people by promoting scientific study of the aging process, publishing information for professionals about aging, and bringing together groups interested in aging research. Publishes a bimonthly journal.

International Association of Addictions and Offender Counseling (IAAOC)
c/o Amer. Association for Counseling and Development
5999 Stevenson Ave.
Alexandria, VA 22304
Phone: (703)823-8900

Membership: Professionals concerned with improving the quality of rehabilitation programs offered to public offenders. Activities: Maintains placement service. Seeks the development of new counseling strategies and of research to support these counseling approaches. Bestows awards.

International Council of Psychologists (ICP)
c/o Patricia J. Fontes, Ph.D.
PO Box 62
Hopkinton, RI 02833-0062
Phone: (608)238-5373

Membership: Psychologists and individuals professionally active in fields allied to psychology. **Purpose:** Seeks to advance psychology and further the application of its scientific findings. Conducts continuing education in the field. **Publication(s):** *Directory*, biennial. • *International Psychologist*, quarterly.

International Educator's Institute (IEI)
PO Box 103
West Bridgewater, MA 02379
Phone: (508)580-1880
Fax: (508)580-2992

Activities: Facilitates the placement of teachers and administrators in American, British, and international schools. Seeks to create a network that provides for professional development opportunities and improved financial security of members. Provides job placement assistance; offers advice and information on international school news, recent educational developments, and investment, consumer, and professional development opportunities. Makes available insurance and travel benefits. Operates International Schools Internship Program. Bestows awards.

National Academic Advising Association (NACADA)
Kansas State University
Bluemont Hall, 446
Manhattan, KS 66506
Phone: (913)532-5717
Fax: (913)532-7304

Membership: Academic program advisers, faculty, administrators, counselors, and others concerned with the intellectual, personal, and career development of students in all types of postsecondary educational institutions. Activities: Maintains placement service. Provides a forum for discussion, debate, and exchange of ideas regarding academic advising. Serves as advocate for standards and quality programs in academic advising. Operates consultants bureau to evaluate advising services on college campuses. Bestows scholarships and annual awards for outstanding advising programs, for individual advisers, and research on advising. Conducts professional training and holds personal and professional development workshops in conjunction with conferences. Maintains archives and speakers' bureau.

National Association for Developmental Education (NADE)
PO Box 5922
North Suburban, IL 60197-5922
Phone: (708)794-6258
Fax: (312)794-6243

Membership: Teachers, counselors, and administrators of developmental education at the postsecondary level. (Developmental education programs set behavioral/learning objectives for students based on what can be expected of them given the cycle of human growth and development. At the postsecondary level, programs are designed to assist students who are lacking in educational experience or learning skills necessary for successful performance at their academic level.) Activities: Provides job placement services and maintains placement committee. Conducts professional developmental workshops; offers scholarships for research, study, and professional development.

National Association of School Psychologists (NASP)
8455 Colesville Rd., Ste. 1000
Silver Spring, MD 20910
Phone: (301)608-0500
Fax: (301)608-2514

Membership: School psychologists. Activities: Maintains placement service. Serves the mental health and educational needs of all children and youth; encourages and provides opportunities for professional growth of individual members; informs the public on the services and practice of school psychology; advances the standards of the profession. Operates national school psychologist certification system. Provides library. Conducts workshops and symposia.

National Association of Social Workers (NASW)
750 1st St., NE, Ste. 700
Washington, DC 20002
Phone: (202)408-8600
Toll-free: 800-638-8799
Fax: (301)587-1321

Membership: Regular members are persons who hold a minimum of a baccalaureate degree in social work. Associate members are persons engaged in social work who have a baccalaureate degree in another field. Student members are persons enrolled in accredited (by the Council on Social Work Education) graduate or undergraduate social work programs. **Purpose:** To create professional standards for social work practice; advocate sound public social policies through political and legislative action; provide a wide range of membership services, including continuing education opportunities and an extensive professional program. Operates National Center for Social Policy and Practice. Maintains library of 4000 volumes; conducts research. Presents National Public Citizen of the Year and National Social Worker of the Year awards; compiles statistics. **Publication(s):** *Health and Social Work*, quarterly. • *Legislative Alert*, periodic. • *NASW News*, 10/year. • *Social Work*, bimonthly. • *Social Work in Education: A Journal for Social Workers in Schools*, quarterly. • *Social Work Research and Abstracts*, quarterly. • Also publishes *Encyclopedia of Social Work*, *Social Workers Dictionary*, *Psycho Social Aspects of AIDS*, and other books, periodicals, and catalog.

National Career Development Association (NCDA)
c/o American Association for Counseling and Development
5999 Stevenson Ave.
Alexandria, VA 22304
Phone: (703)823-9800

Membership: Professionals and others interested in career development or counseling in various work environments. Activities: Maintains placement service. Provides training and other services to counselors, guidance personnel, and professionals working in schools, colleges, military services, private practice, and business and community agencies. Conducts research programs; bestows awards. A division of the American Association for Counseling and Development.

> The United States economy is projected to provide 24 million more jobs in 2005 than it did in 1990, an increase of 20 percent.
>
> Source: *Occupational Outlook Quarterly*

National Council on Family Relations
Family and Health Section
3989 Central Ave. NE, Ste. 550
Minneapolis, MN 55421
Phone: (612)781-9331
Fax: (612)781-9348

Membership: Health and education professionals. **Purpose:** Serves as a forum for all professionals involved in interdisciplinary work in the family and health fields. Presents clinical research and educational programs at NCFR conferences. **Publication(s):** *Family Relations*, quarterly. • *Journal of Marriage and Family*, quarterly. • *The Report*, quarterly.

National Council on Rehabilitation Education (NCRE)
c/o Dr. Garth Eldredge
Department of Special Education
Utah State University
Logan, UT 84322-2865
Phone: (801)750-3241
Fax: (801)750-3572

Membership: Academic institutions and organizations; professional educators, researchers, and students. Activities: Sponsors placement service. Disseminates information and provides forum for discussion. Provides specialized education service. Compiles statistics. Serves as an advisory body to the National Rehabilitation Association and the Rehabilitation Services Administration; works closely with other agencies and associations in the field.

National Employment Counselors Association (NECA)
c/o American Association for Counseling and Development
5999 Stevenson Ave.
Alexandria, VA 22304
Phone: (703)823-9800
Fax: (703)823-0252

Membership: Those engaged in employment counseling, counselor education, research, administration or supervision in business and industry, colleges and universities, and federal and state governments; students. Activities: Conducts placement service. Offers professional leadership and development services; provides opportunities for professional growth through workshops and special projects. Bestows awards. A division of the American Association for Counseling and Development.

National Hospice Organization (NHO)
1901 N. Moore St., Ste. 901
Arlington, VA 22209
Phone: (703)243-5900

The organization is made up of hospices and individuals interested in the promotion of the hospice concept and program of care. It promotes standards of care in program planning and implementation, monitors healthcare legislation and regulation relevant to hospice care. The group publishes an annual guide, a quarterly journal, and monthly newsletter.

National Organization for Human Service Education (NOHSE)
Box 6257
Fitchburg State Coll.
Fitchburg, MA 01420
Phone: (508)345-2151

Membership: Human service professionals, faculty, and students. **Purpose:** To foster excellence in teaching, research and curriculum planning in the human service area; to encourage and support the development of local, state, and national human services organizations; to aid faculty and professional members in their career development. Provides a medium for cooperation and communication among members; maintains registry of qualified consultants in human service education. Conducts professional development workshop; operates speakers' bureau. Grants scholarships; bestows McNeer Memorial Award and research awards. **Publication(s):** *Journal of Human Service Education*, annual. • *Membership Directory*, periodic. • *National Organization for Human Service Education—Link*, quarterly. • Also publishes brochure.

National Rehabilitation Association (NRA)
633 S. Washington St.
Alexandria, VA 22314
Phone: (703)836-0850
Fax: (703)836-2209

Membership: Physicians, counselors, therapists, disability examiners, vocational evaluators, and others interested in rehabilitation of persons with disabilities. Activities: Maintains Job Placement Division. Sponsors Graduate Literary Awards Contest. Conducts legislative activities; develops accessibility guidelines; offers specialized education.

National Staff Development and Training Association (NSDTA)
810 1st St., NE, Ste. 500
Washington, DC 20002-4205
Phone: (202)682-0100

Membership: Social welfare workers engaged in staff development and training. Activities: Offers placement services. Provides technical assistance. Maintains speakers' bureau. Affiliated With: American Public Welfare Association.

North American Association of Christians in Social Work (NACSW)
Box S-90
St. Davids, PA 19087
Phone: (215)687-5777

Membership: Professional social workers and related professionals; students; and interested individuals. Activities: Maintains employment service. Purpose is to provide opportunities for Christian fellowship, growth, learning, outreach, and witness. Promotes a Christian world view in social work and social welfare and encourages awareness within the Christian community of human need and of social work as a means for ministering to this need. Holds regional seminars, evening meetings, one-day conferences, and small study and support group meetings. Compiles statistics; operates speakers' bureau; bestows awards.

> Four out of five companies say their employees can't write well. But only 21 percent of corporate training aims at writing skills.
>
> Source: *U.S. News & World Report*

PACT Training
PO Box 106
New Kingston, NY 12459
Phone: (914)586-3992

Membership: Human service practitioners including police officers, social workers, physicians, nurses, counselors, educators, and theatre professionals. **Purpose:** Purpose is to utilize role-play techniques in training people to handle and negotiate sensitive and critical situations such as hostage negotiations, death and dying, child abuse, domestic violence, and work conflicts. Conducts training programs for those working for airlines, corporations, police and criminal justice agencies, security departments, hospitals, social service agencies, geriatric centers, medical and nursing schools, and educational institutions; these programs include structured improvisations and dramatizations of crisis and conflict situations that require outside intervention. Bestows awards.

Psychology Society (PS)
100 Beekman St.
New York, NY 10038-1810
Phone: (212)285-1872

Membership: Professional membership is limited to psychologists who have a doctorate and are certified/licensed as such in the state where they practice. Associate membership is intended for teachers and researchers as well as persons who will attain professional status shortly. Activities: Maintains placement service for members and recent graduates. Has established a referral service for laypeople and operates an information bureau to answer inquiries of authors, media, and students. Seeks to further the use of psychology in therapy, family and social problems, behavior modification, and treatment of drug abusers and prisoners. Encourages the use of psychology in the solution of social and political conflicts. Sponsors biennial overseas trip to enable members to observe other programs and institutions. Collaborates with other associations. Evaluates programs in the use of psychology. Recommends legislation; presents awards.

Society for the Advancement of Social Psychology (SASP)
c/o Dr. Frank Dane
Dept. of Psychology
Mercer University
Macon, GA 31207
Phone: (912)752-2972
Fax: (912)752-2108

Membership: Social psychologists and students in social psychology. Activities: Operates placement service. Advances social psychology as a profession by facilitating communication among social psychologists and improving dissemination and utilization of social psychological knowledge. Hosts social hours; bestows awards; maintains speakers' bureau.

Employment Agencies and Search Firms

Academy Medical Personnel Services
571 High St.
Worthington, OH 43085
Phone: (614)848-6011

Employment agency. Fills openings on a regular or temporary basis.

Arbor Associates
15 Court Sq., Ste. 1050
Boston, MA 02108
Phone: (617)227-8829

Handles temporary placements.

Davis-Smith Medical Employment Service, Inc.
24725 W. 12 Mile Rd.
No. 2302 Lockdale Office Plaza
Southfield, MI 48034
Phone: (313)354-4100

Employment agency. Executive search firm.

Eden Personnel, Inc.
280 Madison Rd., Rm. 202
New York, NY 10016
Phone: (212)685-8600

Employment agency. Places individuals in regular or temporary positions.

Educational Placement Service
3500 N. Causeway Blvd., Ste. 1450
Metairie, LA 70002
Phone: (504)833-8278

Employment agency. Focuses on teaching, administrative, and education-related openings.

G.A. Agency
108 N. Union Ave.
Cranford, NJ 07016
Phone: (908)272-2080
Fax: (908)272-2962

Employment agency.

Harper Associates-Detroit, Inc.
29870 Middlebelt
Farmington Hills, MI 48334
Phone: (313)932-1170

Employment agency.

Health and Science Center
PO Box 213
Lima, PA 19037
Phone: (215)891-0794

Employment agency. Executive search firm.

Independent Educational Services
353 Nassau St.
Princeton, NJ 08540
Phone: (609)921-6195

Nonprofit teacher recruitment bureau. Furnishes to independent (private) schools dossiers of qualified candidates for teaching and administrative positions. Offers to teachers and prospective teachers information concerning current requirements and qualifications for positions in the field of education and vacancies for which they qualify. Conducts periodic salary and statistical studies. Offers specialized placement workshops, consulting, and in-service programs to independent schools.

Janamar Nurses
1200 N. Eldorado Pl.
D-430
Tucson, AZ 85715
Phone: (602)722-2600

Employment agency. Provides regular or temporary placement of staff.

Kimberly Quality Care
4010 DuPont Cir., Ste. 275
Louisville, KY 40207
Phone: (502)893-8888

Employment agency. Provides temporary staffing for some positions.

Ocean Personnel Agency
PO Box 698
Malibu, CA 90265
Phone: (213)451-8183

Employment agency.

Pasadena Nurses Registry
1000 E. Walnut St., Ste. 212
Pasadena, CA 91106
Phone: (818)792-2103

Employment agency.

Professional Placement Associates, Inc.
11 Rye Ridge Plaza
Port Chester, NY 10573
Phone: (914)939-1195
Fax: (914)939-1959

Employment agency.

Travcorps, Inc.
40 Eastern Ave.
Malden, MA 02148
Phone: (617)322-2600

Places staff in temporary assignments.

Underhill Personnel Service
1147 S. Edgewood Ave.
Jacksonville, FL 32205
Phone: (904)388-7645

Employment agency. Handles temporary and regular placement of staff.

A career path should not be restrictive—there should be forks in the path, allowing you to adapt as changes occur within professional and personal lifestyles. The best intentions can go astray, leading to discouragement and disillusionment if alternative paths have not been prepared.

Source: *The Canadian Nurse*

Career Guides

American Hospital Association (AHA)
840 N. Lake Shore Dr.
Chicago, IL 60611
Phone: (312)280-6000
Toll-free: 800-621-6712
Fax: (312)280-5979

Membership: Individuals and health care institutions including hospitals, health care systems, and pre- and postacute health care delivery organizations. **Purpose:** Is dedicated to promoting the welfare of the public through its leadership and assistance to its members in the provision of better health services for all people. Carries out research and education projects in such areas as health care administration, hospital economics, and community relations; represents hospitals in national legislation; offers programs for institutional effectiveness review, technology assessment, and hospital administrative services to hospitals; conducts educational programs furthering the in-service education of hospital personnel; collects and analyzes data; furnishes multimedia educational materials; maintains 44,000 volume health care administration library, and biographical archive. Bestows awards. **Publication(s):** *AHANews*, weekly. • *Guide to the Health Care Field*, annual. • *Hospital Statistics*, annual. • *Hospitals*, biweekly.

MENTAL HEALTH CAREER DIRECTORY

Being a Counselor: Directions and Challenges
Brooke/Cole Publishing Co.
511 Forest Lodge Rd.
Pacific Grove, CA 93950-5098
Phone: (408)373-0728
Toll-free: 800-876-2350
Fax: (408)375-6414

Jeannette A. Brown and Robert H. Pate, Jr., editors. 1983. Includes bibliographies and indexes.

Career Choices for the 90's for Students of Psychology
Walker and Co.
720 Fifth Ave.
New York, NY 10019
Phone: (212)265-3632
Toll-free: 800-289-2553
Fax: (212)307-1764

1990. Offers alternatives for students of psychology. Gives information about the outlook and competition for entry-level candidates. Provides job-hunting tips.

> In all cases, the people with an edge will be those who know how to use a computer to do their jobs more efficiently, who can present ideas cogently and who work well in teams.
>
> Source: U.S. News & World Report

Career Information Center
Glencoe Publishing Co.
15319 Chatsworth St.
Mission Hills, CA 91345
Phone: (818)898-1391
Toll-free: 800-423-9534

Richard Lidz and Linda Perrin, editorial directors. Fourth edition, 1990. A multi-volume set that profiles over 600 occupations. Each occupational profile describes job duties, educational requirements, advancement possibilities, employment outlook, working conditions, earnings and benefits, and where to write for more information.

Career Ladders: An Approach to Professional Productivity and Job Satisfaction
American Nurses Association Cabinet on Nursing Services
600 Maryland Ave., NW
Washington, DC 20024-2571
Phone: (202)554-4444
Fax: (202)544-2262

American Nurses' Association, Cabinet on Nursing Services. 1984.

Careers in Psychology: Your Options are Open
American Psychological Association
750 1st St., NE
Washington, DC 20036
Phone: (202)336-5500

Pamela G. Armstrong, producer, director. 1990. Describes what psychologists do, where they work, and employment outlook. Gives advice on career planning and educational preparation. Gives an overview of specializations in psychology and career opportunities on the associate, bachelor, and master's level.

Careers in Social Work
National Association of Social Workers (NASW)
750 1st St., NE, Ste. 700
Washington, DC 20002
Phone: (202)408-8600
Toll-free: 800-752-3590

1993. Describes career opportunities in mental health, child welfare, health care, public welfare, schools, family service, services to the aged, industry, business, labor, and corrections. Includes information on how to enter the profession, and educational preparation.

Counseling as a Profession
Accelerated Development, Inc., Publishers
3808 W. Kilgore
Muncie, IN 47304-4896
Phone: (317)284-7511
Toll-free: 800-222-1166
Fax: (317)284-2535

Nicholas A. Vacc and Larry Loesch. 1987. Explains the expectations, activities, and behaviors of professional counselors. Covers counseling theory and practice, career development, assessment and measurement, consultation, research, and trends in professional counseling.

The Encyclopedia of Careers and Vocational Guidance
J. G. Ferguson Publishing Co.
200 W. Monroe, Ste. 250
Chicago, IL 60606
Phone: (312)580-5480

William E. Hopke, editor-in-chief. Ninth edition, 1993. Four-volume set that profiles 900 occupations and describes job trends in 71 industries. Includes career description, educational requirements, history of the job, methods of entry, advancement, employment outlook, earnings, conditions of work, social and psychological factors, and sources of further information.

Guide to Federal Jobs
Resource Directories
3361 Executive Pkwy.
Toledo, OH 43606
Phone: (419)536-5353
Toll-free: 800-274-8515
Fax: (419)536-7056

Rod W. Durgin, editor. Third edition, 1992. Contains information on finding and applying for federal jobs. Describes more than 200 professional and technical jobs for college graduates. Covers the nature of the work, salary, and geographic location. Lists college majors preferred for that occupation. Section one describes the function and work of government agencies that hire the most significant number of college graduates.

Human Services?... That Must Be So Rewarding
Paul H. Brookes Publishing Company
PO Box 10624
Baltimore, MD 21285-0624
Phone: 800-638-3775

Gail S. Bernstein and Judith A. Halaszyn. 1989. Includes a bibliography and an index.

Opportunities in Counseling and Development Careers
National Textbook Co.
NTC Publishing Group
4255 W. Touhy Ave.
Lincolnwood, IL 60646-1975
Phone: (708)679-5500
Toll-free: 800-323-4900

Neale Baxter. 1990. This book describes different types of counselors, including rehabilitation and school. For each counseling field, gives a description of the work, employment outlook, salary, benefits, working conditions, entry requirements, and a career ladder. Explores history and current issues in counseling.

Opportunities in Gerontology Careers
National Textbook Co.
NTC Publishing Group
4255 W. Touhy Ave.
Lincolnwood, IL 60646-1975
Phone: (708)679-5500
Toll-free: 800-323-4900

Williams, Ellen. 1987. Gives a broad overview of career opportunities in gerontology in many fields. Suggest training needed and internships and volunteer opportunities. Lists gerontology-related associations. Gives sources of additional information.

There are two types of ads: open (the company identified) and blind. Open ads are great for job-hunters. They give you the opportunity to do some investigation on the firm. Be sure to tailor your cover letter with your knowledge of the company. If you're lucky, you may uncover a contact.

Source: *Business Monday/Detroit Free Press*

Opportunities in Psychology Careers
National Textbook Co.
NTC Publishing Group
4255 W. Touhy Ave.
Lincolnwood, IL 60646-1975
Phone: (708)679-5500
Toll-free: 800-323-4900

Charles M. Super and Donald Super. Fifth edition, 1988. Defines the field of psychology. Discusses employment outlook, rewards, education required, areas within the field of psychology, and job hunting. Lists scientific and professional organizations, accredited doctoral programs, and internships for clinical and counseling psychology.

Opportunities in Social Work Careers
National Textbook Co.
NTC Publishing Group
4255 W. Touhy Ave.
Lincolnwood, IL 60646-1975
Phone: (708)679-5500
Toll-free: 800-323-4900

Renee Wittenberg. 1988. Describes the skills required for a job in social work, educational preparation, work settings and related careers. Lists additional resources.

> By the end of this decade, 85 percent of all new entrants into the workforce will be women, minorities and immigrants, and they will bring with them very different cultures and values.
>
> Source: *Television Quarterly*

Police Psychologist
Vocational Biographies, Inc.
PO Box 31
Sauk Centre, MN 56378-0031
Phone: (612)352-6516

1988. Four-page pamphlet containing a personal narrative about a worker's job, work likes and dislikes, career path from high school to the present, education and training, the rewards and frustrations, and the effects of the job on the rest of the worker's life. The data file portion of this pamphlet gives a concise occupational summary, including work description, working conditions, places of employment, personal characteristics, education and training, job outlook, and salary range.

Prison Social Worker
Vocational Biographies, Inc.
PO Box 31
Sauk Centre, MN 56378-0031
Phone: (612)352-6516

1988. Four-page pamphlet containing a personal narrative about a worker's job, work likes and dislikes, career path from high school to the present, education and training, the rewards and frustrations, and the effects of the job on the rest of the worker's life. The data file portion of this pamphlet gives a concise occupational summary, including work description, working conditions, places of employment, personal characteristics, education and training, job outlook, and salary range.

Psychologist
Careers, Inc.
PO Box 135
Largo, FL 34649-0135
Phone: (813)584-7333
Toll-free: 800-726-0441

1992. Eight-page brief offering the definition, history, duties, working conditions, personal qualifications, educational requirements, earnings, hours, employment outlook, advancement, and careers related to this position.

Psychologist, Clinical
Careers, Inc.
PO Box 135
Largo, FL 34649-0135
Phone: (813)584-7333
Toll-free: 800-726-0441

1992. Two-page occupational summary card describing duties, working conditions, personal qualifications, training, earnings and hours, employment outlook, places of employment, related careers, and where to write for more information.

Psychologist, School
Careers, Inc.
PO Box 135
Largo, FL 34649-0135
Phone: (813)584-7333
Toll-free: 800-726-0441

1991. Two-page occupational summary card describing duties, working conditions, personal qualifications, training, earnings and hours, employment outlook, places of employment, related careers, and where to write for more information.

Psychologists
Chronicle Guidance Publications, Inc.
66 Aurora St.
PO Box 1190
Moravia, NY 13118-1190
Phone: (315)497-0330
Toll-free: 800-622-7284

1991. Career brief describing the nature of the job, working conditions, hours and earnings, education and training, licensure, certification, unions, personal qualifications, social and psychological factors, location, employment outlook, entry methods, advancement, and related occupations.

Psychology as a Health Care Profession
American Psychological Associaton (APA)
750 1st St., NE
Washington, DC 20002
Phone: (202)336-5500

1986. Discusses the psychologist's role in the health-care field and describes places of employment.

School Counselors
Chronicle Guidance Publications, Inc.
66 Aurora St.
PO Box 1190
Moravia, NY 13118-1190
Phone: (315)497-0330
Toll-free: 800-622-7284

1991. Career brief describing the nature of the job, working conditions, hours and earnings, education and training, licensure, certification, unions, personal qualifications, social and psychological factors, location, employment outlook, entry methods, advancement, and related occupations.

School Psychologists
Chronicle Guidance Publications, Inc.
66 Aurora St.
PO Box 1190
Moravia, NY 13118-1190
Phone: (315)497-0330
Toll-free: 800-622-7284

1992. Career brief describing the nature of the job, working conditions, hours and earnings, education and training, licensure, certification, unions, personal qualifications, social and psychological factors, location, employment outlook, entry methods, advancement, and related occupations.

School Social Work: A Growing Resource in Education
National Associaton of Social Workers (NASW)
750 1st St., NE, Ste. 700
Washington, DC 20002
Phone: (202)408-8600

Describes social work practice in the schools and in special education. Covers professional values, standards, and educational and professional background.

School Social Workers
Chronicle Guidance Publications, Inc.
Aurora St. Extension
PO Box 1190
Moravia, NY 13118-1190
Phone: (315)497-0330
Toll-free: 800-622-7284

1989. Career brief describing the nature of the job, working conditions, hours and earnings, education and training, licensure, certification, unions, personal qualifications, social and psychological factors, location, employment outlook, entry methods, advancement, and related occupations.

Women are nearly as likely as men to have many types of postsecondary degrees, but men hold professional degrees and docto rates at more than double the rate of women.

Source: *The Wall Street Journal*

Social Worker, Clinical
Careers, Inc.
PO Box 135
Largo, FL 34649-0135
Phone: (813)584-7333
Toll-free: 800-726-0441

1991. Two-page occupational summary card describing duties, working conditions, personal qualifications, training, earnings and hours, employment outlook, places of employment, related careers, and where to write for more information.

Social Worker, Medical
Careers, Inc.
PO Box 135
Largo, FL 34649-0135
Phone: (813)584-7333
Toll-free: 800-726-0441

1990. Two-page occupational summary card describing duties, working conditions, personal qualifications, training, earnings and hours, employment outlook, places of employment,

MENTAL HEALTH CAREER DIRECTORY

related careers, and where to write for more information.

Social Worker, School
Careers, Inc.
PO Box 135
Largo, FL 34649-0135
Phone: (813)584-7333
Toll-free: 800-726-0441

1990. Two-page occupational summary card describing duties, working conditions, personal qualifications, training, earnings and hours, employment outlook, places of employment, related careers, and where to write for more information.

> Schools increasingly employ social workers to help with some of the developmental and educational problems facing children and teachers. They often are able to provide the early support many children need to become secure, self-sufficient adults.
>
> Source: National Association of Social Workers

Social Workers
Chronicle Guidance Publications, Inc.
66 Aurora St. Extension
PO Box 1190
Moravia, NY 13118-1190
Phone: (315)497-0330
Toll-free: 800-622-7284

1992. Career brief describing the nature of the job, working conditions, hours and earnings, education and training, licensure, certification, unions, personal qualifications, social and psychological factors, location, employment outlook, entry methods, advancement, and related occupations.

Social Workers
Careers, Inc.
PO Box 135
Largo, FL 34649-0135
Phone: (813)584-7333
Toll-free: 800-726-0441

1989. Eight-page brief offering the definition, history, duties, working conditions, personal qualifications, educational requirements, earnings, hours, employment outlook, advancement, and careers related to this position.

VGM's Careers Encyclopedia
National Textbook Co.
4255 W. Touhy Ave.
Lincolnwood, IL 60646-1975
Phone: (708)679-5500

Norback, Craig T., editor. Third edition, 1991. Profiles 180 occupations. Describes job duties, places of employment, working conditions, qualifications, education and training, advancement potential, and salary for each occupation.

What Is Counseling and Human Development?
American Association for Counseling and Development (AACD)
5999 Stevenson Ave.
Alexandria, VA 22304
Phone: (703)823-9800

Eight-panel brochure describing what counselors do, where they work, the training and education required, and certification.

Professional and Trade Periodicals

Advance
Association for Advancement of Psychology
PO Box 38129
Colorado Springs, CO 80937
Phone: (719)520-0688
Toll-free: 800-869-6595
Fax: (719)520-0375

Stephen Pfeiffer, Ph.D., editor. Quarterly. Concerned with the advancement of psychology. Details the Association's work to represent the interests of professional, social, and scientific psychologists in the public policy arena.

AHANews (AHA)
American Hospital Association (AHA)
840 N. Lake Shore Dr.
Chicago, IL 60611
Phone: (312)280-6000
Weekly.

American Hospital Association—Outreach
American Hospital Association
840 N. Lake Shore Dr.
Chicago, IL 60611
Phone: (312)280-5921

Editor(s): Marilyn Canna. Bimonthly. Analyzes the factors influencing market supply, demand, and competition.

Annual Review of Psychology
Annual Reviews, Inc.
4139 El Camino Way
PO Box 10139
Palo Alto, CA 94303-0897
Phone: (415)493-4400

Mark R. Rosencwig and Lyman W. Porter, editors. Annual.

AssemblyLine
Natl. Assembly of National Voluntary Health & Social Welfare
1319 F St., NW
Washington, DC 20004
Phone: (202)347-2080

Quarterly. Attempts to foster intercommunication and interaction among national voluntary health and social welfare agencies. Discusses topics relating to the impact of voluntarism on human needs, especially in regard to individual health and social welfare agencies.

Career Development Quarterly
American Counseling Association
5999 Stevenson Ave.
Alexandria, VA 22304
Phone: (703)823-9800
Toll-free: (315)423-5282
Fax: (703)823-0252

Mark L. Savickas, editor. Quarterly. Journal for career counseling and career education professionals in schools, colleges, private practice, government agencies, personnel departments in business and industry, and employment counseling centers.

Child and Adolescent Social Work Journal
Human Sciences Press
233 Spring St.
New York, NY 10013
Phone: (212)620-8000

Florence Lieberman, editor. Bimonthly. Journal covering social work with children.

The Counseling Psychologist
Sage Periodicals Press
2455 Teller Rd.
Newbury Park, CA 91320
Phone: (805)499-0721
Fax: (805)499-0871

Gerald L. Stone, editor. Quarterly. Journal on psychological counseling.

Whether you're looking for your next job or your first job, networking must be a key element of your search. More jobs are found by networking than through any other source.

Source: *Business Monday/Detroit Free Press*

Developmental Psychology
American Psychological Association
750 1st St., NE
Washington, DC 20002-4242
Phone: (202)336-5500

Carolyn Waxler, editor. Six issues/year. Journal presenting empirical contributions that advance knowledge and theory about human psychological growth and development from infancy to old age.

Elementary School Guidance & Counseling
American Counseling Association
5999 Stevenson Ave.
Alexandria, VA 22304
Phone: (703)823-9800
Fax: (703)823-0252

Stephen Brooks, director of advertising. Four issues/year. Journal covering guidance program evaluation, development of new applications for theoretical ideas, and current research in elementary counseling.

Family Service America—Newswire
Family Service America
17000 W. Lake Park Dr.
Park Place
Milwaukee, WI 53224
Phone: (414)359-1040

Editor(s): Eva Augustin Rumph and Paula J.

CAREER RESOURCES

MENTAL HEALTH CAREER DIRECTORY

Purcell. Quarterly. Carries news of programs and services of the association and member family service agencies. Covers stories on issues related to families, social services, and other non-profit issues.

International Academy of Behavioral Medicine, Counseling, and Psychotherapy—Newsletter
International Academy of Behavioral Medicine, Counseling, and Psychotherapy
6750 Hillcrest Plaza, Ste. 304
Dallas, TX 75230
Phone: (214)458-8334

Editor(s): George R. Mount, Ph.D. Quarterly. Publishes research articles in the field of behavioral medicine, "the systematic application of various principles of behavioral science to health care problems."

Some companies use creative gimmicks to motivate workers. Each year, John Brady Design Consultants, Pittsburgh, gives a jar of 12 marbles to its 18 employees, a different color for each person. Over the year, employees give the marbles as rewards to co-workers who help them out or achieve great feats. At year's end, the firm can see who recognizes others and who doesn't.

Source: *The Wall Street Journal*

International Psychologist
International Council of Psychologists, Inc.
c/o Dr. Carleton Shay
Education Foundations Department
California State University
Los Angeles, CA 90032
Phone: (213)343-4336

Dr. Carleton B. Shay, editor. Quarterly. Publishes news of the professional and scientific activities of the Council while promoting better understanding within the profession. Also contains official announcements and reports of the International Council.

NASW News
National Association of Social Workers
7981 Eastern Ave.
Silver Spring, MD 20910
Phone: (301)565-0333
Fax: (301)587-1321

Tabloid reporting on development in the social work profession. It includes updates on social policy developments in such areas as child welfare, AIDS, Medicaid, and housing. The publication lists educational and employment opportunities.

Psychological Science
Cambridge University Press
40 W. 20th St.
New York, NY 10011
Phone: (914)937-9600

William K. Estes, editor. Six issues/year. Scientific research journal of the American Psychological Society.

The School Counselor
American Assn. for Counseling and Development
5999 Stevenson Ave.
Alexandria, VA 22304
Phone: (703)823-9800
Fax: (703)823-0252

Stephen Brooks, advertising manager. Five issues/year. Journal covering current issues affecting teens, and how counselors can deal with them.

Basic Reference Guides

ABA Membership Directory
Association for Behavior Analysis (ABA)
258 Wood Hall
Western Michigan University
Kalamazoo, MI 49008
Phone: (616)387-4494
Fax: (616)387-4457

Biennial.

AChemS Membership Directory
Association for Chemoreception Sciences (AChemS)
c/o Panacer Associates
229 Westridge Dr.
Tallahassee, FL 32304
Phone: (215)898-2084

Annual.

Acute Psychiatric Care: An Occupational Therapy Guide to Exercises in Daily Living Skills
Slack, Inc.
6900 Grove Rd.
Thorofare, NJ 08086
Phone: (609)848-1000

Patricia L. Hughes and Linda Mullins. 1981. Includes bibliographical references.

Addiction & Recovery's National Treatment Resource Issue
International Publishing Group
4959 Commerce Pkwy.
Cleveland, OH 44125
Phone: (216)464-1210
Fax: (216)464-1835

Annual. $20.00/single issue. Formerly National Treatment Directory.

AGPA Directory
American Group Practice Association (AGPA)
1422 Duke St.
Alexandria, VA 22314
Phone: (703)838-0033

Annual, January. $125.00. Covers: About 300 private group medical practices and their professional staffs, totalling about 23,000 physicians. Entries include: Group member name, address, phone, names of administrator and other executives, names of physicians listed by medical specialties. Arrangement: Alphabetical. Indexes: Group location, personal name.

AHA Directory of Health Care Professionals
American Hospital Association
840 N. Lake Shore Dr.
Chicago, IL 60611
Phone: (312)280-5957

Annual, May. Covers over 161,000 hospital professionals and 4,000 health care system professionals.

AHA Guide to the Health Care Field
Data Services Business Group
American Hospital Association
840 N. Lake Shore Dr.
Chicago, IL 60611
Phone: (312)280-5957

Annual, July. Covers hospitals, multi-health care systems, freestanding ambulatory surgery centers, psychiatric facilities, long-term care facilities, substance abuse programs, hospices, Health Maintenance Organizations (HMOs), and other health-related organizations.

> One way to improve your chances in the job hunt is to define "you" as broadly as possible.... Defining yourself in terms of your skills rather than your job history is the key.
>
> Source: *Business Monday/Detroit Free Press*

AHSSPPE Membership Directory
Association on Handicapped Student Service Programs in Postsecondary Education (AHSSPPE)
PO Box 21192
Columbus, OH 43221
Phone: (614)488-4972

Annual.

The AJN Guide to Nursing Career Opportunities
American Journal of Nursing Co.
555 W. 57th St.
New York, NY 10019
Phone: (212)582-8820

Annual. Gives career planning, self-assessment, and job hunting advice. This is primarily a listing of hospitals and health centers. Profiles on each hospital describe the facilities, professional climate, and benefits.

American Association for Correctional Psychology Directory
American Association for Correctional Psychology
c/o Robert R. Smith
College of Graduate Studies, Counseling Program
University of West Virginia
Institute, WV 25112
Phone: (304)766-1929

Continuously updated. Covers: 400 mental

CAREER RESOURCES

health professionals engaged in correctional and rehabilitative work in prisons, reformatories, juvenile institutions, probation and parole agencies, and in other aspects of criminal justice. Entries include: Name, affiliation, address, phone. Arrangement: Alphabetical.

American Hospital Association—Guide to the Health Care Field
American Hospital Association (AHA)
840 N. Lakeshore Dr.
Chicago, IL 60611
Phone: (312)280-5957

Annual, July. $195.00; payment with order. Covers: 7,000 hospitals, long-term care facilities, and multihospital systems; individual members; and 1,800 health-related organizations. Entries include: For hospitals - Facility name, address, phone, administrator's name, number of beds, facilities and services, other statistics. For multihospital systems -Headquarters name, address, phone, chief executive. Arrangement: Hospitals are geographical; members are alphabetical. Indexes: Subject.

> At the same time that whale-size firms are whacking away the blubber, a net of 1.9 million new jobs will be created this year 1992, estimates Dun & Bradstreet, and 80 percent of them will be at companies with fewer than 100 employees.
>
> Source: U.S. News & World Report

American Journal of Nursing—Directory of Nursing Organizations Issue
American Journal of Nursing Company
555 W. 57th St.
New York, NY 10019
Phone: (212)582-8820
Fax: (212)586-5462

Annual, April. $4.00. Publication includes: Directory of nursing organizations and agencies. Entries include: Name, address, names of officers or nursing representative. Arrangement: Classified by type of organization.

AMP Membership Directory
Association for Media Psychology (AMP)
228 Santa Monica Blvd.
Ste. 4
Santa Monica, CA 90401
Phone: (213)394-4546
Fax: (213)394-4546

Periodic.

APA Membership Register
American Psychological Association (APA)
1200 17th St., NW
Washington, DC 20036
Phone: (202)955-7600
Fax: (703)525-5191

Periodic. $35.00/issue.

ASC Member Directory
American Society of Criminology (ASC)
1314 Kinnear Rd., Ste. 212
Columbus, OH 43212
Phone: (614)292-9207
Fax: (614)292-6767

Annual. Free to members.

Association for School, College and University Staffing Directory of Membership
Association for School, College and University Staffing
1600 Dodge Ave.
S-330
Evanston, IL 60201-3451
Phone: (708)864-1999
Fax: (708)864-8303

Annual, winter. $20.00. Covers: Includes about 450 school district personnel officers and/or superintendents responsible for hiring professional staff. Entries include: Institution name, address, phone, contact name. Arrangement: Geographical. Indexes: Personal name, subject-field of teacher training.

AWP Membership Directory
Association for Women in Psychology (AWP)
c/o Angela R. Gillem, Ph.D.
Haverford College
370 Lancaster Ave.
Haverford, PA 19041-1392

Annual.

Behavior Modification in Therapeutic Recreation: An Introductory Learning Manual
Venture Publishing, Inc.
1999 Capo Ave.
State College, PA 16801
Phone: (814)234-4561

John Dattilo and William D. Murphy. 1987. Includes a bibliography.

Billian's Hospital Blue Book
Billian Publishing Co.
2100 Powers Ferry Rd., Ste. 300
Atlanta, GA 30339
Phone: (404)955-5656

Annual, spring. $95.00, plus $4.50 shipping. Covers more than 7,100 hospitals. Entries include name of hospital, accreditation, mailing address, phone, number of beds, type of facility (nonprofit, general, state, etc.); list of administrative personnel and chiefs of medical services, with titles.

Boarding Schools Directory
Committee on Boarding Schools
National Association of Independent Schools (NAIS)
75 Federal St.
Boston, MA 02110
Phone: (617)451-2444
Fax: (617)482-3913

Annual, September. Free. Covers: 245 boarding schools that are members of the National Association of Independent Schools. Entries include: School name, address, phone, contact name, grades for which boarding students are accepted, enrollment, brief description. Arrangement: Classified by type of school. Indexes: Geographical.

Christian Schools International Directory
Christian Schools International
PO Box 8709
3350 E. Paris Ave., SE
Grand Rapids, MI 49512
Phone: (616)957-1070
Fax: (616)957-5022

Annual, November. $45.00. Covers: Nearly 425 Reformed Christian elementary and secondary schools; related associations, and societies without schools. Entries include: For schools - School name, address, phone; name, title, and address of officers; names of faculty members. Arrangement: Geographical.

CLC Directory
Child Life Council (CLC)
7910 Woodmont Ave., Ste. 300
Bethesda, MD 20895

Periodic.

> Interview proactively. Make a list of questions you'd like answered. Target the company's current and future plans, the job and where it could lead. You'll have the chance to ask most of them if you tie them into the answers you give on similar topics.
>
> Source: *Business Monday/Detroit Free Press*

Concise Encyclopedia of Psychology
John Wiley and Sons, Inc.
605 Third Ave.
New York, NY 10158
Phone: (212)850-6000

Raymond J. Corsini and George W. Albee, editors. 1987. Includes a bibliography. Illustrated.

Continuing Education for Gerontological Careers
Council on Social Work Education
1600 Duke St.
Alexandria, VA 22314
Phone: (703)683-8080

Roberta R. Greene. 1988. Includes bibliographies.

CPC National Directory: Who's Who in Career Planning, Placement, and Recruitment
College Placement Council (CPC)
62 Highland Ave.
Bethlehem, PA 18017
Phone: (215)868-1421

Annual. Free to members; $47.95/year for nonmembers.

MENTAL HEALTH CAREER DIRECTORY

CWLA Directory of Member Agencies
Child Welfare League of America (CWLA)
440 1st St., NW, Ste. 310
Washington, DC 20001
Phone: (202)638-2952

Semiannual. Free to members; $14.00 for nonmembers. Includes calendar of events.

Dictionary of Concepts in General Psychology
Greenwood Press, Inc.
88 Post Rd., W.
PO Box 5007
Westport, CT 06881
Phone: (203)226-3571
Fax: (203)222-1502

John A. Popplestone and Marion White McPherson. 1988. Contains short articles on concepts in behavioral psychology and includes references for further reading.

Scientists and environmentalists are warning that our natural environment is deteriorating at an alarming rate. The social work profession has the theoretical base and practice skills to respond to the social dimensions of environmental issues at the local, national, and international levels.

Source: *Social Work*

Directory of Adventure Alternatives in Corrections, Mental Health & Special Populations
Association for Experiential Education
Box 249-CU
Boulder, CO 80309
Phone: (303)492-1547
Fax: (303)492-7090

Irregular; latest edition 1988. $12.00. Covers: About 115 organizations and agencies providing programs which link traditional therapeutic strategies with alternative practices to treat children and adults who have corrections, substance abuse, or mental health problems, or are physically or mentally handicapped. Entries include: Organization name, address, phone, name of director, description of program, and coded indication of target population location, sex, and age. Arrangement: Alphabetical. Indexes: Geographical.

Directory of Catholic Charities, Agencies and Institutions in the United States, Puerto Rico
Catholic Charities USA
1731 King St., Ste. 200
Alexandria, VA 22314
Phone: (703)549-1390

Biennial, odd years. $35.00; $20.00 for members. Covers: Nearly 1,200 affiliated Catholic community and social service agencies and residential and non-residential institutions and facilities. Listings include diocesan agencies, institutions for the elderly, handicapped, and youth, Catholic schools of social work, and state Catholic conferences. Entries include: Organization name, address, name and title of director, phone. Arrangement: Classified by type of organization, then geographical by diocese.

Directory of Christian Social Welfare Agencies in the U.S.
North American Association of Christians in Social Work (NACSW)
Box S-90
St. Davids, PA 19087
Phone: (215)687-5777

Directory of Counseling Services
International Association of Counseling Services
101 S. Whiting St., Ste. 211
Alexandria, VA 22304
Phone: (703)823-9840

Annual, September. $50.00, payment with order. Covers: About 200 accredited services in the United States and Canada concerned with psychological, educational, and vocational counseling, including those at colleges and universities, community and technical colleges, and public and private agencies. Entries include: Name, address, phone, hours of operation, director's name, service, clientele served. Arrangement: Geographical.

Directory of Employment Opportunities in the Federal Government

Arco Publishing Company
Simon and Schuster, Inc.
15 Columbus Circle
Order Dept., 16th Fl.
New York, NY 10023
Phone: (212)373-8931
Fax: (212)767-5852

1985. $24.95. Covers: Federal agencies offering employment opportunities in the U.S. government. Entries include: Agency name and address, geographical area served, subsidiary and branch names and locations, eligibility requirements, application and testing procedures, and job descriptions. Arrangement: Alphabetical. Indexes: Department name, position title, subject (occupational categories).

Directory of Hospital Personnel

Medical Device Register
5 Paragon Dr.
Montvale, NJ 07645-1725

Annual. $279.00, plus $5.00 shipping. Covers: 50,000 executives at hospitals with more than 200 beds. Entries include: Name of hospital, address, phone, number of beds, type of hospital, names and titles of key department heads and staff. Arrangement: Geographical. Indexes: Hospital name, personnel, hospital size.

Directory of Jewish Health and Welfare Agencies

Council of Jewish Federations
730 Broadway, 2nd Fl.
New York, NY 10003
Phone: (212)475-5000
Fax: (212)529-5842

Biennial, March of even years. $10.00. Covers: Health and welfare services for individuals and families, children, youth, and adults; central agencies for Jewish education; vocational services; housing and nursing homes for the elderly; hospitals; and other specialized services supported partly or wholly by Jewish federations in the United States and Canada. Entries include: Organization or facility name, address, phone, name of director. Arrangement: Geographical.

Directory of Nursing Homes

Oryx Press
4041 N. Central, No. 700
Phoenix, AZ 85012
Phone: (602)265-2651
Fax: (602)253-2741

Reported as triennial; latest edition August 1991. $225.00. Covers: 16,259 state-licensed long-term care facilities. Entries include: Name of facility, address, phone, licensure status, number of beds; many listings also include name of administrator and health services supervisor; number of nursing, dietary, and auxiliary staff members; availability of social, recreational, and religious programs; and medicaid/medicare certification status. Arrangement: Geographical. Indexes: Facility name.

Selecting a boss who is a good match for your work style can be critical to your job success. The mismatched, or wrong boss, can make your work life miserable, as well as significantly damage your career.

Source: *The Detroit News*

Directory of Public School Systems in the U.S.

Association for School, College and
University Staffing (ASCUS)
c/o High School
1600 Dodge Ave., No. 5-300
Evanston, IL 60204
Phone: (708)864-1999
Fax: (708)864-8303

Annual. $65.00. Lists nearly 15,000 public schools with the name of the individual responsible for hiring, grade levels, and size of each district.

EASNA Membership Directory

Employee Assistance Society of North
America (EASNA)
2728 Phillips
Berkley, MI 48072
Phone: (313)545-3888

Annual. $10.00, for members only.

CAREER RESOURCES

Employment Opportunities
Council for Health and Human Services Ministries (CHHSM)
700 Prospect Ave. E.
Cleveland, OH 44115
Phone: (216)736-2250
Fax: (216)736-2251

Monthly.

Encyclopedia of Psychology
John Wiley and Sons, Inc.
605 Third Ave.
New York, NY 10158
Phone: (212)850-6000
Toll-free: 800-526-5368

Raymond J. Corsini, editor. Second edition, 1994. Contains articles on different fields of psychology and on psychological topics such as applied, clinical, and theoretical psychology. Includes a bibliography.

Average starting salary for an M.B.A. with a liberal arts bachelor's degree: $35,734. A technical bachelor's degree adds $5,579.

Source: *U.S. News & World Report*

Encyclopedia of Social Work
National Association of Social Workers (NASW)
750 1st St., NE, Ste. 700
Washington, DC 20002
Phone: (202)408-8600
Toll-free: 800-227-3590

Anne Minahon, editor in chief. Eighteenth edition, 1987. Contains articles on social work practice, social issues and problems, and social institutions.

The Encyclopedic Dictionary of Psychology
Dushkin Publishing Group, Inc.
Sluice Dock
Guilford, CT 06437
Phone: (203)453-4351

Terry Pettijohn, editor. Fourth edition, 1991. Illustrated.

Eponyms in Psychology: A Dictionary and Biographical Sourcebook
Greenwood Press, Inc.
88 Post Rd., W.
PO Box 5007
Westport, CT 06881
Phone: (203)226-3571

Leonard Zusne. 1987. Defines 1800 psychological eponyms— a term or process named after an individual.

Federal Personnel Office Directory
Federal Reports, Inc.
1010 Vermont Ave., NW, Ste. 408
Washington, DC 20005
Phone: (202)393-3311
Fax: (202)393-1553

Biennial, March of even years. $27.00. Covers: Over 1,500 federal government personnel offices that hire people for federal jobs; limited international coverage. Entries include: Government agency name, address, phone, description of services, restrictions for employment eligibility, branch office names and locations. Includes information on federal recruitment programs for disabled persons, women and minorities, veterans, students, and summer employment. Arrangement: Geographical, classified by department or agency.

Federal Staff Directory
Staff Directories Ltd.
Box 62
Mount Vernon, VA 22121-0062
Phone: (703)739-0900
Fax: (703)765-1300

Semiannual, December and July. $59.00. Covers: 30,000 persons in federal government offices and independent agencies, with biographies of 2,500 key executives; includes officials at policy level in agencies of the Office of the President, Cabinet-level departments, independent and regulatory agencies, military commands, federal information centers, and libraries, and United States attorneys, marshals, and ambassadors. Entries include: Name, title, location (indicating building, address, and room), phone. Arrangement: By department or agency. Indexes: Personal name, subject.

FSA—Directory of Member Agencies
Family Service America (FSA)
11700 West Lake Park Dr.
Milwaukee, WI 53224
Phone: (414)359-1040
Fax: (414)359-1074

Annual. Free to each member, headquarters and branch; $250.00 for nonmembers; $40.00 for nonprofit organizations. Lists accredited, provisional, and affiliate member agencies by state.

Handbook of Clinical Adult Psychology
Gower Publishing Co.
Old Post Rd.
Brookfield, VT 05036
Phone: (802)276-3162

S.J. Lindsay and G.E. Powell. 1987.

The Handbook of Clinical Psychology: Theory, Research and Practice
Dorsey Press
c/o Wadsworth, Inc.
10 Davis Dr.
Belmont, CA 94002
Phone: (415)595-2350
Toll-free: 800-245-7524

Eugene C. Walker, editor. 1983. Reviews current research and clinical practice.

Handbook of Private Schools
Porter Sargent Publishers, Inc.
11 Beacon St.
Boston, MA 02108
Phone: (617)523-1670
Fax: (617)523-1021

Annual, June. $65.00, plus $2.41 shipping. Covers: 1,800 elementary and secondary boarding and day schools in the United States. Entries include: School name, address, enrollment, facilities, names of administrators, fees, descriptions of school offerings. Arrangement: Geographical.

Handbook of Social Psychology
Lawrence Erlbaum Associates, Inc.
365 Broadway
Hillsdale, NJ 07642
Phone: (201)666-4110

Gardner Lindzey and Elliot Aronson, editors. Third edition, 1985. Summarizes current research in psychology.

Handbook of Vocational Psychology
Lawrence Erlbaum Associates, Inc.
365 Broadway
Hillsdale, NJ 07642
Phone: (201)666-4110
Fax: (201)666-2394

W. Bruce Walsh, and Samuel H. Osipow, editors. 1983. Includes indexes.

Citicorp is changing the way it uses interns, as are other companies. Instead of providing opportunities for students to examine various career paths, employers are taking a closer look at them as potential full-time employees. This means giving interns more responsibility.

Source: *Fortune*

Hospital Market Atlas
SMG Marketing Group, Inc.
1342 N. LaSalle Dr.
Chicago, IL 60610
Phone: (312)642-3026
Fax: (312)642-9729

Biennial. $595.00, postpaid; payment with order. Covers: Over 8,200 hospitals, clinical laboratories, hospital systems, group purchasing organizations, health maintenance organizations, outpatient surgery centers, and diagnostic imaging centers. Entries include: Hospital or organization name, address, phone, management, type of hospital service, number of beds, admissions, surgical operations, and emergency room visits. Arrangement: Geographical.

Hospital Phone Book
U.S. Directory Service
655 NW 128th St.
Miami, FL 33168
Phone: (305)769-1700

Irregular; previous edition 1988; latest edition 1991/92. Covers about 7,975 hospitals, including military and other federal facilities.

CAREER RESOURCES

MENTAL HEALTH CAREER DIRECTORY

Hospital Phone Book
Reed Reference Publishing
121 Chanlon Rd.
New Providence, RI 07974
Toll-free: 800-521-8110

Contains thousands of numbers and basic information on hospitals around the country.

Nothing can be more frustrating than getting typecast at work. You can get typecast in a certain job or image. Then, when you're ready to move up or into a different area of expertise, you can't get anyone to see you in a different way.... One technique to change your image is to dress in a more professional manner. You must also position yourself with people who can help you. One good way is to become active in a professional group, which also can provide you with good contacts and news of opportunities throughout your industry.

Source: *Business Monday/Detroit Free Press*

Hospitals Directory
American Business Directories, Inc.
American Business Information, Inc.
5711 S. 86th Circle
Omaha, NE 68127
Phone: (402)593-4600
Fax: (402)331-1505

Annual. $415.00, payment with order. Number of listings: 10,020. Entries include: Name, address, phone (including area code), year first in 'Yellow Pages.' Arrangement: Geographical.

ICP Directory
International Council of Psychologists (ICP)
c/o Patricia J. Fontes, Ph.D.
PO Box 62
Hopkinton, RI 02833-0062
Phone: (401)377-3092
Fax: (401)377-6013

Biennial.

Medical and Health Information Directory
Gale Research Inc.
835 Penobscot Bldg.
Detroit, MI 48226
Phone: (313)961-2242
Fax: (313)961-6241

Three volumes. Each volume published separately on a biennial basis; volume 1, latest edition 1991; volume 2, latest edition 1992; volume 3, latest edition 1992. $195.00 per volume; $480.00 for the three-volume set. Covers: In volume 1, medical and health oriented associations, organizations, institutions, and government agencies, including health maintenance organizations (HMOs), preferred provider organizations (PPOs), insurance companies, pharmaceutical companies, research centers, and medical and allied health schools. In volume 2, medical book publishers; medical periodicals, review serials, etc.; audiovisual producers and services, medical libraries and information centers, and computerized information systems and services. In volume 3, clinics, treatment centers, care programs, and counseling/diagnostic services for 30 subject areas (drawn from specialized lists published by governments and associations). Entries include: Institution, service, or firm name, address, phone; many include names of key personnel and, when pertinent, descriptive annotation. Arrangement: Classified by activity, service, etc. Indexes: Each volume has a complete master name and keyword index.

Mental Health Directory
National Institute of Mental Health
Public Health Service
Department of Health and Human Services
5600 Fishers Ln., Rm. 15C-05
Rockville, MD 20857
Phone: (301)443-4513

Irregular; latest edition 1990. $23.00. Send orders to: Superintendent of Documents, U.S. Government Printing Office, Washington, DC 20402 (202-783-3238). Covers: Hospitals, treatment centers, outpatient clinics, day/night facilities, residential treatment centers for emotionally disturbed children, residential supportive programs such as halfway houses, and mental health centers offering mental health assistance; not included are substance abuse programs, Veteran's Administration programs, nursing homes, programs for the developmentally disabled, and organizations in which fees are retained by individual members. Entries include: Name, address, phone. Arrangement: Geographical.

Mental Health Services
American Business Directories, Inc.
American Business Information, Inc.
5711 S. 86th Circle
Omaha, NE 68127
Phone: (402)593-4600
Fax: (402)331-1505

Annual. $485.00, payment with order. Number of listings: 13,586. Entries include: Name, address, phone (including area code), year first in 'Yellow Pages.' Arrangement: Geographical.

NASP Membership Directory
National Association of School Psychologists (NASP)
8455 Colesville Rd., Ste. 1000
Silver Spring, MD 20910
Phone: (301)608-0500
Fax: (301)608-2514

Biennial.

National Directory of Children & Youth Services
Marion L. Peterson, Publisher
Box 1837
Longmont, CO 80502
Phone: (303)776-7539

Annual. $67.00, plus $5.00 shipping. Covers: Child and youth-oriented social services, health and mental health services, and juvenile court and youth advocacy services in state and private agencies, major cities, and 3,100 counties; also covers runaway youth centers, child abuse projects, congressional committees, clearinghouses, and national organizations concerned with child health and welfare. Entries include: Agency listings include agency name, address, phone, names of principal executives and staff, description of services. Arrangement: Geographical.

National Directory of Internships
National Society for Internships and Experiential Education
3509 Haworth Dr., Ste. 207
Raleigh, NC 27609-7229
Phone: (919)787-3263

Covers more than 30,000 educational internship opportunities in 75 fields with over 650 organizations in the United States. Includes information on deadlines, application procedures, contact names, and eligibility requirements.

National Directory of Private Social Agencies
Croner Publications, Inc.
34 Jericho Tpke.
Jericho, NY 11753
Phone: (516)333-9085
Fax: (516)338-4986

Base edition supplied upon order; monthly updates. $74.95, plus $4.95 shipping; including updates. Number of listings: Over 15,000. Entries include: Agency name, address, phone, description of services. Arrangement: Geographical. Indexes: Service, agency type.

Some people will find the training they need right at the office. American companies desperate to produce more with fewer, better-skilled workers now are pumping $30 billion annually into employee-training programs that run the gamut from basic computer courses to company-sponsored M.B.A. degrees.

Source: U.S. News & World Report

NCRE Membership Directory
National Council on Rehabilitation Education (NCRE)
c/o Dr. Garth Eldredge
Department of Special Education
Utah State University
Logan, UT 84322-2865
Phone: (801)750-3241
Fax: (801)750-3572

Annual.

NOHSE Membership Directory
National Organization for Human Service Education (NOHSE)
Box 6257
Fitchburg State College
Fitchburg, MA 01420
Phone: (508)345-2151

Periodic.

NSDTA Directory
National Staff Development and Training Association (NSDTA)
810 1st St., NE, Ste. 500
Washington, DC 20002-4205
Phone: (202)682-0100

Annual. Membership directory; includes titles,

MENTAL HEALTH CAREER DIRECTORY

addresses, and program responsibilities; also includes names by state.

Nurses and Nurses Registries

American Business Directories, Inc.
American Business Information, Inc.
5711 S. 86th Circle
Omaha, NE 68127
Phone: (402)593-4600
Fax: (402)331-1505

Annual. $450.00, payment with order. Number of listings: 12,049. Entries include: Name, address, phone (including area code), year first in 'Yellow Pages.' Arrangement: Geographical.

Jeffrey A. Sonnenfeld, an Emory University management professor, divides US corporations into 4 categories: the Baseball Team—advertising, entertainment, investment banking, software, biotech research, and other industries based on fad, fashion, new technologies, and novelty; the Club—utilities, government agencies, airlines, banks, and other organizations that tend to produce strong generalists; the Academy—manufacturers in electronics, pharmaceuticals, office products, autos, and consumer products; and the Fortress—companies in fields such as publishing, hotels, retailing, textiles, and natural resources.

Nursing Career Directory

Springhouse Corporation
1111 Bethlehem Pike
Springhouse, PA 19477
Phone: (215)646-8700

Annual, January. Free; restricted circulation. Covers: Nonprofit and investor-owned hospitals and departments of the United States government which hire nurses. Does not report specific positions available. Entries include: Unit name, location, areas of nursing specialization, educational requirements for nurses, licensing, facilities, benefits, etc. Arrangement: Geographical.

Nursingworld Journal Nursing Job Guide

Prime National Publishing Corporation
470 Boston Post Rd.
Weston, MA 02193
Phone: (617)899-2702
Fax: (617)899-4361

Annual, January. $85.00. Covers: Over 7,000 hospitals and medical centers, infirmaries, government hospitals, and other hospitals in the United States; in tabular format, provides information about each facility which would be of interest to nurses considering employment there, but does not list specific openings. Entries include: Hospital name, address, phone, name of nurse recruiter; number of beds, number of admissions, number of patient days, type of control, whether a teaching institution; nurses salary range; nursing specialties utilized; list of fringe benefits; whether relocation assistance is given; educational opportunities; special programs. Arrangement: Geographical.

Private Independent Schools

Bunting and Lyon, Inc.
238 N. Main St.
Wallingford, CT 06492
Phone: (203)269-3333

Annual, April. $92.00. Covers: Nearly 1,200 elementary and secondary private schools and summer programs in 45 states and 39 countries. Entries include: School name, address, phone, enrollment, tuition and other fees, scholarship information, headmaster's name and educational background, director of admissions, regional accreditation, description of programs, curriculum, activities. Arrangement: Geographical. Indexes: School name.

Psychology: Principles and Applications

Prentice-Hall, Inc.
200 Old Tappan Rd.
Old Tappan, NJ 07675
Phone: (201)592-2000

Stephen Worchel and Wayne Shebilske. Fourth edition, 1992. Describes the major subfields of psychology. Covers the application of psychology to fields such as law and health. Explains various psychological theories and their applications.

Psychology Society Membership List
Psychology Society (PS)
100 Beekman St.
New York, NY 10038-1810
Phone: (212)285-1872

Biennial.

Public Welfare Directory
American Public Welfare Association
810 1st St., NE, Ste. 500
Washington, DC 20002
Phone: (202)682-0100

Annual, August. $70.00, plus $3.00 shipping; payment with order. Covers: International, federal, state, territorial, county, and major municipal human service agencies; coverage includes Canadian federal and provincial agencies. Entries include: Agency name, address, phone, names of key personnel, type of service or clientele. Arrangement: Geographical.

Register of Clinical Social Workers
National Association of Social Workers (NASW)
7981 Eastern Ave.
Silver Spring, MD 20910
Phone: (301)565-0333
Fax: (301)587-1321

Biennial. $66.00/copy. Directory listing qualified clinical social workers; arranged geographically.

SASP Membership Directory
Society for the Advancement of Social Psychology (SASP)
c/o Dr. Frank Dane
Dept. of Psychology
Mercer University
Macon, GA 31207
Phone: (912)752-2972
Fax: (912)752-2108

Periodic.

Skills for Direct Practice in Social Work
Columbia University Press
562 W. 113th St.
New York, NY 10025
Phone: (212)316-7100
Toll-free: 800-944-8648

Ruth R. Middleman. 1990.

The Social Work Dictionary
National Association of Social Workers (NASW)
750 1st St., NE
Washington, DC 20002
Phone: (202)408-8600
Toll-free: 800-752-3590

Robert L. Barker. Second edition, 1991. Defines common terms in social work and related fields.

Social Work Practice: A Generalist Approach
Simon & Schuster, Inc.
Simon & Schuster Bldg.
1230 Avenue of the Americas
New York, NY 10020
Phone: (212)698-7000

Louise C. Johnson. Fourth edition, 1991. Introductory text written for the social worker. Presents current and historical literature. Covers human development, human diversity, and social systems theory.

A computer can make it easier to customize your resume. If you store your resume on a computer disk, you can copy it and rearrange it by skills, job chronology or almost any other method, customizing it for each job you apply for.

Source: *Business Monday/Detroit Free Press*

Social Work Speaks; NASW Policy Statements
National Association of Social Workers (NASW)
7981 Eastern Ave.
Silver Spring, MD 20910
Phone: (301)565-0333
Toll-free: 800-752-3590

Second edition, 1991.

State Vocational Rehabilitation Agencies
Office of Special Education and Rehabilitative Services
Department of Education
330 C St., SW
Washington, DC 20202
Phone: (202)732-1370

Three times a year; April, August, and

CAREER RESOURCES

December. Free. Covers: State government agencies responsible for vocational rehabilitation activities, including those for the blind. Entries include: Agency name, address, phone, name and title of director, federal Rehabilitation Services Administration region number. Arrangement: Geographical.

Stevens' Handbook of Experimental Psychology
John Wiley and Sons, Inc.
605 Third Ave.
New York, NY 10158
Phone: (212)850-6000
Toll-free: 800-526-5368

Richard C. Atkinson, Richard J. Hernstein, and Gardner Lindzey, editors. Second edition, 1988. Covers perception, motivation, learning, and cognition.

Faster than average employment growth for social workers is expected in response to the needs of a growing and aging population, as well as increasing concern about services for the mentally ill, the mentally retarded, and families in crisis. Employment in hospitals is expected to grow due to greater emphasis on discharge planning.

U.S. Hospitals: The Future of Health Care
Deloitte & Touche
125 Summer St.
Boston, MA 02110
Phone: (617)261-8000

1990. Survey of 25 per cent of all acute care hospitals in the United States. The report describes financial losses, low occupancy rates, and nursing shortages.

U.S. Medical Directory
U.S. Directory Service, Publishers
655 NW 128th St.
PO Box 68-1700
Miami, FL 33168
Phone: (305)769-1700
Fax: (305)769-0548

Latest edition 1989. $150.00, plus $5.00 shipping. Covers: Medical doctors, hospitals, nursing facilities, medical research laboratories, poison control centers, medical schools and libraries, and other medical services, organizations, facilities, and institutes.

Who's Who among Human Services Professionals
National Reference Institute
3004 Glenview Rd.
Wilmette, IL 60091
Phone: (708)441-2387

Biennial, February of even years. $69.95. Covers: Nearly 20,000 human service professionals, in such fields as nursing, counseling, social work, psychology, audiology, and speech pathology. Entries include: Name, address, education, work experience, professional association memberships. Arrangement: Alphabetical. Indexes: Geographical, field of specialization.

Who's Who in American Nursing
Society of Nursing Professionals
3004 Glenview Rd.
Wilmette, IL 60091
Phone: (708)441-2387

Biennial, March of odd years. $69.95. Covers: Approximately 30,000 nursing professionals, including educators, administrators, deans of nursing, directors of nursing, nurse practitioners, clinical supervisors, and others. Entries include: Name, address, personal history, area of specialization, professional experience, education, professional organization membership, and other data. Arrangement: Alphabetical. Indexes: Geographical, specialization.

Master Index

Master Index

The Master Index provides comprehensive access to all four sections of the Directory by citing all subjects, organizations, publications, and services listed throughout in a single alphabetic sequence. The index also includes inversions on significant words appearing in cited organization, publication, and service names. For example, "Ward's Business Directory of U.S. Private and Public Companies" could also be listed in the index under "Companies; Ward's Business Directory of U.S. Private and Public."

AAHA Provider News 295
ABA Membership Directory 326
ABA Newsletter 295
Academic Advising Association (NACADA); National 315
Academic Journal: The Educators' Employment Magazine 295
Academy Medical Personnel Services 318
AChemS Membership Directory 327
Acute Psychiatric Care: An Occupational Therapy Guide to Exercises in Daily Living Skills 327
Addiction & Recovery 295
Addiction & Recovery's National Treatment Resource Issue 327
Adolescent Counselor 296
Advance 324
Advances in Nursing Science 296

Aging; American Association of Homes for the 305
AGPA Directory 327
AHA Directory of Health Care Professionals 327
AHA Guide to the Health Care Field 327
AHANews 324
AHSSPPE Membership Directory 327
AICS Compass 296
The AJN Guide to Nursing Career Opportunities 327
Alabama Department of Human Resources 221
Alabama State Department of Mental Health and Mental Retardation 221
Alamo Mental Health Association 289
Alaska Department of Health and Social Services 289

Alaska Division of Alcoholism and Drug
    Abuse 289
Alaska Division of Family and Youth Services
    222
Alaska Division of Mental Health and
    Developmental Disabilities 222
Alaska Psychiatric Institute 222
*Alcoholism, Clinical and Experimental
    Research* 296
Alta Bates-Herrick Hospital 223
Alternatives Inc. 223
Alton Mental Health and Developmental
    Center 223
American Annals of the Deaf 296
American Art Therapy Association 304
*American Association for Correctional
    Psychology Directory* 327
American Association for Counseling and
    Development (AACD) 304
American Association for Marriage and
    Family Therapy 305
*American Association for Marriage Therapy
    Journal* 296
American Association of Homes for the Aging
    305
American Association of Industrial Social
    Workers 305
American Association of Mental Health
    Professionals in Corrections 305
American Biodyne Inc. 223
American City and County 296
American Counseling Association 306
American Hospital Association 319
*American Hospital Association—Guide to the
    Health Care Field* 328
American Hospital Association—Outreach 325
American Humanics 306
American Journal of Art Therapy 296
American Journal of Mental Deficiency 296
American Journal of Nursing 296
*American Journal of Nursing—Directory of
    Nursing Organizations Issue* 328
American Journal of Psychology 296
American Journal of Public Health 296
American Medical Association 306
American Medical International Inc. - AMI
    Brookwood Medical Center 224
American Mental Health Counselors
    Association 307
The American Nurse 297
American Psychiatric Association 307

American Psychological Association 307
American Psychologist 297
American Psychology Management Inc. -
    Hurst Associates Inc. 224
American Public Health Association (APHA)
    308
American Rehabilitation Counseling
    Association 308
American School Counselor Association 308
American School Health Association (ASHA)
    308
American Society of Criminology (ASC) 309
American Treatment Centers Inc. 224
AMP Membership Directory 328
Annual Review of Psychology 325
APA Membership Register 328
The APA Monitor 297
Applied developmental psychologist
    career paths 50, 51
    responsibilities of 48
Applied developmental psychology
    definition of 48
Arbor Associates 318
ARCA News 297
Arizona Division of Behavioral Health
    Services 225
Arizona Division of Family Health Services
    225
Arizona State Hospital 225
Arkansas Department of Human Services 289
Arkansas Division of Alcohol and Drug Abuse
    Prevention 225
Arkansas Division of Mental Health Services -
    Arkansas State Hospital 225
Art therapist
    career paths 43
    certification procedure of 43
    entry-level responsibilities of 43-44
    personal qualifications 44
Art therapy
    archetypal 39, 40
    career preparation for 43
    college preparation for 43
    drawbacks of 44
    forms of 39
    internships in 43
    Native American 39
    salaries 44
    traditional 39
Art Therapy; American Journal of 296
Art Therapy Association; American 304

ASC Member Directory 328
ASCUS Annual: Job Search Handbook for Educators 297
Asian American Psychological Association (AAPA) 309
AssemblyLine 325
Assistant professor
  salaries 123
Association for Behavior Analysis (ABA) 309
Association for Chemoreception Sciences (AChemS) 309
Association for Holistic Health (AHH) 309
Association for Humanistic Education and Development (AHEAD) 310
Association for Media Psychology (AMP) 310
Association for Multicultural Counseling and Development (AMCD) 310
Association for School, College and University Staffing Directory of Membership 328
Association for Specialists in Group Work (ASGW) 310
Association for Women in Psychology 311
Association of Black Psychologists 311
Association of Mental Health Administrators 311
Association of Mental Health Practitioners With Disabilities (AMHPD) 311
Association on Handicapped Student Service Programs in Postsecondary Education (AHSSPPE) 312
Associations
  importance of 145
Augusta Mental Health Institute 226
Austin State Hospital 289
AWP Membership Directory 328
AWP Newsletter 297
Baltimore Addictions Treatment Center 289
Bangor Mental Health Institute 226
Baptist Rehabilitation Institute of Arkansas 226
Bay Area Recovery Centers Inc. 226
Behavior Analysis (ABA); Association for 309
Behavior Modification in Therapeutic Recreation: An Introductory Learning Manual 329
Behavioral Medicine, Counseling, and Psychotherapy—Newsletter, International Academy of 326
Behavioral Medicine; Journal of 301
Being a Counselor: Directions and Challenges 320

Bellevue Hospital Center 289
Benefits 152
Billian's Hospital Blue Book 329
Black Psychologists; Association of 311
Boarding Schools Directory 329
Bradford at Birmingham for Adults 289
Bradman Therapy Centers 289
Bridgewater State Hospital 226
Bristol Hospital, Inc. 226
Butler Hospital 226
California Department of Alcohol and Drug Programs 227
California Department of Developmental Services 227
California Department of Mental Health 289
California Department of Social Services 227
California Health and Welfare Agency - Office of the Secretary 227
Camargo Manor Inc. 227
Camarillo State Hospital and Center 228
Camelot Care Center, Inc. 228
Care Options 289
Career Choices for the 90's for Students of Psychology 320
Career Development Association (NCDA); National 315
Career Development Quarterly 325
Career Information Center 320
Career Ladders: An Approach to Professional Productivity and Job Satisfaction 320
Career objective
  establishing a 146
Career Opportunities; Federal 299
Career Planning, Placement, and Recruitment; CPC National Directory: Who's Who in 329
Career Planning, Placement, and Recruitment; Spotlight: On 304
Careers and Vocational Guidance; The Encyclopedia of 321
Careers Encyclopedia; VGM's 324
Careers in Psychology: Your Options are Open 320
Careers in Social Work 320
Caretenders HealthCorp 228
CareUnit Clinics of Washington 228
CareUnit Hospital of Cincinnati 229
CareUnit of Colorado 229
CareUnit of South Florida Inc.
Carpenter HealthCare Systems 229
Catalyst 297

MASTER INDEX

343

Catholic Charities, Agencies and Institutions in the United States, Puerto Rico; Directory of 330
Catlett Corp. 229
CENAPS Corp. 229
Center of Behavioral Therapy P.C. 230
Centrac - Care Inc. 230
Central State Hospital 230
Certified Employee Assistance Professional exam 101
Champions Psychiatric Treatment Center 230
Charter Hospital of the East Valley 230
Charter Medical Corp. 231
Chemoreception Sciences (AChemS); Association for 309
Cherry Hospital 289
Chicago-Read Mental Health Center 231
Child and Adolescent Social Work Journal 325
Child Life Council (CLC) 312
Child Welfare: Journal of Policy, Practice, and Program 297
Child Welfare League of America (CWLA) 312
Child welfare worker
 benefits of 85
 career paths 84
 challenges of 82
 educational requirements of 82
 employer expectations of 83
 job expectations of 82, 83
 responsibilities of 81
 salaries 84
 travel requirements of 84
Children & Youth Services; National Directory of 335
Children's Home of Detroit 231
Children's Hospital of Orange County 231
Choate Mental Health and Developmental Center 232
Christian Medical Foundation International (CMF) 312
Christian Schools International Directory 329
Christian Social Welfare Agencies in the U.S.; Directory of 330
Christians in Social Work (NACSW); North American Association of 317
The Chronicle of Higher Education 298
CLC Directory 329
Clinical Nurse Specialist 298
Clinical psychology
 benefits of 53

career paths 55
career preparation for 54
college preparation for 53-54
definition of 53
fellowships in 55
getting started in 55
graduate-level 54
growth of 55
internships in 54
junior clinical psychologist-in-training 54
licensing procedures 55
practicums in 54
salaries 55
specialties in 54
CMG Health Inc. 232
Cognitive Rehabilitation 298
College degree
 importance of 140
College for Human Services 312
College professor
 salaries 123
Colmery-O'Neil Department of Veterans Affairs Medical Center 232
Colorado Alcohol and Drug Abuse Division 290
Colorado Division of Mental Health 290
Colorado State Department of Social Services 290
Colorado State Hospital 232
Columbia Health Systems Inc. 232
Community Jobs 298
Community Lifecare Enterprises 233
Community Mental Health Journal 298
Community organizer
 benefits of 135
 personal qualifications 135
 role of 132, 133
 salaries 135
 working conditions 131
Community organizing
 career paths 135
 challenges of 135
 college preparation for 134
 definition of 131
 getting started in 133
 graduate-level 134
 history of 132
 internships in 134
 job titles 135
 opportunities in 133
 professional organizations 135

purpose of 131
undergraduate level 134
Community Psychiatric Centers 233
Comprehensive Aging Services Inc. 233
Concise Encyclopedia of Psychology 329
Connecticut Department of Human Resources 290
Connecticut State Department of Mental Health 233
Connecticut Valley Hospital 234
Consortium of Social Science Associations 313
Contact Inc. 234
Contemporary Psychology 298
Continuing Education for Gerontological Careers 329
Coral Ridge Psychiatric Hospital 234
Coreance Inc. 234
Cornerstone of Recovery, Inc. 290
Correctional Psychology Directory; American Association for 327
Corrections; American Association of Mental Health Professionals in 305
Corrections, Mental Health & Special Populations; Directory of Adventure Alternatives in 330
Council for Health and Human Services Ministries (CHHSM) 313
Council on Social Work Education 313
Counseling and Development (AACD); American Association for 304
Counseling and Development (AMCD); Association for Multicultural 310
Counseling and Development Careers; Opportunities in 321
Counseling and Human Development; What Is 324
Counseling, and Psychotherapy—Newsletter, International Academy of Behavioral Medicine, 326
Counseling as a Profession 320
Counseling Association; American 306
Counseling Association; American Rehabilitation 308
Counseling; Elementary School Guidance & 325
Counseling (IAAOC); International Association of Addictions and Offender
The Counseling Psychologist 325

Counseling psychologist
in a counseling center 3
in private practice 3
responsibilities of 3
the role of 1
typical working day 3
Counseling psychology
benefits of 4
career paths 3
career preparation for 2
graduate-level 2
growth of 4
internships in 2
salaries 3
specialties in 3
Counseling Services; Directory of 330
The Counselor 298
Counselor, Adolescent 296
Counselor Association; American School 308
Counselor: Directions and Challenges; Being a 320
Counselor, Professional 303
Counselor, The School 326
Counselors Association (NECA); National Employment 316
Counselors; School 323
CPADN Newsletter 298
CPC National Directory: Who's Who in Career Planning, Placement, and Recruitment 329
CPC St. Johns River Hospital 234
The Criminologist 299
Criminology (ASC); American Society of 309
Current Openings in Education in U.S.A. 299
CWLA Directory of Member Agencies 330
Danville State Hospital 290
Davis-Smith Medical Employment Service, Inc. 318
Day Treatment Center of Dallas 234
De Paul Hospital 235
Delaware Curative Workshop 235
Delaware Department of Health and Social Services 235
Delaware State Hospital - Division of Alcoholism, Drug Abuse and Mental Health 235
Detroit Central City Community Mental Health, Inc. 290
Developmental psychologist
challenges of 47
in academia 50
responsibilities of 47, 48

salaries 51
Developmental Psychology 325
    applied developmental psychology 48, 50, 51
    definition of 47
    educational requirements of 49
    future of 51
    post-doctoral fellowships in 49
    post-graduate level 49
Devereux Center in Arizona 236
Dictionary of Concepts in General Psychology 330
Directory of Adventure Alternatives in Corrections, Mental Health & Special Populations 330
Directory of Catholic Charities, Agencies and Institutions in the United States, Puerto Rico... 330
Directory of Christian Social Welfare Agencies in the U.S. 330
Directory of Counseling Services 330
Directory of Employment Opportunities in the Federal Government 331
Directory of Hospital Personnel 331
Directory of Jewish Health and Welfare Agencies 331
Directory of Nursing Homes 331
Directory of Public School Systems in the U.S. 331
Disabilities; NRA Newsletter: Committed to Enhancing the Lives of Persons with 302
District of Columbia Alcohol and Drug Abuse Services 236
District of Columbia Commission on Mental Health Services 236
District of Columbia Commission on Social Services 236
Diversion Associates 236
EAP Digest 299
EASNA Membership Directory 331
East Louisiana State Hospital 237
East Mississippi State Hospital 290
Eastwood Clinic 237
Eden Personnel, Inc. 318
Edgewood Children's Center 237
Education (AHSSPPE); Association on Handicapped Student Service Programs in Postsecondary 312
Education and Development (AHEAD); Association for Humanistic 310
Education; The Chronicle of Higher 298

Education in U.S.A.; Current Openings in 299
Education (NADE); National Association for Developmental 315
Educational Placement Service
Educational Services; Independent 318
Educators; ASCUS Annual: Job Search Handbook for 297
Educators' Employment Magazine; Academic Journal: The 295
Educator's Institute (IEI); International 314
Educators; Job Search Handbook for 300
Elementary School Guidance & Counseling 325
Elgin Mental Health Center 237
Employee Assistance 299
Employee assistance counselor
    career advancement 102
    career preparation for 101
    challenges of 102
    educational preparation for 101
    personal qualifications 101
    salaries 101-102
    working conditions 102
Employee Assistance Programs 19
    career paths 100
    external 99
    internal 99
    job titles and descriptions 100
    on-the-job training in 101
    purpose of 99
    types of 99, 100
Employment Counselors Association (NECA); National 316
Employment criteria 149, 151
Employment Listing Service Bulletin; National 301
Employment Opportunities 332
Employment Opportunities in the Federal Government; Directory of 331
Employment Service, Inc.; Davis-Smith Medical 318
Employment Support Center (ESC) 313
The Encyclopedia of Careers and Vocational Guidance 321
Encyclopedia of Psychology 332
Encyclopedia of Social Work 332
The Encyclopedic Dictionary of Psychology 332
Englewood Hospital 237
Eponyms in Psychology: A Dictionary and Biographical Sourcebook 332
Evansville State Hospital 237
Ewing Residential Treatment Center 238

Exceptional Children 299
Fairbanks Hospital, Inc. 238
Fairfield Hills Hospital 238
Fairfield Hospital for Psychiatric and Addictive Disease Medicine 238
Families in Society 299
Family psychologist
  beliefs of 12
  career preparation for 13
  personal qualifications 14
  salaries 13
  vs. other psychologists 13
Family psychology
  career opportunities in 11
  entry-level opportunities in 13
  evolution of 11
  future of 12
  getting started in 13
Family Relations; National Council on - Family and Health Section 316
Family Service America (FSA) 314
Family Service America—Newswire 325
The Family Therapy News 299
Federal Career Opportunities 299
Federal Jobs Digest 300
Federal Personnel Office Directory 332
Federal Staff Directory 332
Florida Department of Health and Rehabilitative Services 239
  Alcohol, Drug Abuse and Mental Health Program Office 239
Florida State Hospital 239
Foreign Faculty and Administrative Openings 300
Forensic psychologist
  career paths 62-63
  career preparation for 63
  college preparation for 63
  educational requirements of 62
  personal qualifications 65
  responsibilities of 62
  salaries 65
Forensic psychology
  career opportunities in 62
  definition of 61
  Diplomate in 63
  future of 66
  graduate-level 63, 64
  internships in 64
  joint degree programs in 64
  postdoctoral level 65

  professional associations in 63
Forsythe-Stokes Mental Health Center 239
Fort Logan Mental Health Center 239
Four Winds Chicago LP 240
Friends Recovery Center 240
FSA—Directory of Member Agencies 333
Fulton State Hospital 290
G.A. Agency 318
The Gables 240
Genesis Health Ventures 240
Georgia Department of Human Resources 290
Georgia Division of Mental Health, Mental Retardation and Substance Abuse 240
Georgia Mental Health Institute 241
Geriatric and Medical Centers Inc. 241
Geriatric care management
  opportunities in 117
  salaries 118
  working conditions 118
Gerontological Careers; Continuing Education for 329
Gerontological Society of America
Gerontology
  growth of 119
  opportunities in 117
Gerontology Careers; Opportunities in 321
Glass Mental Health Centers Inc. - Glass Substance Abuse Programs 290
Glenbeigh Hospital of Cleveland 241
Glenbeigh Inc. 241
Good Neighbor Services Inc. 242
Gracie Square Hospital 242
Grady Memorial Hospital 242
Greater Bridgeport Community Mental Health Center 242
Greenleaf Health Systems 242
Greenville Health Corp. Pain Therapy Centers 243
Greystone Park Psychiatric Hospital 290
Griffin Memorial Hospital 290
Group Work (ASGW); Association for Specialists in 310
Guide to Federal Jobs 321
Guidepost 300
Hamot Health Systems Inc. 243
Handbook of Clinical Adult Psychology 333
The Handbook of Clinical Psychology: Theory, Research and Practice 333
Handbook of Private Schools 333
Handbook of Social Psychology 333
Handbook of Vocational Psychology 333

Handicapped Student Service Programs in Postsecondary Education (AHSSPPE); Association on 312
Harper Associates-Detroit, Inc. 318
Hawaii Adult Mental Health Division 243
Hawaii Alcohol and Drug Abuse Division 290
Hawaii Department of Human Services, Health Care Administration Division, Medicaid 243
HCA Psychiatric Co. 244
HCA Rockford Center 244
Health and Human Services Ministries (CHHSM); Council for 313
Health and Science Center 318
Health and Social Work 300
Health and Welfare Agencies; Directory of Jewish 331
Health Association (ASHA); American School 308
Health Care and Retirement Corp. 244
Health Care Field; AHA Guide to the 327
Health Care Professionals; AHA Directory of 327
Health Management Associates Inc. 244
Healthcare International Inc. 244
Healthcare; Modern 301
Helian Health Group Inc. 244
Highland Ridge Hospital 244
Holistic Health (AHH); Association for 309
Horizon Healthcare Corp. 245
Hospice Organization; National 316
Hospital & Community Psychiatry 300
Hospital Association; American 319
Hospital Association—Guide to the Health Care Field; American 328
Hospital Association—Outreach; American 325
Hospital Blue Book; Billian's 329
Hospital Corporation of America 245
Hospital Market Atlas 333
Hospital Personnel; Directory of 331
Hospital Phone Book 333
Hospital Tribune 300
Hospitals 300
Hospitals Directory 334
Hospitals: The Future of Health Care; U.S. 338
Houston Day Hospital 290
Howard University Hospital 245
Human Service Education; National Organization for 316
Human Services; College for 312

Human Services Professionals; Who's Who Among 338
Human Services?...That Must Be So Rewarding 321
Humanics; American 306
Humanistic Education and Development (AHEAD); Association for 310
ICP Directory 334
Idaho Department of Health and Welfare - Division of Health 245
Idaho Division of Family and Children's Services, Substance Abuse Program 246
Ideal company profile 149
Illinois Department of Mental Health and Developmental Disabilities 246
Illinois Department of Public Aid 246
Impact Drug and Alcohol Treatment center 246
Independent Educational Services 318
Indiana Department of Human Services 247
Indiana Department of Public Welfare 247
Indiana Family and Social Services Administration - Division of Mental Health 247
Infant mental health
    clinical course work in 78
    definition of 77
    history of 77
Infant mental health specialist
    career paths 78
    career preparation for 78
    personal qualifications 78
    responsibilities of 79
    salaries 79-80
Information gathering
    through publications 146
Informational interviews 152
    definition of 154
    example of an 155
    letters to send when seeking 193
    vs. job interviews 154
Integrated Health Services Inc. 247
Intercare Inc. 247
Intermountain Health Care Inc. 247
International Academy of Behavioral Medicine, Counseling, and Psychotherapy— Newsletter 326
International Association of Addictions and Offender Counseling (IAAOC) 314
International Council of Psychologists 314
International Educator's Institute (IEI) 314

International Psychologist 326
Internships; National Directory of 335
Interviews
    preparation for 141
Interwest Medical Corp. 248
Iowa Department of Human Services 248
Iowa Division of Mental Health/Mental Retardation/Mental Disabilities 248
Iowa Division of Substance Abuse and Health Promotion 248
J and Company Inc. 249
Jackson Recovery Center 249
Janamar Nurses 319
Jefferson Alcohol and Drug Abuse Center 290
Jewish Board of Family and Children's Services, Inc. 249
Jewish Communal Service; Journal of 301
Jewish Health and Welfare Agencies; Directory of 331
Job applications 217
Job interviews 152
    answering questions at 212
    following up on 211
    format of 211
    how to behave at 209
    how to dress for 209
    how to prepare for 206
    illegal questions at 216
    importance of 205
    importance of doing research before 207
    questions commonly asked at 212, 215
    questions for you to ask at 215
    selection vs. screening 208
    vs. informational interview 154
    what to avoid at 210
    what to take with you 209
Job Search Handbook for Educators 300
Job Search Process 139
    steps in the 140
    when to start the 141
Jobs Digest; Federal 300
John Umstead Hospital 290
Journal of Applied Psychology 301
Journal of Behavioral Medicine 301
Journal of Jewish Communal Service 301
Journal of Psychology 301
Journal of Psychosocial Nursing and Mental Health Services 301
Journal of the American Academy of Nurse Practitioners 301
Justice Resource Institute, Inc. 249

Kalamazoo Regional Psychiatric Hospital 249
Kansas Mental Health and Retardation Services 249
Kansas State Department of Social and Rehabilitation Services 250
Kendall Healthcare Properties Inc. 250
Kentucky Department for Mental Health/Mental Retardation Services 250
Kentucky Department for Social Insurance 250
Kimberly Quality Care 319
Koala Hospital 251
Labor unions 152
Lakeshore Mental Health Institute 290
Larned State Hospital 251
Letters
    examples of 194
    for an informational interview 193
    for blanket prospecting 192
    for networking 193
    of thanks 193
    questions to answer before preparing 189
    rules to follow when sending 191
    types of 189
    when answering an ad 192
    when inquiring about job openings 192
    when to send 191
Life Care Centers of America Inc. 251
Life care communities
    opportunities in 119
Lincoln Regional Center 291
Living Centers of America 251
Logansport State Hospital 251
Long-term care
    opportunities in 118
    salaries 118
Louisiana Office for Prevention and Recovery from Alcohol and Drug Abuse 252
Louisiana Office of Human Services 252
The Lutheran 301
Lutheran Social Services of Iowa 252
Madison State Hospital 252
Maine Bureau of Mental Health 291
Maine Department of Human Services 253
Manhattan Alcoholism Treatment Center 253
Manhattan Children's Psychiatric Center 253
Manor Care Inc. 253
Marlboro Psychiatric Hospital 291
Marriage and family therapist
    career advancement 95
    continuing education 95

in academia 19
in alcohol and substance abuse programs 19
in hospitals and clinics 19
in the business sector 19
independent contracting 96, 98
responsibilities of 15
salaries 19, 98
Marriage and family therapy
assistantships in 18
campus interviews 17
college preparation for 94, 96
definition of 15
divorce counseling 97
educational requirements 16
future of 98
getting started in 94
graduate-level 16, 17, 18
history of 15
licensing procedure in 96
opportunities in 19
reasons for entering 93
resumes 17
specialties in 93
state regulation of 96
subspecialties in 97
Marriage and Family Therapy; American Association for 305
Marriage Therapy Journal; American Association for 296
Maryland Alcohol and Drug Abuse Administration 253
Maryland Developmental Disabilities Administration 254
Maryland Mental Hygiene Administration 254
Maryland Social Services Administration 254
Massachusetts Bureau of Substance Abuse Services 254
Massachusetts Department of Mental Health 254
Massachusetts Department of Public Welfare 254
Mayview State Hospital 291
MCC Managed Behavioral Care Inc. 254
McLean Hospital 255
Medfield Center Corp. 255
Medical and Health Information Directory 334
Medical Association; American 306
Medical Directory; U.S. 338
Medical Employment Service, Inc.; Davis-Smith 318

Medical Foundation International (CMF); Christian 312
Medical Personnel Services; Academy 318
Medical school 67
Medical University of South Carolina 255
Mediplex Rehab-Camden - Institute of Brain Injury Rehabilitation Research and Training 256
Memorial Medical Center 256
Mental Deficiency; American Journal of 296
Mental Health Administrators; Association of 311
Mental Health & Special Populations; Directory of Adventure Alternatives in Corrections, 330
Mental Health Center of Jacksonville Inc. 256
Mental Health Counselors Association; American 307
Mental Health Directory 334
Mental Health Institute 256
Mental Health Journal; Community 298
Mental Health Practitioners With Disabilities (AMHPD); Association of 311
Mental Health Professionals in Corrections; American Association of 305
Mental Health Services 335
Mental Health Services; Journal of Psychosocial Nursing and 301
Mental Retardation 301
Mercy Hospital Medical Center 257
Mercy Psychiatric Institute 257
Mercy Services for Aging 257
Metropolitan State Hospital 257
Meyer Rehabilitation Institute - University of Nebraska Medical Center 257
Michigan Department of Mental Health 258
Michigan Department of Social Services 258
Michigan Health Care Corp. 258
Michigan Office of Substance Abuse Services - Michigan Department of Public Health 258
Mid-America Health Centers 258
Middle Tennessee Mental Health Institute 291
Miller Medical Group PC 259
Milwaukee County Mental Health Complex 291
Minnesota Department of Human Services 259
Minorities in psychology
career opportunities for 31

college counselor 30
college preparation for 27
financial aid 28
graduate level 29
importance of 31
salaries 31
state practicing regulation 31
use of a mentor 29
Mississippi Department of Human Services 259
Mississippi Department of Mental Health 259
Missouri Department of Mental Health 259
Missouri Division of Maternal, Child and Family Health 260
Mobile Mental Health Center, Inc. 260
Modern Healthcare 301
Montana Department of Family Services 260
Montana Department of Social and Rehabilitation Services 261
Moose Lake Regional Treatment Center 291
Mount Rogers Community Service Board 261
Mount Sinai Hospital 261
Mountainview Hospital 261
Multicultural Counseling and Development (AMCD); Association for 310
Muscatatuck State Developmental Center 262
Music therapist
    career opportunities for 35, 36
    certification procedure of 35
    responsibilities of 33
    salaries 36
    typical working day 36
Music therapy
    career preparation for 34
    definition of 33
    educational preparation for 34
    graduate-level 34
    growth of 36
    history of 37
    internships in 34
Napa State Hospital 262
NASP Membership Directory 335
NASW News 301, 326
National Academic Advising Association (NACADA) 315
National Association for Developmental Education (NADE) 315
National Association of School Psychologists (NASP) 315
National Association of Social Workers 315

National Career Development Association (NCDA) 315
National Council on Family Relations - Family and Health Section 316
National Council on Rehabilitation Education (NCRE) 316
National Directory of Children & Youth Services 335
National Directory of Internships 335
National Directory of Private Social Agencies 335
National Employment Counselors Association (NECA) 316
National Employment Listing Service Bulletin 301
National Expert Care Consultants, Inc. 262
National Hospice Organization 316
National Medical Enterprises - Psychiatric Institutes of America 263
National Medical Enterprises Inc. 263
National Organization for Human Service Education 316
National Rehabilitation Association (NRA) 317
National Staff Development and Training Association (NSDTA) 317
National Weekly Bulletin 302
The Nation's Health 302
Native American art therapy
    college programs in 42, 45
    process of 40
    role of 39
NCRE Membership Directory 335
Nebraska State Department of Social Services 263
Networking 152
    definition of 152
    history of 153
    how to do it 153
    letters to send when 193
    reasons for 159
    rules to follow when 158
    who to include when 153
NeuroCare Inc. 263
Neuropsychologist
    career preparation for 59
    college preparation for 58
    responsibilities of 58
    salaries 60
    typical working day 57-58
    working conditions 57

Neuropsychology
    definition of 57
    graduate-level 58, 59
    growth of 60
    internships in 59
    post-doctoral training 59
    professional organizations in 59
    specialties in 58
Nevada Mental Health Institute 291
Nevada Mental Hygiene and Mental Retardation Division 264
Nevada Welfare Division 264
New Beginnings of Northwest 291
New Center Community Mental Health Services 264
New Dimensions, Inc. 264
New Directions, Inc. 264
New Hampshire Department of Health and Human Services 265
New Hampshire Division of Mental Health and Developmental Services 265
New Hampshire Hospital 291
New Jersey Division of Family Health Services 291
New Jersey Family Development 291
New Life Treatment Centers Inc. 265
New Medico Associates Inc. 265
New Mexico Human Services Department 291
New Mexico Social Services Division 265
New York Office of Mental Retardation and Developmental Disabilities 266
New York State Department of Social Services 266
New York State Division of Substance Abuse 266
New York State Office of Mental Health 291
NOHSE Membership Directory 335
Non-Profit Organizations; Opportunities in 303
The NonProfit Times 302
Norrell Health Care Inc. 266
Norristown State Hospital 291
North American Association of Christians in Social Work (NACSW) 317
North Carolina Division of Medical Assistance 267
North Carolina Division of Mental Health, Developmental Disabilities, and Substance Abuse Services 267
North Dakota Department of Human Services 267

North Dakota Mental Health Services - Department of Human Services 267
Northern Virginia Doctors Hospital Corp. 268
Northville Regional Psychiatric Hospital 268
NRA Newsletter: Committed to Enhancing the Lives of Persons with Disabilities 302
NSDTA Directory 335
Nu-Med Inc. 268
Nurse; The American 297
Nurse Practitioner 302
Nurse Practitioner Forum 302
Nurse Practitioners; Journal of the American Academy of 301
Nurse Specialist; Clinical 298
Nurses and Nurses Registries 336
Nurses; Janamar 319
Nurses Registry; Pasadena 319
Nursing '92 302
Nursing, American Journal of 296
Nursing & Health Care 302
Nursing & Health; Research in 304
Nursing and Mental Health Services; Journal of Psychosocial 301
Nursing Career Directory 336
Nursing Career Opportunities; The AJN Guide to 327
Nursing—Directory of Nursing Organizations Issue; American Journal of 328
Nursing Economics 302
Nursing Homes; Directory of 331
Nursing Management 302
Nursing Outlook 303
Nursing Research 303
Nursing Science; Advances in 296
Nursing; Who's Who in American 338
Nursing World Journal 303
Nursingworld Journal Nursing Job Guide 336
Oak Hill Nursing Homes 291
Occupational Therapy Guide to Exercises in Daily Living Skills; Acute Psychiatric Care: An 327
Ocean Personnel Agency 319
Ohio Department of Alcohol and Drug Addiction Services 268
Ohio Department of Human Services 269
Ohio Department of Mental Health 269
Oklahoma Department of Human Services 269
Oklahoma Department of Mental Health 269
Omnilife Systems Inc. 269

Opportunities in Counseling and Development Careers 321
Opportunities in Gerontology Careers 321
Opportunities in Non-Profit Organizations 303
Opportunities in Psychology Careers 321
Opportunities in Social Work Careers 322
OptimumCare Corp. 270
Oregon Adult and Family Services Division 270
Oregon Mental Health and Developmental Disability Services Division 270
Oregon Office of Alcohol and Drug Abuse Programs 270
Oregon State Hospital 291
PACT Training 317
Parc Place 271
Pasadena Nurses Registry 319
Patton State Hospital 271
Penn Recovery Systems, Inc. 271
Pennsylvania Department of Public Welfare 271
Pennsylvania Drug and Alcohol Programs 272
Personnel Agency; Ocean 319
Personnel; Directory of Hospital 331
Personnel, Inc.; Eden 318
Personnel Office Directory; Federal 332
Personnel Service; Underhill 319
Personnel Services; Academy Medical 318
Perspectives in Psychiatric Care 303
Petrie Method 272
G. Pierce Wood Memorial Hospital 272
Pinecrest State School 272
Placement Associates, Inc.; Professional 319
Planned Behavioral Health Care Inc. 272
Polestar 272
Police Psychologist 322
Policy practitioner
    college preparation for 127
    employer expectations 128
    salaries 129
    typical working day 129
    working conditions 129
The Presbyterian Hospital 273
Preventive Lifestyles Inc. 273
Princeton Diagnostic Laboratories of America Inc. 273
Princeton Psychiatric Recovery Network 273
Prison Social Worker 322
Private Independent Schools 336
Professional Counselor 303
Professional Placement Associates, Inc. 319

Professional Report of the National Rehabilitation Counseling Association 303
Promotion 151
Psychemedics Corp.
Psychiatric Annals 303
Psychiatric Association; American 307
Psychiatric Care; Perspectives in 303
Psychiatric Institute of Washington 273
Psychiatric News 303
Psychiatry
    career paths 68
    evolution of 67
    medical school 67
    opportunities in 68
    personal qualifications 68
    residency training in 68
    salaries 68
    specialties in 68
    use of psychotherapy in 68
Psychiatry, Hospital & Community 300
Psychiatry resident
    job description 68
    salaries 68
Psychological Association (AAPA); Asian American 309
Psychological Association; American 307
Psychological Bulletin 303
Psychological Science 326
Psychologist 322
Psychologist; American 297
Psychologist, Clinical 322
Psychologist; The Counseling 325
Psychologist; International 326
Psychologist; Police 322
Psychologist, School 322
Psychologists 322
Psychologists; Association of Black 311
Psychologists; International Council of 314
Psychologists (NASP); National Association of School 315
Psychologists; School 323
Psychology
    career preparation for 22
    educational requirements of 22
    graduate-level 22
    growth of 24
    internships in 22
    research opportunities in 22
    specialties in 21
    women in 21

Psychology: A Dictionary and Biographical Sourcebook; *Eponyms in* 332
Psychology; *American Journal of* 296
Psychology (AMP); Association for Media 310
Psychology; *Annual Review of* 325
Psychology as a Health Care Profession 323
Psychology; Association for Women in 311
Psychology; *Career Choices for the 90's for Students of* 320
Psychology Careers; *Opportunities in* 321
Psychology; *Concise Encyclopedia of* 329
Psychology; *Contemporary* 298
Psychology; *Developmental* 325
Psychology; *Dictionary of Concepts in General* 330
Psychology Directory; *American Association for Correctional* 327
Psychology; *Encyclopedia of* 332
Psychology; *Handbook of Clinical Adult* 333
Psychology; *Handbook of Social* 333
Psychology; *Handbook of Vocational* 333
Psychology; *Journal of* 301
Psychology; *Journal of Applied* 301
Psychology: Principles and Applications 336
Psychology professor
    benefits of 23, 24
    career paths 23
    salaries 23
Psychology (SASP); Society for the Advancement of Social 318
Psychology Society Membership List 337
Psychology Society (PS) 317
Psychology; *Stevens' Handbook of Experimental* 338
Psychology Today 303
Psychology: Your Options are Open; *Careers in* 320
The Psychotherapy Bulletin 304
Psychotherapy—Newsletter, *International Academy of Behavioral Medicine, Counseling, and* 326
PsychWest 274
Public Health; *American Journal of* 296
Public Health Association (APHA); American 308
Public Welfare Directory 337
Publications
    importance of 146
Quincy Mental Health Center 274
Ramsay Health Care, Inc. - Cumberland Hospital 274

Ramsey Health Care 274
Record keeping
    example of 157
    importance of 157
Referrals 152
Register of Clinical Social Workers 337
Rehab Systems Co. 275
Rehabilitation Agencies; *State Vocational* 337
Rehabilitation Association (NRA); National 317
Rehabilitation; *Cognitive* 298
Rehabilitation Counseling Association; American 308
Rehabilitation Counseling Association; Professional Report of the National 303
Rehabilitation Education (NCRE); National Council on 316
Rehabilitation Today 304
ReLife Inc. 275
Reproductive Institute Inc. 291
Research in Nursing & Health 304
Resume
    chronological format 164
    examples of a 171
    for psychology and social work positions 161
    functional format 164
    how to prepare a 161
    importance of a 161
    organizing your data before preparing a 164
    rules to follow when preparing a 161, 164
    targeted format 164
    using power words in a 169
    what not to include in a 169
    what to include in a 165, 168
Resume Data Input Sheets 167
    how to fill out 167
Rhode Island Department of Human Services 275
Rhode Island Department of Mental Health, Retardation and Hospitals 275
Richmond State Hospital 275
Rivendell of America Inc. 275
RN 304
Roosevelt Warm Springs Institute for Rehabilitation 275
Rusk State Hospital 292
Rye Psychiatric Hospital Center Inc. 276
Safe Recovery Systems Inc. 276
Saint Elizabeth's Hospital 276

St. John's Hospital, Inc. 292
St. Joseph Mercy Hospitals of Macomb 276
St. Joseph's Home for Children 292
St. Michael's Hospital 277
St. Peter Regional Treatment Center 292
Salary 151
San Diego County Psychiatric Hospital 277
San Pablo Treatment Center 277
SASP Membership Directory 337
School counseling
    educational requirements of 30
The School Counselor 326
School Counselors 323
School Psychologists 323
School social work 87
    crisis intervention services 88
    graduate-level 88
    preventive mental health services 88
    special education staff composition 89
    working conditions 91
School Social Work: A Growing Resource in Education 323
School social worker
    benefits of 89, 91
    career advancement 89
    career paths 89
    drawbacks of 89
    educational requirements of 88
    role of 87
    salaries 89
    working in general education 90
    working in special education 90
School Social Workers 323
School Systems in the U.S.; Directory of Public 331
Second opinion
    importance of 143
Self-evaluation form
    creating a 142
    example of a 143
Self-evaluation process 141
Senior centers
    opportunities in 119
    salaries 119
Senior Living Centers Inc. 277
SHARE, Psychiatric Day Treatment Center, Inc. 277
Sinai Health Care System 278
Skills for Direct Practice in Social Work 337
Social Agencies; National Directory of Private 335

Social Science Associations; Consortium of 313
Social Service Jobs 304
Social Welfare Agencies in the U.S.; Directory of Christian 330
Social Work 304
Social work
    definition of 71
    future of 74
    private practice 73, 74
    vs. other helping professions 71
Social Work: A Growing Resource in Education; School 323
Social Work; Careers in 320
Social Work Careers; Opportunities in 322
The Social Work Dictionary 337
Social Work Education; Council on 313
Social Work; Encyclopedia of 332
Social Work; Health and 300
Social Work Journal; Child and Adolescent 325
Social Work (NACSW); North American Association of Christians in 317
Social work policy and planning
    benefits of 129
    entry-level position 128
    future of 129
    graduate-level 128
    importance of experience in 128
    policy practitioner 127
Social Work Practice: A Generalist Approach 337
Social work research
    assistant in 122
    career preparation for 122, 124
    definition of 121
    educational preparation for 122
    future of 124
Social work researcher
    graduate level 122
    importance of computer skills 124
    in a hospital setting 122
    in academia 123
    in large organizations 123
    opportunities for 123
    personal qualifications 124
    responsibilities of 123
    salaries 123
Social Work; Skills for Direct Practice in 337
Social Work Speaks; NASW Policy Statements 337

Social worker
　career opportunities for 71, 73, 105
　career preparation for 72
　graduate level 72
　personal qualifications 74
Social Worker, Clinical 323
Social worker in corrections
　benefits of 111
　career advancement 115
　career opportunities for 112, 115
　career paths 111, 115
　career preparation for 112, 114
　challenges of 116
　educational requirements of 114
　personal qualifications 112
　responsibilities of 114
　salaries 114
　typical working day 114
　working conditions 113, 114
Social worker in physical therapy
　benefits of 109
　career opportunities for 108
　college preparation for 107
　future of 109
　graduate-level 108
　internships 107
　personal qualifications 109
　responsibilities of 106
　salaries 108
　typical working day 106
　working conditions 108
Social Worker, Medical 323
Social Worker, Prison 322
Social Worker, School 324
Social Workers 324
Social Workers; American Association of Industrial 305
Social Workers; National Association of 315
Social Workers; Register of Clinical 337
Social Workers; School 323
Society for the Advancement of Social Psychology (SASP) 318
South Carolina Commission on Alcohol and Drug Abuse 278
South Carolina Department of Social Services 278
South Carolina State Department of Mental Health 278
South Carolina State Hospital 292
South Dakota Department of Social Services 279

South Dakota Division of Alcohol and Drug Abuse 292
South Dakota Division of Developmental Disabilities 279
Southboro Medical Group Inc. 279
Spectrum Programs Inc. 292
Spotlight: On Career Planning, Placement, and Recruitment 304
Staff Development and Training Association (NSDTA); National 317
State child welfare agency
　agency director 82
　interviewing 83
　regional director 82
　Social Services Worker I 83-84
　Social Services Worker II 83-84
　structure of 82
　supervisor 82
State Vocational Rehabilitation Agencies 337
Stevens' Handbook of Experimental Psychology 338
Stockton Developmental Center 279
Stormont-Vail Regional Medical Center 279
Substance abuse counseling
　drawbacks of 7
　history of 5
　large vs. small programs 6
　working conditions 7
Substance abuse counselor
　career options for 9
　career paths 8
　career preparation for 8
　certification procedure of 9
　college preparation for 8
　getting started in 8-9
　internships 9
　job expectations of 7
　responsibilities of 6
　salaries 6-7
　typical working day 7
Summit Health Ltd. 280
Talbott Recovery System, Inc. 292
Teaching Exceptional Children 304
Tennessee Bureau of Alcohol and Drug Abuse Services 280
Tennessee Social Services 280
Tennessee State Department of Human Services 292
Terrell State Hospital 292
Texas Department of Human Services 280

Texas Department of Mental Health and
    Mental Retardation 281
*Therapeutic Recreation: An Introductory
    Learning Manual; Behavior Modification in*
    329
Therapy News; The Family 299
Tinley Park Mental Health Center 281
TME Inc. 281
Toledo Mental Health Center 281
Topeka State Hospital 281
A Touch of Care 292
Training 151
Travcorps, Inc. 319
Treatment Center; Moose Lake Regional 291
Treatment Center; St. Peter Regional 292
Tri-State Regional Rehabilitation Hospital 282
UMS Corp. 282
Underhill Personnel Service 319
United Behavioral Systems Inc. 282
U.S. Behavioral Health 282
U.S. Hospitals: The Future of Health Care 338
U.S. Medical Directory 338
Universal Health Services Inc. 283
Utah Department of Human Services 283
Utah Division of Substance Abuse 283
Utah Mental Health 283
Utah State Hospital 292
VA Medical Center 284
Vari-Care Inc. 284
Vermont Agency of Human Services 284
Vermont Department of Mental Health and
    Mental Retardation 284
Vermont Department of Social Welfare 285
Vermont Office of Alcohol and Drug Abuse
    Programs 285
Vermont State Hospital 292
VGM's Careers Encyclopedia 324

Village at Manor Park 285
Virginia Department of Mental Health, Mental
    Retardation and Substance Abuse Services
    285
Virginia Department of Social Services 286
Vista Del Mar Child and Family Services 286
Walter P. Carter Community Mental
    Health/Retardation Center 286
Washington Division of Alcohol and
    Substance Abuse 286
Washington Hospital Center 287
Washington State Department of Social and
    Health Services 287
Wausau Hospital 287
West Virginia Bureau of Human Resources
    287
West Virginia Division on Alcoholism and
    Drug Abuse 288
Western Reserve Psychiatric Habilitation
    Center 292
Western State Hospital 288, 292
Weston Hospital 292
What Is Counseling and Human Development
    324
*Who's Who Among Human Services
    Professionals* 338
Who's Who in American Nursing 338
Wichita Falls State Hospital 292
Willow Creek Hospital and Treatment Center
    288
Wisconsin Department of Health and Social
    Services 288
Women in Psychology; Association for 311
Woodhull Medical & Mental Health Center
    288
Wyoming Department of Family Services 288
Wyoming State Hospital 292